Fighting Corruption in Eastern Europe

Anti-corruption programmes, projects and campaigns have come to constitute an essential aspect of good governance promotion over the last two decades. The post-communist countries in Eastern Europe have presented one of the first key targets of transnational anti-corruption efforts, and indeed most of these countries have shown an impressive record of respective measures. Yet path-breaking institutional and policy developments have not set in before the mid-2000s both at the international level and in most Eastern European countries. Are these the beginnings of a mutually synergetic success story?

In order to answer this question, we need to better understand the complex interplay between the international and domestic domains in this policy field and geographic region. This book provides in-depth and comparative insights about this interplay, with a particular focus on the involvement of domestic social movements, governmental political machines and international legal mechanisms. We find that, on all three levels of analysis, political and material interests of relevant actors are complemented and at times contradicted by normative claims. Moreover, at the interfaces of the three levels, coincidental and spontaneous developments have largely outweighed systematic implementation and coordination of anti-corruption strategies.

This book is based on a special issue of *Global Crime*.

Diana Schmidt-Pfister is a researcher at the Centre of Excellence 'Cultural Foundations of Integration' at the University of Konstanz, Germany. Her research focuses on normative change at the nexus of governance and culture. Her book *Transnational Advocacy on the Ground* (Manchester University Press, 2010) assesses transnational anti-corruption promotion in Russia.

Holger Moroff is DAAD professor of political science at the University of North Carolina in Chapel Hill. His research and publications focus on comparative political corruption and the internationalization of anti-corruption regimes as well as on security theories and European integration.

Fighting Corruption in Eastern Europe

A Multi-level Perspective

Edited by
Diana Schmidt-Pfister and Holger Moroff

Routledge
Taylor & Francis Group

LONDON AND NEW YORK

First published 2012
by Routledge
2 Park Square, Milton Park, Abingdon, Oxon, OX14 4RN

Simultaneously published in the USA and Canada
by Routledge
711 Third Avenue, New York, NY 10017

Routledge is an imprint of the Taylor & Francis Group, an informa business

British Library Cataloguing in Publication Data
A catalogue record for this book is available from the British Library

ISBN13: 978-0-415-50299-3

Typeset in Times New Roman
by Taylor & Francis Books

Publisher's Note
The publisher would like to make readers aware that the chapters in this book may be referred to as articles as they are identical to the articles published in the special issue. The publisher accepts responsibility for any inconsistencies that may have arisen in the course of preparing this volume for print.

Printed and bound in Great Britain by the MPG Books Group

Contents

III Critical Reflections

IV Conclusion

Preface

It is by now commonly acknowledged that we still need to better understand the broader contexts both for corruption to operate and for anti-corruption efforts to take root. Two years ago, when our authors submitted their original contributions for our special issue "Anti-Corruption for Eastern Europe" (*Global Crime,* Vol. 11, Issue 2, May 2010), we were convinced that we offered an overdue and up-to-date compendium of well-conceptualised and empirically grounded studies about anti-corruption efforts at the intersections of various sets of contexts: the transnational anti-corruption sphere, post-communist governments, and post-communist civil societies. Since then, controversial debates among practitioners and scholars have continued about how to best fight corruption at the international, regional, national and local levels.

The invitation to re-issue our special issue as a book confirms the persistent relevance of our compilation. Importantly, with its special focus on the dynamics of transnational anti-corruption efforts, it presents an essential supplement to the ever-growing pile of handbooks on the facets of corruption itself. With the benefit of hindsight, we may today confirm that our previous general conclusions hold true: within the Eastern European countries, major breakthroughs have been seen where relevant external, national and civic actions coincided. The most decisive potential for effective anti-corruption reforms, however, resides with the post-communist governments. External pressure on governments, foreign funding for domestic civil societies, and rivalries between countries or among political factions within countries, are all highly decisive factors. But it depends on the situational constellation of contextual circumstances whether they advance or hinder the promotion of anti-corruption policies in a particular country at a particular time.

Since a common thread in the case studies compiled here is the ideally vital but actually limited role of post-communist civil societies, and since the global anti-corruption venture has now moved even further towards intergovernmental action, a new chapter has been devoted to the question of civil society involvement. Moreover, three major developments have been shaping anti-corruption discourses and practices more recently. They are reflected in the mass demonstrations against the regime in Russia, that is perceived as corrupt, as well as in the instrumentalisation of anti-corruption measures for the purpose of punishing political rivals, as seen in Ukraine and Hungary. A third aspect has come to the fore in the wake of the public debt and financial crises, which have already lead to more external and internal oversight of public budgets and administrations with direct consequences for anti-corruption policies. These new aspects and various cyclical dimensions of anti-corruption processes are analysed in our new concluding chapter.

We are deeply indebted to all our authors for joining us in reflecting the relevancy of our general and case-specific conclusions and for feeding their expert knowledge into our final theses. We are also grateful to Taylor & Francis for inviting the re-issuance of our special issue as a book and to the Center of Excellence "Cultural Foundations of Integration" at the University of Konstanz as well as to the University of North Carolina at Chapel Hill for providing us with highly productive institutional environments.

Anti-corruption movements, mechanisms, and machines – an introduction

Holger Moroff[a] and Diana Schmidt-Pfister[b]

[a]Department of Political Science, University of North Carolina at Chapel Hill, Chapel Hill, NC, USA; [b]Center of Excellence EXC 16 'Cultural Foundations of Integration', University of Konstanz, Konstanz, Germany

Anticorruption programmes, projects and campaigns have come to constitute an essential aspect of furthering good governance over the last two decades. This article provides a conceptual framework for studying anticorruption efforts and it assesses their nature and impacts across Eastern Europe by focusing on the interplay between the international and domestic domains. More precisely, it differentiates between domestic social movements, governmental political machines and international legal mechanisms. These three levels of analysis – domestic civil society, national governments and international society – provide a meaningful general basis for comparing a variety of anti-corruption efforts. On all three levels, political and material interests of relevant actors are complemented by normative arguments. In assessing the case studies in this volume, this article concludes that, at the interfaces of the three levels, coincidental and spontaneous breakthroughs have largely outweighed systematic implementation of appropriate anticorruption strategies. It further stresses that broad societal support for anticorruption remains essential for the success of any international or governmental initiatives.

Promotion of democracy and good governance are established policies of various international organisations, governments, and NGOs. Anti-corruption programmes, projects, and campaigns have come to constitute an essential aspect of furthering good governance over the last two decades. The post-communist countries in Eastern Europe have presented key targets of such efforts, and indeed most of these countries have shown an impressive record of domestic anti-corruption measures. But how do external structures and agents influence anti-corruption efforts in post-communist countries? How are domestic responses feeding back into the global fight against corruption? And what kind of structures and agents have become involved at both national and international levels at all? These are the core questions that this special issue approaches. They are highly relevant when looking at a policy field and at a region where 'change' has been a central parameter. Not only transnational anti-corruption efforts have been evolving and have taken various forms since the early 1990s, but also the relations between West and East have been changing and the domestic transformations in the various Eastern European countries have, irrespective of a shared communist legacy, proceeded in manifold ways. As the articles compiled here show, these dynamic international and domestic contexts have been conducive to coincidental and spontaneous breakthroughs rather than systematic implementation of appropriate anti-corruption strategies.

This special issue has sprung from a panel on 'Prevention of organised crime and corruption: International efforts in post-communist countries' that we organised at the fourth European Consortium for Political Research (ECPR) General Conference in Pisa 2007. By that time we found it vital to launch a fresh appraisal of the nature and implications of anti-corruption programmes across this region with regard to the two inseparable sides of this coin, namely, the international and the domestic sides of fighting corruption. Much has been written on corruption and crime in Eastern Europe. We have also seen dispersed analyses of anti-corruption efforts at the international level and in selected, mostly single country cases. Yet a compendium of well-conceptualised and empirically grounded studies on the range of such efforts across this region was missing. This volume now brings together a number of senior and junior scholars from different national backgrounds who have long been working on these issues from different disciplinary perspectives (political science, international relations, European integration, comparative politics, area studies, sociology, and anthropology). All authors have been guided by the common conceptual premise to explore more attentively the complex interplay between international and domestic factors, structures, and agents in the anti-corruption field. Moreover, country case studies (Part III) are supplemented by contributions about the approaches of international actors and about the analytical challenge of measuring the experiences and the perceptions of corruption (Part II) and by critical reflections about the nature and mixed successes of the global anti-corruption venture in general (Part IV). During the evolution of this volume and the various case studies over the last 3 years, it became more and more apparent that the domestic experiences with anti-corruption must be further differentiated by looking at governments and civil societies separately. This has led us to reconceptualise the interplay between domestic and international efforts and introduce further differentiations on both levels, as outlined further below.

Contexts

Efforts of preventing transnational crime and corruption have expanded greatly in recent years. An international policy environment has been shaped by International Financial Institutions (IFIs), the United Nations, the Organisation for Economic Cooperation and Development (OECD), the Council of Europe (CoE), the European Union (EU), and the United States. These efforts have been bolstered by the advocacy and awareness-raising activities of international non-governmental organisations (NGOs), most notably Transparency International (TI) and domestic civil society as well as by new areas of legal, investigatory, and prosecutorial co-operation between Western European and Eastern European countries. Certainly, many legislative and cooperative measures remain too new for definitive judgements about the successes of particular policies or projects. Still, policy-makers and academics can draw on multiple data sources and a collection of cases that have emerged over the last two decades to analyse more systematically the multiple processes at work and to reflect on the usefulness of conceptual approaches towards studying transnational anti-corruption promotion. As the contributions in this issue underline, it is not only that corruption and crime themselves are putting strains on domestic development and international relations, but also the many political, economic, technical, cultural, and moral aspects involved in collaborative counter-efforts of international bodies and domestic actors are posing diverse new challenges.

In the post-communist transformation countries, in particular, the issue of corruption and crime has continued to receive large amounts of attention from international bodies, Western countries, and the media. This has included a growing set of issues, ranging from concerns about democratisation, investment, and the rule of law to international and security affairs. Corruption has been deemed to hinder democratisation, to facilitate transnational organised crime and terrorism, but also to foster unpredictability in foreign policy-making and for foreign investments. On a regional European level, particularly in the course of the 2004 and 2007 Eastern enlargements of the European Union, new international security concerns have been raised about an expansion of organised crime from Russia and the Balkans. But also the governments in some Eastern European countries came to view corruption as a national security issue, as it has been the key to popular dissatisfaction ultimately leading to a number of revolutions, such as Georgia's Rose Revolution in 2003, Ukraine's Orange Revolution in 2004, and Kyrgyzstan's Tulip Revolution in 2005. At the same time, and somewhat paradoxical, in the eyes of some international actors domestic political stability has become an important precondition for promoting anti-corruption reforms.

The scholarly literature contains many cautionary notes about the potentially limited success or even negative implications of anti-corruption programmes in Eastern Europe and Central Asia.[1] On the one hand, this stands in sharp contrast not only to the normative and optimistic perspective of most anti-corruption programmes in practice but also to another body of literature presenting mainly success stories about the promotion of international norms in fields such as human rights or the environment.[2] On the other hand, the reservations about anti-corruption promotion in Eastern Europe are in line with recurring arguments about the possibly negative implications of anti-corruption measures elsewhere[3] and with recent contributions pointing to the more complex questions regarding external democratic norm promotion in Eastern Europe and Eurasia.[4] The special issue moves beyond this rather contradictory state of research by looking more deeply into anti-corruption efforts in different Eastern European countries. Moreover, national responsiveness towards

---

1. For example, Virginie Coulloudon, 'Russia's Distorted Anticorruption Campaigns', in *Political Corruption in Transition. A Sceptic's Handbook*, ed. Stephen Kotkin and András Sajó (Budapest/New York: CEU Press, 2002), 187–206; Ivan Krastev, *Shifting Obsessions. Three Essays on the Politics of Anticorruption* (Budapest/New York: CEU Press, 2004); Steven Sampson, 'Integrity Warriors: Global Morality and the Anti-Corruption Movement in the Balkans', in *Corruption. Anthropological Perspectives*, ed. Dieter Haller and Chris Shore (London/Ann Arbor, MI, USA: Pluto Press Ltd., 2005), 103–30; or Franklin Steves and Alan Rousso, 'Anti-Corruption Programmes in Post-Communist Transition Countries and Changes in the Business Environment, 1999–2002' (working paper No. 85, European Bank for Reconstruction and Development, London, 2004).
2. Especially, Margaret E. Keck and Kathryn Sikkink, *Activists Beyond Borders. Advocacy Networks in International Politics* (Ithaca/London: Cornell University Press, 1998) and Thomas Risse, Stephen C. Ropp, and Kathryn Sikkink, eds., *The Power of Human Rights. International Norms and Domestic Change* (Cambridge: Cambridge University Press, 1999).
3. Especially, Frank Anechiarico and James B. Jacobs, *The Pursuit of Absolute Integrity. How Corruption Control Makes Government Ineffective* (Chicago/London: The University of Chicago Press, 1996); but also on the potential abuse of anti-corruption campaigns under non-democratic conditions, Samuel Huntington, *Political Order in Changing Societies* (London/New Haven: Yale University Press, 1968).
4. For example, Christopher Lord and Erika Harris, *Democracy in the New Europe* (Houndmills and New York: Palgrave Macmillan, 2006); Amichai Magen and Leonardo Morlino, *International Actors, Democratization and the Rule of Law. Anchoring democracy?* (New York and London: Routledge, 2009), or Sarah E. Mendelson and John K. Glenn, eds., *The Power and Limits of NGOs. A Critical Look at Building Democracy in Eastern Europe and Eurasia* (New York, Chichester, West Sussex: Columbia University Press, 2002).

international anti-corruption efforts seems to vary with the degree of desired association with the European Union. Our selection of country studies with different relations to the European Union provides cases in point: Some of the countries studied have struggled to move from candidates to members (Hungary, Poland, Bulgaria, and Romania) and still face some scrutiny as far as the transparent use of EU funds is concerned, others are now participating in the European Neighbourhood Policy (ENP) (Georgia, Ukraine).

Concepts

In this research endeavour we set out to study the interplay between international and domestic anti-corruption efforts. First results of the case studies showed that there has been an enormous transfer of resources and ideas from the international to the domestic level and that indeed a range of domestic measures have been undertaken in response. But many measures, both external and domestic, have been taken in parallel or have merely coincided rather than being based on strategic coordination. Moreover, the studies in this volume indicate that anti-corruption efforts are pursued by using techniques of social movements from below, international legal and financial mechanisms from above, or the means of governmental machines from within national administrations.[5] In the light of these tentative findings, we suggest to adjust the general conceptual approach of studying anti-corruption efforts by moving from two to three levels of analysis: the levels of domestic civil society, national government, and international society. Such a three-pronged approach lends itself to the study of anti-corruption efforts in general and provides a structured prism for comparing the multifaceted nature of various anti-corruption policies and campaigns.

Relevant actors on the first level are mainly NGOs of which there are home-grown as well as externally induced and funded ones, with some having strong connections to political opposition parties. These NGOs are often perceived and portrayed by Western and international donors as public spirited, non-profit enterprises. However, within their domestic contexts, NGOs in Eastern Europe also present an essential means of attracting foreign and domestic funding to generate income. This latter aspect seems reinforced with regard to anti-corruption efforts, which has grown into a global industry employing now countless anti-corruption professionals and involving immeasurable monetary resources.[6] Thus, it is difficult to tell whether activists are motivated by conviction, material benefits, or both. National businesses and business associations can also be found in this group of civil society, either genuinely supporting anti-extortion efforts or staging such activity for

---

5. Our machine concept refers to (party) political systems that use ideally independent bureaucracies to further the power political interests of the political leadership, rather than to bureaucratic politics which may involve turf wars not permeated by political interests. It is characterised by a spoils system of patronage and clientelism within and between the administrative and political levels of government. Machine politics is different from bureaucratic politics in that the latter refers to turf wars in and between various bureaucracies without them necessarily being permeated by party-book civil servants nor driven by (party) political interests. International organisations and NGOs can evince self-interested bureaucratic behaviour and politics to further the power, income, and careers of those working for them, but since they are usually independent from domestic (party) political forces they are not part of the machine politics played out on that level.

6. Estimates of the monetary weight of the anti-corruption industry range from many millions (Sampson, this issue) up to many billions of dollars [Bryane Michael, 'The Evolution of the Anti-Corruption Industry in the Third Wave of Anti-Corruption Work' (paper presented at the conference 'International Anti-Corruption Regimes in Europe', Konstanz, Germany, July 24, 2009)].

various public relations reasons, for example, to divert from their own corrupt practices which can then be blamed more easily on individual company employees, thus serving as a cover up for any structural or top level corruption. Again, it is difficult to assess their real motives. As domestic civil society might have connections to international NGOs, to international organisations, to national and foreign governments alike, they can be well interconnected with the other two levels. Some governments and international organisations support and thus influence NGOs at home and abroad to varying degrees, thus undercutting the notion of a separate and truly independent and intrinsically motivated sphere of civil society. In general, civil society seems to be a much employed but rarely defined concept, thus tempting both international organisations and advocacy scholars to fill this blank by looking for the ideal in the unfamiliar and under-*volonté générale*, one would not need a democracy as a system of political competition among various parties and interest groups. They are all part of a civil society or rather various civil societies. This is especially important to recognise as the development of collective action groups, parties, NGOs, and intermediary organisations in post-communist Eastern Europe differ sharply from the development of these groups in older Western democracies.

The second level consists of national governments, their agencies and administrations, politicians, and political parties. That is the group of power holders whose anti-corruption efforts can be internally motivated by power struggles among political factions, or by legitimacy crises brought about by social anti-corruption movements from below, and successful scandalisations of high-profile or pervasive corruption cases. Governmental anti-corruption measures can also be externally induced through international conventions and organisations or by international awareness-raising, such as through corruption perception indices or regular monitoring schemes. Whether national governments pursue anti-corruption efforts out of a genuine belief in the rule of law and the importance of a level playing field, or to merely please international donors and investors, or even to develop a weapon against political opponents is, once again, very difficult to ascertain. Often their policies are motivated by a mixture of the above reasons.

On the third level we find an international society made up of international organisations, international NGOs, transnational actors such as private foundations, think tanks, multinational businesses, and some very active Western governments. They can also foster anti-corruption efforts for manifold reasons that are difficult to tell apart. Besides a genuine belief in the merits of these policies, it might be a bureaucratic interest in gaining a new field of activity for an international organisation or a government department, or an interest in using such policies as a means of influencing developments in other countries. Anti-corruption efforts may also be employed by large exporting nations as a tool to help their companies compete abroad, or as a way to internationalise their legal standards for business conduct and accounting rules.

On all three levels, material or power political interests in anti-corruption policies are complemented by regulatory, normative, and moral arguments. Although all actors can play various roles on all three levels, civil society is closely associated with social movements and seems to carry the greatest legitimacy in the anti-corruption discourse. International organisations have developed legal and financial mechanisms in the form of conventions and conditionality regimes, whereas national governments instituted anti-corruption measures and administrations that in some cases are part of or used by the broader power political machine. Studying the interaction patterns of these actors on all three levels is revealing the actual workings of international anti-corruption regimes in general as well as in the national and regional setting of Eastern Europe in particular.

Our approach not only contributes to a better understanding of anti-corruption policies in and for a particular region but also speaks to a wider theoretical debate within comparative politics and international relations. It asks what impact the international system has on domestic politics and looks at the interdependence between the international, governmental, and civil society levels. This approach can be linked to Peter Gourevitch's concept of the 'second-image-reversed'[7] as it studies international factors causing domestic outcomes. In the field of comparative politics, Jon Pevehouse used this analysis for his influential study on externally induced processes of democratisation, which is relevant for the study of corruption in so far as it presupposes a normative theory of (legitimate) representation and democracy.[8] In international relations, both liberal and constructivist theoretical approaches build upon the second-image-reversed concept as well.[9] The same applies to issue-oriented studies focusing on norm diffusion – of which international anti-corruption regimes are more recent examples – and on the impact of international norms on domestic human rights policies.[10] Anti-corruption policies are also straddling the international–domestic divide not only through 'two-level-games'[11] in which national governments can play the international and the domestic levels off against each other and thus gain greater independence but also by the way how international discourses are used for domestic power purposes by governments, oppositions, the media, and civil society.

Civil society especially is often treated as universalism's assistant parochial partner, helping international norms to take root domestically – sometimes in lockstep with but more often in opposition to national governments. In this way the 'two-level game' is stood on its head by having the international level and the level of domestic civil society joining forces in cornering obstinate national governments and forcing them to change their policies and behaviour. According to conventional wisdom, civil societies, transnational NGOs, and researchers engaged in advocacy scholarship (some professionally by working for IFIs or think tanks, some from a more disinterested academic base) form an epistemic community that has the capacity of supplanting states in shaping discourses and norms for the international society.

In the anti-corruption field, we find such a 'contractual bond' between international organisations (as well as some Western governments) and domestic NGOs mainly in development and transition countries. The NGOs are thus becoming associated with policies of international organisations, certain norm entrepreneurial governments, and strong international NGOs which are usually based in countries with such strong norm entrepreneurial governments.[12] This in turn can be readily exploited by recalcitrant national governments through painting those NGOs and their cause as a Trojan horse of subversive foreign powers.

---

7. Peter Gourevitch, 'Second Image Reversed: The International Sources of Domestic Politics', *International Organization* 32 (1978): 886.

8. on Pevehouse, *Democracy from Above: Regional Organizations and Democratization* (New York/Cambridge: Cambridge University Press, 2005).

9. A general and comprehensive overview is provided by Robert Keohane and Helen Milner, *Internationalization and Domestic Politics* (New York/Cambridge: Cambridge University Press, 1996).

10. For example, Risse, Ropp, and Sikkink, *Power of Human Rights*.

11. Peter Evans, Harold Jacobson, and Robert Putnam, *Double-Edged Diplomacy: International Bargaining and Domestic Politics* (Berkeley: University of California Press, 1993).

12. For the disciplining effect of this constellation see Graham Burchell, 'Liberal Government and Techniques of the Self', in *Foucault and Political Reason*, ed. Andrew Barry, Thomas Osborne, and Nicholas Rose (London: UCI Press, 1996), 29.

On the contrary, IFIs, other international organisations, and norm entrepreneurial states are also directly addressing the governments of a 'target' state. Domestic civil societies often remain excluded from this diplomatic sphere that concerns loans and assistance provided to governments – made conditional upon the state's corruption situation or offered in support for governmental anti-corruption initiatives – investigatory and prosecutorial cooperation, or country-to-country peer review monitoring. Many studies have been conducted about the active support of non-state actors in advancing the case for international policies and regimes, especially with regard to environmental and human rights norms.[13] However, hardly any such studies exist for the intricate interplay between the domestic civil society, the national governmental and the international level concerning anti-corruption efforts.[14] This special issue provides empirical evidence and insights that allow for new theoretical conclusions about these complex interaction patterns in Eastern Europe.

Contents

The contributions compiled here demonstrate that national and international anti-corruption efforts are deeply intertwined, albeit not necessarily strategically coordinated. Although many domestic measures have been undertaken in response to external anti-corruption promotion, progress has often been triggered by unforeseen synergies between international mechanisms, domestic power struggles, and the engagement of some advocacy groups and civil society. Indicating that anti-corruption promotion is still in its very early stages, crucial policy developments and breakthroughs have been rather recent in many countries, such as new anti-corruption drives in Poland in 2002, in Ukraine in 2005, or in Hungary in 2007. Yet also the international policy and advocacy environment has gained more substance only throughout the early 2000s, when the international conventions entered into force and TI began to take roots across Eastern Europe through National Chapters.[15]

Major insights derived from the contributions to this volume can be structured along the three levels of analysis identified earlier. At international society level that is the third level of analysis, Sebastian Wolf identifies Group of States against Corruption (GRECO's) and the OCED's monitorings as major mechanisms of anti-corruption promotion through regular and highly formalised evaluation procedures. Although they take place mainly in interaction with governments of Eastern European countries and though these have displayed a better implementation record of GRECO recommendations than Western (European) countries, they seem to show little practical enforcement and follow-up efforts. Thus the symbolic legal mechanisms are in place but they have little impact on the perception of corruption which remains as high as before. Tanja Börzel, Andreas Stahn, and Yasemin Pamuk look at the EU's actions in the region and outline how it has mainstreamed anti-corruption promotion by incorporating it into various aspects of the ENP.

---

13. Especially, Keck and Sikkink, *Activists Beyond Borders*; Risse, Ropp, and Sikkink, *Power of Human Rights*.

14. For a rare example, see Diana Schmidt-Pfister, *Transnational Advocacy on the Ground. Against Corruption in Russia?* (Manchester: Manchester University Press, forthcoming 2010).

15. The OECD Anti-Bribery Convention entered into force in 1999, the CoE Criminal Law Convention on Corruption in 2002, the CoE Civil Law Convention in 2003, and the UN Convention Against Corruption in 2005. Efforts to set up TI National Chapters in Eastern Europe only started in 1996, and the majority of Chapters in this region became formally accredited by the TI Secretariat after 2000 (with the exceptions of Poland, Slovakia, Latvia, Bulgaria, Czech Republic, and Kazakhstan).

However, without a clear membership option and without further context-specific differentiation, the European Union's Action Plans remain very broad and thus necessarily vague blueprints rather than effective tools for exerting pressure about concrete anti-corruption measures. Despite a formal commitment to promoting the involvement of civil society in anti-corruption reforms, the European Union might also strengthen (potentially corrupt) governments and administrations more than it does civil society and forces that should keep governments in check. This can be attributed to the intergovernmental design of the ENP in which power holders are the main interlocutors. On the societal level that is the first level of analysis, Richard Rose and William Mishler find that citizens' perception of corruption in Russia depends more on the state of the economy than on anything else, suggesting a certain pragmatism about judging the governance system and its politicians. Whatever works and makes citizens feel that they are on average better off than before is fine. This corresponds very well to the concept of output legitimacy in which equal and transparent participation in the governance process (input legitimacy) is less important than the effective problem-solving capacity of these processes. Given that international actors tend to use measures of the perception of corruption (such as the CPI) as a key point of reference, this article cautions against the assumption that they provide good proxy indicators for the actual level of corruption in any country. Using survey data from the New Russia Barometer, the authors find that the perception of corruption is not based on firsthand experiences of paying bribes.

The country case studies presented in Part III dive deeper into the complex linkage between various externally induced anti-corruption measures and home-grown initiatives resulting from bottom-up pressures such as mass protests or special local efforts, or from top-down politico-administrative elite projects – on both genuine grounds and as instrumentalised pretexts for power political purposes.

As Agnes Batory shows for Hungary, civil society seems to take over from the European Union as the main driving force behind anti-corruption, thus suggesting a shift from international mechanisms to social movements. As in most other studies, the impact of the electoral cycle is highlighted. It might turn the issue of corruption into an overly politicised campaign item or elections may break a previously created anti-corruption momentum. Kaja Gadowska's article on Poland buttresses what was ascertained earlier by Wolf, namely, that even though symbolic legal mechanisms induced by the international level are in place, they remain ineffective due to a lack of implementation because of machine politics on the national level. Moreover, as shown by Kalin Ivanov for Bulgaria and Romania, popular outrage and scandalisation of corruption cases on the by domestic civil society may be mixed with cynical resignation. A particular challenge to the EU policy on the international level seems to tailor the anti-corruption approach to domestic circumstances while remaining neutral in the context of party politics on the national level. Furthermore, as demonstrated in this and other cases (e.g. Georgia), rivalries between countries and concerns about the international image may either fuel or hamper anti-corruption promotion.

In the post-Soviet countries, the role of the European Union becomes marginal and a Soviet heritage seems to prevail at both the governmental and societal levels. Yet especially at the latter, corruption as well as the shadow economy are deemed socially accepted forms of resistance against an all encroaching state. In the case of Georgia, Lilli di Puppo looks at how the anti-corruption discourse is appropriated in many ways on the second level. It is employed as a means of power and machine politics, as a way of improving the image of a post-revolutionary government that seems willing to fight corruption but is reluctant to subscribe to international instruments. At the first level, NGOs seem often more accountable to foreign donors than to a domestic constituency. Fighting corruption can be a fundraising strategy for professional NGO activists. Some of their highly qualified staff have moved to the second level and have taken government posts and taken over government positions on anti-corruption policies. Åse Grødeland turns to the case of Ukraine, where measures taken by the Yushchenko government clearly represent responses to requirements made by the international community. However, elite perceptions demonstrate that international anti-corruption requirements are not properly adjusted to the local context.

Not least, the various domestic developments in this region have to be considered against the backdrop of a consolidating aggregate of global discourses, structures, and practices. Referring to this aggregate as a global anti-corruption industry, Steve Sampson turns to a concluding and critical reflection about its changing nature and ambivalent implications. It becomes clear that, regardless of the unique intensity of anti-corruption efforts over the past 15 years, the global anti-corruption venture is still in its infancy when it comes to the question of effectiveness.

Conclusions

At the third level, the European Union had a direct influence on this policy field and geographic region, although its main leverage was confined to the 2004 and 2007 EU Eastern enlargements and to the candidate countries. The bar had been set higher during the second round (see Bulgaria and Romania), and Ivanov predicts that it may be raised even further for future entrants. However, after acceding to the European Union, membership conditionality loses its momentum, even though the European Union may still exert influence by freezing funds over concerns of corruption (such as in the case of Bulgaria). The OECD, in turn, had a limited role in this region because only Bulgaria, Hungary, and Poland are members and have signed the OECD Anti-Bribery Convention. Almost all countries studied have subscribed to the CoE and UN conventions and GRECO monitoring will thus play a major role. However, on the first level a domestic constituency is needed to ensure that the implementation of legal codes is followed up by their adequate enforcement.

More general insights derived from the present studies are that new governments seem more likely to initiate new anti-corruption campaigns as witnessed in Hungary, Georgia, and Ukraine. At this second level, rivalries between countries or among political factions within countries – depending on the heat of the moment – may advance or hinder the promotion of anti-corruption policies. In this regard, Hungary, Bulgaria, Romania, and Ukraine provide cases in point. On the third level, external actors seem most concerned about stability and administrative continuity in these countries, fearing that domestic party politics, especially around elections, or even staff rotation in the bureaucracy may disturb established working relations with traditional interlocutors, and thus seek to strengthen any administration, regardless of their records in good or bad governance

Despite different theoretical approaches, case selections and interpretations, a surprising consensus emerges from the various studies compiled in this issue. The vital role of a broad societal constituency in anti-corruption efforts seems essential even for more technical international anti-corruption approaches to take roots and for domestic efforts to be successful beyond the governmentally staged façade and instrumentalisation in political contests. So far, the approaches of international organisations seem to buttress the governments' executives and political parties in power by focusing on training officials and cooperating with governments in setting up legal and administrative anti-corruption outfits, thus by default and design neglecting the civil society components within the domestic contexts.

Notes on contributors

Diana Schmidt-Pfister is a researcher at the Centre of Excellence 16 'Cultural Foundations of Integration' at the University of Konstanz, Germany. She has extensively researched and published on anti-corruption efforts in post-Soviet countries, with a particular view to the entanglement of international, domestic, and local initiatives. In this regard, her book *Transnational Advocacy on the Ground* (Manchester University Press, forthcoming 2010) discusses the nature and implications of such multi-level ventures in Russia during the authoritarian Putin era. Her research interests further include good governance, crime prevention, and scientific integrity.

Holger Moroff is a visiting DAAD professor at the University of North Carolina in Chapel Hill and was a lecturer in political science at Friedrich Schiller University of Jena. He has published extensively on comparative political corruption, the internationalisation of anti-corruption regimes, and on corruption reporting in print media. He places pervasive corruption within the new security agenda in international relations on which he edited the book *European Soft Security Policies* (2002) and published numerous articles on EU foreign policy towards Eastern Europe and Russia. His current research focuses on the interlocking effects of major international anti-corruption regimes.

Assessing Eastern Europe's anti-corruption performance: views from the Council of Europe, OECD, and Transparency International

Sebastian Wolf

Department of Politics and Management, University of Konstanz, Konstanz, Germany

This article compares the results of Council of Europe and Organisation for Economic Co-operation and Development (OECD) anti-corruption monitoring reports to two Transparency International instruments, the Corruption Perceptions Index and the OECD Anti-Bribery Convention Progress Report. It constructs and applies a simple typology (four-cell matrix) consisting of the combinations of good/deficient implementation of international anti-corruption provisions and high/low level of perceived corruption. As the sources and the comparative method used cannot prove causality, the article introduces three ideal types of interpretation to discuss the relevance of the anti-corruption regulatory framework in both domestic and cross-border anti-corruption policies. In the conclusion it is argued that there is a specific Eastern European pattern of anti-corruption performance that implies a need for new strategies.

Introduction

The Council of Europe (CoE) and the Organisation for Economic Co-operation and Development (OECD) have been engaged in the fight against corruption for more than a decade[1] and have issued dozens of country reports on anti-corruption policies in Eastern and Western European countries.[2] The same goes for Transparency International (TI), the leading anti-corruption non-governmental organisation (NGO),[3] and its numerous national chapters. These

---

1. For contributions on the early years of CoE and OECD anti-corruption policies, see Guy de Vel and Peter Csonka, 'The Council of Europe Activities Against Corruption', in *Corruption, Integrity and Law Enforcement*, ed. Cyrille Fijnaut and Leo Huberts (The Hague: Kluwer Law International, 2002), 361–80, and Gemma Aiolfi and Mark Pieth, 'How to Make a Convention Work: The Organization for Economic Co-operation and Development Recommendation and Convention on Bribery as an Example of a New Horizon in International Law', in *Corruption, Integrity and Law Enforcement*, ed. Cyrille Fijnaut and Leo Huberts (The Hague: Kluwer Law International, 2002), 349–60. For current initiatives, see Sebastian Wolf, *Der Beitrag internationaler und supranationaler Organisationen zur Korruptionsbekämpfung in den Mitgliedstaaten* (Speyer: Deutsches Forschungsinstitut für öffentliche Verwaltung Speyer, 2007), and the organisations' websites http://www.coe.int/t/dg1/Greco/Default_en.asp and http://www.oecd.org/topic/0,3373,en_2649_37447_1_1_1_1_37447,00.html (accessed February 23, 2009).
2. For the purposes of this article, the term 'Eastern Europe' includes post-communist countries of Central Europe, Eastern Europe, and South Eastern Europe. It is based on a broad notion of 'Europe' like the concept of the CoE.
3. See Peter Eigen, *The Web of Corruption. How a Global Movement Fights Graft* (Berlin: Druckhaus, 2008), and http://www.transparency.org (accessed February 23, 2009).

three organisations have used and are still using different methods to assess anti-corruption efforts, and they apply their specific approaches indiscriminatingly to both Eastern and Western European countries as well as non-European countries. At the same time, the European Union (EU), because of its rather discriminatory approach,[4] has published only few monitoring data on corruption and anti-corruption performance in Western Europe.[5] Focusing on the key question 'Is there a specific Eastern European pattern of anti-corruption performance?', this article compares corruption-related international evaluations of Eastern and Western European countries. In this specific area, CoE and OECD are the two international organisations (IOs) that provide the most coherent and comprehensive data.[6] Because of its asymmetric and selective data basis, the EU, albeit an important actor in the fight against corruption in Eastern Europe,[7] is not dealt with in the following sections.[8]

Given the countless detailed country reports published by the CoE's and OECD's anti-corruption monitoring bodies – 'Group of States Against Corruption' (GRECO) and 'Working Group on Bribery in International Business Transactions' (OECD Working Group) – and the bulk of indices and other assessments by TI, this article can only provide a short overview and show general trends. Its aim is twofold: On the one hand, it compares results of GRECO and OECD monitoring reports to TI instruments such as the 'Corruption Perceptions Index' (CPI) and the 'OECD Anti-Bribery Convention Progress Report'.

---

4. See, for example, Andrea Tivig and Andreas Maurer, 'Die EU-Antikorruptionspolitik. Erfolgs-bedingungen einer Korruptionsbekämpfung auf mehreren Ebenen', *SWP Discussion Paper* no. 3 (2006): 53. Whereas the European Commission has published many reports on anti-corruption policies of pre-accession countries and even some 'new members' (Bulgaria and Romania), it is more or less silent about the situation in the (old) member-states. One might argue that the EU is not meant to produce reports on the anti-corruption performance of its older members, but some of the affected Eastern European countries have already blamed the EU for its discriminatory approach (double standards) and suggested EU evaluations of every member state based on common standards (see Wolf, *Der Beitrag internationaler und supranationaler Organisationen*, 78).
5. Such as the two reports on the implementation of the Convention on the protection of the European Communities' financial interests and its protocols [COM(2004) 1299 and COM(2008) 77] and the report on the implementation of the Council Framework Decision on combating corruption in the private sector [COM(2007) 328].
6. The CoE and OECD, unlike the EU, evaluate all members of their respective anti-corruption working groups in the same way. Moreover, they base their anti-corruption monitoring on a clear and broad set of commonly agreed principles and provisions. Finally, their reports are much more detailed than the EU reports because the EU does not provide individual country reports on Western European member states.
7. It is obviously difficult to assess the real impact of the EU's anti-corruption policy on Eastern Europe. The Union's role is certainly not restricted to rather abstract anti-corruption discourses or to the European Anti-Fraud Office's work to protect the EU's financial interests (see Tivig and Maurer, 'Die EU-Antikorruptionspolitik'). Because of the economical advantages connected with EU accession, the Union is able to offer more positive incentives for effective anti-corruption measures than other International Organisations (Wolf, *Der Beitrag internationaler und supranationaler Organisationen*, 55). It seems that at least the EU Twinning Projects, in which 'embedded' experts from the old member states help to improve Eastern European anti-corruption policies, have positive practical effects, see Cornelia Gädigk, 'Möglichkeiten der Korruptionsbekämpfung im Rahmen von EU-Twinning-Projekten', in *Korruption. Ansätze zur präventiven und repressiven Bekämpfung korruptiver Strukturen*, ed. Hartmut Brenneisen and Alexander Hahn (Berlin: LIT, 2008), 103–18. For a recent political initiative by MEPs (supported by civil society organisations) to improve the EU's anti-corruption policy, see http://www.stopcorruption.eu (accessed March 5, 2010).
8. For a comprehensive critical analysis of corruption and anti-corruption policies in the EU, see Carolyn M. Warner, *The Best System Money Can Buy. Corruption in the European Union* (Ithaca and London: Cornell University Press, 2007).

On the other hand, it looks for specific Eastern European and/or Western European patterns of perceived corruption and anti-corruption policies on a rather abstract level.

The next section briefly introduces the different approaches used by GRECO, the OECD Working Group, and TI. As to the relationship between perceived corruption and compliance with international anti-corruption provisions, it presents a typology and three different types of interpretation. Then domestic corruption in Eastern and Western Europe is looked at, drawing on GRECO country reports and CPI scores. The following section deals with foreign corruption by contrasting OECD Working Group reports with TI's OECD Convention Progress Report. In the conclusion it is argued that there is a specific Eastern European pattern of anti-corruption performance that implies a need for new strategies.

Assessing anti-corruption performance: different approaches and interpretations

It is always difficult to evaluate the extent of a certain crime in a given state and the success of countervailing measures. But as corruption is a so-called victimless crime, it is even more difficult to measure the degree of corruption in a country than the spread of other crimes.[9] There simply is no manageable way to find out the real extent of domestic or foreign corruption. However, there are some methods to measure aspects or phenomena that are believed to be more or less closely connected with the actual degree of corruption.[10] GRECO and the OECD Working Group evaluate the implementation of international anti-corruption provisions by using peer review mechanisms.[11] By contrast, TI's CPI is based on experts' perceptions about the level of corruption in certain countries.[12] TI's OECD Anti-Bribery Convention Progress Reports mainly draw on the numbers of prosecutions and judicial investigations related to foreign corrupt practices.

All these approaches are using nation states as basic units. Moreover, they assume that a good regulatory framework is likely to reduce the real extent of corruption, whereas non-compliance with certain institutional and legal standards is said to have a negative impact.[13]

---

9. Dieter Dölling, 'Grundlagen der Korruptionsprävention', in *Handbuch der Korruptionsprävention*, ed. Dieter Dölling (München: C. H. Beck, 2007), 6.

10. Vito Tanzi, 'Corruption Around the World. Causes, Consequences, Scope, and Cures', *IMF Staff Papers* 45, no. 4 (1998): 559–94.

11. In both organisations, an evaluation team (consisting of representatives of two or three member states, assisted by the respective secretariat) prepares a draft report on the basis of answers to a questionnaire and findings from a country on-site visit. Then the draft report is discussed, revised, and adopted by the plenum of member states. On the OECD Working Group's review procedure, see Nicola Bonucci, 'Monitoring and Follow-up', in *The OECD Convention on Bribery*, ed. Mark Pieth, Lucinda A. Low, and Peter J. Cullen (Cambridge: Cambridge University Press, 2007), 445–75. On GRECO's evaluation mechanism, see Wolf, *Der Beitrag internationaler und supranationaler Organisationen*, 38–41. For a general analysis of the peer review method in an international organisation, see Fabrizio Pagani, 'Peer Review: A Tool for Co-Operation and Change. An Analysis of an OECD Working Method' (OECD working paper), http://www.oecd.org/dataoecd/33/16/1955285.pdf (accessed February 13, 2009).

12. For comprehensive information on the CPI, see the 'Internet Center for Corruption Research', http://www.icgg.org/corruption.cpi_2008.html (accessed February 13, 2009).

13. See Transparency International, 'Persistently High Corruption in Low-Income Countries Amounts to an "Ongoing Humanitarian Disaster"' (CPI 2008 Press Release), http://www.transparency.org/news_room/latest_news/press_releases/2008/2008_09_23_cpi_2008_en (accessed February 24, 2009), and GRECO, 'The Fight against Corruption: A Priority for the Council of Europe', http://www.coe.int/t/dg1/greco/general/1.%20The%20Fight%20against%20Corruption%20-%20A%20Priority%20for%20the%20CoE_en.asp (accessed February 24, 2009). For an analysis that tends to

However, the exact interrelation between (real and perceived) corruption and compliance with international anti-corruption provisions is unclear.[14] For example, in one country, a high level of perceived corruption may be mainly the result of inadequate regulation in the areas of administrative, competition, and/or criminal law. In another country, however, a high level of perceived corruption may have been the reason that pushed a government to enact anti-corruption legislation based on international standards, but it is questionable whether how and when such laws will work. Aside from that, the absence of prosecutions and judicial investigations is mostly seen as an indicator of ineffective regulation.[15] Yet this same criterion is invoked by some authors to argue that the deterrent function of anti-corruption provisions is working.[16] Thus, lack of prosecutions can be interpreted as a sign of either effective or ineffective anti-corruption performance.

This article mainly analyses how Eastern and Western European states cluster according to two criteria, perceived corruption and compliance with international anti-corruption provisions. It is not intended to explain causal interrelations between these two factors.[17] Nevertheless, it seems useful to work with different ideal types of interpretation that offer competing explanations for the interrelation between the level of perceived corruption and the quality of the regulatory framework. If one takes perceived corruption as a dependent variable, as most studies do,[18] three main ideal types of interpretation can be distinguished:

(1) The regulatory framework 'matters most', that is, it is the only factor or the only key factor that influences the level of perceived corruption;
(2) The regulatory framework 'does matter' to a certain degree, but other factors also have significant impact on the level of perceived corruption[19];
(3) The regulatory framework 'does not matter': it does not have a (significant) impact on the level of perceived corruption.

---

oversimplify the relationship between CPI scores and formal compliance with (or just ratification of) anti-corruption provisions, see Andreas Tiemann, 'The United Nations Convention Against Corruption – Does it Work?' (bachelor's thesis, University of Konstanz, 2008).

14. Even the notion of 'compliance' is rather vague. In CoE's, OECD's, and TI's view, compliance is not only exact formal implementation of international provisions (enactment of law), but also actual law enforcement. Although early international anti-corruption monitoring has concentrated on assessing mostly formal implementation (as these data are easier to collect and to evaluate, and assessment is less intrusive), recent monitoring also looks at law enforcement (e.g. case law and number of prosecutions, investigations, and convictions). However, even the precise interrelation between 'actual' compliance and (real and perceived) corruption is nebulous.

15. See Transparency International, 'OECD Anti-Bribery Convention Progress Report 2008', 8, http://www.transparency.org/global_priorities/international_conventions (accessed February 24, 2009), and Daniel K. Tarullo, 'The Limits of Institutional Design: Implementing the OECD Anti-Bribery Convention', *Virginia Journal of International Law* 44 (2004): 665–710.

16. Mark Pieth, 'Staatliche Intervention und Selbstregulierung der Wirtschaft', in *Festschrift für Klaus Lüderssen*, ed. Cornelius Prittwitz (Baden-Baden: Nomos, 2002), 326.

17. The article's main sources (anti-corruption monitoring reports and an index on perceived corruption) cannot provide explanations for such causal interrelations.

18. It is also possible to see compliance with international anti-corruption provisions as dependent variable, that is, to explain the quality of the legal framework with current or past levels of perceived corruption (see Conclusion).

19. For this conception, see, for example, Tanzi, 'Corruption Around the World', 565–78.

Table 1 shows a typology consisting of the four combinations of good/deficient implementation of international anti-corruption provisions and high/low level of perceived corruption as seen by these three ideal types of interpretation.[20]

The following sections first describe how Eastern and Western European states cluster with regard to the typology. Then it is discussed whether the three ideal types of interpretation offer convincing explanations for the observed distribution of countries.

Patterns of domestic corruption and anti-corruption performance

GRECO evaluation reports[21] provide deep insights into national policies that aim to fight domestic corruption.[22] Because of the bulk of CoE anti-corruption provisions (three Council recommendations, two conventions, and an additional protocol[23]) and the time it takes to ratify and implement these instruments, GRECO monitoring consists of several multi-year evaluation rounds. In each round, the implementation of selected standards is evaluated[24] in all participating countries.[25] Approximately 2 years after the publication of a country's evaluation report, which contains a couple of recommendations, a compliance report is issued. In this report, the implementation of each recommendation is assessed.[26] Another 2 years or so later, an addendum to the compliance report is adopted that terminates the country's evaluation in that round. The first evaluation round has focused on a small number of rather modest anti-corruption principles.[27] Thus, nearly all states that were

20. It is emphasised once again that this article does not postulate a specific causal (or temporal) interrelation between perceived corruption and compliance with international anti-corruption provisions (cf. supra notes 14 and 17), but rather uses the three ideal types of interpretation as analytical tools.

21. All country reports are available at http://www.coe.int/t/dg1/greco/evaluations/index_en.asp (accessed December 5, 2008; subsequent reports are not taken into account in the following analysis). GRECO cannot publish a report without the consent of the respective national government. Until now, all governments have agreed to the publication sooner or later.

22. For selected country analyses based on GRECO reports see Wolf, *Der Beitrag internationaler und supranationaler Organisationen*.

23. These documents are available at http://www.coe.int/t/dg1/greco/documents/instruments_en.asp (accessed February 24, 2009).

24. 'A team of experts is appointed by GRECO for the evaluation of a particular member. The analysis of the situation in each country is carried out on the basis of written replies to a questionnaire and information gathered in meetings with public officials and representatives of civil society during an on-site visit to the country. Following the on-site visit, the team of experts drafts a report that is communicated to the country under scrutiny for comments before it is finally submitted to GRECO for examination and adoption', see http://www.coe.int/t/dghl/monitoring/greco/general/4.%20How%20 does%20GRECO%20work_en.asp (accessed May 15, 2009).

25. GRECO currently has 46 members: all CoE member states – apart from Liechtenstein and San Marino – and the United States. Countries that later become GRECO members undergo joint first and second round evaluations. Thus, their specific evaluation and compliance reports have a broader basis and cannot be directly compared to the reports of older GRECO members, at least from a quantitative perspective. These states (Andorra, Armenia, Austria, Azerbaijan, Italy, Monaco, Montenegro, Russia, Serbia, Switzerland, Turkey, and Ukraine) are therefore not included in the calculations in Tables 2 and 3. Moreover, this article only deals with the first two evaluation rounds. The third evaluation round (launched in 2007) is not included since there are only a few evaluation reports so far (Estonia, Finland, Iceland, Latvia, Luxembourg, Netherlands, Slovakia, Slovenia, United Kingdom) and not a single compliance report.

26. The following 'marks' are used by GRECO to assess the implementation: 'satisfactorily implemented', 'dealt with in a satisfactory manner', 'partly implemented', 'not implemented'.

27. Three principles out of the CoE's 'Twenty Guiding Principles for the fight against corruption' have been selected by GRECO: *Principle 3* (to ensure that those in charge of the prevention, investigation, prosecution and adjudication of corruption offences enjoy the independence and autonomy

Table 1. A typology of the relationship between compliance with international anti-corruption provisions and perceived corruption as well as three different interpretations.

Interpretation	Rather low level of perceived corruption			Rather high level of perceived corruption		
	A	B	C	A	B	C
Rather good implementation of international anti-corruption provisions	Low level of perceived corruption because of good regulatory framework	Low level of perceived corruption because of good regulatory framework and other factors	Low level of perceived corruption because of factors other than the regulatory framework	Good regulatory framework will lead to a low level of perceived corruption in the future	Good regulatory framework cannot outweigh other factors that cause a high level of perceived corruption	High level of perceived corruption because of factors other than the regulatory framework
Rather deficient implementation of international anti-corruption provisions	Level of perceived corruption will raise in the future because of bad regulatory framework	Other factors outweigh bad regulatory framework	Low level of perceived corruption because of factors other than the regulatory framework	High level of perceived corruption because of bad regulatory framework	High level of perceived corruption because of bad regulatory framework and other factors	High level of perceived corruption because of factors other than the regulatory framework

included in the first evaluation round got positive (addenda to) compliance reports. Table 2, as well as Tables 3 and 5, shows aggregated data, that is, total numbers of monitoring recommendations and evaluations for two or three groups of countries. Additional information about individual country performance is provided in the Appendix.

As to the implementation of GRECO first-round recommendations, the (quantitative) performance of the included Eastern and Western European countries is more or less equal, especially with regard to percentages of compliance.[28] The addenda to the compliance reports show that both groups have improved their performance after the publication of the respective compliance reports. The Eastern European states' implementation record is slightly better at both stages, but this difference is only marginal. On the contrary, Eastern European countries had to implement much more recommendations than Western European GRECO members. From this point of view, their performance is more impressive than the Western European countries' implementation record. However, one must add that the Eastern European country Georgia is the only state so far that had to undergo a (rather short) non-compliance procedure because of significant shortcomings in the initial implementation of GRECO recommendations.[29]

The second evaluation round is not finished yet. Only five addenda to compliance reports have been issued by now.[30] Countries that lack a compliance report so far are not included in Tables 3 and 4. In this round, the implementation of much more as well as much more demanding CoE anti-corruption provisions is evaluated.[31] Both Eastern and

---

appropriate to their functions, are free from improper influence and have effective means for gathering evidence, protecting the persons who help the authorities in combating corruption and preserving the confidentiality of investigations), *Principle 6* (to limit immunity from investigation, prosecution or adjudication of corruption offences to the degree necessary in a democratic society), and *Principle 7* (to promote the specialisation of persons or bodies in charge of fighting corruption and to provide them with appropriate means and training to perform their tasks).

28. A disadvantage of this quantitative approach is that the recommendations are not weighted: a state might comply, for example, with eight rather negligible recommendations while not implementing two crucial recommendations. However, such extreme cases are rare, and weighting of policy recommendations might involve new methodological problems. Even GRECO uses an unweighted quantitative approach (e.g. 'GRECO concludes that State X has implemented satisfactorily or dealt with in a satisfactory manner half of the recommendations contained in the Second Round Evaluation Report').

29. See Appendix Table A2 for the results of both Georgia's regular compliance report and its special second compliance report. The first disastrous report that triggered the non-compliance procedure is available at http://www.coe.int/t/dg1/greco/evaluations/round1/GrecoRC1(2003)12_Georgia_EN.pdf (accessed February 26, 2009).

30. Because of the small number of addenda to compliance reports adopted so far (Finland, Luxembourg, Poland, Slovakia, and Slovenia), they are not included in Table 3. The third evaluation round has been launched in 2007, which means that the evaluation rounds are overlapping. For some GRECO members, the third evaluation round reports have already been published, although even second round compliance reports of other members have not been adopted yet. This is due to the high number of member states and the different dates of joining GRECO.

31. The following Guiding Principles have been selected by GRECO: *Principle 4* (to provide appropriate measures for the seizure and deprivation of the proceeds of corruption offences), *Principle 5* (to provide appropriate measures to prevent legal persons being used to shield corruption offences), *Principle 8* (to ensure that the fiscal legislation and the authorities in charge of implementing it contribute to combating corruption in an effective and co-ordinated manner, in particular by denying tax deductibility, under the law or in practice, for bribes or other expenses linked to corruption offences), *Principle 9* (to ensure that the organisation, functioning, and decision-making processes of public administrations take into account the need to combat corruption, in particular by ensuring as much transparency as is consistent with the need to achieve effectiveness), *Principle 10* (to ensure that the rules relating to the rights and duties of public officials take into account the requirements of the fight

Table 2. GRECO first evaluation round.

	Evaluation report recommendations	Compliance report				Addendum to compl. report			
		Satisfactorily implemented	Satisfactory manner	Partly implemented	Not implemented	Satisfactorily implemented	Satisfactory manner	Partly implemented	Not implemented
17 Western European countries and USA[a]	166 (average: 9.2)	90 (54%)	30 (18%)	39 (23%)	7 (4%)	101 (61%)	43 (26%)	20 (12%)	2 (1%)
16 (South) Eastern European countries[b]	233 (average: 14.6)	128 (55%)	44 (19%)	52 (22%)	9 (4%)	154 (66%)	56 (24%)	20 (9%)	3 (1%)

Note: [a]Belgium, Cyprus, Denmark, Finland, France, Germany, Greece, Iceland, Ireland, Luxembourg, Malta, Netherlands, Norway, Portugal, Spain, Sweden, United Kingdom, and United States.
[b]Albania, Bosnia-Herzegovina, Bulgaria, Croatia, Czech Republic, Estonia, Georgia, Hungary, Latvia, Lithuania, Macedonia, Moldova, Poland, Romania, Slovakia, and Slovenia.

Table 3. CPI 2008 and GRECO second evaluation round.

	CPI 2008 average score (on a 1–10 scale)	GRECO evaluation report recommendations	GRECO compliance report			
			Satisfactorily implemented	Satisfactory manner	Partly implemented	Not implemented
Seventeen Western European countries[a]	7.6	121 (average: 7.1)	36 (30%)	26 (21%)	45 (37%)	14 (12%)
Thirteen (South) Eastern European countries[b]	4.7	160 (average: 12.3)	48 (30%)	40 (25%)	51 (32%)	21 (13%)

Note: [a]Belgium, Cyprus, Denmark, Finland, France, Germany, Greece, Iceland, Ireland, Luxembourg, Malta, Netherlands, Norway, Portugal, Spain, Sweden, and United Kingdom (no addenda to compliance reports adopted yet).
[b]Albania, Bulgaria, Croatia, Czech Republic, Estonia, Hungary, Latvia, Lithuania, Macedonia, Poland, Romania, Slovakia, and Slovenia (no addenda to compliance reports adopted yet).

Table 4. Perceived corruption and implementation records according to CPI and GRECO data.

	Rather high CPI score 2008	Rather low CPI score 2008
Rather good GRECO implementation record	(1) Denmark, Estonia, Finland, France, Germany, Ireland, Netherlands, Norway, Portugal, Slovenia, Sweden, United Kingdom	(2) Albania, Armenia, Bulgaria, Czech Republic, Croatia, Greece, Hungary, Lithuania, Macedonia, Poland, Slovakia
Rather deficient GRECO implementation record	(3) Belgium, Cyprus, Iceland, Luxembourg, Spain	(4) Latvia, Malta, Romania, Serbia, Turkey

Western European countries perform worse than in the first round. On the basis of the first round results, one may assume that the implementation record of both groups of countries will improve until the publication of the addenda to compliance reports, albeit only to a small extent. This remains to be seen. At least, there has been no non-compliance procedure in the second round so far. Once again, the Eastern European states' implementation record is slightly better, but the difference in percentages is rather marginal. Table 3 also provides information about the average CPI 2008 scores. There is a significant gap between Eastern and Western Europe with respect to the level of perceived corruption.[32]

A comparison of the countries' GRECO compliance record with the CPI 2008 results reveals that most Western European countries score rather high on both the CPI and the implementation of GRECO recommendations whereas most Eastern European countries do not. Table 4 shows that only two Eastern European countries (Estonia and Slovenia) can be found in cell 1.[33] The majority of Eastern European states scores low on the CPI but has good GRECO implementation results. Greece is the (South) Western European deviant case in cell 2. A small group of solely Western European countries has a weak implementation record but good CPI scores (cell 3). Finally, there is a mixed group that shows the combination of rather low CPI scores and poor implementation of GRECO recommendations (cell 4).

As to the three ideal types of interpretation introduced in the previous section, type A (regulatory framework matters most) seems to provide a convincing explanation for most Western European countries. From this point of view, low levels of perceived corruption are the results of good anti-corruption regulatory frameworks (cell 1). Moreover, according to this line of argumentation, deficient implementation of international anti-corruption standards has caused the poor CPI scores of the countries in cell 4. However, type A reasoning is hardly persuasive with regard to the countries in cells 2 and 3: It is not likely that

---

against corruption and provide for appropriate and effective disciplinary measures; promote further specification of the behaviour expected from public officials by appropriate means, such as codes of conduct), and *Principle 19* (to ensure that in every aspect of the fight against corruption, the possible connections with organised crime and money laundering are taken into account), as well as complementing provisions of the CoE Criminal Law Convention on Corruption (Art. 13, 14, 18, 19, 23).

32. The CPI 2008 is available at http://www.transparency.org/policy_research/surveys_indices/cpi (accessed February 24, 2009). This article works with the CPI, as many studies, despite its weaknesses. For a recent analysis on bias in perceptions based indices, see Jörn Ege, 'Systematische Verzerrungen bei wahrnehmungsbasierten Indizes politischer Korruption' (bachelor's thesis, University of Konstanz, 2008).

33. For the purposes of this study, countries with a CPI score above the average (6.1) of all countries included in Table 4 are considered to have a 'rather high' CPI score. States that implemented less than half of their GRECO recommendations in either Round 1 or Round 2 are considered to have a 'rather deficient' implementation record.

the levels of perceived corruption in the Western European countries in cell 3 will raise just because of bad GRECO implementation records. As to the majority of Eastern European countries situated in cell 2, many of them have adopted commendable regulatory frameworks based on international provisions already several years ago, but levels of perceived corruption are still high. With regard to these cases, type B interpretation (regulatory framework does matter to a certain degree) and type C interpretation (regulatory framework does not matter) offer more convincing explanations. It seems that the levels of perceived corruption of Western European countries in cell 3 are hardly (or not) influenced by their deficient regulatory frameworks. Conversely, factors other than the quality of the regulatory framework appear to cause low CPI scores in most Eastern European countries under consideration (cell 2).

As mentioned above, this article does not intend to explain causal interrelations. But from the distribution of countries according to our four-cell typology and from the tentative discussion of ideal types of interpretation, it is feasible to conclude that Eastern and Western European countries show diverging patterns regarding the combination of corruption perceptions and anti-corruption measures. The next section analyses how countries cluster in the area of foreign corruption as evaluated by the OECD and TI.

Patterns of foreign corruption and anti-corruption performance

The OECD's anti-corruption policy deals with fighting corruption in the public sector, bribery and export credits, governance and development, and tax treatment of bribes. Since 1994, it puts special emphasis on combating bribery of foreign public officials in international business transactions.[34] The detailed monitoring reports adopted and published by the OECD Working Group on Bribery in International Business Transactions[35] cover several aspects that are relevant for both domestic and foreign anti-corruption measures.[36] As the number and scope of OECD anti-corruption provisions that are subject to peer review are rather limited (mainly a short convention and two Council recommendations[37]), the OECD Working Group's monitoring does not consist of several separate evaluation rounds. There have been, however, two monitoring phases so far:[38] In Phase 1, a country's implementing legislation is assessed ('desk review'); Phase 2, which includes on-site visits, shall evaluate whether the practical enforcement of this legislation is effective. In each phase, the implementation of all standards included in the OECD Anti-Bribery Convention and two Council recommendations[39] is evaluated in all participating

---

34. See Aiolfi and Pieth, 'How to Make a Convention Work'.
35. All country reports are available at http://www.oecd.org/document/24/0,3343,en_2649_34859_ 1933144_1_1_1_1,00.html (accessed December 5, 2008, subsequent reports are not taken into account in the following analysis). Unlike GRECO, the OECD Working Group can publish a report without the consent of the examined country.
36. For selected country analyses based on OECD Working Group reports see Wolf, *Der Beitrag internationaler und supranationaler Organisationen.*
37. These documents are available at http://www.oecd.org/document/21/0,3343,en_2649_34859_ 2017813_1_1_1_1,00.html (accessed February 24, 2009). For an in-depth legal analysis of the OECD Anti-Bribery Convention and complementing instruments, see Mark Pieth, Lucinda A. Low, and Peter J. Cullen, eds., *The OECD Convention on Bribery* (Cambridge: Cambridge University Press, 2007).
38. A new monitoring phase 3 will start in late 2009 or 2010.
39. The core provision is laid down in Art. 1 of the Convention: 'Each Party shall take such measures as may be necessary to establish that it is a criminal offence under its law for any person intentionally to offer, promise or give any undue pecuniary or other advantage, whether directly or through

countries.[40] Two to three years after the publication of a country's Phase 2 Report, which contains a couple of recommendations, the OECD Working Group issues a report on progress.[41] In this report, the implementation of each recommendation is assessed.[42] Like GRECO, the OECD Working Group has a non-compliance procedure. It is called Phase 1bis or Phase 2bis and is used more often than the GRECO non-compliance mechanism so far. No Eastern European state had to undergo such a procedure until now, but several Western countries like Luxembourg, Japan, and the United Kingdom did.[43]

Table 5 shows the performance of Working Group members according to the Phase 2 monitoring reports. It also provides the main conclusions from TI's OECD Anti-Bribery Convention Progress Report 2008. In this report, TI mainly draws on numbers of foreign bribery cases and investigations to assess whether there is 'significant enforcement' in the states that are parties to the Convention.[44]

Because of the small number of Eastern European countries in this part of our analysis, only tentative conclusions can be made. Again, Eastern European states show a better implementation record than Western European countries. They are the only geographical group of states that have implemented slightly more than half of the Phase 2 recommendations so far. It is striking that Western European countries have not implemented nearly a third of their recommendations compared with just a sixth in Eastern Europe. TI's progress report, however, shows a different picture: When it comes to the practical enforcement of foreign bribery legislation, Western European countries and non-European states perform better than Eastern European countries.

---

intermediaries, to a foreign public official, for that official or for a third party, in order that the official act or refrain from acting in relation to the performance of official duties, in order to obtain or retain business or other improper advantage in the conduct of international business'. Other important provisions include the liability of legal persons, effective sanctions, money laundering, accounting, and tax deductibility of bribes.

40. The OECD Working Group currently has 38 members: all OECD member states and Argentina, Brazil, Bulgaria, Chile, Estonia, Israel, Slovenia, and South Africa.

41. The OECD Working Group's system of peer review is similar to GRECO's monitoring mechanism (see supra notes 11 and 24). First, an evaluation team is appointed and a questionnaire is sent to the country under evaluation. Then, 'Phase 2 involves one week of intensive meetings in the examined country with key actors from government, law enforcement authorities, business, trade unions and civil society. With input from these actors, the Working Group assesses how effective that country's anti-foreign bribery laws are in practice', see http://www.oecd.org/document/5/0,3343,en_2649_34859_35430021_1_1_1_1,00.html (accessed May 19, 2009). For a detailed analysis, see Bonucci, 'Monitoring and Follow-up'.

42. The following 'marks' are used by the Working Group to assess the implementation: 'satisfactorily implemented', 'partly implemented', 'not implemented'. In some early reports, the Working Group decided that a few recommendations just need 'further consideration'.

43. As to the consequences of the non-compliance mechanism, Luxembourg has taken some small positive steps and Japan 'has made significant progress'. But 'the Group is disappointed and seriously concerned with the unsatisfactory implementation of the Convention by the UK'. On Luxembourg, see http://www.oecd.org/dataoecd/4/21/40322335.pdf, on Japan, see http://www.oecd.org/dataoecd/49/44/39591489.pdf, and on the United Kingdom, see http://www.oecd.org/dataoecd/23/20/41515077.pdf (accessed May 19, 2009).

44. One might ask why this article does not draw on TI's Bribe Payers Index (BPI), a perceptions based index focussing on bribery in international business transactions, http://www.transparency.org/news_room/latest_news/press_releases/2008/bpi_2008_en (accessed February 24, 2009). Firstly, the BPI does not cover Eastern European countries apart from Russia, which is neither a OECD member state nor a voluntary member of the OECD Working Group. Secondly, it seems appropriate to use the TI report because this is the main instrument that TI particularly developed for the OECD overseas bribery context.

Table 5. TI progress report and OECD working group phase 2 monitoring.

	TI Report 2008 significant enforcement?	OECD Phase 2 number of recommendations	OECD Phase 2 progress report			
			Satisfactorily implemented	Partly implemented	Not implemented	Further consideration/other
Thirteen Western European countries[a]	Yes: 10 countries[b] No: 2 countries	177 (average: 13.6)	83 (47%)	38 (21%)	54 (31%)	2 (1%)
Three Eastern European countries[c]	Yes: 1 country No: 2 countries	63 (average: 21.0)	32 (51%)	18 (29%)	10 (16%)	3 (5%)
Five other working group members[d]	Yes: 3 countries No: 2 countries	88 (average: 17.6)	40.5 (46%)	27 (31%)	15.5 (18%)	5 (6%)

Note: Countries that lack a Phase 2 Progress Report so far are not included in this table (e.g. the following Eastern European states: Czech Republic, Estonia, Poland, and Slovenia). The same goes for countries that undergo the non-compliance procedure (Luxembourg, Japan, and United Kingdom) because their specific reports cannot be compared to regular Phase 2 progress reports, at least from a quantitative perspective. However, Japan and United Kingdom are included in Table 6 as they have obviously shown rather deficient implementation records. Luxembourg is not included because it is not dealt with in the TI report.
[a]Austria, Belgium, Denmark, Finland, France, Germany, Greece, Iceland, Italy, Norway, Spain, Sweden, Switzerland.
[b]Iceland is not dealt with in the TI report.
[c]Bulgaria, Hungary, and Slovakia.
[d]Australia, Canada, Korea, Mexico, and United States.

Table 6. Implementation and enforcement records according to OECD and TI data.

	Significant enforcement according to TI report	Little or no enforcement according to TI report
Rather good OECD working group implementation record	(1) Australia, Belgium, France, Germany, Korea, Norway, Sweden, United States	(2) Austria, Slovakia
Rather deficient OECD working group implementation record	(3) Denmark, Finland, Hungary, Italy, Spain, Switzerland	(4) Bulgaria, Canada, Greece, Mexico, Japan, United Kingdom

Table 6 shows how Working Group members cluster along the two dimensions good/ deficient Working Group implementation record[45] and significant/no significant enforcement according to TI. It is remarkable that non-European states can only be found in cells 1 and 4. This means that they show either a good implementation record and significant enforcement (cell 1) or a deficient implementation as well as little or no enforcement (cell 4). By contrast, Western European countries can be found in each of the four cells. Nearly the same goes for the small number of Eastern European countries under consideration, but there is no Eastern European state in cell 1. Just two neighbouring countries (Austria and Slovakia) show the combination of a good implementation record and little enforcement (cell 2). Some Western European states and Hungary have a significant number of prosecutions despite deficient implementing legislation (cell 3). A geographically mixed group of states shows both a poor implementation record and no significant enforcement (cell 4).

Although the IOs and NGO sources used in this section differ from those dealt with in the previous section, the three ideal types of interpretation on the relevance of the anti-corruption regulatory framework can also be applied to the context of foreign corruption. Contrary to the case of domestic corruption, type A interpretation (regulatory framework matters most) does not seem to provide a convincing explanation for most Western European countries as they can be found in each cell of the matrix. This type of interpretation assumes that a good regulatory framework causes significant enforcement whereas a deficient regulatory framework implies little or no prosecutions and investigations. In particular, type A reasoning cannot explain why a range of Western European countries show a significant number of prosecutions despite deficient implementing legislation. However, non-European countries perfectly fit in type A's line of argumentation because they just cluster in either cell 1 or 4. Because of the small number of Eastern European countries included in this part of our analysis, it does not make sense to apply the different types of interpretation to this group of states. As to the Western European countries, type B interpretation (regulatory framework does matter to a certain degree) and type C interpretation (regulatory framework does not matter) seem to offer more convincing explanations than type A because there is no eye-catching cluster of countries that might suggest the assumption that the regulatory framework is of particular importance for the practical enforcement.

---

45. For the purposes of this study, states that have satisfactorily implemented less than half of their OECD Working Group Phase 2 recommendations are considered to have a rather deficient implementation record.

Conclusion

This article has compared the results of GRECO and OECD Working Group monitoring reports to two TI instruments, the CPI and the OECD Anti-Bribery Convention Progress Report.[46] It has constructed and applied a simple typology (four-cell matrix) consisting of the combinations of good/deficient implementation of international anti-corruption provisions and high/low level of perceived corruption. As the sources and the comparative method used cannot prove causality, the article has introduced three ideal types of interpretation to discuss the potential contribution of the anti-corruption regulatory framework in reducing domestic and cross-border corruption. Without any doubt, OECD and CoE anti-corruption hard and soft law and monitoring mechanisms have influenced many national policies which aim to fight corruption. The country reports of both organisations show that member states have formally implemented numerous international provisions.[47] However, significant regulatory gaps in a number of countries remain. The peer-review method applied by both organisations is rigorous (and somewhat costly[48]). Without this strict methodology, implementation records would certainly be worse.[49] Nevertheless, TI's evaluation instruments show different results than OECD and GRECO reports. The mixed picture for both Eastern and Western European countries can only be interpreted with caution.

A conventional line of argumentation, which assumes that a good regulatory framework based on international standards is the key factor to determine anti-corruption performance, seems to provide a plausible explanation for Western European countries in the domestic context, but not in the area of fighting corruption abroad. In contrast, most Eastern European states do not cluster in accordance with this type of interpretation's hypotheses as to domestic anti-corruption policies, whereas the small data basis does not allow conclusions regarding the cross-border context. It is striking that a majority of Eastern European countries scores low on the CPI since several years, despite better implementation of GRECO recommendations (i.e. a better regulatory framework) than many Western European states.[50]

---

46. It is remarkable that the country reports issued by the different organisations do not mention each other. This might be a strategy to insist on the independence (and importance) of each monitoring mechanism. But there is a certain degree of co-operation between GRECO and the OECD Working Group (e.g. the Working Group's secretariat sends observers to GRECO meetings). In many cases, GRECO and Working Group evaluations show similar results where the areas of examined anti-corruption measures overlap. However, diverging views do occur in some instances (e.g. the Working Group is much more sceptical than GRECO about the German maximum monetary sanction for legal persons).

47. For detailed results, see the Appendix (Tables A1–A7).

48. Participation in OECD and CoE anti-corruption monitoring bodies costs considerable administrative resources. For example, authorities of Liechtenstein plausibly state that the micro-state has not joined GRECO because it can hardly afford to burden its few officials with GRECO work (i.e. to analyse and comment on hundreds of draft reports and send own experts to GRECO meetings and on-site country visits). Andorra and Monaco, however, have recently joined GRECO. But unlike Liechtenstein, they have not ratified the UN Convention Against Corruption. Thus, it seems that micro-states focus their limited administrative resources on selected international anti-corruption activities.

49. This is why TI fights for a UN anti-corruption monitoring mechanism that is similar to GRECO's and OECD Working Group's procedures, see http://www.transparency.org/global_priorities/international_conventions (accessed May 20, 2009). If the Conference of the States Parties to the UN Convention Against Corruption fails to establish an effective review mechanism, it might be useful to re-focus on CoE and OECD. More countries should sign the OECD anti-bribery convention and join the Working Group (see Sebastian Wolf, 'Internationale Korruptionsbekämpfung. Anmerkungen zum zehnjährigen Jubiläum des OECD-Bestechungsübereinkommens', *Kritische Justiz* 41 (2008): 376).

50. For a similar conclusion based on different data, see Tivig and Maurer, 'Die EU-Antikorruptionspolitik', 53.

Moreover, Eastern European countries slightly better legally implement OECD Working Group recommendations than Western European and non-European states but show little or no practical enforcement. Thus, it remains unclear whether Eastern European 'OECD members lack either the will or the capacity to meet their obligations'.[51]

As the time span of this study is rather limited, it might be that in the long run, perceptions of corruption in Eastern Europe could significantly improve with the implementation and enforcement of anti-corruption measures. Only the future will tell which of the types of interpretation about the relevance of compliance with international anti-corruption provisions has the most explanatory power. This study introduced a model of analysis that requires further testing and refining in the future. But for the time being, the preliminary results presented here could indicate that the importance of regulatory frameworks based on international standards is particularly limited when it comes to anti-corruption performance in Eastern Europe. One might even question the conventional relationship between dependent and independent variable: In most Eastern European countries,[52] a certain level of perceived corruption appears to be the reason for implementing a specific regulatory framework, not the other way around. Therefore, it seems that both IOs and NGOs should focus their efforts in fighting corruption in Eastern Europe more on other corruption-related factors than simple compliance with legal and institutional anti-corruption standards.[53] However, these other factors that contribute to the extent of corruption in a society (such as cultural aspects) are much more difficult to identify and to deal with.[54] Nonetheless, the more IOs and transnational actors stick to the traditional legal and institutional compliance approach, although this policy does not seem to work in Eastern Europe since a couple of years, the more this strategy might become symbolic politics.

Acknowledgements

The author thanks Diana Schmidt-Pfister, Steven Sampson, and two anonymous referees for valuable comments and recommendations.

Notes on contributor

Sebastian Wolf holds a Master's degree in Political Science from the University of Darmstadt and a Master's degree in European law from Saarland University. He received his PhD from the University of Darmstadt in 2005. From 2005 to 2007, he worked at the German Research Institute for Public Administration, Speyer. Since 2007, he is a postdoctoral researcher at the University of Konstanz, Department of Politics and Management. His research interests are international anti-corruption regimes, law and politics, and European integration. Sebastian Wolf is a board member of the German chapter of Transparency International since 2007.

---

51. Tarullo, 'The Limits of Institutional Design', 683.
52. It might be useful to investigate why Estonia and Slovenia perform like many Western European states whereas most Eastern European countries do not.
53. This article has mainly dealt with the criteria developed and applied by GRECO, the OECD Working Group, and TI in their reports. The exploration of other corruption-related factors is beyond the focus of this study.
54. For a comprehensive research project that explores the goodness of fit between institutional (top-down) anti-corruption concepts and (bottom-up) perceptions of corruption in several Eastern and Western European societies, see Dirk Tänzler, Konstadinos Maras, and Angelos Giannakopoulos, 'Crime and Culture. Breaking New Ground in Corruption Research', *Crime & Culture Discussion Paper Series* no. 1 (2007), http://www.uni-konstanz.de/crimeandculture/docs/Discussion_Paper_No_1_Project_Presentation_June_2007.pdf (accessed February 24, 2009).

Appendix

Table A1.   GRECO first evaluation round – detailed results for Western European countries.

	Evaluation report recommendations	Compliance report				Addendum to compliance report			
		Satisfactorily implemented	Satisfactory manner	Partly implemented	Not implemented	Satisfactorily implemented	Satisfactory manner	Partly implemented	Not implemented
Belgium	14	14	0	0	0	14	0	0	0
Cyprus	10	6	0	4	0	7	1	2	0
Denmark	4	3	0	1	0	3	0	1	0
Finland	8	5	1	2	0	7	1	0	0
France	10	6	0	4	0	7	0	3	0
Germany	6	1	2	3	0	1	3	2	0
Greece	10	7	2	1	0	7	3	0	0
Iceland	3	0	1	2	0	1	1	1	0
Ireland	8	5	0	3	0	5	1	2	0
Luxembourg	12	4	0	3	5	5	3	4	0
Malta	15	10	3	2	0	10	3	2	0
Netherlands	7	2	3	2	0	3	4	0	0
Norway	5	4	0	1	0	5	0	0	0
Portugal	12	8	2	1	1	9	2	0	1
Spain	10	2	4	4	0	3	5	2	0
Sweden	8	4	3	1	0	4	4	0	0
United Kingdom	12	6	2	3	1	7	3	1	1
United States	12	3	7	2	0	3	9	0	0
Total	166	90 (54%)	30 (18%)	39 (23%)	7 (4%)	101 (61%)	43 (26%)	20 (12%)	2 (1%)

Table A2. GRECO first evaluation round – detailed results for (South) Eastern European countries.

	Evaluation report recommendations	Compliance report				Addendum to compliance report			
		Satisfactorily implemented	Satisfactory manner	Partly implemented	Not implemented	Satisfactorily implemented	Satisfactory manner	Partly implemented	Not implemented
Albania	11	4	1	6	0	8	3	0	0
Bosnia and Herzegovina	18	10	5	3	0	10	5	3	0
Bulgaria	14	8	4	2	0	10	4	0	0
Croatia	16	6	2	6	2	10	4	2	0
Czech Republic	9	5	2	2	0	6	2	1	0
Estonia	12	4	5	3	0	5	7	0	0
Georgia	25 Regular report	0	2	16	7	5	13	5	2
	25 Special report	5	12	6	2				
Hungary	11	7	2	1	1	7	3	1	0
Latvia	15	10	1	3	1	10	3	2	0
Lithuania	10	9	0	1	0	9	0	1	0
Moldova	14	6	4	3	1	9	4	1	0
Poland	17	8	5	4	0	9	6	2	0
Romania	13	12	0	1	0	13	0	0	0
Slovakia	19	15	0	4	0	19	0	0	0
Slovenia	12	9	0	3	0	10	1	1	0
Macedonia	17	10	1	4	2	14	1	1	1
Total	233	128 (55%)	44 (19%)	52 (22%)	9 (4%)	154 (66%)	56 (24%)	20 (9%)	3 (1%)

Table A3. CPI 2008 and GRECO second evaluation round – detailed results for Western European countries.

	CPI 2008 average score (on a 1–10 scale)	GRECO evaluation report recommendations	GRECO compliance report			
			Satisfactorily implemented	Satisfactory manner	Partly implemented	Not implemented
Belgium	7.3	9	2	1	4	2
Cyprus	6.4	10	3	2	2	3
Denmark	9.3	6	0	3	1	2
Finland	9.0	4	3	0	1	0
France	6.9	6	2	1	2	1
Germany	7.9	6	2	2	2	0
Greece	4.7	10	3	2	3	2
Iceland	8.9	6	1	1	2	2
Ireland	7.7	6	3	1	2	0
Luxembourg	8.3	13	2	1	9	1
Malta	5.8	7	1	2	4	0
Netherlands	8.9	6	2	1	3	0
Norway	7.9	4	2	2	0	0
Portugal	6.1	10	2	4	4	0
Spain	6.5	6	2	0	4	0
Sweden	9.3	5	4	0	0	1
United Kingdom	7.7	7	2	3	2	0
Total	Average: 7.6	121	36 (30%)	26 (21%)	45 (37%)	14 (12%)

Table A4. CPI 2008 and GRECO second evaluation round – detailed results for (South) Eastern European countries.

	CPI 2008 average score (on a 1–10 scale)	GRECO evaluation report recommendations	GRECO compliance report			
			Satisfactorily implemented	Satisfactory manner	Partly implemented	Not implemented
Albania	3.4	13	5	2	4	2
Bulgaria	3.6	11	5	2	3	1
Croatia	4.4	11	5	1	3	2
Czech Republic	5.2	12	5	1	4	2
Estonia	6.6	15	1	9	3	2
Hungary	5.1	12	3	3	4	2
Latvia	5.0	13	1	4	5	3
Lithuania	4.6	8	4	3	1	0
Poland	4.6	9	5	2	1	1
Romania	3.8	15	4	2	6	3
Slovakia	5.0	17	2	6	7	2
Slovenia	6.7	10	2	2	6	0
Macedonia	3.6	14	6	3	4	1
Total	Average: 4.7	160	48 (30%)	40 (25%)	51 (32%)	21 (13%)

Table A5. TI progress report and OECD working group Phase 2 monitoring – detailed results for Western European countries.

	TI report 2008 significant enforcement?	OECD Phase 2 number of recommendations	OECD Phase 2 progress report			
			Satisfactorily implemented	Partly implemented	Not implemented	Further consideration/other
Austria	No	19	10	1	8	0
Belgium	Yes	16	9	3	4	0
Denmark	Yes	13	2	4	7	0
Finland	Yes	9	4	3	2	0
France	Yes	13	12	1	0	0
Germany	Yes	8	5	1	2	0
Greece	No	15	7	4	4	0
Iceland	Not included	10	3	2	5	0
Italy	Yes	11	2	4	3	2
Norway	Yes	11	11	0	0	0
Spain	Yes	23	5	4	14	0
Sweden	Yes	19	11	3	5	0
Switzerland	Yes	10	2	8	0	0
Total	Yes: 10 countries No: 2 countries	177	83 (47%)	38 (21%)	54 (31%)	2 (1%)

Table A6. TI progress report and OECD working group Phase 2 monitoring – detailed results for Eastern European countries.

	TI report 2008 significant enforcement?	OECD Phase 2 number of recommendations	OECD Phase 2 progress report			
			Satisfactorily implemented	Partly implemented	Not implemented	Further consideration/other
Bulgaria	No	17	8	5	2	2
Hungary	Yes	23	8	9	6	0
Slovakia	No	23	16	4	2	1
Total	Yes: 1 country No: 2 countries	63	32 (51%)	18 (29%)	10 (16%)	3 (5%)

Table A7. TI progress report and OECD working group Phase 2 monitoring – detailed results for non-European countries.

	TI report 2008 significant enforcement?	OECD Phase 2 number of recommendations	OECD Phase 2 progress report			
			Satisfactorily implemented	Partly implemented	Not implemented	Further consideration/other
Australia	Yes	22	12	8	2	0
Canada	No	16	4	7	3	2
Korea	Yes	14	7	3	4	0
Mexico	No	22	10.5	7	4.5	0
United States	Yes	14	7	2	2	3
Total	Yes: 3 countries No: 2 countries	88	40.5 (46%)	27 (31%)	15.5 (18%)	5 (6%)

The European Union and the fight against corruption in its near abroad: can it make a difference?

Tanja A. Börzel[a], Andreas Stahn[b] and Yasemin Pamuk[b]

[a]Center for European Integration, Freie Universität Berlin, Berlin, Germany;
[b]DFG Collaborative Research Center 700, Freie Universität Berlin, Berlin, Germany

This article sheds light on the European Union's (EU) efforts to facilitate the fight against corruption and promote good governance through the European Neighbourhood Policy (ENP). Our analysis shows that the level of corruption in the Eastern Neighbourhood is strongly connected to the success of democratic and economic reforms. The ENP theoretically corresponds to the complex nature of the phenomenon by placing equal emphasis on strengthening state institutions, restructuring the economy, and pushing for democratic reforms. As the EU, however, by and large seeks cooperation with state actors and pursues a 'one-size-fits-all' approach mostly based on 'soft' mechanisms such as socialisation and capacity-building, the implementation of politically sensitive reforms seems to be unlikely. Moreover, the EU potentially allows its partner governments to 'pick and chose' from the overall reform agenda and evade real political and economic change towards better governance.

Introduction

With the 'big bang' enlargement in 2004, the European Union (EU) started to spur political and economic reforms in Eastern Europe and promote the fight against corruption and for good governance. As its borders moved eastwards, the EU has developed a new foreign policy framework for those countries in the East and in the South that do not have a membership perspective in the near future. The European Neighbourhood Policy (ENP) aims at developing 'a zone of prosperity and a friendly neighbourhood – a "ring of friends" – with whom the EU enjoys close, peaceful, and co-operative relations'.[1]

However, many scholars questioned whether the ENP would contribute to reform processes in the EU's partner countries in the same way as the EU's enlargement policy did. On the one hand, doubts have been raised, whether the ENP is sufficiently equipped

The article draws on research conducted in the project 'Good Governance without the Shadow of Hierarchy? The European Neighbourhood Policy and Anti-Corruption Measures in the Southern Caucasus', which is part of the SFB 700 'Governance in Areas of Limited Statehood', funded by the Deutsche Forschungsgemeinschaft (http://www.sfb-governance.de/en/teilprojekte/projektbereich_b/b2/index.html).
1. European Commission, *Wider Europe – Neighbourhood: A New Framework for Relations with Our Eastern and Southern Neighbours*, 2003, COM (2003) 104 final, 4.

and provides enough incentives to substitute for the 'membership carrot'.[2] On the other hand, the ENP countries pose a much bigger challenge to the EU as the necessity of political and economic reforms has been much greater than it had been in Central Eastern Europe.[3]

All the Eastern Neighbours of the EU – including Armenia, Azerbaijan, Georgia, Moldova, Ukraine, and potentially Belarus – seriously suffer from bad governance.[4] Compared to the Central Eastern European countries, state institutions are weaker, corruption levels much higher, and arbitrary rule abounds. None of these states can be considered a consolidated democracy and some are still far from being a functioning market economy.[5] Moreover, some of them even face challenges to their territorial integrity.

In this article, we aim at shedding light on how the EU has sought to address bad governance in its neighbourhood focusing on the fight against corruption as the most prominent problem. More specifically, we ask whether the EU has developed strategies adaptive to the transition context of its Eastern Neighbours.

Our analysis will show that the EU pursues a 'one-size-fits-all' strategy[6] principally pushing for reform measures in all important areas associated with the fight against corruption. However, the quite uniform strategy of the EU to improve governance has hardly been fitted to the transition context or 'to each country's specific circumstances'.[7] Because higher corruption levels go hand in hand with (semi-)authoritarian rule as well as insufficient market reform, we conclude that an approach which more strongly focuses enhancing pluralism and the accountability of the political regime(s) would require increasing the overall effectiveness of the EU's anti-corruption efforts. To this end, the EU could press for greater opportunities of civil society actors and business in domestic decision-making and implementation processes as well as their formal incorporation in the political dialogue between the EU and its Eastern Neighbours.

To state our argument, the first part of our article gives a short overview of the (re-)emergence of corruption in post-communist countries. It shows that the phenomenon of corruption and the success and failure of the democratic and economic transition processes in the Eastern Neighbourhood of the EU are inextricably linked with each other. Moreover, common patterns of corruption in the EU's Eastern Neighbourhood often involve vested interests of political and economic elites, who have little incentive to change.

---

2. Judith Kelley, 'New Wine in Old Wineskins: Promoting Political Reforms through the New European Neighbourhood Policy', *Journal of Common Market Studies* 44, no. 1 (2006): 29–55; Amichai Magen, 'The Shadow of Enlargement: Can the European Union Neighbourhood Policy Achieve Compliance?' *Columbia Journal of European Law* 12, no. 2 (2006): 495–538.

3. Frank Schimmelfennig, 'Europeanization Beyond Europe', *Living Reviews in European Governance* 1, no. 1 (2007), http://www.livingreviews.org/lreg-2009-3 (accessed March 3, 2010).

4. Tanja A. Börzel, Yasemin Pamuk, and Andreas Stahn, 'The European Union and the Promotion of Good Governance in Its near Abroad. One Size Fits All?' (SFB-Governance Working Paper Series, no. 18, 2008).

5. Jeffrey S. Kopstein and David A. Reilly, 'Geographic Diffusion and the Transformation of the Post-Communist World', *World Politics* 53 (2000): 1–37; Daniel Gros and Alfred Steinherr, *Economic Transition in Central and Eastern Europe. Planting the Seeds* (Cambridge: Cambridge University Press, 2004).

6. Tanja A. Börzel and Thomas Risse, 'One Size Fits All! EU Policies for the Promotion of Human Rights, Democracy and the Rule of Law' (paper presented at the Workshop on Democracy Promotion, CDDRL, Stanford University, Stanford, CA, October 4–5, 2004).

7. European Commission, *European Neighbourhood Policy. Strategy Paper*, 2004, COM (2004) 373 final, 14.

The second part of our article develops an analytical framework that distinguishes three basic reform options for the fight against corruption. We argue that external actors, such as the EU, can focus on strengthening state institutions, restructuring the economy, or pushing for democratic reforms. Moreover, they can either cooperate with state actors or seek to (also) involve business and civil society. Finally, we discuss various instruments and influence mechanisms through which reforms can effectively be promoted. Given the prevalence of state capture and (semi-)authoritarianism in the EU's Eastern Neighbourhood, we conclude that the EU should place great emphasis on increasing the accountability of the political regime through democratic reforms. Moreover, as governments may be unwilling to reform, the diffusion of principles such as the rule of law, transparency, and accountability through non-state actors that have an interest in pressing for real change might be of equal importance.

The third part explores which stance on the fight against corruption the EU has actually adopted in the framework of its ENP and which channels and instruments it has used. Moreover, we shed light on potential country-specific variation in the bilateral relations between the EU and its partner countries. We show that the EU has developed an ambitious reform agenda with and for each partner government, which pays equal attention to democratic and economic reforms, and to strengthening efficiency and effectiveness of the states. Additionally, the EU increasingly demands from its partners to involve non-state actors. However, when it comes to the practical application of the channels and instruments at the EU's disposal, it largely restricts itself to socialisation and capacity-building efforts with state actors, which mutes its efforts to fight corruption in neighbourhood countries.

Corruption in transition countries

Corruption – widely defined as the abuse of public power for the private benefit – poses a serious challenge for EU's Eastern Neighbours. According to the Corruption Perceptions Index (CPI) of Transparency International, which can be regarded a rough proxy for illustrating the pervasiveness of that problem, all the respective countries suffer from exceptionally high levels of corruption (Table 1).

The prevalence of corruption in the EU's Eastern Neighbourhood, however, does not come as a surprise, given the numerous variables the literature considers to correlate with corruption. Although it is often difficult to establish clear causality and identify the mechanisms at work,[8] many scholars agree that corruption is more likely to evolve in fairly specific political, economic, and cultural settings. Corruption can be bread by, first, features of the political system, such as authoritarianism and limited political freedoms, the

Table 1. Perceptions of corruption in the EU's Eastern Neighbourhood.

	Armenia	Azerbaijan	Belarus	Georgia	Moldova	Ukraine
Individual scores	2.9	1.9	2.0	3.9	2.9	2.5
Rank out of 180 countries	109th	158th	151th	67th	109th	134th

Source: Transparency International Corruption Perceptions Index 2008.

8. Johann Graf Lambsdorff, 'Corruption in Empirical Research – A Review' (Transparency International Working Paper, Transparency International, November 1999), 2.

organisational structure of the state, and its administrative capacities.[9] Second, corruption has been associated with economies in which a smooth functioning of the market is distorted by frequent and arbitrary state interventions, and businesses face an exhaustive and intransparent regulatory framework in particular with regard to licensing, taxing, customs, and public procurement as well as competition.[10] Finally, the literature points to cultural explanations of corruption, such as religion, culturally determined attitudes or gender issues.[11]

In the transition context of (Central) Eastern Europe and the Former Soviet Union, explanatory factors of all three dimensions coincide and even tend to reinforce each other. On the one hand, many scholars argue that post-communist countries are in general more prone to corruption.[12] In their view, the communist past – in which patterns of corruption even helped to balance dysfunctions of the planned economies – continues to affect the societies by the persistence of old personal networks, habits, and practises.[13] On the other hand, all of these countries were expected to quickly engage in a simultaneous transition towards democracy and market economy as well as in nation-building efforts after the fall of communism.[14] The dismantling of the *ancien régime* and uncertainty over the political and economic institutions to come also provided many-fold new opportunities to engage in rent-seeking and asset-grabbing activities.[15]

Twenty years after the fall of the Berlin Wall, one can draw some conclusions on the individual transition dynamics and outcomes as well as the respective state of corruption. These can be illustrated best by a comparison between the successor states of the Soviet Union and those Central Eastern European Countries (CEEC) that entered the EU in 2004 and 2006, respectively. Figure 1 suggests that the CEEC have been far more successful in adopting comprehensive political and economic reforms.[16] By contrast, most of the Newly

9. Ce Shen and John B. Wiliamson, 'Corruption, Democracy, Economic Freedom, and State Strength: A Cross-National Analysis', *International Journal of Comparative Sociology* 46, no. 4 (2005): 327–45; Daniel Treisman, 'Postcommunist Corruption', in *Political Economy of Transition and Development: Institutions, Politics, and Policies*, ed. Jan Fidrmuc and Nauro Campos (Norwell: Kluwer Academic Publishers, 2003); and Wayne Sandholtz and William Koetzle, 'Accounting for Corruption: Economic Structure, Democracy, and Trade', *International Studies Quarterly* 44 (2000): 31–50.

10. Shen and Wiliamson, 'Corruption, Democracy, Economic Freedom, and State Strength'; Treisman, 'Postcommunist Corruption'; Sandholtz and Koetzle, 'Accounting for Corruption'; and Kimberly Ann Elliott, ed., *Corruption and the Global Economy* (Washington, DC: Institute for International Economics, 1997).

11. Lambsdorff, 'Corruption in Empirical Research'; Wayne Sandholtz and Rein Taagepera, 'Corruption, Culture, and Communism', *Review of Sociology* 15, no. 1 (2005): 109–31; and Treisman, 'Postcommunist Corruption'.

12. Sandholtz and Taagepera, 'Corruption, Culture, and Communism'; Mancur Olsen, 'Why the Transition from Communism is so Difficult', *Eastern Economic Journal* 21, no. 4 (1995): 437–61.

13. Rasma Karklins, *The System Made Me Do It: Corruption in Post-Communist Societies* (New York and London: M. E. Sharpe, 2005); Sandholtz and Taagepera, 'Corruption, Culture, and Communism'.

14. Claus Offe, 'Capitalism by Democratic Design? Democratic Theory Facing the Triple Transition in East Central Europe', *Social Research* 58, no. 4 (1991): 865–92.

15. Richard Lotspeich, 'Crime in the Transition Economies', *Europe-Asia Studies* 47, no. 4 (1995): 555–89.

16. The scores presented are average values for both groups of countries, based on the Freedom House *Political Rights* & *Civil Liberties* indices (democratic transition), the sub-index *Economic Transition* of the Bertelsmann Transformation Index (BTI) and the Transparency International *Corruption Perceptions Index* from 2008. The respective values of the Baltic States have been included into the CEEC-dataset, as they acceded the European Union in 2004. For a discussion of the strength and weaknesses of such governance indices cf. for example: Daniel Kaufmann and Aart Kraay, 'Governance Indicators: Where We Are, Where Should We Be Going?' (World Bank Policy

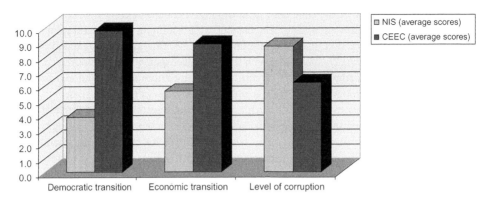

Figure 1. Corruption and the political and economic transition.

Independent States (NIS) remained half-way stuck in transition or even reversed their initial reform efforts.[17]

The greatest gap between the CEEC and the NIS obviously concerns the transition to
democracy, followed by the comprehensiveness of economic reforms. At the same time,
corruption levels in the NIS are comparatively higher than in the CEEC.

Examining the causal links between corruption and the different transition paths, many
scholars initially restricted their focus to the economic dimension. They argued that it was
'the partial nature of many economic reforms'[18] or 'half-baked, poorly designed, inade-
quately implemented market reforms'[19] that laid the foundations for the extraordinary
growth of corruption and organised crime in many countries of the region. By contrast, the
virtue of political reforms had been largely neglected or restricted to the mere necessity of
strengthening weak judicial and law enforcement agencies. Democratic progress was even
expected to hamper the economic transition because 'frustrations with economic performance and distribution' under the condition of 'democratic politics' may have blocked or
distorted 'the road to privatisation and hence marketisation'.[20]

This initial assumption, however, proved to be misleading. Hellmann's influential
study on the link between democracy and economic reform in post-communist transitions
helps to explain the causal chain. He convincingly demonstrated that (Central) Eastern
European governments that were democratically elected and remained under democratic
control also initiated more substantive economic reforms. Conversely, those governments
that faced less electoral pressure from the public 'have made, at best, only partial progress
in reforming their economies'.[21] Thus, in many post-communist countries it has been the
lack of democratic control that allowed political elites and businessmen to benefit from
the economic distortions that they have caused by the politics of partial reforms. To phrase

Research Working Paper 4370, Washington, DC, 2008); Dirk Berg-Schlosser, 'Concepts, Measure-
ments, and Sub-Types in Democratization Research', in *Democratization. The State of the Art*, ed.
Dirk Berg-Schlosser (Opladen: Budrich, 2007).
17. Thomas Carothers, 'The End of the Transition Paradigm', *Journal of Democracy* 13, no. 1 (2002):
5–21.
18. Lotspeich, 'Crime in the Transition Economies', 580.
19. Daniel Kaufmann, 'Corruption: The Facts', *Foreign Policy* 107 (1997): 114–31, 122.
20. Offe, 'Capitalism by Democratic Design?'.
21. Joel S. Hellman, 'Winner Takes All: The Politics of Partial Reform in Postcommunist Transitions',
World Politics 50, no. 2 (1998): 203–34, 232.

it with Sandholtz and Koetzle, 'participants in corruption benefit precisely because they rigged the system in their favor'.[22]

Empirically, researchers of the World Bank have provided further evidence for these complex causal chains. They distinguished different forms of corruption such as 'state capture' and 'administrative corruption'.[23] The former refers to the abuse of political power to shape rules and regulations in the interest of a small political or economic elite, whereas the latter applies to intentionally created distortions in the implementation of rules and regulations by state officials.[24] Comparing the prevalence of either form in the CEEC and the NIS, the World Bank shows that many NIS suffer from higher levels of state capture that render them a particularly difficult context for facilitating the fighting against corruption from the outside.[25]

Fighting against corruption from the outside: approaches, channels, and instruments

The EU like any other external actor engaged in seeking to fight corruption in third countries faces a number of choices. To become effective, the design of an external intervention is decisive. It entails, firstly, determining areas that most urgently need to be reformed and promoting measures that yield effective results. Secondly, it is necessary to decide on the actors to cooperate with. Thirdly, the instruments with which anti-corruption measures are being promoted play a major role. To be sure, the fight against corruption is a domestic matter, and it is certainly a difficult task to contribute to effective domestic change for the better from the outside. However, any potentially effective strategy requires careful consideration of the political and economic context of the target country, the nature of corruption, and its root causes.

In this section we explore in greater detail the choices the EU has in designing its anti-corruption and good governance agenda for the Eastern Neighbours. The exposure of the various options and entry points primarily will allow the systematic mapping of the EU's actual efforts in the empirical cross-country analysis in the following section.

Approaches

In general, the literature recommends a combination of different measures aiming at improving control of corruption and reducing incentives for corrupt activities. These measures can roughly be grouped into three different approaches that differ with regard to the actors concerned and the mechanism employed.

---

22. Sandholtz and Koetzle, 'Accounting for Corruption', 48.
23. This distinction largely resembles the rough and most common typology in the literature that differentiates between highly centralised grand corruption and rather decentralised administrative corruption. Cf. Arvind K. Jain, 'Corruption: A Review', *Journal of Economic Surveys* 15, no. 1 (2002): 71–121; Kimberly Ann Elliott, 'Corruption as an International Policy Problem: Overview and Recommendations', in *Corruption and the Global Economy*, ed. Kimberly Ann Elliott (Washington, DC, 1997), 175–236; and Susan Rose-Ackerman, 'Democracy and "Grand Corruption"', *International Social Science Journal* 48, no. 3 (1996): 365–80.
24. World Bank, *Anticorruption in Transition. A Contribution to the Policy Debate* (Washington, DC, 2000).
25. James H. Anderson and Cheryl W. Gray, 'Anticorruption in Transition 3 – Who is Succeeding . . . and Why?' (World Bank Report, Washington, 2006).

The first approach aims at fighting corruption in the administration and the public sector. It largely concerns the reform of the state and its administration[26] by providing institutional checks that facilitate the detection and the subsequent punishing of corrupt behaviour.[27] 'This approach might include the establishment of internal monitoring units in bureaucracies, protecting whistleblowers, and, more generally, the creation of anti-corruption agencies or commissions'.[28] At the same time, it aims at strengthening the prosecution of corrupt behaviour by legal reforms and measures that strengthen the judiciary and particularly the role of prosecutors. Granting the independence of the judiciary and monitoring units from the executive is of utmost importance, as they could otherwise be used as an 'instrument of repression, rather than a force for clean government'.[29] We also subsume measures that aim at strengthening professionalism and professional ethics in the administration under this approach. The *reform of the state approach* largely rest on an idea of 'self-control' and incentives to constrain corrupt behaviour within the public administration by the officials themselves.

The second approach is related to the regulative framework of, and state activities in, the economic sphere.[30] It is based on the assumption that excessive and non-transparent regulations with regard to taxes, customs, or licensing provide incentives for corrupt behaviour among businesses in their interaction with the state.[31] The often distorting role of state activities in the economic sector and the negative consequences of monopolies are a major concern, too. Respective countermeasures comprise deregulation, liberalisation, and privatisation as well as efforts aiming at strengthening competition and enhancing transparency for instance with regard to public procurement.[32] The *reform of the economy approach* therefore largely intends to remove opportunities for corrupt behaviour through altering the incentives of private businesses (and opportunities for state actors) to distort markets.

Finally, the third approach aims at improving governance processes, by empowering non-state actors. It focuses on the interaction between state and non-state actors – in a more general way. It seeks to make decision-making and implementation processes more transparent, accountable, and gives non-state actors and individuals a greater say with regard to rules and regulations.[33] In contrast to the first approach, it rests on society's control over government, rather than government controlling itself. We call this a *democratic*

---

26. Rose-Ackerman, 'Democracy and "Grand Corruption"'; Michael Johnston, 'Corruption and Democratic Consolidation' (paper presented at the Conference on Democracy and Corruption, Shelby Cullom Davis Center for Historical Studies Princeton University, Princeton, NJ, March 12, 1999).

27. Vito Tanzi, 'Corruption Around the World: Causes, Consequences, Scope, and Cures', in *Governance, Corruption & Economic Performance*, ed. George T. Abed and Sanjeev Gupta (Washington, DC: International Monetary Fund, 2002).

28. George T. Abed and Hamid R. Davoodi, 'Corruption, Structural Reforms, and Economic Performance in Transition Countries', in *Governance, Corruption & Economic Performance*, ed. George T. Abed and Sanjeev Gupta (Washington, DC: International Monetary Fund, 2002), 5.

29. Rose-Ackerman, 'Democracy and "Grand Corruption"', 373.

30. Abed and Davoodi, 'Corruption, Structural Reforms, and Economic Performance in Transition Countries'; Rose-Ackerman, 'Democracy and "Grand Corruption"'.

31. Tanzi, 'Corruption Around the World'.

32. Joel S. Hellman, Geraint Jones, and Daniel Kaufmann, *'Seize the State, Seize the Day': State Capture, Corruption and Influence in Transition*, 2444 (Washington, DC, 2000); Abed and Davoodi, 'Corruption, Structural Reforms, and Economic Performance in Transition Countries'; and Shen and Wiliamson, 'Corruption, Democracy, Economic Freedom, and State Strength'.

33. Hellman, Jones and Kaufmann, *'Seize the State, Seize the Day'*; Johnston, 'Corruption and Democratic Consolidation'; and Daniel Lederman, Norman Loayza, and Rodrigo Reis Soares, 'Accountability and Corruption. Political Institutions Matter' (World Bank Policy Research Working Paper 2708, Washington, DC, 2001).

Table 2.   Anti-corruption approaches and wider implications.

Anti-corruption approaches	Goal	Legitimacy	Opportunities for non-state actors to participate
Reform of the state	Increasing internal control (monitoring & persecution)	Measures predominantly increase output legitimacy → efficient and effective provision of services through the state	Low
Reform of the economy	Reducing incentives for corrupt activities	Measures predominantly increase output legitimacy → economic development	Medium
Democratic reforms	Increasing external control (awareness raising & monitoring)	Increasing input legitimacy → ensuring public voice & accountability	High

reform approach because it necessitates respect for civil liberties as well as a vibrant civil society and a vigilant-free press. The third approach has some connections with the first, as democratic accountability also refers to the separation of powers and more specifically to the independence of the judiciary to become effective.[34] Apart from strengthening the very foundations of democracy, measures that increase the relevance of external control also embrace awareness rising to alter societal acceptance of corrupt behaviour and counter political fatigue.[35]

The actual choice of approaches has wider implications with regard to the questions of legitimacy and the role of society in facilitating intended reforms. Legitimacy has two dimensions.[36] Output legitimacy refers to the extent to which the effects of political decisions are perceived to be in the interest of the people, whereas input legitimacy requires political decisions to correspond to the preferences of affected people. Therefore, the *reform of the state* and the *reform of the economy* approaches mostly increase output legitimacy by improving the efficiency and effectiveness in the provision of public goods and removing obstacles for investment and growth. *Democratic reforms*, by contrast, do not only serve the aim of fighting corruption with second-order effects on output legitimacy, but also directly increase input legitimacy. Thus, by choosing the *democratic reforms* approach, external actors automatically contribute to good governance in a broader sense (cf. Table 2).[37]

The role of society is an equally important issue with regard to the choice of one or the other approach. Although the state is mainly in charge of formulating and implementing reforms in all three areas, there is growing empirical evidence that 'new modes of governance', that is, patterns of cooperation between state and non-state actors offer a viable alternative to hierarchical and monopolised decision-making.[38] The main assumption of

34. Rose-Ackerman, 'Democracy and "Grand Corruption"'.

35. Alejandro Moreno, 'Corruption and Democracy: A Cultural Assessment', *Comparative Sociology* 1, no. 3–4 (2002): 495–507.

36. Fritz W. Scharpf, *Governing Europe. Effective and Legitimate?* (Oxford: Oxford University Press, 1999).

37. Börzel, Pamuk, and Stahn, 'European Union and the Promotion of Good Governance'.

38. Thomas Risse and Ursula Lehmkuhl, 'Regieren ohne Staat? Governance in Räumen begrenzter Staatlichkeit', in *Schriften Zur Governance-Forschung*, vol. 10, ed. Thomas Risse and Ursula Lehmkuhl (Baden-Baden: Nomos, 2007).

this kind of research is that the pooling of resources of state and non-state actors such as interest organisations or private businesses might contribute to an efficient, effective, and even inclusive formulation and implementation of collectively binding norms.[39]

Although non-state actors can principally cooperate on reforms in each of the three areas, they are only likely to be empowered by the *economic* and *democratic reforms* approaches (cf. Table 2).

Efforts aiming at increasing economic competition and reducing the role of the state in the economy, for instance, are likely to increase the sheer number of enterprises that have an interest in cooperating with the state on future economic policies. *Democratic reforms* lay the very foundations for political engagement of individuals or intermediate actors. Strengthening state institutions, by contrast, tends to increase the autonomy of public actors and can bolster their (repressive) capacities to control society, particularly in regimes that have not made or completed the transition to democracy.

Channels and instruments

External actors can implement their approach(es) through different channels, depending on whether they decide to involve non-state actors or not. When opting for the intergovernmental channel, they exclusively cooperate with the state actors. Alternatively, external actors can seek to trigger and influence domestic reform processes through transnational channels through societal actors in the target state.[40] Forging broader reform coalitions comprising reform-oriented political elites, state officials, and non-state actors is likely to increase the overall acceptance and effectiveness of anti-corruption measures. In countries under authoritarian rule or with a prevalence of 'state capture', the transnational channel or at least the demand to empower and include non-state actors in the formulation and implementation of anti-corruption reforms may even be the only option for external actors to get things changed.

The political context in which the fight against corruption shall be facilitated is also extremely relevant for the instruments chosen by an external actor. The ultimate goal of external anti-corruption interventions through whatever approaches and channels is to get relevant reforms implemented. Based on whether target countries are considered to be incapable or unwilling to enact domestic change, external actors can choose between different instruments to get their policies work.[41]

If lacking capacities is considered the main problem, transferring financial and technical resources or training is key.[42] If states predominantly lack the will to comply with external requirements as they imply high costs, both economic and political, external actors can either induce recalcitrant states into compliance by using *conditionality*, that is,

39. Renate Mayntz and Fritz W. Scharpf, eds., Gesellschaftliche Selbstregulierung und Politische Steuerung (Frankfurt a. M.: Campus, 1995); Adrienne Héritier, 'New Modes of Governance in Europe: Increasing Political Capacity and Policy Effectiveness?' in *The State of the European Union, 6 – Law, Politics, and Society*, ed. Tanja A. Börzel and Rachel Cichowski (Oxford: Oxford University Press, 2003).

40. Schimmelfennig, 'Europeanization Beyond Europe', 6.

41. Börzel, Pamuk, and Stahn, 'European Union and the Promotion of Good Governance'.

42. Abram Chayes and Antonia Handler Chayes, 'On Compliance', *International Organization* 47, no. 2 (1993): 175–205; Abram Chayes, Antonia Handler Chayes, and Ronald B. Mitchell, 'Managing Compliance: A Comparative Perspective', in *Engaging Countries: Strengthening Compliance with International Environmental Accords*, ed. Edith Brown Weiss and Harold K. Jacobsen (Cambridge: MIT Press, 1998).

Table 3.   Toolkit of external actors.

Instrument	Mechanism of influence
Assistance	Capacity and institution building
Conditionality	Manipulation of cost-benefit calculations
Political dialogue	Social learning and persuasion

by offering negative (sanctions) and positive (rewards) incentives,[43] or seek to change their preferences through socialisation processes (*political dialogue*) based on persuasion and social learning.[44] Accordingly, the toolkit of external actors consists of positive and negative incentives (conditionality), persuasion (political dialogue), and capacity building (assistance) (Table 3).

In a nutshell, external actors face three major choices to promote the fight against corruption in third countries. First, regarding the overall *approach*, they can concentrate on either reforms of the state, reforms of the economy, or democratic reforms. The second choice concerns the *channels* through which anti-corruption reforms shall be promoted. External actors can either cooperate with the governments of third states or seek to diffuse their reform goals through non-state actors. Third, external actors can make use of three different *instruments* to promote anti-corruption reforms. Assistance mainly addresses lacking capacities of state or non-state actors. Conditionality seeks to alter the preferences of such actors. Political dialogue rests on social learning and persuasion.

Given the complexity of corruption in transition countries as well as the embeddedness of corruption in the political system itself, we argue that EU should place great emphasis on the *democratic reform* approach as well as on the inclusion of non-state actors in order to forge broader reform coalitions. Moreover, because elite corruption and the danger of state capture are high[45] there should be serious doubts whether capacity building or socialisation efforts vis-à-vis their partner government suffice to push them to the formulation and implementation of substantial anti-corruption reforms.

The next part analyses that approaches, channels and instruments the EU actually uses within the framework of the ENP and whether these are likely to facilitate the fight against corruption.

Fighting corruption in the Eastern Neighbourhood of the EU

The fight against corruption in the Western NIS and states of the Southern Caucasus is a core element of the youngest foreign policy framework of the EU – the ENP. The ENP has been established as a common policy framework for those states at the borders of the enlarged EU that do not have a medium or even long-term perspective to join. Between 2004 and 2006, 12 new member states entered the EU, 10 of which were post-communist countries from Central Eastern Europe. Already on the verge of this 'big bang' enlargement the

43. George W. Downs, 'Enforcement and the Evolution of Cooperation', *Michigan Journal of International Law* 19, no. 2 (1998): 319–44; James D. Fearon, 'Bargaining, Enforcement and International Cooperation', *International Organization* 52, no. 2 (1998): 269–305.

44. Jeffrey T. Checkel, 'Why Comply? Social Learning and European Identity Change', *International Organization* 55, no. 3 (2001): 553–88; Thomas Risse, 'International Norms and Domestic Change: Arguing and Communicative Behavior in the Human Rights Area', *Politics and Society* 27, no. 4 (1999): 526–56.

45. World Bank, *Anticorruption in Transition*.

European Commission began elaborate the ENP that ought to integrate its 'new' neighbours in the East and its 'old' neighbours in the South under a common roof. As regards the Eastern Neighbours, these efforts have been additionally spurred by a certain 'enlargement fatigue'[46] particularly among the 'old' member states. Fearing an 'enlargement automatism' once the Western NIS would simply follow the path of the CEEC and apply for membership,[47] they opted for the development of the ENP as a viable alternative. Simultaneously, the EU and its member states became increasingly aware of the security risks emanating from the internal conflicts, bad governance and wide-spread corruption in its Eastern Neighbourhood.

As its borders moved eastwards, the EU was first of all motivated by a vital interest in increasing security and stability at its new borders, also in advancing trade and economic relations with its 'near abroad'. The ultimate aim was to establish 'a zone of prosperity and a friendly neighbourhood – a "ring of friends" with whom the EU enjoys close, peaceful and co-operative relations'.[48] To reach these goals, the EU has sought to initiate reform dynamics comparable to those in the CEEC during the accession negotiations, despite the absence of the 'membership carrot', which has proved to be successful in promoting reforms in Central Eastern Europe.

Institutionally, the ENP did not start from scratch.[49] As regards the NIS, the EU has begun to develop its relations with these countries soon after the fall of communism and the subsequent dissolution of the Soviet Union in 1991. Initially, it issued a large assistance package that concentrated on supporting the ongoing transition processes by advancing economic reforms through capacity-building measures.[50] In a second step, the EU sought to formalise its relations with the Technical Assistance for the Commonwealth of Indepentdent States (TACIS) countries. Hence in the period between 1997 and 1999 nine bilateral Partnership and Cooperation Agreements (PCA) entered into force. Belarus also signed such an agreement in 1996, but the EU has so far abstained from ratifying it, because of the growing authoritarianism under President Lukashenka. Thus, Belarus, takes a special position as a country that is on the one hand regarded to be a neighbourhood country, but lacks on the other hand one of the very foundations on which the ENP is built.

With minor variations, the PCAs were designed to further support the transition of the NIS to efficient and effective state institutions, full-fledged market economies and – to a lesser extent – to liberal democracies.[51] Both aspects were neither explicitly linked to a broader good governance agenda nor to the fight against corruption during the 1990s. Increasing EU attention to governance-related principles such as the rule of law, however,

---

46. Karen E. Smith, 'The Outsiders: The European Neighbourhood Policy', *International Affairs* 81, no. 4 (2005): 757–73, 758; Martin Dangerfield, 'The EU and Post-Communist Europe: One Approach or Several?' *Journal of Communist Studies and Transition Politics* 23, no. 4 (2008): 478–500.
47. Barbara Lippert, *The Discussion on EU Neighbourhood Policy – Concepts, Reform Proposals, and National Positions* (Berlin: FES International Policy Analysis, 2007).
48. European Commission, *Wider Europe – Neighbourhood*, 4.
49. Smith, 'The Outsiders: The European Neighbourhood Policy'.
50. The Technical Assistance for the Commonwealth of Independent States (TACIS) programme included Armenia, Azerbaijan, Belarus, Georgia, Kazakhstan, Kyrgyzstan, Moldova, Tajikistan, Turkmenistan, Ukraine, Uzbekistan, and Russia. Mongolia joined the programme from 1993–2003.
51. Christophe Hillion, 'Introduction to the Partnership and Cooperation Agreements', in *EU Enlargement. The Constitutional Impact at EU and National Level*, ed. Alfred E. Kellermann, Jaap W. de Zwaan, and Jenö Czuczai (The Hague: TMC Asser Press, 2001); Roman Petrov, 'The Partnership and Co-Operation Agreements with the Newly Independent States', in *Handbook on European Enlargement*, ed. Andrea Ott and Kirstin Ingles (The Hague: TMC Asser Press, 2002), 175–96.

became apparent in the programming of TACIS, which was the primary instrument for fostering the implementation of the PCAs.[52]

The ENP can be understood as an attempt of the EU to give fresh impetus into the relations with its neighbours and their reform agendas. In view of the great reform lags of the Eastern Neighbours compared to the accession countries, the promotion of good governance and the fight against corruption have become of utmost importance.[53] Moreover, as political concerns and objectives have been growing the ENP has been established as 'a very sophisticated policy' built on a 'wide range of instruments'[54] in order to meet the expectations. Jointly agreed Action Plans that copy the logic of the accession partnerships in the EU's enlargement policy are at the institutional core of the ENP.[55] Although they are not legally binding agreements, they formulate concrete reform objectives particularly in governance-related areas as well as detailed priorities for action. These blueprints for reform have been flanked with an intensified political dialogue, additional incentives as well as increasing levels of assistance.

Anti-corruption approaches in the Action Plans

The Eastern dimension of the ENP originally comprised Ukraine, Moldova and potentially Belarus, the inclusion of which has been made conditional on substantial democratic progress.[56] In 2004, however, the European Commission (successfully) suggested to further expand the ENP to the three states of the Southern Caucasus, Armenia, Azerbaijan, and Georgia.[57] In preparation of the negotiations on the Action Plans with their partner governments, the European Commission launched a series of Country Reports that give account of the political and socio-economic situation of each neighbourhood country. The reports of the Eastern Neighbourhood countries regarded corruption and other governance-related issues such as undemocratic elections, an inefficient and often not sufficiently independent judiciary as well as limited respect to civil liberties to be serious concerns.[58] Additionally, the Country Reports pay great attention to shortcomings in regulatory framework of the economy.

The sub-sections on corruption summarise the international commitments of the respective states, their participation in specific international anti-corruption networks, such as the Group of States against Corruption (GRECO) – a platform that has been established by the Council of Europe, and the legal and institutional efforts taken by the respective governments in order to effectively fight corruption. These reflections largely correspond to the *reform of the state* approach, although the EU had placed them into the general context of the democratic state of affairs and regards corruption to be particularly detrimental to the

---

52. Cf. in this respect the much more detailed reform-objectives in the Council Regulation 99/2000 (December 29, 1999) compared to those of the Council Regulation 1279/96 (June 25, 1996).

53. Tanja A. Börzel, Yasemin Pamuk, and Andreas Stahn, *'Good Governance in the European Union'*, *Berliner Arbeitspapiere zur Europäischen Integration*, Center of European Studies, no. 5 (Berlin: Freie Universität Berlin, 2007).

54. Marise Cremona and Gabriella Meloni, 'Introduction', in *The European Neighbourhood Policy. A Framework for Modernisation*, ed. Marise Cremona and Gabriella Meloni (EUI Working Papers, LAW 2007/21, Florence, 2007), 1.

55. Kelley, 'New Wine in Old Wineskins'; Magen, 'Shadow of Enlargement'

56. European Commission, *On Strengthening the European Neighbourhood Policy*, 2006, COM (2006) 726 final.

57. European Commission, 'European Neighbourhood Policy'.

58. The individual Country Reports can be accessed under http://ec.europa.eu/world/enp/documents_de.htm (accessed January 25, 2009).

Table 4.   Corruption in the Country Reports.

	Corruption	Related areas mentioned
Armenia	Serious concern (high level)	Judiciary; Civil Service; Criminal Code; Economy; Customs; Taxation; Education
Azerbaijan	Serious problem (very high level)	Civil Service; Criminal Code; Economy; Privatisation & Land Reform; Taxation
Belarus	–	–
Georgia	Very high level	Civil Service; Customs; Energy Sector; Education
Moldova	High level	Judiciary; Taxation; Economy; Trade
Ukraine	*Not specified*	Judiciary; Economy; Trade

Sources: Own compilation based on the individual Country Reports.

business climate, investment, and growth. Table 4 summarises the European Commission's notion of corruption in the Eastern Neighbourhood countries as well as those areas to which the problem of corruption has additionally been linked.

The Action Plans that are based on these initial country assessments had been adopted in December 2004 in the cases of Ukraine and Moldova. The Southern Caucasus States followed in November 2006. In all cases, the Action Plans provide very comprehensive and ambitious roadmaps for reform reflecting the complex and multi-faceted nature of governance. The sheer number of individual measures in the various areas touched adds up to about 300.[59]

The Action Plans display major similarities with regard to the content, and – more specifically – the anti-corruption approaches.[60] As in the Country Reports, the fight against corruption has rather narrowly been interpreted on first sight, although they are either placed in the context of economic or democratic reforms. Measures to be taken, first of all concern the formulation, implementation or revision of national anti-corruption strategies. Secondly, the Action Plans – in particular those of the Southern Caucasus states – require the neighbourhood countries to accede, ratify or implement international conventions that are related to the fight against corruption such as the UN convention on Corruption, the Council of Europe Criminal and Civil Law Conventions or the OECD Convention on combating bribery of Foreign Public Officials in International Business Transactions. Thirdly, the countries are requested to join international anti-corruption networks such as GRECO and implement their recommendations in order to advance legislative or institutional reforms in this regard. Finally, except for Moldova, each ENP country has some additional provisions that largely concentrate on promoting anti-corruption measures within the administration and/or the law enforcement agencies or improving the legal framework for the prosecution of corruption-related crimes. These provisions, however, vary both with regard to their specificity and scope. As in the Country Reports, the sections concerned with the fight against corruption largely concentrate on measures that correspond to a *reform of the state* approach (cf. Table 5). Nevertheless, the Action Plans of Armenia, Georgia and Moldova additionally require the EU's partner governments to involve non-state actors in their anti-corruption efforts. By contrast, the Action Plans of Ukraine and, astonishingly, Azerbaijan, which had still been urged to cooperate with 'civil society and

---

59. On the general structure of the Action Plans as well as the issues touched see also Smith, 'The Outsiders: The European Neighbourhood Policy' and Lippert, *Discussion on EU Neighbourhood Policy*.
60. The individual Action Plans can be accessed under http://ec.europa.eu/world/enp/documents_de.htm (accessed January 25, 2009).

Table 5.   Anti-corruption measures in the Action Plans.

	Specific anti-corruption measures[a]	Active non-state actor participation
Armenia	• Review implementation of the national Anti-Corruption Strategy • Ensure prosecution and conviction of corruption-related offences • Reform of Criminal Code in line with international standards • Establish anti-corruption measures within the law enforcement agencies • Monitor the declaration of assets and income by officials • Establish sanctions in case of wrong declarations • Implement GRECO – recommendations • Establish of administrative courts • Increase the salary of judges • Implement the Codes of Ethics for judges and prosecutors (including monitoring)	Envisaged
Azerbaijan	• Enforce the anti-corruption law and the State Programme on fighting corruption • Ensure conformity of Criminal Code in line with international standards • Improve the normative-legislative framework in line with international standards • Implement GRECO – recommendations	–
Georgia	• Implement the national Anti-Corruption Strategy • Accede or ratify international conventions and ensure conformity that the domestic legislation is in line with the international instruments • Establish anti-corruption measures within the law enforcement agencies • Implement GRECO – recommendations	Envisaged
Moldova	• Improve the business climate [. . .] by the fight against corruption • Implement GRECO – recommendations • Implement measures of the the Stability Pact Anti-Corruption Initiative • Implement the National Strategy on prevention and combating corruption	Envisaged
Ukraine	• Improve the business climate [. . .] by the fight against corruption • Join GRECO and implement recommendations • Revise national Anti-Corruption Strategy • Promote transparency & accountability in the administration • Reform the civil service in line with European Standards • Implement measures of the JHA scoreboard	–

Note: [a]The individual bullet points have been largely re-formulated and/or abridged by the authors.
Sources: Own compilation based on the individual Action Plans.

NGOs' (Country Report AZ) on corruption-related reforms in its Country Report, do not contain such an explicit demand.

Apart from the very specific bundles of measures that ought to facilitate fight against corruption through the *reform of the state* approach, the Action Plans further require changes in both the regulative framework of the economy and democracy.

Table 6. Economic reforms in the Action Plans.

	Armenia	Azerbaijan	Georgia	Moldova	Ukraine
Taxation	x	x	x	x	x
Customs	x	x	x	x	x
Public procurement	x	x	x	x	x
Privatisation		x	x	x	x
Competition	x	x	x	x	x
Business conditions	x	x	x	x	x
SME-development	x	x	x	x	x

Sources: Own compilation based on the individual Action Plans of each country.

As regards the *reform of the economy* approach, the Action Plans of the Eastern Neighbourhood countries touch upon almost all areas that have been regarded as a contribution to the fight against corruption (cf. Table 6).

First of all, the neighbourhood countries shall improve their business and investment climate by fostering 'the conditions to starting a business, hiring and firing workers, registering property, getting credit, protecting investors, enforcing contracts, [and] closing a business'[61]. Further actions to be taken aim at increasing transparency and competition in the area of public procurement, advancing privatisation (except for Armenia), increasing fair competition in particular through heightened transparency of state aid as well as improving the conditions for development of small and medium size enterprises (SMEs). Finally, each Action Plan contains a number of reforms regarding taxation and customs. These entail, on the one hand, the clarification and simplification of respective rules and procedures as well as administrative reforms within the responsible authorities. In general, the *reform of the economy* approach has been closely tied to the *reform of the state* approach, as the complementary provision to 'enhance institutional and administrative capacities' is 'scattered throughout'[62] the documents.

The *democratic reform* approach also figures prominently in the Action Plans. In all cases they include provisions that aim at improving the electoral legislation and/or the conduct of elections, and generally ensuring the separation of powers in particular with a view to the independence and professionalism of the judiciary. Moreover, the ENP countries are required to foster the development of political parties and/or civil society and increase respect for human rights and civil liberties. More specifically, the EU paid great attention to the development of independent media – which would be a great contribution to the fight against corruption. In some cases, such as Azerbaijan, the provisions for laying the foundation for democratic change are, however, coined in more general terms or the scope of the measures is less broad than in others. Table 7 summarises the findings with regard to key provisions of the democratic reform approach in Eastern Neighbourhood countries' Action Plans.

In a nutshell, the Action Plans are very comprehensive blueprints for political and economic reforms. As regards the fight against corruption, they provide suggestions that correspond to the three principal anti-corruption approaches in almost equal measure. Moreover, at least in three cases, the involvement of non-state actors in defining, implementing or monitoring anti-corruption measures is explicitly demanded. Thus, the ENP

---

61. See the respective clauses in the Action Plans of Armenia and Azerbaijan (Priority Area 4) and Georgia (Priority Area 2). Cf. also the Action Plans of Ukraine and Moldova.
62. Smith, 'The Outsiders: The European Neighbourhood Policy', 764.

Table 7. Democratic reforms in the Action Plans.

	Armenia	Azerbaijan	Georgia	Moldova	Ukraine
Conduct of Elections/Electoral framework	x	x	x	x	x
Separation of Powers (Independence of Judiciary)	x	(x)	x	(x)	(x)
Reform of the Judiciary	x	x	x	x	x
Strengthen the Parliament			x	x	
Pluralism/Party Development	x		x		x
Civil Society Development/ Freedom of Association/Assembly	x	x		x	x
Freedom of Expression/ Development of independent Media	x	x	x	x	x
Human Rights Ombudsman	x	x	x		
Minority Rights	x	x	x	x	x

Sources: Own compilation based on the individual Action Plans.

addresses the problem of corruption in a holistic way and the Eastern Neighbourhood states have committed themselves to respective reforms. To what extent these reforms really materialise depends to a great extent on the channels and the instruments of which the EU makes use to achieve compliance.

The implementation of the Action Plans

Over the last 20 years, the EU has developed a universal toolkit for almost all its foreign policy frameworks.[63] The ENP and its predecessor policies are no exception. This 'one size fits all approach' combines all three instruments – political dialogue, conditionality and assistance – that we have introduced above.[64] However, with the setting up of the ambitious Action Plans, the EU has readjusted its instruments accordingly.

As the ENP generally seeks to 'reinforce relations between the EU and partner countries', the EU has placed great emphasis on increasing the partner government's commitment to reform through an intensification of the political dialogue. Rather than imposing 'a pre-determined set of priorities',[65] the EU entered into intensive negotiations on the content of the Action Plans. Consent on the reform agenda and the use of a 'partnership language'[66] on the part of EU Officials have been part of a strategy to enhance 'ownership'[67] among the ENP countries. At the same time, however, the EU has consistently stressed the basic 'commitment to common values comprising the rule of law, good governance, the respect for human rights, including minority rights, the promotion of good neighbourly relations, and the principles of market economy and sustainable development',[68] which has certainly not been negotiable. To 'legitimise' the demands for reform in areas closely linked to normative and potentially disputed questions, such as the fight against corruption or human rights, the EU has additionally sought to refer 'to international norms'[69] or demand

63. Börzel, Pamuk, and Stahn, 'European Union and the Promotion of Good Governance'.
64. Börzel and Risse, 'One Size Fits All!'
65. European Commission, 'European Neighbourhood Policy', 8.
66. Kelley, 'New Wine in Old Wineskins', 39.
67. European Commission, 'European Neighbourhood Policy', 8.
68. Ibid., 3.
69. Kelley, 'New Wine in Old Wineskins', 40.

participation in international networks. One way or the other, it remains an open question whether the respective priority areas and actions have been included into the Action Plan on the basis of real commitment or as part of 'package deal'. Nevertheless, they provide a point of reference for assessing the state of implementation.

The actual implementation and operationalisation of the measures has equally been made an issue of political dialogue. A regular review has been assigned to the Cooperation Councils and their Committees and sub-committees that had already been established under the PCAs.[70] Thus, the implementation process enshrines the joint ownership principle in a similar way as the negotiations on the Action Plans. Part of the political dialogue is the translation of the priorities for action into concrete measures. Particularly with regard to the governance-related areas of reform, this process is hampered by the often vague and very broad definition of the reform goals and the lacking definition of time frames and responsible agencies in the Action Plans. To break down the reform goals into more concrete steps, the European Commission has therefore put forward non-papers – so-called Action Plan Implementation Tools – that are to be discussed with their partner governments. Still, in many areas they remain too vague and are open to interpretation.[71] When the European Commission for instance urged Georgia to take steps to effectively ensure the separation of powers in 2007, Georgian officials responded by referring to the respective article of the Constitution.[72]

One way to increase pressure on the governments of the Western NIS and the Southern Caucasus states in governance-related areas would have been the inclusion of non-state actors in the pursuit of political dialogue. The recourse on existing communication channels, however, has implied little change for the role of non-state actors. Unlike in other foreign policy frameworks, such as the partnership between the African, Caribbean and Pacific Group of States and the European Community, the EU has refrained from enhancing their status within the political dialogue.[73] Accordingly, the EU missed the chance to actually clarify the very vague and general demand for non-state actor inclusion in anti-corruption and other efforts on a tripartite basis, which could well have contributed to more effective discussions on which concrete reform steps are of most priority and how they can be implemented best – particularly in those ENP countries, where public voice is restricted.

Conditionality is the second major instrument of the ENP and – with a view on the potential impact – probably the most disputed among scholars and practitioners. Theoretically, the EU has flanked the ENP with various types of conditionality reaching from carrots that ought to reward reform progress[74] to sticks with regard to violations of the PCA.[75] In both cases, however, conditionality lacks specificity and clear benchmarks for its application. Positive conditionality, for example, has been very vaguely tied to progress in

70. Hillion, 'Introduction to the Partnership and Cooperation Agreements'.
71. OSGF, Georgia and the European Neighborhood Policy. Perspectives and Challenges, Tbilisi, 2007.
72. Interview with an official of the European Commission, November 2007.
73. Börzel, Pamuk, and Stahn, *'Good Governance in the European Union'*.
74. More specifically, the EU offers new enhanced bilateral agreements providing for a stake in the internal market that could eventually be 'expanded to include all elements of the European Economic Area' (Lippert, *'Discussion on EU Neighbourhood Policy'*, 9). Other incentives include visa facilitation, the promotion of 'people to people' contacts, enhanced bilateral or multilateral cooperation in different sectors such transport, energy, the opening-up of Community programs and agencies for participation as well as an intensified cooperation on foreign policy and security issues (European Commission, 'On Strengthening the European Neighbourhood Policy'). Additionally, the EU has set up a so-called governance facility that provides additional funds to those neighbourhood countries that take the lead in implementing their Action Plans.
75. Börzel, Pamuk, and Stahn, 'European Union and the Promotion of Good Governance'.

implementing the Action Plans and the 'extent to which' common 'values are effectively shared'.[76] As the Action Plans cover a broad range of issues, the evaluation of progress is a difficult task. With this lack of clarity, the dilemma emerges to weigh progress in areas of low politics against stagnation or even regress in areas that closely related to good governance, such as the fight against corruption.[77] Additionally, despite the efforts of the EU to enhance the attractiveness of the ENP through positive conditionality, doubts have remained whether these incentives would suffice to effectively improve governance.[78] This discussion remains closely linked to the 'accession perspective debate'[79] and the unclear *finalité* of the relations between the EU and their Eastern Neighbours. As in particular Ukraine has consistently insisted on a membership perspective, the inclusion in the ENP has been regarded at best as temporary policy framework bringing Ukraine closer to accession.[80] So far, Ukraine has been the only country in the Eastern dimension that has been offered significant rewards acknowledging progress the country has made in the implementation of its Action Plan, in particular with regard to democratic and economic reforms. On this basis, the EU started negotiations on a new enhanced agreement envisaging a free trade area and deeper economic integration.[81] Moreover, the EU has provided additional assistance through the governance facility based on the same notion. Despite the positive evaluation of Ukraine's progress underlying the provision of rewards, however, there are still significant doubts whether democracy in Ukraine has really consolidated: Even the European Commission regrets the lack of judicial independence or endemic corruption – which is seen as 'the main challenge [. . .] to progress'.[82] Thus, in the case of Ukraine, the EU decided to reward a country that has done comparatively better than others, but by no means sufficiently implemented reforms that effectively tackle the issue of bad governance and corruption.

Negative conditionality and its application, by contrast, are closely linked to the question, 'how to deal with "countries of concern" '.[83] Particularly with a view to state democracy, human rights, and high level corruption in some of the Eastern Neighbourhood states, this is a delicate question. The EU's answer has so far been very ambiguous (cf. Table 8).

On the one hand, the EU refrained from ratifying the PCA of Belarus and did not officially include it into the ENP framework for its democratic mal-performance. On the other hand, none of those states, with which the EU concluded a PCA and an ENP Action Plan, has been targeted by comparable measures, although upon democratic and economic conditionality has even been bilaterally agreed.[84] Each of the PCAs contains safeguard

---

76. European Commission, *Wider Europe – Neighbourhood*, 3.

77. Judith Kelley, *Ethnic Politics in Europe: Power of Norms and Incentives* (Princeton: Princeton University Press, 2004); Kelley, 'New Wine in Old Wineskins'.

78. Magen, 'Shadow of Enlargement'.

79. Lippert, 'Discussion on EU Neighbourhood Policy', 7.

80. Michael Emerson, Gergana Noutcheva, and Nicu Popescu, 'European Neighbourhood Policy Two Years On: Time Indeed for an "ENP Plus"', in CEPS Policy Brief, No. 126, Brussels, 2007; Viktor Yushchenko, Ukraine Following 'Road Map' to EU, 2007, in Interview with EuroNews, March 16, 2007.

81. Benita Ferrero-Waldner, EU-Ukraine Start Negotiations on New Enhanced Agreement, IP/07/275, Brussels, 2007.

82. European Commission, *Implementation of the European Neighbourhood Policy in 2007. Progress Report Ukraine*, SEC (2008) 402, Brussels, 2008, 2.

83. Smith, 'The Outsiders: The European Neighbourhood Policy', 769.

84. It is, for example, difficult to determine significant differences between Belarus and Azerbaijan with regard to the state of democracy, human rights or the level of corruption that could account for the very distinct type of relations between both countries and the EU. Cf. Jan Boonstra, How Serious Is the EU About Supporting Democracy and Human Rights in Azerbaijan, Madrid, 2008.

Table 8.   Application of conditionality.

	Application/enforcement of conditionality	Justification
Armenia	–	
Azerbaijan	–	
Belarus	• 1997: ratification of PCA stalled • 2004: sanctions (visa ban for four officials) • 2006: sanctions (visa ban extended to 41 officials including the President, additional freezing of assets) • 2008: lifting of visa ban (except for our officials)	• Lack of democracy • Human rights abuses
Georgia	• 2003: restrictions with regard to the provision of TACIS funds incl. additional criteria for implementation of funds	• Lack of reform commitment • Corruption • Suspected involvement of state officials in organised crime
Moldova	–	
Ukraine	• 2007: provision of additional assistance through governance facility • 2007: start of negotiations on an enhanced agreement	• Progress in PCA/Action Plan implementation (i.e. democracy & rule of law – but not specifically with regard to fighting corruption or improving the business climate)

Sources: Own compilation.

clauses that allow for taking 'appropriate measures' in case of violations of essential elements to the agreements. The essential elements clause of all Eastern Neighbourhood countries comprises respect for democratic principles, human rights, and of market economy. Good governance, by contrast, has not been made formally subject to conditionality, although the European Commission increasingly considers it to be a common value.[85]

Georgia has been the only Eastern Neighbourhood country where the EU at least reinforced negative conditionality with regard to the provision of assistance. In 2003, the EU responded to growing insecurity of its own staff because of organised crime and high-level corruption by almost completely reviewing its assistance strategy.[86] Assistance ought to be only provided for measures where the Georgian government displayed a clear commitment to cooperation. Additionally, the EU made assistance largely conditional upon the involvement of non-state actors – which has been unique in the relations with the Eastern Neighbourhood countries.

Conditionality thus appears to be a key instrument of the ENP. It theoretically allows both rewarding progress and punishing regress – which might have been central to altering the incentive structure of governments that are less committed to implementing the politically sensitive reforms they have agreed upon in the Action Plans. At a closer look, however, the EU has not really operationalised conditionality. In the absence of clear benchmarks measuring both progress and stagnation/regress, coherent and comprehensible differentiation between the Eastern Neighbourhood countries is impossible, which in turn may well weaken the inclination of the Eastern Neighbourhood states to really tackle issues such as the fight against corruption.

---

85. Börzel, Pamuk, and Stahn, 'European Union and the Promotion of Good Governance'.
86. European Commission, *Wider Europe – Neighbourhood.*

Table 9.   TACIS and ENPI assistance levels compared.

Nat. allocation (million €)		Armenia	Belarus	Azerbaijan	Georgia	Moldova	Ukraine
2007–2010	Democratic Governance	29.52	/	30	31.5	52.4–73.4	148.2
	Regulatory Reform	29.52	/	32	31.5	31.5–41.9	148.2
	Total	98.4	20	92	120.4	209.7	494
2004–2006	Institutional, Legal & Administrative Reforms	13.5	/	17	11.5	23	110
	Private Sector Development	/	/	13	/	13	60
	Total	20	10	30	24	42	212

Sources: Own compilation based on the National Indicative Programmes for 2004–2006 and 2007–2010 for each country.

The third major instrument, assistance, has undergone the greatest change since the introduction of the ENP. Simultaneously, it is – together with the political dialogue – of highest importance for the actual implementation of the good governance agenda of the EU.[87] For that reason, the European Commission proposed in 2003 the introduction of new financial instrument, the European Neighbourhood and Partnership Instrument (ENPI), which was to displace the 'old' TACIS and MEDA[88] assistance programmes for the Eastern and Southern dimension of the ENP, respectively. Until the new financial perspective covering the period 2007–2013 became effective, however, the EU still relied on the predecessor instruments. A comparison of the last programming of TACIS and the current programming of ENPI reveals four major changes. Firstly, assistance levels have at least increased two-fold, in the case of Georgia even five-fold (cf. Table 9).[89]

Secondly, the new assistance programme brought about a significant change towards corruption-sensitive approaches and measures. This can be illustrated best in the case of Azerbaijan. Under TACIS, EU assistance supported projects that would in general match the *reform of state* and the *reform of the economy* approaches, such as the modernisation of the tax or customs system. However, an increase of transparency or accountability was not made an explicit goal of any reform measure in the programming of assistance for 2004–2006. By contrast, the programming document covering the period 2007–2010 refers eleven times to transparency and six times to accountability in description of goals, indicators or prospective impacts of governance-related reforms.[90]

Thirdly, the introduction of ENPI led to a greater alignment of EU assistance with reform goals of the Action Plans and the incorporated anti-corruption approaches. Whereas in 2004 assistance programming only in the cases of Moldova and Ukraine and Georgia systematically addressed the area of human rights, civil liberties and civil society

87. European Commission, 'European Neighbourhood Policy'.
88. Financial and technical measures to accompany the reform of economic and social structures in the frame work of the Euro-Mediterranean Partnership.
89. Cf. the respective TACIS and ENPI National Indicative Programmes for 2004–2006 and 2007–2010. These can be accessed under http://ec.europa.eu/external_relations/enp/index_en.htm (accessed January 25, 2009).
90. Cf. Azerbaijan's TACIS National Indicative Programme for 2004–2006 and the ENPI National Indicative Programme 2007–2010.

Table 10. TACIS and ENPI priorities for assistance compared.

Priorities for assistance		Armenia	Azerbaijan	Georgia	Moldova	Ukraine
2007–2010	Reform of Public Administration/Finance Management/Civil Service	x	x	x	x	x
	Reform of the Judiciary	x	x	x	x	x
	HR & CL, Civil Society	x	x	x	x	x
	Approximation of legislation (inter alia in the areas of trade, company law, competition, public procurement, taxation, customs)	x	x	x	x	x
2004–2006	Reform of Public Administration/Finance Management/Civil Service				(x)	x
	Reform of the Judiciary			x	(x)	x
	HR & CL, Civil Society	(x)		x	x	x
	Approximation of legislation (inter alia in the areas of trade, company law, competition, public procurement, taxation, customs)	x	x	(x)	x	x

Sources: Own compilation based on the National Indicative Programmes for 2004–2006 and 2007–2010 for each country.

development, the programming documents for 2007–2010 for each country include a section devoted to the *democratic reforms* approach.[91] With the introduction of ENPI, the EU significantly expanded the focus of corruption-sensitive reforms in the other areas. The programming of ENPI funds supports judicial reforms, reform of the public administration such as civil service reform or public finance management, or measures aiming at improving the business and investment climate equally in each Eastern Neighbourhood country (cf. Table 10). Thus, the combination of the trinity of anti-corruption approaches reflected in the Action Plans has been mainstreamed in EU-assistance. Simultaneously, the problem of lacking differentiation among the countries shows in the provision of assistance. Because of the broadly defined areas for assistance, the Eastern European Neighbourhood governments can in principle benefit from measures that for instance strengthen law enforcement capacities or improve the collection of revenues, without paying too much attention to the effectiveness of reforms supported by EU assistance in other areas – particularly in the area of democratisation.

Finally, unlike TACIS, ENPI at least allows for a direct incorporation of non-state actors.[92] Thus, the transnational channel can at least be activated through capacity-building measures. In the long term, this kind of support may well lead to increasing 'public voice' and thereby strengthening the overall effectiveness of the EU's programme.

---

91. Ukraine's and Moldova's Action Plan was concluded in the same year, which may have led to some adjustment with regard to the provision of TACIS funds. The emphasis in on civil society development Georgia's TACIS NIP, by contrast, has been part the exceptional assistance strategy that the EU specifically drew up in order largely circumvent the Georgian government.

92. Cf. the up-grading of civil society actors in the Council Regulation 1638/2006 (October 24, 2006) compared to the Council Regulation 99/2000 (December 29, 1999).

Conclusion

This article aimed at shedding light on the EU's efforts to facilitate the fight against corruption and promote good governance in its Eastern Neighbourhood. The first part analysed the very specific setting of transition countries and the interrelatedness of the success of democratic and economic reforms, on the one hand, and increasing control of corruption, on the other.

In part two we took account of the different approaches, the channels of influence and the instruments that can be used for that purpose. More specifically, we distinguished between a r*eform of the state*, a *reform of the economy*, and a *democratic reforms* approach. These can be promoted from the outside through socialisation, the setting of incentives or capacity-building measures. Additionally, the inclusion of non-state actors in defining, implementing and monitoring reforms increases the prospective effectiveness of any measure adopted.

Part three used our framework to trace the EU's actual application of approaches, channels and instruments in a systematic cross-country analysis. We focused on the Western NIS, Belarus, Moldova, and Ukraine as well as the Southern Caucasus states, Armenia, Azerbaijan and Georgia, all of which already participate or are potential participants of the youngest and most ambitious foreign policy framework of the EU – the ENP.

Our empirical analysis shows that the EU has indeed deeply incorporated the promotion of good governance and the fight against corruption into the ENP. Except for Belarus, the EU concluded with each Eastern Neighbourhood country comprehensive blueprints for reform – so-called Action Plans – that yield a very holistic perspective on bad governance and corruption and in most cases provide for non-state actor inclusion with regard to anti-corruption reforms. Additionally, the jointly agreed priorities for action match all three fundamental anti-corruption approaches identified. However, whether the ENP can really contribute to an effective implementation of governance-related reforms remains questionable.

In general, the EU has once more made use of its universal foreign policy toolkit consisting of political dialogue, conditionality and assistance in the ENP. The overall strategy of the EU is based on principles such as partnership and joint ownership – which indicates the EU's preference for socialisation techniques, support through capacity-building and the provision of rewards. This cooperative stance may work well, when governments are already inclined to reform or when the rewards far outweigh the costs of reform for the governments. In the EU's Eastern Neighbourhood, however, where corruption and bad governance are rooted in the political and economic systems, the prospective success of such a strategy is limited. In the absence of the big 'membership carrot' for the EU's Eastern Neighbours, the EU's offer of deeper economic integration in return for better governance may not suffice. But even if it does, the ENP does not adequately provide for differentiation based on performance. Anti-corruption and governance-related reform goals of the Action Plan have been rather vaguely defined; the reform objectives lack prioritisation and concrete benchmarks that have to be reached.

Thus, rather than conditionality, political dialogue and assistance are the instruments central to the actual implementation of the ENP Action Plans. Both certainly take into account the large array of reform objectives including the three fundamental anti-corruption approaches – *reform of state*, *reform of the economy*, and *democratic reforms*. Additionally, overall coherence of assistance, that is equal support to each approach in each neighbourhood country, has grown – despite the need for differentiation and prioritisation. This again shows the EU's clear preference for a broad governance-related reform agenda – but it leaves it largely up to the partner governments to decide in which areas they want to engage. Aggravating this problem is the fact that there are no mechanisms to ensure the participation of non-state actors in defining, implementing or monitoring governance-related reforms. Although such cooperation has been demanded in the Action Plans with regard to the fight against corruption and other reform objectives, the concrete role of non-state actors remains weakly defined. They do neither regularly participate in the political dialogue nor is their inclusion in any way subject to conditionality.

To conclude, in the absence of domestic and external pressure, the Eastern European partner governments of the EU are likely to 'pick and choose' from the overall reform agenda and circumvent reforms that would impede their political manoeuvrability, particularly with regard to advancing democratisation and the rule of law. With a lack of accountability to either the EU or their own societies, we see little chance that the *reform of the state* or *reforms of the economy* approaches can become effective in reducing corruption in these states.

Acknowledgements

We thank Steven Sampson and the two anonymous reviewers for their helpful comments. We are also grateful to Esther Ademmer for her excellent research assistance.

Notes on contributors

Tanja A. Börzel is a professor of political science and holds the Chair for European Integration at the Otto-Suhr-Institut for Political Science, Freie Universität Berlin. Together with Thomas Risse, she directs the Research College 'The Transformative Power of Europe'. Her research focus and teaching experience lie in the field of Institutional Theory and Governance, European Integration, and Comparative Politics with a focus on Europe. She mainly concentrates on questions of governance and institutional change as a result of Europeanisation as well as on the diffusion of European ideas and policies within and outside of the EU.

Andreas Stahn is a research associate with the research centre (SFB) 700 'Governance in Areas of Limited Statehood'. His research focuses on EU and US foreign policy, particularly in the areas of democracy promotion and good governance. Andreas Stahn holds degrees in political science as well as Russian and East European Studies. He is a member of the research project B2 'Good Governance without the Shadow of Hierarchy? The EU Neighbourhood Policy and Anti-Corruption Measures in the Southern Caucasus'.

Yasemin Pamuk is a research associate with the research centre (SFB) 700 'Governance in Areas of Limited Statehood'. Her PhD focuses on the role of informal institutions in areas of limited statehood in the former Soviet Union. She holds degrees in Islamic Studies and Political Science from Heidelberg University and Turkic Studies from Université Marc Bloch Strasbourg. Yasemin Pamuk is a member of the research project B2 'Good Governance without the Shadow of Hierarchy? The EU Neighbourhood Policy and Anti-Corruption Measures in the Southern Caucasus'.

Post-accession malaise? EU conditionality, domestic politics and anti-corruption policy in Hungary

Agnes Batory

Department of Public Policy, Central European University, Budapest, Hungary

Corruption in the then candidate countries of Central and Eastern Europe was a major concern for the European Union (EU) before its 2004 enlargement. This concern and its expression in the conditionality of membership constituted strong incentives for the candidate countries' governments to control corruption – or more precisely to take control measures that could be communicated to the European Union. A common assumption in the literature is that with the removal by accession of these incentives anti-corruption efforts would not be maintained at their pre-accession level. But is this really the case? Or have other influences from international organisations, domestic politics or civil society taken over to provide impetus for further corruption control interventions? This article considers these questions with respect to Hungary and finds that while some of the post-2004 measures have been a response to the country's international commitments, there have also been important domestic sources of reform. The results are, however, limited: despite the country's relatively smooth path to the European Union, membership of all the major international legal instruments and three major reform packages since 2000, corruption seems no less prevalent than it was a decade before.

Introduction

It is almost commonplace for articles dealing with corruption and anti-corruption to start by remarking on what is normally described as an explosion of interest in the subject in the past decade.[1] And indeed, in no other part of the world is 'corruption eruption' as aptly observed as in the former communist countries of Central and Eastern Europe: a recent study found an approximately sevenfold increase in press coverage of corruption in six East Central European (ECE) countries between 1996 and 2004, a higher growth than anywhere else around the globe.[2] Reflecting increasing salience in the political and public discourse, scholarly attention has kept apace, with numerous academic articles and books looking at corruption in the ECE context. In addition to the themes generally discussed in the literature, such as the relationship of corruption with development, democracy and democratisation, this

---

1. The author is chairman of the Board of Transparency International Hungary (TI-H). This article was written in a personal (academic) capacity; the views expressed in the following do not necessarily represent those of TI-H.
2. Alexandru Grigorescu, 'The Corruption Eruption in East-Central Europe: The Increased Salience of Corruption and the Role of International Organizations', *East European Politics and Societies* 20 (2006): 527. For the purposes of this article, ECE refers to the post-communist member states of the EU.

body of work has contributed insights into the impact of the 'post-communist condition', i.e. the economic, political and cultural legacies of state socialist regimes in countries of the region. Perhaps unsurprisingly, these scholarly analyses have tended to focus on the causes, consequences and manifestations of corruption in a transition setting, rather than on corruption control, and particularly corruption control post-transition, which is the focus of this article.[3]

The policy relevance of the topic is obvious. Anti-corruption has been on the rise, in both rhetoric and practice. There is probably no government in ECE countries that does not claim to be tough on graft, and it is difficult to think of elections in living memory where pledges to root out corruption (normally portrayed as something political opponents, and they alone, indulge in) did not constitute a major theme, if not the central part, of campaigns. While this could be easily dismissed as 'all talk', governments have also taken action to show commitment: ECE countries have typically ratified all major international legal instruments, adopted national anti-corruption strategies, passed or amended relevant domestic legislation and many also established dedicated anti-corruption agencies or judicial bodies. The context has also changed as compared with the transition years in the 1990s. On the one hand, many of the structural conditions that provide fertile ground for corruption in transition – most notably large-scale privatisation and the foundation and/or adaptation of political parties to competitive politics – are no longer present, which should provide a (more) favourable environment for control efforts. On the other hand, the race for EU membership, which provided impetus to reform, to some degree, in every country of the region, is over. Moreover, in the era of EU membership new corruption risks have emerged, particularly those associated with the administration of structural funds from the Union.

These developments invite a re-consideration of anti-corruption initiatives in ECE countries. Much of the existing literature assumes that domestic reform – not only in anti-corruption but also more broadly – was largely a result of external pressure from the European Union, or, as one study puts it, that ECE governments were 'driven to change'.[4] On the basis of these incentive-based understandings of conditionality one would expect that whatever political will existed for fighting corruption pre-accession would not be sustained once EU membership is achieved. This is particularly the case in policy areas such as corruption which were included among the political conditions of accession but where, not being part of the acquis, the Commission has little leverage.[5] But have governmental anti-corruption initiatives really lost momentum? And if the impact of conditionality was indeed so great, what other domestic or international influences might there be at play, possibly making up for (decreased) EU pressure post-accession?

The purpose of this article is to explore these questions with respect to Hungary. The country case is particularly suitable for analysing the interplay of international and national influences and in particular assessing the impact of EU conditionality, as the same

---

3. See, e.g., William L. Miller, Ase Grodeland, and Tatyana Y. Koshechkina, *A Culture of Corruption: Coping with Government in Post-Communist Europe* (Budapest/New York: CEU Press, 2001); Stephen Kotkin and Andras Sajo, ed., *Political Corruption in Transition: A Skeptic's Handbook* (Budapest/New York: CEU Press, 2002); and Rasma Karlkins, *The System Made Me Do It: Corruption in Post-Communist Societies* (London: M.E. Sharpe, 2005).
4. Antoaneta Dimitrova, ed. *Driven to change: The European Union's enlargement viewed from the East* (Manchester: Manchester University Press, 2004). It should be noted that while incentive-based conditionality explanations are still dominant, they were found insufficient for explaining post-accession developments in a number of recent studies. See particularly Rachel A. Epstein and Ulrich Sedelmeier, 'Beyond Conditionality: International Institutions in Postcommunist Europe after Enlargement', *Journal of European Public Policy* 15 (2008): 795–805, and other articles in the same issue.
5. Epstein and Sedelmeier, 'Beyond Conditionality', 798.

major political party has been in power in both the pre- and the post-accession period (from mid-2002 to 2008 in a coalition, then as a minority government). This should allow for controlling for shifts in policy that naturally arise in the wake of changes in government. In addition to the academic literature, the article draws on a wide range of policy documents, including legislation and (draft) strategic documents, as well as assessments from international organisations, International Non-Governmental Organisations (INGOs) and a small number of interviews, which provided important background information.

The article is divided into five sections. The following section discusses the relationship of democratisation and corruption, setting the background for corruption control efforts and teasing out synergies and possible contradictions with EU conditionality. This section also sets the Hungarian experience in comparative perspective. The third section provides background to the country case, describing the corruption situation and general conditions for control efforts. The fourth section then reviews notable governmental anti-corruption initiatives and assesses the factors that may have shaped them. A brief section concludes, arguing that while there is indeed evidence of a post-accession fatigue, simple incentive-based conditionality explanations apply only with some qualifications. The post-2004 efforts have been in part a response to the country's international commitments, but there have also been important domestic sources of reform. The combined result of conditionality and domestic influences is, however, quite limited: despite the country's relatively smooth path to the European Union, membership of all the major international legal instruments and three major anti-corruption reform packages since 2000, corruption seems no less prevalent than it was a decade before.

Democratisation, conditionality and corruption

Measuring corruption is clearly not without its problems, and perception-based indices in particular have come under increasing criticism in recent years.[6] Nonetheless, the Corruption Perceptions Index (CPI) of Transparency International (TI) is probably the best known indicator used internationally. According to this source, as of 2008 the new EU member states continued to be perceived as fairly corrupt, albeit with considerable cross-country variation (between a score of 6.7 for Slovenia and 3.6 for Bulgaria in 2008, where 1 indicates very corrupt and 10 very clean).[7]

Yet, observations from the literature would lead to the expectation that, following an initial worsening of the situation in the early phases of transition, corruption should be on the retreat.[8] The initial increase of corruption is due to several factors.[9] One is the state of

---

6. See, e.g., Endre Sik, 'The Bad, the Worse and the Worst: Guesstimating the Level of Corruption', in *Political Corruption in Transition*, ed. Stephen Kotkin and Andras Sajó, (Budapest/New York: CEU Press, 2002), 91–115; Fredrik Galtung, 'Measuring the Immeasurable: Boundaries and Functions of (Macro) Corruption Indices', in *Measuring Corruption*, ed. Charles Sampford, Fredrik Galtung, Arthur Shacklock, and Carmel Connors (London: Ashgate, 2006); and Diana Schmidt-Pfister, 'Transnational Anti-Corruption Advocacy: A Multi-Level Analysis of Civic Action in Russia' in *Governments, NGOs and Anti-Corruption: The New Integrity Warriors*, ed. Luís de Sousa, Peter Larmour, and Barry Hindess (London: Routledge, 2008), 140.
7. The CPI is available at Transparency International's website at www.transparency.org.
8. See Hung-En Sung, 'Democracy and Political Corruption: A Cross-national Comparison', *Crime Law and Social Change* 41 (2004): 179–94; Bo Rothstein, 'Anti-Corruption: A Big Bang Theory' (Working Paper 2007/3, QoG/Goteborg University, 2007); and Hanna Back and Axel Hadenius, 'Democracy and State Capacity: Exploring a J-Shaped Relationship', *Governance* 21 (2008): 1–24.
9. See generally Jonathan Moran, 'Democratic Transitions and Forms of Corruption', *Crime, Law and Social Change* 36 (2001): 379–93.

flux in norms and values, whereby the written and unwritten rules that governed citizens' and bureaucrats' behaviour under communism are undermined, but not yet superseded by, as Lovell puts it, the new 'rational-legal form of rule' (supposedly) ushered in by the transitions.[10] This weakness is compounded by low administrative capacity in transition states, which inhibits governments from implementing policies and enforcing the new rules of the game. The rule of law is further undermined by both incentives and new opportunities for the misappropriation of public assets. The transition from central planning to the market economy, which accompanied the political changes in post-communist countries, redefines the boundary between private and public on which the definition of corruption as is commonly understood rests. Political parties need resources for campaigns and cronies – what Moran described as 'the development of machine politics' and much earlier Huntington simply as party building,[11] – and those with existing networks and influence stand to benefit from the large-scale privatisation by manipulating the distribution of state assets.[12] Thus, in addition to the petty bribery citizens engage in as part of a day-to-day survival strategy, transition creates an environment in which new forms of grand corruption can flourish, seemingly with impunity.[13]

In the case of genuine democratisation – i.e. one which does not stop at the establishment of formal procedures such as periodic elections – these are however seen, like the conditions that they grow out of, transitory phenomena. 'Control from above' is slowly reinserted by the government through law enforcement, and supplemented with 'control from below', provided by civil society actors that gradually grow and strengthen as the new regime matures towards open, consolidated democracy.[14] In other words, in later stages of transition, accountability mechanisms are expected to kick in and become fully operational, thus creating the conditions for clean(er) public life.

Crucially, the dominant strand of the literature considers integration into international frameworks generally, and integration into the European Union specifically, as augmenting this process towards greater accountability and transparency and thus reducing corruption – or even as an essential condition for the institutionalisation of accountability and control mechanisms. Previous research identified two principal modes by which influence from the international to the national realm may be transmitted: a normative mode whereby domestic actors internalise prevailing international norms that stigmatise corruption and an economic mode which largely relies on incentives.[15] Both the normative and the economic modes work principally on elites/governments ('control from above'), but a third influence can also be identified in the sense that actors in the international realm may also provide support to civil society actors directly, thereby simultaneously strengthening capacity for 'control from below'.

---

10. David Lovell, 'Corruption and a Transitional Phenomenon: Understanding Endemic Corruption in Postcommunist States', in *Corruption: Anthropological perspectives*, ed. Dieter Haller and Chris Shore (London: Pluto Press, 2005), 77.

11. Moran, 'Democratic Transitions', 381; Samuel P Huntington, 'Modernization and Corruption', in *Political Corruption: A Handbook*, ed. Arnold J. Heidenheimer, Michael Johnston and Victor de LeVine (New Brunswick: Transaction, 1989/1993), 59–71.

12. See, e.g., Quentin Reed, 'Corruption in Privatization: The Dangers of 'Neo-Liberal' Privatization' in *Political corruption in transition*, ed. Stephen Kotkin and Andras Sajó, (Budapest/New York: CEU Press, 2002), 261–85.

13. Miller et al., *A Culture of Corruption* and Karlkins, *The System Made Me Do It*.

14. Back and Hadenius, 'Democracy and State Capacity'.

15. Wayne Sandholtz and Mark M. Gray, 'International Integration and National Corruption', *International Organization* 57 (2003): 761–800.

Interventions to promote anti-corruption by intergovernmental organisations and the European Union from the 1990s in ECE countries at first sight seem to tick all these boxes. All major intergovernmental organisations as well as bilateral development agencies were present in the region with various initiatives that utilised normative pressure, economic incentives, capacity building for both the civil service and NGOs or a combination of all of these. To mention a few (without attempting to be exhaustive), these included peer review within the framework of the Group of States Against Corruption (GRECO) established in 1998 by the Council of Europe, diagnostics and capacity building by the World Bank and standard setting by the OECD Convention on Combating Bribery of Foreign Public Officials in International Business.[16] Various EU member states also participated in the so-called twinning projects with government agencies in candidate countries financed under EU pre-accession assistance.

However, arguably it was the conditionality of EU membership that played the most important role in anti-corruption in ECE. Conditionality involved regular assessment, in the form of annual reports by the European Commission, of candidate countries' preparedness in meeting the Union's membership criteria, set by the Copenhagen European Council of June 1993. Crucially, although corruption control was not explicitly mentioned among the Copenhagen criteria, the Commission considered it to be covered by membership conditionality along with a number of other areas in which the Union itself does not have common rules or competencies.[17] The justification is that widespread corruption 'can (directly or indirectly) impact on each of the three areas evaluated by the Commission, undermining implementation of the acquis communautaire, the smooth functioning of the single market, and the quality of democratic institutions and core democratic values the Union seeks to represent'.[18] Nonetheless, the link was closest, and hence corruption was normally discussed in connection with the so-called political criteria, which require the stability of institutions guaranteeing democracy, the rule of law, human rights and respect for and protection of minorities.[19]

Concerns with corruption prominently featured in virtually all country monitoring reports issued by the Commission and played a major part in excluding Romania and Bulgaria from the group of 2004 entrants. The reports essentially acted as checklists of tasks for negotiating governments the Commission would come back to year after year until each task could be ticked off. In this, the instrument combined normative pressure by setting standards and clear benchmarks for meeting them, and both material and non-material incentives, with EU membership as the ultimate prize. Incentives were found to work best in terms of producing domestic reform when the Union's commitment to enlargement was seen to be credible (i.e. particularly after the opening of accession negotiations) and when the costs of compliance with the conditions in the candidate countries were for the negotiating governments bearable.[20] Empirical studies have linked peaks in the intensity of

---

16. For an overview of these see Grigorescu, 'Corruption Eruption'.

17. For the general point see Bernard Steunenberg and Antoaneta Dimitrova, 'Compliance in the EU Enlargement Process: The Limits of Conditionality', *European Integration Online Papers (EIoP)* 11, no. 5 (2007): 4.

18. Summary of the report of the Open Society Institute's EU Map program on corruption and anti-corruption, http://www.eumap.org/topics/corruption (accessed December 5, 2008).

19. Transparency International, 'Corruption and the EU Accession Process', 2006, www.transparency.org/content/download/6337/37673/file/Corruption_and_the_EU_accession_process.pdf (accessed December 15, 2008).

20. See generally Frank Schimmelfennig and Ulrich Sedelmeier, *The Europeanization of Central and Eastern Europe* (Ithaca and London: Cornell University Press, 2005).

anti-corruption legislation to the proximity of accession, concluding that probable but not yet certain accession was associated with bursts of activity on behalf of candidate country governments.[21]

Indeed, the 1998–2002 period of accession negotiations saw a significant amount of legislation adopted by the candidates in the anti-corruption field, including the adoption of standards established by international organisations other than the European Union, such as the Council of Europe's Criminal Law Convention on Corruption.[22] There was a wave of national anti-corruption strategies developed by ECE governments prior to the 2004 enlargement, starting with the Czech Republic in 1999, Slovakia in 2001 and followed by Bulgaria, Romania and Hungary in 2001.[23] By several accounts,[24] among the international organisations present in the region the European Union was the most influential from the opening of accession negotiations to their conclusion. Grigorsescu's study indicates that every second time the word 'corruption' was mentioned in the press in ECE countries, the European Union was mentioned 'in the same breath' – which leads him to conclude that the increase in the salience of the issue was 'due almost solely to the discussions involving the European Union'.[25]

Although the general conclusion thus seems to be that the European Union was highly successful in putting the issue on the agenda and that the 'accession process had on the whole had a major positive impact on candidate States' legal and institutional frameworks for fighting against corruption',[26] EU conditionality has also been subject to criticism on both normative and pragmatic grounds. The main normative criticism is that of double standards – i.e. setting the bar for membership higher for candidates than for existing members.[27] This line of criticism speaks to a body of literature, exemplified by Ivan Krastev's work or a recent volume edited by de Sousa et al., which questions the efficacy, legitimacy and benevolence of interventions by international organisations and INGOs such as the European Union, the World Bank or TI, which are seen to promote a particular self-motivated agenda dressed up as good governance.[28] An example cited of double standards in anti-corruption is that, as of 2006, the Council of Europe convention was ratified by only half of the EU-15, and yet the Commission successfully 'induced' negotiating ECE governments to ratify the convention before they joined the Union.[29]

A second, pragmatic criticism is that conditionality over-emphasised the adoption of laws and institutions, whereas less attention was paid to whether and how legislation was actually implemented and to what effect.[30] The conditionality literature describes this as symbolic compliance[31] – i.e. candidate governments simply ticking off Commission requirements without any serious effort made to affect changes on the ground. A Bulgarian

---

21. World Bank (James Anderson and Cheryl Gray), *Anti-Corruption in Transition 3: Who Is Succeeding and Why* (Washington: The World Bank, 2006), 81.
22. Grigorescu, 'Corruption Eruption', 538.
23. Ibid., 548.
24. Including the World Bank's flagship Anti-Corruption in Transition.
25. Grigorescu, 'Corruption Eruption', 543 and 544.
26. EUmap summary.
27. See, e.g., Transparency International, 'Corruption and the EU Accession Process'.
28. Ivan Krastev, 'When "Should" Does Not Imply "Can": The Making of the Washington Consensus on Corruption', in *Shifting Obsessions: Three Essays on the Politics of Anti-Corruption* (Budapest/New York: CEU Press, 2004) and de Sousa et al., ed. *Governments, NGOs and Anti-Corruption*.
29. Grigorescu, 'Corruption Eruption', 538.
30. Karlkins, *The System Made Me Do It*, 168 and Grigorescu, 'Corruption Eruption', 548.
31. Steunenberg and Dimitrova, 'Compliance in EU Enlargement'.

analyst, for instance, found that anti-corruption measures introduced in that country in response to EU pressure are 'now largely forgotten, the few investigations into high level corruption that were initiated have since stalled, and public cynicism has increased'.[32] For others, and with respect to other new member states, the situation may not seem quite so bleak. Although the CPI is not suitable for indicating trends, particularly trends from one year to the next, the around or over one full point improvement (on a ten-point scale) since the beginning of the decade in the scores of Latvia, Estonia, Slovakia, the Czech Republic and Slovenia gives at least some indication that levels of corruption are perceived to have decreased, to some extent, in a number of countries by 2007.

Yet another concern about conditionality, raised by INGOs such as TI and the Open Society Institute (OSI), was the absence of a clear framework and sufficiently systematic approach specifically relating to anti-corruption. On the one hand, this led to a 'perception that countries were not treated equally', with higher demands placed on some candidates than others.[33] On the other hand, and perhaps more importantly, the absence of an EU monitoring mechanism and mandate means that the Commission has limited means for dealing with corruption in the existing member states. Consequently, the European Union may lose all leverage on countries once they join – or perhaps even before. Work by Steunenberg and Dimitrova suggests that the 'expiration date' of conditionality arrives when the Commission ceases to maintain uncertainty about the outcome: after the Union commits itself by setting the date of accession, compliance by candidate states decreases sharply across all policy areas.[34] The safeguard clauses put in place with respect to the first group of post-communist member states were designed to maintain a degree of uncertainty and thereby provide the European Union with some leverage.[35] The introduction of the Cooperation and Verification Mechanism (CVM),[36] largely because of corruption concerns, in relation to Bulgaria and Romania was also clearly an attempt by the European Union to address the limited shelf-life of conditionality post-accession.

However, research into whether the pattern of a drop in compliance indeed holds with respect to the 2004 entrants' anti-corruption efforts is patchy and points to divergent outcomes across countries. Geoffrey Pridham observes that in Slovakia 'since EU entry a lack of urgency has been evident and most ministries have reduced their [anti-corruption] activity', whereas in Latvia a 'new momentum was created' post-accession by a combination of domestic factors.[37] The crucial question is, of course, which kind of experience has been more common, and if indeed a new momentum was created, what was it due to – domestic actors coming to the fore to exercise 'control from below', international pressure from other sources or something else. The following sections consider these questions in more detail with respect to the Hungarian case, first giving an indication of the severity of corruption in the country and describing the context and conditions for control efforts from both below and above.

32. Boyko Todorov, 'Anti-Corruption Measures as Political Criteria for EU Accession: Lessons from the Bulgarian Experience', *U4 Brief*, February 2008, 5, www.u4.no/themes/political-corruption (accessed December 15, 2008).

33. Transparency International, 'Corruption and the EU Accession Process'.

34. Steunenberg and Dimitrova, 'Compliance in EU Enlargement'. cf. Epstein and Sedelmeier, 'Beyond Conditionality'; and Ulrich Sedelmeier, 'After Conditionality: Post-Accession Compliance with EU Law in East Central Europe', *Journal of European Public Policy* 15 (2008): 806–25.

35. Ibid.

36. See generally the European Commission's website on the CVM, http://ec.europa.eu/dgs/secretariat_general/cvm/index_en.htm (accessed December 15, 2008).

37. Geoffrey Pridham, 'The EU's Political Conditionality and Post-Accession Tendencies: Comparisons from Slovakia and Latvia', *Journal of Common Market Studies* 46 (2008): 365–87.

Corruption in Hungary: the state of affairs

Hungary is a country of approximately 10 million and as of 2008 the fourth biggest economy among the new member states. It is a parliamentary democracy characterised, since the mid-1990s, by the competition of two major parties: the centre-left Socialist Party and the rightist catch-all party Fidesz-Hungarian Civic Alliance. In addition to these two, three smaller parties – the liberal Alliance of Free Democrats, the conservative Democratic Forum and the Christian-Democratic People's Party – were represented in the parliament in the 2006–2010 term. In terms of government stability, Hungary stood out among the other new democracies in ECE countries for much of the post-communist period although it has experienced considerable political turbulence since 2008, when the Alliance of Free Democrats quit their coalition with the Socialists. The latter party was in office from 2002, having been re-elected in 2006, and following the departure of the Free Democrats in 2008 formed a minority government. This was replaced in April 2009 by an 'expert government', appointed to manage the fallout from the global economic crisis and supported by the Socialists and Free Democrats in Parliament.

The issue of corruption often featured in political discourse, particularly in the wake of scandals involving politicians or individuals associated with one party or another. The scandals provided ample opportunity for political opponents to discredit each other or question each other's commitment to corruption control. The topic that came to the fore on each of these occasions was the reform of party financing. According to independent experts, campaign spending regularly exceeded the statutory limit by as much as 90%,[38] indicating that the parties had very large undeclared revenues.[39] While the parties agreed on the need to change the law, as of 2008 the constitutionally required qualified majority support did not materialise in the parliament for any specific reform proposal – despite the fact that pledges to curb corruption were common features of the parties' campaigns ahead of elections.

A number of NGOs have been active in putting, or keeping, the fight against corruption on the agenda. These include civil rights organisations and think tanks, which deal with the issue as part of their portfolio, and TI's national chapter as perhaps the most visible (although not the only) organisation with an exclusive focus on anti-corruption. TI first started operating in Hungary as an association in 1999 but was wound up in 2005 due to lack of funding. In 2006, a new national chapter was founded in the form of a foundation (its official status in 2008 was 'chapter in formation'). The organisation was most noticeable in connection with the annual publication of the CPI, which tended to generate a flurry of media attention and comments by parties and other civil society organisations alike. A recent comprehensive National Integrity System (NIS) study by the organisation identified party financing, public procurement and local government as the most corruption-prone areas and the insufficient implementation and enforcement of existing laws as the principal cross-cutting problem.[40]

In terms of the prevalence of corruption, the attention the issue received was certainly not unjustified. Hungary's CPI score was around 5 out of 10 year after year (apart from the first, 1996 issue of the index, where it was even less), which – as media reactions often stressed – showed the country to be perceived as somewhat less corrupt than the majority of the other ECE countries but more corrupt than, for instance, Slovenia or Estonia. Survey data, on the

---

38. Laszlo Majtenyi of the Eotvos Karoly Institute, article referred to available at http://www.ekint.org/ekint/ekint.tevekenysegek.page?tevekenyseg=8 (accessed December 15, 2008).
39. Transparency International Hungary/Eszter Kosa and Noemi Alexa, eds., *Corruption Risks in Hungary: National Integrity System Country Study* 2007. Part one (Budapest: Transparency International Hungary, 2007).
40. Ibid.

other hand, consistently indicated that corruption was widespread in the country. In 2003–2004, almost 5% of Hungarian respondents of the International Crime Victims Survey reported having encountered bribe-taking by (street-level) public officials.[41] In a 2007 Gallup survey, 9% of respondents reported that a bribe was asked or expected for a service they were entitled to receive.[42] While, according to a Eurobarometer survey conducted in the same year, 95% of Hungarians believed that corruption was a major problem in the country (one of the highest proportions in the EU-27),[43] social condemnation of everyday forms of corruption was not particularly high. The 1999 edition of the World Values Survey found that only 53% of respondents thought that accepting a bribe in the course of one's duties was never acceptable, and while 65% thought the same about cheating on one's taxes (a comparable illicit behaviour), 78% believed that 'almost all' their compatriots nonetheless engaged in this practice.[44]

The number of cases of corruption-related crimes, official bribery and abuse of influence, dealt with by the police was very low, end even dropped from a high of 728 cases in 2002 to just 425 in 2006.[45] This is however as, or more, plausibly explained by low rates of reporting and discovery as an actual drop in corruption-related crime. Survey data certainly did not show any sign of improvement in how respondents perceived the situation in the course of the past decade. As mentioned, Hungary's CPI score did not change significantly (it was 5 in 1998, and remained 5.1 ten years later), while the proportion of ordinary people believing that corruption was a 'very serious problem' actually grew from 39% in 2003 to 43% in 2007.[46] Consequently, whatever corruption control efforts took place, they produced no perceptible change on the ground, at least not to the extent that survey methods would be able to detect them. The following section considers what these control efforts consisted of and what may have been the main drivers of reform.

Anti-corruption initiatives

What has actually happened in the anti-corruption field? In the light of the public opinion data referred to above, it would be tempting to answer 'not much', but perceptions may simply have been too slow to change. Many legal regulations have been tightened, some loopholes closed and the range of publicly available information has grown.[47] Since the beginning of the current decade, there have been three distinct periods when anti-corruption activities intensified although no long-term plan has been carried out consistently. As expressed in the latest publicly available draft (the sixth) of the 2008 Anti-corruption strategy (as of early 2009, awaiting adoption by the cabinet), 'governmental attention to the problem since regime change has at times increased or decreased'.[48]

---

41. Jan van Dijk, John van Kesteren, and Paul Smit, *Criminal Victimisation in International Perspective: Key Findings from the 2004–2005 ICVS and EU ICS* (Tilburg, the Netherlands: Tilburg University, 2007), 90.
42. Reference to a fall 2007 Gallup survey in the Anti-Corruption Coordination Body's (ACB) 'Anti-Corruption Strategy', draft 6, accessed at the website of the Ministry of Justice and Law Enforcement, http://www.irm.gov.hu/?mi=1&katid=304&id=330&cikkid=4453 (accessed December 10, 2008).
43. European Commission, 'The Attitudes of Europeans Towards Corruption', *Special Eurobarometer*, No. 291, April 2008.
44. World Values Survey data viewed at http://www.worldvaluessurvey.org/(accessed March 8, 2010).
45. Criminal statistics in ACB, 'Anti-Corruption Strategy', 31.
46. Gallup Survey, ibid., 24.
47. For an inventory of anti-corruption and transparency promotion measures see ACB, 'Anti-corruption strategy', and TI Hungary, Corruption Risks in Hungary.
48. ACB, 'Anti-Corruption Strategy', 10.

The intention to formulate some sort of systematic anti-corruption policy as such dates back to the end of the 1990s.[49] The Minister of Justice of the Fidesz-led coalition of 1998–2002, Ibolya David, signed a memorandum of understanding with the United Nations Office for Drug Control and Crime Prevention, agreeing in 1999 for Hungary to become a test case of the UN's Global Programme against Corruption. According to the report on the pilot study on Hungary, the initiation of the Programme coincided with the government's efforts to produce a national anti-corruption strategy, to which the UN organs were to lend their expertise. Hungary was praised, in the words of the UN official in charge, for 'setting an example for the rest of the world in openly confronting this issue'.[50] The strategy was eventually adopted as a government resolution in 2001, setting a long list of tasks reflecting the international organisations' recommendations, among which those requiring specific changes in criminal law were later largely adopted.[51] Many others of a more general nature, however, seem to have been forgotten or not prioritised, including the creation of a dedicated 'anti-corruption body' to prepare and monitor relevant policies, as the parties geared up to fight the 2002 elections.

Following the elections, a Socialist-Free Democrat government replaced Fidesz and its coalition partners in office, and – albeit along somewhat different lines than foreseen by the 2001 resolution – another burst of activity in 2002 and 2003 followed. Perhaps most importantly, the new government established a high-level governmental organ with an explicit anti-corruption mandate, a state secretariat dedicated to the transparent management of public finances within the Prime Minister's Office. The state secretariat drew on limited in-house corruption control expertise, but the government at least tried to overcome this shortcoming by the establishment (officially with a February 2004 resolution) of the Advisory Body for Corruption-free Public Life. The Advisory Body was headed by the state secretary for public finances and composed of the representatives of various ministries and law enforcement agencies as well as experts and NGO delegates.

In 2003, Parliament also unanimously adopted the so-called Glass Pockets Act, a collection of miscellaneous transparency-promoting and anti-corruption measures, which was generally well received. In the same year, a new Ethical Council of the Republic was created to oversee the drafting of a code of conduct for high-ranking officials and civil servants. By and during this time, Hungary's integration into the major international organs was also completed, and in 2003 Budapest hosted a major conference on corruption jointly organised by the Prime Minister's Office and the United Nations Office on Drugs and Crime.[52]

By late 2004, however, the momentum was largely lost, which seems to be connected to two major developments. First, EU monitoring of Hungary and the other 2004 entrants finished in 2003. In previous years, the Commission's annual monitoring reports (published following the first Opinion recommending the opening of accession negotiations in 1997) consistently stressed corruption as a problem the Hungarian government needed to

---

49. The problem of corruption received some attention earlier too in the context of efforts to reduce the size of the black economy, as seen in, e.g., the 1994 creation of a Coordination Committee for the Protection of the Economy.
50. United Nations Global Programme against Corruption, 'Joint Project Against Corruption in the Republic of Hungary: Preliminary Assessment and Feedback on the Corruption Pilot Study', March 2000, 12, http://www.unodc.org/pdf/crime/corruption_hungary_wp_prelim%20.pdf (accessed December 15, 2008).
51. ACB, 'Anti-Corruption Strategy'.
52. Ibid., 19. The OECD convention was introduced into domestic law in 2000, and the Council of Europe conventions in 2002 and 2004, respectively. The UN convention entered into force somewhat later, in 2005.

address. This criticism clearly played an important part in bringing the first anti-corruption strategy of 2001 about – in fact EU Map, the OSI monitoring programme found that the approach the strategy takes was 'designed largely to address EU concerns'. Yet, EU pressure did not cease in response to the 2001 strategy. Rather, the Commission continued to prompt the government to take action and even its 'parting words' in the last, end of 2003 report were that '[t]he fight against corruption should continue to receive high priority, in particular through the rapid implementation of the "glass-pocket" programme that was adopted in April 2003.'[53]

The second development took place in domestic politics. In the wake of the governing Socialists' poor performance in the first European elections in 2004, Prime Minister Peter Medgyessy was replaced by Ferenc Gyurcsany (also of the Socialist Party). The internal power dynamics within the party changed, and the Public Finance State Secretariat fell victim to a government reshuffle following the new prime minister taking office. The state secretariat's operation had been subject to considerable criticism (for instance on grounds of objectivity in selecting matters to pursue), but regardless of the questions about its effectiveness, its liquidation was a setback in terms of losing the institutional locus of anti-corruption.

The combined effect of these two developments was that anti-corruption dropped lower down on the policy agenda. TI Hungary's study finds that, despite the Commission's explicit requirement, 'the subsequent implementation of the [Glass Pockets] Act has been patchy'.[54] The code of conduct the Ethical Council had been developing for the civil service was not introduced, the Advisory Body ceased to function and generally whatever policy-making activity had been taking place earlier reduced to a bare minimum.[55] This is not to say that no anti-corruption-related work was conducted at all, but rather that there was no governmental 'champion of reform' who would have invested political capital in the issue. Activities in the period between 2004 and 2006 were consequently low profile and seemed largely to have stemmed from the need to meet Hungary's existing international obligations towards the OECD, the Council of Europe/Greco and the UN agencies. This was ensured by a small team of civil servants in the Ministry of Justice.

Well after the 2006 elections returned the Socialists and Prime Minister Gyurcsany to office, governmental anti-corruption policy activity slowly picked up again. A June 2007 government resolution (No. 1037/2007) was adopted on 'tasks related to the fight against corruption'. The short document's preamble made reference to Hungary's 'international treaty obligations' and 'the importance of addressing and preventing corruption phenomena for the economic competitiveness and international standing' of the country. It called on the Minister of Justice and Law Enforcement to prepare a new, long-term anti-corruption strategy and a short-term action plan by the end of 2007, 'implementing the relevant recommendations' of the UN, GRECO and the OECD. The resolution also established the Anti-Corruption Coordinatory Body (ACB) to assist in this task, with representation of the main ministries, public bodies outside the executive branch such as the State Audit Office and the Office of the relevant Parliamentary Commissioner, as well as NGOs and experts. In October 2007, the government announced the 'New Order and Freedom' programme,

---

53. European Commission, *Comprehensive Monitoring Report on Hungary's Preparations for Membership* (Brussels: European Commission, 2003), http://eur-lex.europa.eu/LexUriServ/LexU-riServ.do?uri=CELEX:52003SC1205:EN:HTML (accessed December 5, 2008).
54. TI Hungary, *Corruption Risks in Hungary*, 24.
55. One important exception was the 2005 adoption of an Act of Parliament on electronic Freedom of Information to supplement the existing FOI legislation from the early 1990s.

aiming, among others, to shrink the grey economy and corruption. In the same month, the prime minister personally announced an action plan, which became known as the 'cleanliness pack', calling for the reform of party financing, 'Europe's strictest conflict of interest regulations', routine asset monitoring for high-level civil servants and more transparency in Members' of Parliament incomes.[56]

These developments are clearly unexpected if one assumes that EU conditionality is the sole driving force of anti-corruption measures, although here, too, the reference to Hungary's international legal obligations indicates that they were not motivated by domestic factors alone. Two rather different dynamics explain this third high(er) intensity phase of anti-corruption. The high-profile 'cleanliness package' is clearly political in nature both in its macro-level aims (such as the reform of party financing) and its motivation. The prime minister's announcement of the package – much of which subsequently fell through, not having received sufficient cross-party support from the parliamentary parties – followed on the heels of a highly publicised corruption scandal involving a former Socialist MP, in connection with which the opposition raised the question of the prime minister's personal involvement (or tacit knowledge). In his announcement Ferenc Gyurcsany himself mentioned the scandal as the backdrop to his proposals, suggesting that rather than bringing up similar cases involving the opposition parties – the 'usual' blame-game – it was time to address the underlying causes.[57]

In contrast, the summer 2007 government resolution and the ensuing work on a long-term anti-corruption strategy seems to have been a result not of high-level political leadership, but rather a low-key, but in its impact no less significant, initiative of civil servants who had been given the task of the day-to-day management of the policy area in the Ministry of Justice. Having been given the portfolio, this small team first tried to re-activate the Advisory Body created a few years prior, and when it became clear that the body was unsuited for spearheading a new initiative, it put forward the idea of a tripartite (government – public watchdog and control organisations – civil society) body, the ACB. The cabinet agreed to the plan, but the absence of a 'high level patron' is detectable in the fact that the government resolution (No. 1037/2007) approved only a single civil service position for the additional tasks the ACB's operation would generate at the Ministry of Justice. The body was also given a very small budget.[58] Nonetheless, the ACB was convened and, in accordance with its mandate, produced several drafts of a new, detailed national anti-corruption strategy, including one the body considered ready for adoption by the government.

The initiative from within the civil service was assisted by mild international pressure, expressed partly indirectly through the monitoring mechanisms of the relevant international organisations and partly directly from the so-called Transparency Working Group, established in 2007 by the ambassadors to Hungary of a number of 'old' EU member states, the United States, Japan and Canada. Officially, the Group's aim was 'to share the experience of their governments in the field of transparency and to offer practical advice and solutions to Hungary'.[59] In practice, the ambassadors used their influence to lobby the Hungarian government for anti-corruption reforms through formal and informal channels

---

56. The prime minister's speech at the press conference of 1 October 2007; accessed at the website of his office at http://www.miniszterelnok.hu/mss/alpha?do=2&st=1&pg=2&m10_doc=1334 (accessed December 5, 2008).

57. Ibid.

58. 'Democratic Forum Suggests 100-Fold Increase of ACB's Budget', http://www.nepszava.hu/default.asp?cCenter=article.asp&nID=919676

59. See 'Ambassadors for Transparency' at the US embassy's website, http://hungary.usembassy.gov/transparency.html (accessed December 17, 2008).

and supported NGOs such as TI-H do the same.[60] The Group seems to have grown out of a longer-standing concern of investors from the OECD countries with corruption and corruption's impact on their businesses in Hungary, which prompted for instance the American Chamber of Commerce to establish a transparency committee. The Group closely observed the ACB's work, for instance by commenting on an earlier draft of the anti-corruption strategy.

Last but not least, civil society clearly played a role in raising awareness, keeping anti-corruption on the agenda and in more substantive ways. A small number of NGO representatives were active participants in the work of the ACB until December 2008, when they quit in protest over lack of progress on the adoption of the anti-corruption strategy.[61] A coalition of local NGOs and INGOs worked to move the parties over the political impasse over the reform of party financing. The 'Joint initiative for a more transparent party financing system'[62] organised a media campaign to publicise the findings of an earlier independent study conducted by think tank Eotvos Karoly Institute, which had in 2007 tried to directly mediate among the parties in the hope of generating sufficiently wide support for new regulations. The local chapter of TI conducted a comprehensive corruption risk assessment, which was partly sponsored and then used by the ambassadors of the Transparency Working Group in their negotiations with the government and also generated high media coverage on the release of the global TI products such as the CPI. In short, a post-accession revival of anti-corruption occurred even in the absence of conditionality, thanks to a coalition of international, non-governmental and governmental actors, although in the latter case the impetus came from within the administration rather than political leadership.

Conclusion

It is difficult to judge the impact of this diverse set of actors, and particularly whether their influence can replace EU conditionality in prompting changes in the long run. Membership conditionality clearly focused ECE governments' minds on the goals the Commission identified, whereas the impetuses from domestic politics, civil society and intergovernmental organisations were more diffuse and at times, in terms of concrete policy prescriptions and set priorities, even contradictory. The end of EU monitoring and the country's official membership status was followed by a slump in anti-corruption activity, which seems to indicate that the conditionality of membership had indeed been the primary force behind various governments' anti-corruption resolve.

On the other hand, conditionality mainly translated into adopting or amending pieces of legislation, rather than into the development and consistent implementation of a long-term, sustainable strategy that would be capable of tackling more impervious structures of corruption. In other words, measures were primarily motivated by, and tailored to, the objective of 'ticking the box' for the Commission. Moreover, other international organisations were also influential, particularly UN agencies and the Council of Europe. Crucially, these organisations left a (more) lasting legacy in the sense of integrating countries into a web of legal obligations, locking in governments at least to the extent that anti-corruption could

60. Transparency International, 'Corruption Risks', 150.

61. Transparency International Hungary press release, http://www.transparency.hu/files/lem-ondo%20nyilatkozat_TI.pdf (accessed December 15, 2008).

62. The initiative's website is at http://www.kampanyfinanszirozas.hu/index.php?oldal=in-english (accessed March 8, 2010).

not completely disappear from the political radar screen even in the absence of more direct pressure from the European Union.

However, as Yves Meny put it, intergovernmental organisations 'might bark a lot; but they do not bite much'.[63] They lack a credible sanction, the possibility of withholding something highly desirable like EU membership was and therefore can only work in combination with domestically rooted factors. In Hungary, some of these endogenous drivers were present and the issue of corruption did consequently reappear on the agenda post-accession. This development was due to domestic party political contestation perhaps best described as the politics of scandal and a combination of low-key influences from the administration itself and civil society activism, aided by international actors working on the ground. Amidst recent changes of government and the ensuing state of flux in political leadership it is too early to judge whether 'control from below' really has the potential to play a more significant role. The long delay in the official adoption of the long-term anti-corruption strategy indicates that the impetus may have been lost again. Nonetheless, the very fact that there was a post-2004 wave gives some grounds for at least questioning the conclusion that, in the words of a recent study, 'there is really no substitute for the European Union in terms of projecting an issue on the national agenda'.[64] In the case of Hungary accession thus may have been less of a watershed than incentive-based conditionality explanations suggest.

The Hungarian case also points to a factor that is perhaps undeservedly neglected in the academic literature: the impact of the electoral cycle. The political build-up to elections seems to drain administrations of the energy and commitment to systematically addressing corruption and provides incentives to political parties both in government and opposition for using the issue as part of smear campaigns against opponents. This both discredits anti-corruption as a worthy political goal, in that it politicises corruption in the worst sense and makes it difficult for actors outside government to frame it as a policy issue that should be tackled through targeted, sustainable interventions the same way other social problems are. Rather than building on foundations already in place, changes of government break whatever momentum was created earlier on, causing measures to be left un- or only partially implemented as new governments decide to take a different approach to addressing the problem.

While this is clearly not unique to anti-corruption, the *ad hoc* nature and suspected political motivation of interventions is particularly damaging in anti-corruption policy, because they undermine the credibility of interventions of any kind in this area. Perfunctory measures create expectations but fail to deliver, which leaves citizens, in Hungary and elsewhere, with the impression that nothing ever changes on the ground and that corruption consequently cannot be combated. This sense of futility and malaise in turn undermines the social support for change that would be essential for future control efforts to succeed.

Notes on contributor

Agnes Batory is Associate Professor at the Department of Public Policy and a Research Fellow of the Centre for Policy Studies at the Central European University in Budapest. She has a PhD from the University of Cambridge. She is co-editor of a book on voting behaviour in European elections and author of a research monograph, *The politics of EU accession*, published by Manchester University Press. Her current research interests include anti-corruption, EU politics and cohesion policy.

---

63. Yves Meny, 'Foreword', in de Souza et al., *Governments, NGOs and Anti-Corruption*, xvii.
64. Grigorescu, 'Corruption Eruption', 549.

National and international anti-corruption efforts: the case of Poland

Kaja Gadowska

Institute of Sociology, Jagiellonian University, Krakow, Poland

This article's objective is to analyse the influence of international anti-corruption pressure on national measures aimed at combating corruption in Poland. First, the change in perception of corruption in Poland will be addressed, along with a short discussion on attempts to reduce its scope. Second, the anti-corruption measures of international organisations, such as the United Nations, the organisation for economic co-operation and development (OECD), the Council of Europe, Group of States against Corruption and the European Union, as well as international Conventions adopted and ratified by Poland will be examined. Third, the role of state and non-governmental institutions involved in the fight against corruption in Poland will be reviewed. Finally, the process of implementing governmental anti-corruption strategies will be analysed, with a particular focus on the introduction of legislative changes that are aimed at limiting corruption through the processes of legal modernisation and harmonisation. This article argues that from among the many initiatives undertaken by various international institutions combating corruption in Poland, the most effective was found to be pressure exerted by the European Union. Poland's eagerness to enter the European Union, and to make use of structural funds after accession, forced the country's elected governments to implement certain recommendations of the European Commission regarding anti-corruption policy. However, these activities had, to a certain degree, a facade-like character and were addressed to fulfil the formal requirements of the European Commission instead of serving as a genuine effort to curb corruption. Even though corruption has been officially considered a serious social problem, which needs to be combated and many anti-corruption measures have been implemented, the effects of the actions undertaken by consecutive Polish governments are not fully satisfactory. Also, anti-corruption slogans have been instrumentally used to fight against political opponents. From another perspective, the activities of Polish non-governmental organisations have contributed to a visible reduction in social tolerance for corruption. Although public opinion research shows that the level of corruption is slowly decreasing in Poland and the country's position in the Corruption Perception Index is systematically improving, it is uncertain how strongly rooted this positive tendency will find itself in the long term.

Introduction

The phenomenon of corruption has always been present in social life. It has existed in ancient Rome, flourished in the Republic of Florence and the Polish-Lithuanian Commonwealth of the seventeenth and eighteenth centuries, constituted the basis of centrally steered communist economies and is still present in today's global market world.[1] For the majority of its history, the fight against corruption was carried out independently by individual states. It was only in the early 1990s that the international community recognised corruption as a global problem, requiring unification and intensification of efforts at the international level. Many international organisations are involved in the fight against corruption, which has resulted in the creation of many recommendations and legally binding documents.[2]

The seriousness of corruption as a social and political pathology is recognised by the citizens of the European Union. Seventy-two per cent of EU inhabitants agree that corruption is a severe problem in their country. More than 9 out of 10 Greek (94%), Czech (93%), Hungarian (93%), Portuguese (91%) and Slovenian (91%) citizens share this concern for corruption.[3] Similarly, 88% of Poles agree that corruption is a serious problem, while 76% think that preventing and fighting international corruption would be more efficient if decided upon at the systemic level of the European Union, rather than at the level of independent states.

According to the Corruption Perception Index (CPI) published by Transparency International (TI) in 2005, Poland was ranked as the most corrupt of the eight new Central and Eastern EU member states. From this time, we observe that the level of corruption is slowly if not systematically decreasing in the country. The latest 2008 CPI ranks Poland as the 58th least corrupt state in the world (out of 180 analysed countries), with a score of 4.6 (Table 1). In general, the level of corruption is much higher in new member states that

Table 1.   Poland in Transparency International's CPI.

Year	Number of countries researched	Poland's ranking	CPI
2008	180	58	4.6
2007	180	61	4.2
2006	163	61	3.7
2005	159	70	3.4
2004	146	67	3.5
2003	133	64	3.6
2002	102	45	4.0
2001	91	44	4.1
2000	90	43	4.1
1999	99	44	4.2
1998	85	39	4.6
1997	52	29	5.08
1996	54	22	5.57

1. The notion of corruption appeared in the works of Greek philosophers Plato and Aristotle, as well as the writings of Machiavelli and Montesquieu, though these authors related corruption more to the moral condition of a society than to individual actions. Antoni Z. Kamiński and Bartłomiej Kamiński, *Korupcja rządów. Państwa pokomunistyczne wobec globalizacji* [Corruption of governments. Post-communist states and globalisation] (Warsaw: Wydawnictwo TRIO, ISP PAN, 2004), 23–9.
2. Celina Nowak, *Dostosowanie prawa polskiego do instrumentów międzynarodowych dotyczących korupcji – raport* [Adaptation of the Polish legal system to the international anti-corruption instruments] (Warsaw: Batory Foundation, 2004), 2, http://www.batory.org.pl/doc/kor_instr.pdf (accessed February 8, 2010).
3. European Commission, 'Opinions on Organised, Cross-Border Crime and Corruption', *Special Eurobarometer*, March 2006, http://ec.europa.eu/public_opinion/archives/ebs/ebs_245_sum_en.pdf (accessed February 8, 2010).

joined the European Union in 2004 or later, with Romania and Bulgaria considered to be the most corrupt.[4]

Public opinion polls show that Poles consider corruption a systemic feature of the public sphere. In 2003, 91% of Poles thought that nepotism and favouritism held sway in public offices, 85% considered that issues of interest can be handled through the appreciation related to a bribe and 71% believed that many high-level public officials take undue advantages from their public functions. Sixty-seven per cent of all respondents were convinced that it was common for public officials and politicians to transfer funds to their own political parties. The following year, in 2004, 64% of Poles considered corruption to be most widely spread among politicians, party-activists, members of the parliament and councillors, 39% in central public offices while 29% in local and regional government offices. Thirty-seven per cent of respondents indicated that healthcare is the most corrupt area, and 42% expressed their belief that corruption is most common in courts and prosecutor's offices. In 2007, 58% of Poles indicated healthcare as the most common area of corruption, whereas only 44% regarded politicians, party-activists, members of the parliament and councillors as the most corrupt. Thirty-one per cent of respondents indicated that corruption is most widely spread in central public offices, 25% in local and regional government offices and 30% in courts and prosecutors' offices. After a 2-year period, in 2009, 55% of Poles expressed their belief that corruption takes place most frequently among politicians, party-activists, members of the parliament and councillors, whereas 54% of respondents indicated that the area of healthcare is the most corrupt. At the same time 27% of respondents considered corruption to be most widely spread in central public offices, 28% in local and regional government offices and 29% in courts and prosecutors' offices.[5]

Despite being common, corruption in communist Poland was not considered a social problem until 1989. Before the beginning of systemic transition, public discussion of corruption stood against the interests of the communist party. Because of chronic deficits within the centrally planned economy (a shortage economy), bribery became an integral part of the system, facilitating everyday existence. Corruption served a regulating function, which eased shortages, and led to a common consent among citizens to use public property for private gains. Corruption became a coping strategy and it was articulated as a part of Polish everyday life and even as a component of the Polish national mentality.[6]

---

4. In 2005, Poland was listed 70th out of 159 states with 3.4 points. This was the worst of the up to date analyses conducted on the country. In 2006, Poland scored 3.7 (the 61st position out of 163 classified countries), whereas in 2007 the country scored 4.2 (the 61st position out of 180 countries). Transparency International, *Corruption Perception Index* (2008), http://www.transparency.org/policy_research/surveys_indices/cpi/2008 (accessed February 8, 2010).

5. CBOS, *Polacy o korupcji, lobbingu i kupowaniu ustaw* [Poles on corruption, lobbying and buying laws] (Warsaw, 2003), http://www.cbos.pl/SPISKOM.POL/2003/K_037_03.PDF (accessed March 9, 2010); CBOS, *Barometr Korupcji* [Corruption Barometer] for Batory Foundation, Anna Kubiak, *Opinia publiczna i posłowie o korupcji* [Public opinion and members of parliament on corruption] (Warsaw, 2004), http://www.batory.org.pl/doc/opinia_korup.pdf (accessed March 9, 2010); CBOS, *Barometr Korupcji* [Corruption Barometer] for Batory Foundation, Anna Kubiak, *Raport z badań* [Research report] (Warsaw, 2007), http://www.batory.org.pl/doc/barometr-korupcji-2007.pdf (accessed March 9, 2010); CBOS, *Opinia społeczna o korupcji w Polsce* [Public opinion on corruption in Poland] (Warsaw, 2009), http://www.cbos.pl/SPISKOM.POL/2009/K_062_09.PDF (accessed March 9, 2010).

6. Deeper determinants of social tolerance for corruption could be traced to Poland's historical experience. Antoni Mączak, *Klientela. Nieformalne systemy władzy w Polsce i Europie XVI-XVIII wieku* [Clientela. Informal governing systems in Poland and Europe in from 16th to 18th century] (Warsaw: Wydawnictwo Scholar, 2000).

Corrupt practices did not automatically come to an end after 1989. The transition from market socialism to free market economy occurred with no crystallised rules clearly delimiting the border between private and public interests. With vast state property and large-scale privatisation, possibilities for effective control over the privatisation process were limited. Political capitalism – the conversion of the previous regime's political capital into economic capital[7] – became a characteristic feature of the new post-communist democracies. Property, in many cases, was accumulated in illegal and unfair ways. The need for rapid privatisation of state property, with Polish capital lacking, entailed turning a blind eye to irregularities and abuse during the process. This unofficial government policy of tolerance for abuse led to the demoralisation of the country's political elites, as well as public officials, who did not regard as reprehensible the obvious conflict of interest resulting from the holding of a public office and owning a company in a business branch regulated by oneself. Dissemination of the saying 'the first million must be stolen', in a sense, extended the social consent to corruption. In the following years of transition, these mechanisms for the private appropriation of public goods were further consolidated. A growing number of media reports concerning corruption scandals involving public elites strengthened a widespread attitude of the omnipresence of corruption in politics. However, surprisingly, in the early 1990s the word 'corruption' was not present in Polish public discourse. In the national daily *Gazeta Wyborcza*, only a few articles containing the word 'corruption' were published in 1990, while 5 years later the number grew to 700 and exceeded 1700 in 2001.[8]

A considerable growth of public interest in the issue of corruption occurred under the rule of the post-communist Democratic Left Alliance (SLD) government as a result of a number of political corruption scandals revealed by the media. The spark occurred with the so-called Rywingate scandal. The scandal began in 2002 and concerned legislative work regarding a law on public radio and television, with prominent left-wing politicians allegedly involved in corrupt activities. To investigate the scandal, the first special Parliamentary Investigative Committee in the democratic history of Poland was established. Detailed media relations of its works presented the public with a clear mechanism of state capture. As a result, the government of Leszek Miller collapsed.[9] Growing public dissatisfaction with corruption led the legislative measures designed to limit it. In the following parliamentary elections anti-corruption rhetoric brought Law and Justice party (PiS) to power. While this political party has had certain successes in the battle against corruption, the anti-corruption slogan soon became in its hands a tool to fight-off political opponents.

Research on corruption shows that its extent is inversely proportional to the economic development level of a given country. Indicators denoting quality of governance, such as social participation in governance and the accountability of authorities, are positively correlated with the gross domestic product. A low quality of governance is increasingly identified as a main barrier to economic development and to the legitimisation of a democratic regime, whereas corruption is cited as one of its worst consequences.[10] Thus, international

---

7. Jadwiga Staniszkis, 'Political Capitalism and Its Dynamics', in *Postkommunism. The Emerging Enigma* (Warszawa: ISP PAN, 1999), chap. 2, 71–97.

8. Grzegorz Makowski, *Korupcja jako problem społeczny* [Corruption as social problem] (Warsawa: Trio, 2008), 15.

9. The influence of these events on the rise of the common belief of the spread of corruption is evident, TNS OBOP, *Korupcja: zmiana w latach 2005–2007* [Corruption: changes in the years 2005–2007] (Warsaw, 2007), http://www.tns-global.pl/archive-report/id/7631 (accessed February 8, 2010).

10. Kamiński and Kamiński, *Korupcja rządów*; Susan Rose-Ackerman, *Korupcja i rządy. Przyczyny, skutki i drogi reform* [Corruption and government. Causes, consequences and reform] (Warsaw: Fundacja Stefana Batorego i Wydawnictwo Sic!, 2001).

institutions have strengthened their pressure upon Polish reformers to tackle the problem and to limit corruption.[11] An acceleration of the process of introducing anti-corruption legislation was brought about by Poland's efforts to enter the European Union and the European Union's demands to reduce corruption.

Contribution of international institutions to limiting corruption in Poland

In the beginning of the twenty-first century, Poland, like most Central and Eastern European countries, started to adjust its legal system to the requirements of instruments created by international organisations. It is currently working on adopting legislation which implements the provisions contained in the international anti-corruption conventions.

The most important conventions ratified by Poland are as follows:

(1) The OECD Convention on Combating Bribery of Foreign Public Officials in International Business Transactions (ratified on 20 December 2000)
(2) The Council of Europe Civil Law Convention on Corruption (ratified on 11 September 2002)
(3) The Council of Europe Criminal Law Convention on Corruption (ratified on 11 December 2002)
(4) The Council of Europe Convention on Laundering, Search, Seizure and Confiscation of the Proceeds from Crime and on the Financing of Terrorism (ratified on 8 August 2007)
(5) The EU Convention on the Fight against Corruption involving Officials of the European Communities or Officials of the EU Member States (ratified on 25 January 2005)
(6) The UN Convention against Corruption (ratified on 15 September 2006)

Ratification of the above-mentioned conventions was a result of actions of several key international organisations aiming at combating corruption. Let me now briefly present their influence upon anti-corruption activities undertaken by Poland.

The World Bank

In the late 1980s, most communist states started to undergo the process of systemic transition to free market economies. A crucial role in this process was played by the so-called Bretton Woods sisters: the World Bank and the International Monetary Fund.[12]

The World Bank has identified corruption as one of the greatest obstacles to economic and social development. It has formulated strategies and recommendations aimed at combating corruption in transition states, designed to strengthen the commitment to tackle corruption.[13] In 1997, the World Bank began to conduct its anti-corruption efforts in

---

11. Aleksander Surdej, 'Sources of Corruption in Post-Communist Poland', in *Political Corruption in Poland*, ed. Kaja Gadowska and Aleksander Surdej (Bremen, Germany: Forschungsstelle Osteuropa Bremen, Arbeitspapiere und Materialien, 2005), no. 65, 5.
12. On the IMF, *The IMF and Good Governance*, http://www.imf.org/external/np/exr/facts/gov.htm (accessed February 8, 2010).
13. Recommended measures include, among others, increasing political accountability, strengthening institutional restraints within the state, strengthening civil society participation, fostering independent media, creating an independent private sector, and reforming public sector management. The World Bank,

Central-Eastern Europe and Central Asia with the design of diagnostic tools to combat corruption. With the main focus on diagnostics, large-scale surveys of citizens, enterprise managers and public officials, aimed to initiate a debate about corruption and to raise the profile of anti-corruption on the reform agenda, have been carried out. Moreover, the World Bank, in cooperation with the European Bank for Reconstruction and Development, has been undertaking a continuous monitoring of corruption in the region through periodic Business Environment and Enterprise Surveys, looking specifically at the quality of the interactions between the state and the private sector. As a result of the research, a series of comprehensive reports drawing on Business Environment and Enterprise Surveys have been published.[14] A specific country report *Corruption in Poland: Review of Priority Areas and Proposals for Action* was published in 1999.[15] The report thoroughly described the main areas of corruption in Poland and referred to the need for public sector reform. It included a review of past anti-corruption efforts, along with some initial general proposals for combating corruption. The necessity of creating an anti-corruption strategy was emphasised. Moreover, the significance of the role of civil society in the design of anti-corruption policy was stressed. Nonetheless, the aim of the report was neither regular monitoring nor providing strict recommendations but to contribute to a starting point for a strategy that could produce results and generate confidence that change was indeed possible.[16] Even though the role of the World Bank in the transformation of the Polish economy was significant (the World Bank, besides financial support, also assisted in developing a series of restructuring programmes, and Poland, taking advantage of loans from the World Bank, had to fulfil specified criteria), factually the impact of this institution on implementing anti-corruption policies in Poland was rather limited. The World Bank experts cooperated with working groups, which had the goal of developing strategies to combat corruption in Poland. Unfortunately, the results from the work of these groups were not utilised. In practice, the use of the World Bank reports amounted to referring to them in academic discussions and in analyses by domestic institutions combating corruption.

United Nations

International governmental organisations, especially those setting specific conditions for their potential future members, are significant players in international relations and have

---

Anticorruption in Transition. A Contribution to the Policy Debate (Washington, DC, 2000), http://lnweb90.worldbank.org/eca/eca.nsf/0/D74DB51B2D46615D8525695B00678C93?OpenDocument (accessed February 8, 2010).

14. The World Bank, *Anticorruption in Transition: A Contribution to the Policy Debate (ACT 1)* (Washington, DC, 2000), http://lnweb90.worldbank.org/eca/eca.nsf/0/D74DB51B2D46615D8525 695B00678C93?OpenDocument (accessed February 8, 2010); The World Bank, *Anticorruption in Transition 2: Corruption in Enterprise-State Interactions in Europe and Central Asia 1999–2002 (ACT 2)* (Washington, DC, 2004), http://publications.worldbank.org/ecommerce/catalog/product? item_id=3788605 (accessed February 8, 2010); and The World Bank, *Anticorruption in Transition 3: Who is Succeeding . . . And Why? (ACT 3)* (Washington, DC, 2006), http://siteresources.world-bank.org/INTECA/Resources/ACT3.pdf (accessed February 8, 2010).

15. The World Bank Warsaw Office, *Corruption in Poland: Review of Priority Areas and Proposals For Action* (October 11, 1999), http://www-wds.worldbank.org/external/default/WDSContentServer/ WDSP/IB/2005/08/17/000090341_20050817144825/Rendered/PDF/333100P0671240Poland1 Corruption01public1.pdf (accessed February 8, 2010).

16. Ibid., 10. To contribute to the elimination of corruption incentives created by a certain institutional environment, the World Bank advocated privatisation, which, in the long run, is considered as a corruption reducing policy. In the short run, however, especially at the beginning of transformation process, the privatisation was itself perceived as a specific form of corruption.

in the last years developed an ever-growing impact on national legislation. Among them, the United Nations is the largest, oldest and considered one of the most influential.

The most important international document on preventing and combating corruption is the UN *Convention against Corruption* (UNCAC). Adopted by the UN General Assembly on 31 October 2003 by Resolution 58/4, it was signed by Poland on 10 December 2003 and ratified on 15 September 2006. According to Article 1 of the Convention, its purposes are to promote and strengthen measures to prevent and combat corruption; to promote, facilitate and support international cooperation and technical assistance in the prevention of and fight against corruption; to promote integrity, accountability and proper management of public affairs and public property.[17]

The UNCAC also requires that states establish institutions to prevent corruption and to enact specialised anti-corruption legislative measures. The document lists a number of other recommendations and propositions of legislative and administrative measures to be fulfilled by each state party. The unique nature of the Convention lies not only in its pursuit of a complex presentation of the problem, but, foremost, in its idea of involving non-governmental and local organisations both in the process of preventing and combating corruption and in disseminating knowledge to society, in general, about the problem of corruption.[18]

Although after the adoption of the Convention, the United Nations organised two sessions of the Conference of the States Parties to the UNCAC devoted to group consultation and a review of the Convention's implementation process, no strict and binding decisions were made. Only a working group was established, which was entrusted with the goal of developing a project that would create a mechanism for monitoring the implementation of the provisions of the Convention by the states. Low-ranking state officials took part in the meetings that attracted no media interests, which illustrates the weakness of this document. Other relevant UN initiatives, such as the Global Forum, designating 9 December as the International Anti-Corruption Day, the UN Global Compact and Democratic Governance as one of the Millennium Development Goals are characterised more with a symbolic and educational, than active nature.

By ratifying the Convention, Poland gave a symbolic expression of its will to combat corruption at the national and international level and of its conviction about the need for international cooperation with the goal of preventing this phenomenon. It is worth noting that as a result of this ratification, Poland undertook legislative efforts aimed at adjusting Polish criminal regulations to the anti-corruption requirements of the Convention. A series of regulations required by the Convention were already present in the Polish legal system. A governmental *Anti-corruption Strategy* was also being realised. From 2005 onwards, as discussed earlier, Poland's position in TI's CPI had improved, though it is difficult to unambiguously assess to what degree this was the result of activities directly related to the ratification of the UNCAC.

---

17. *UN Convention against Corruption* (2003), www.unodc.org/pdf/corruption/publications_ unodc_convention-e.pdf (accessed February 8, 2010). The Convention stipulates criminalisation of corruption offences such as bribery of public officials and in the private sector; embezzlement, misappropriation, or other diversion of property by a public official and in the private sector; trading in influence; abuse of functions; illicit enrichment and laundering of proceeds of crime.

18. Celina Nowak, 'Nowe instrumenty prawa międzynarodowego w walce z korupcją a prawo polskie' [New international legal instruments in the fight against corruption and Polish Law], *Państwo i Prawo* [State and Law], no. 3 (2004): 84.

Organisation for Economic Co-Operation and Development Initiatives

According to the OECD, corruption constitutes a threat to freedom of trade and competition in international business transactions.[19] When the OECD *Convention on Combating Bribery of Foreign Public Officials in International Business Transactions* was adopted on 17 December 1997, Poland immediately signed it and deposited the instrument of ratification with the OECD Secretary-General on 8 September 2000.

According to the Convention, member states decide to establish, under their law, for any company conducting international business, especially multinational corporations, to offer, promise or give any undue advantage to a foreign public official as a criminal offence (active bribery), regardless of the criminal responsibility of public officials in their own countries (passive bribery). Thus, the Convention's provisions only pertain to responsibility for active and not for passive corruption. Regulations of the Convention enforce over its signatories a duty to introduce internal legislation on bribery of foreign public officials. Although the provisions are concerned with only a narrow range of corruption, this aspect is fundamental to economic development and consolidating democratic institutions. For a country to be internationally perceived as prone to corruption has far-reaching consequences. On 4 February 2001, a law implementing provisions of the Convention into Polish legislation (*the Act of 9 September 2000 on the Amendment to the Act – Penal Code, the Act – Code of Penal Proceedings, the Act on Combating Unfair Competition, the Public Procurement Act* and *the Act – Banking Law, Journal of Laws* No. 93 item 1027) was adopted.[20]

According to Article 12 of the Convention, state parties are obliged to cooperate in mutual monitoring of compliance with its provisions, among others by a two-stage review of countries by the OECD Working Group on Bribery in International Business Transactions. The first stage of the review assesses national legislation's compliance with the Convention while the second appraises whether it is being effectively changed by the reviewed state.[21] As a result of the two-phase review, country reports with suitable recommendations are published. The first OECD Working Group report on Poland was published in 2001 and today is highly outdated.[22] In 2007, the second report was adopted by the Working Group.[23] Apart from an evaluation of the application of the Convention, the

---

19. The initiative of complex interest in these problems stems from the United States, who, as the sole OECD member state, accepted internal provisions prohibiting American companies operating abroad, especially in developing countries, from bribing foreign public officials, for example, to be awarded with contracts or higher rewards (*Foreign Corrupt Practices Act* of 1977).

20. The Act establishes as criminal active and passive corruption of foreign public officials (art. 228 par. 6, art. 229 par. 5 of the *Penal Code*), introduces administrative responsibility of legal persons for bribing a person serving public functions (based on the amended *Act on Combating Unfair Competition*) and provisions excluding convicted corruption offenders from public procurement proceedings and concerning international cooperation in accessing information protected by the bank secrecy principle. Currently the responsibility of legal persons is regulated by *the Act on Liability of Collective Subjects for the Acts Forbidden under a Penalty of 28 October 2002* (*Journal of Laws* No. 197, item 1661 with later changes).

21. Initial information on the OECD Anti-Bribery Convention, http://www.oecd.org/about/ 0,3347,en_2649_34859_1_1_1_1_1,00.html (accessed February 8, 2010); Tomasz Grzegorz Grosse, *Działania antykorupcyjne w państwach członkowskich OECD* [Anti-corruption in OECD Member States] (2000), http://www.batory.org.pl/ftp/program/przeciw-korupcji/pk0001.pdf (accessed February 8, 2010).

22. OECD, *Poland. Phase 1. Review of Implementation of the Convention and 1997 Recommendation* (2001), http://www.oecd.org/dataoecd/39/45/2020928.pdf (accessed February 8, 2010).

23. OECD, *Poland. Phase 2. Report on the Application of the Convention on Combating Bribery of Foreign Public Officials in International Business Transactions and the 1997 Revised Recommendation*

report contains a series of recommendations that include a more proactive approach in detecting, investigating and prosecuting cases of foreign bribery and advocates legislative amendments that would clearly confirm that bribes are not tax-deductible. It also advises that Poland should strengthen safeguards for prosecutorial independence to prevent potential risks of undue influence that may arise from the dual role of the Prosecutor General and the Minister of Justice, that is the positions should not be filled simultaneously by the same person; likewise, Poland should consider amendments to the *Act on Liability of Collective Subjects* and should ensure that the *Penal Code* does not contravene the Convention. Moreover, Poland became obligated to prepare an oral follow-up report on the implementation of the recommendations and to submit a written report within 2 years.

Assessing the effectiveness of implementing the OECD Convention in Poland, one must stress that, thanks to its signing, Poland undertook conforming measures and introduced a number of legal amendments preventing corruption. Working Group reports and recommendations proved to be very helpful in this respect.[24]

The Council of Europe and the Group of States against Corruption

Finding a solution to curtail the problem of corruption is one of the important goals of the Council of Europe. The general law concerning anti-corruption consists of the *Criminal Law Convention on Corruption* (of 27 January 1999) with the *Additional Protocol* (2003), and the *Civil Law Convention on Corruption* (of 4 November 1999).[25] Poland ratified the *Criminal Law Convention on Corruption* on 11 December 2002 and the Convention entered into force on 1 April 2003. The *Civil Law Convention on Corruption* was ratified on 11 September 2002; Poland, however, has never signed the *Additional Protocol*.[26]

Group of States against Corruption (GRECO), an organisation specifically concentrated on combating corruption in all of its aspects, was established on 1 May 1999 by the Council of Europe to monitor member states' compliance with the organisation's anticorruption standards. GRECO is responsible for implementation of both of the Council of

---

on *Combating Bribery in International Business Transactions* (2007), http://www.oecd.org/dataoecd/ 3/54/38030514.pdf (accessed February 8, 2010). The report recapitulates the review undertaken in 2006 and is based on information provided by the Polish government, conclusions from a series of meetings with representatives of the judiciary, administration and the private sector held in the Ministry of Justice in 2006, and an on-site visit analysis by an examining team from the OECD.

24. However, though the English versions of the 2001 and 2007 reports are publicly available, only the part on *Recommendations of the Working Group and Follow-up* have been translated into Polish and published on the website of the Ministry of Justice, http://www.ms.gov.pl/oecd/oecd_coop.php (accessed February 8, 2010). Similarly, Poland's replies to the recommendations have never been made public.

25. European Treaty Series – No. 173, *Criminal Law Convention on Corruption,* Strasbourg, 27.01.1999, http://conventions.coe.int/Treaty/EN/Treaties/Html/173.htm (accessed February 8, 2010); European Treaty Series – No. 174, *Civil Law Convention on Corruption,* Strasbourg, 4.11.1999, http://conventions.coe.int/Treaty/en/Treaties/Html/174.htm (accessed February 8, 2010). Another document of the Council of Europe relevant to corruption is a resolution drafted by the Committee of Ministers (97)24 *on the twenty guiding principles for the fight against corruption* (1997). The other instruments are recommendations of the Committee of Ministers to member states *on codes of conduct for public officials* (2000) and *on common rules against corruption in the funding of political parties and electoral campaigns* (2003).

26. The *Criminal Law Convention on Corruption* stipulates criminalisation of a wide range of corruption offences. However, criminal law measures, typically regarded as best in the fight against corruption, do not encompass all problems concerning preventing corruption, which created the need for a civil law Convention, that entered into force in 1999.

Europe Conventions. The most significant aspect of GRECO's activity is carrying out Mutual Evaluation.[27] Its first part, *The First Evaluation Round (2000–2002)*, brought about three reports concerning Poland: 'Evaluation Report on Poland', 'Compliance Report on Poland' and 'Addendum to the Compliance Report on Poland'. The first document (2002) consisted of detailed information on Polish criminal legislation regarding corruption, state bodies and institutions in charge of the fight against corruption. A short analysis contained relevant information about a policy for preventing corruption. The crucial part of the report consisted of 17 recommendations for Poland.[28] The second (2004) and the third (2006) documents touched upon adopting GRECO's recommendations. Although GRECO concluded that a majority of recommendations have been implemented or dealt with in a satisfactory manner, the organisation requested additional information on implementation of the remaining recommendations.

The *Second Evaluation Round (2003–2006)* was constructed in a similar manner although the 'Evaluation Report on Poland' (2004) involved three main themes: proceeds of corruption, public administration and corruption and legal persons and corruption. Similarly, GRECO addressed a list of nine recommendations for Poland.[29] Moreover, GRECO invited Polish authorities to present a report on the implementation of the recommendations by the end of 2005. The 'Compliance Report on Poland' (2006) stated that Poland has implemented or dealt with the vast majority of the recommendations satisfactorily. In the 'Addendum to the Compliance Report on Poland' (2008), however, GRECO pointed to a lack of implementation of certain recommendations.[30] Although GRECO invited Polish authorities to translate GRECO reports and publish them in the national language, only small fragments of reports can be found in specialist prosecutorial journals.

---

27. The evaluation procedures involves the collection of information through questionnaires, on-site country visits and discussions with key domestic players, as well as the drafting of evaluation reports that contain recommendations for the evaluated countries. Measures taken to implement recommendations are then assessed by GRECO under a separate compliance procedure. GRECO, *Mutual Evaluation*, http://www.coe.int/t/dghl/monitoring/greco/evaluations/intro_EN.asp (accessed February 8, 2010).

28. These recommendations included developing governmental strategy for combating corruption, establishing a council or designating an existing institution to steer all bodies involved in combating corruption, exchanging information with NGOs to discuss government anti-corruption initiatives, implementing a global training programme aimed at raising awareness among public officials, undertaking steps towards reducing the scope of discretionary powers of administrative officers, adopting codes of conduct for the civil service, and creating a central intelligence database (pp. 24–5), http://www.coe.int/t/dghl/monitoring/greco/evaluations/round1/GrecoEval1(2001)11_Poland_EN.pdf (accessed February 8, 2010).

29. To provide prosecution authorities with coordinated and up-to-date financial and economic information, to establish multidisciplinary teams of experts in the field of combating economic and financial crime, to extend the scope of application of the *Act on Restricting the Pursuit of Business Activity of Persons Performing Public Functions* and of the *Civil Service Act* aimed at prohibiting 'pantouflage' (i.e. improper movement of a public official to the private sector), to amend the *Act on Liability of Collective Subjects for the Acts Forbidden under a Penalty* to include all relevant corruption offences which may lead to the establishment of corporate liability, to establish special training and guidelines for tax authorities concerning the detection of corruption offences (pp. 21–2), http://www.coe.int/t/dghl/monitoring/greco/evaluations/round2/GrecoEval2(2003)6_Poland_EN.pdf (accessed February 8, 2010).

30. To extend the scope of the *Act on Restricting the Pursuit of Business Activity of Persons Performing Public Functions* and the *Civil Service Act* aimed at prohibiting 'pantouflage' (p. 2), http://www.coe.int/t/dghl/monitoring/greco/evaluations/round2/GrecoRC2(2006)5_Add_Poland_EN.pdf (accessed February 8, 2010).

GRECO's most recent *Third Evaluation Round* is currently being conducted since its beginning on 1 January 2007. As previously, in the 'Evaluation Report' (2008) GRECO addressed Poland with a number of recommendations concerning combating corruption.[31]

Thanks to the formula of monitoring the process of implementing its recommendations, GRECO's *Mutual Evaluation* programme encourages countries to undertake any necessary reforms. As a response to GRECO's instructions, Poland introduced a number of anti-corruption legal amendments. Part of the changes, as it was already mentioned, resulted directly from the ratification of the *Criminal Law Convention on Corruption* and the *Civil Law Convention on Corruption*.[32]

In May 2000, the Economic Committee of Poland's Council of Ministers appointed a working group with a view to analysing which measures could be undertaken to improve the prevention of corruption and the efficiency of counter-measures. The group produced a report named 'Tasks in combating the sources of corruption', which constituted one of the most important attempts by the government to formulate a comprehensive anti-corruption strategy, including organisational and legal aspects. Moreover, Poland addressed GRECO's recommendations by adopting the *Anti-corruption Strategy* in September 2002, covering a wide range of sectors and institutions involved in preventing and fighting corruption.[33]

The European Union

Among international organisations involved with combating corruption, the European Union's contribution is especially noteworthy. In connection with its enlargement, the European Union had a tangible opportunity to influence the reduction of corruption in the countries seeking admission to its structure, as the candidate countries had to fulfil requirements formulated by the European Commision. After accession, the diminishing influence of the European Union was partially reinforced by the opportunity of new member states to receive funding from structural funds.

Having been affected by corruption scandals in the early 1990s, the European Union adopted binding anti-corruption measures. Article 29 of the *Treaty on European Union* mentions preventing and combating corruption as examples of the ways of achieving the objective of creating and maintaining a European area of freedom, security and justice. Corruption constitutes one of the types of offences that should be fought against as part of the European Union's third pillar of responsibility, which consists of police and judicial cooperation in criminal matters. Although corruption constitutes one of the crucial accession problems, no strict formal framework to be adopted by candidate countries has been created. The European Union has taken actions aimed at introducing principles of 'good

---

31. Poland was recommended, e.g. to sign and ratify an *Additional Protocol to the Criminal Law Convention on Corruption*, to amend the *Penal Code* with provisions on bribery in the private sector and review the provisions on active trading in influence, as well as to harmonise the provisions on political financing, and to ensure more substantial and pro-active auditing and monitoring of political parties' and election committees' financing (Theme I, p. 22, Theme II, pp. 28–9), http://www.coe.int/t/dghl/monitoring/Greco/evaluations/round3/GrecoEval3(2008)2_Poland_One_EN.pdf (accessed February 8, 2010); http://www.coe.int/t/dghl/monitoring/Greco/evaluations/round3/GrecoEval3(2008)2_Poland_Two_EN.pdf (accessed February 8, 2010).
32. For instance, in November 2003, the *Act on Liability of Collective Subjects* entered into force. Its provisions meet to a large extent the standards laid down in Article 18 of the *Criminal Law Convention on Corruption*.
33. It will be discussed later in this article.

governance' at the Community level. However, attempts to diffuse these measures to the country level and harmonisation of anti-corruption standards in member states do not seem satisfactory. Anti-corruption provisions within the European Union remain scattered and in many cases are not legally binding.

EU legislation concerning the fight against corruption comprises legislative instruments, preparatory acts, as well as European Commission opinions and responses to other acts.[34] Since the early 1990s, the European Union has taken several anti-corruption measures, most importantly, the *Convention on the Protection of the Financial Interests of the European Communities* of 26 July 1995, and the *Convention on the Fight against Corruption involving Officials of the European Communities or Officials of [EU] Member States* of 26 May 1997. Moreover, based on article 3 of the *Treaty on European Union*, the Council of the European Union adopted on 22 December 1998 the *Council's Joint Action* 98/472/JHA *on corruption in the private sector*.[35] Yet, as a legal measure of the European Union's third pillar, the *Joint Action* was not legally binding.

The launch of the European Anti-Fraud Office (OLAF), with large investigative powers, was another important moment in the EU anti-corruption policy. Since its instigation in 1999, it has developed a number of methods of preventing fraud and corruption.[36]

The European Commission assesses to what extent member states comply with international anti-corruption measures. Yet, according to the Open Society Institute, the Commission has not set clear standards concerning corruption and anti-corruption policy for candidate countries.[37] In annual European Commission *Regular Reports*, prepared to evaluate the state of preparations for membership, there are six monitoring criteria: existence and implementation of anti-corruption policy; institutional solutions for implementation and division of tasks between institutions; ethical codes of conduct for public officials; public officials training programmes; incidents of corruption in government and public administration, and reactions of the government towards them; ratification and implementation of Conventions. While criteria concerning international measures, law implementation and enforcement have been evaluated in the same way for all countries, the Commission's assessment has been far from consistent. It has occurred that the Commission has recommended certain measures in one country, at the same time disregarding the same problem in the case of another state, where it could constitute an even more serious threat, as in the case of the assessment of conflict of interests, party financing and lobbying regulations in accessing states.[38]

Evaluation of the progress of candidate countries towards accession was carried out, apart from the Commission's *Regulars Reports*, within the EU Accession Monitoring Programme by the Open Society Institute (now EU Monitoring and Advocacy Programme,

---

34. For a list of regulations, *Access to the European Union Law Eur-Lex*, http://eur-lex.europa.eu/en/dossier/dossier_19.htm (accessed February 8, 2010).
35. The *Joint Action* recommended member states to align legislation of member states on active and passive bribery in the private sector and on the criminal liability of natural persons, as well as to align penalties and sanctions for these offences.
36. For example, an interdisciplinary anti-fraud strategy, principles of cooperation between police forces and the judiciary, transparency in public life and the European arrest warrant, http://europa.eu/legislation_summaries/fight_against_fraud/antifraud_offices/l34008_en.htm (accessed February 8, 2010).
37. Open Society Institute, *Korupcja i polityka antykorupcyjna*. Program Monitoringu Akcesji do Unii Europejskiej [Corruption and Anti-Corruption Policy]. EUMAP, Raporty Krajowe: Polska [Country Reports: Poland], Budapest, 2002, p. 16, http://www.batory.org.pl/ftp/program/przeciw-korupcji/publikacje/inne_publikacje/korupcja_i_polityka_antykorupcyjna.pdf (accessed February 8, 2010).
38. Ibid., 54–8.

EUMAP). In 2002, the EUMAP report evaluated Poland's approach to corruption and anti-corruption policy.[39] Although specific legal amendments were praised (e.g. the 2001 *Electoral Law*), the report also noted that Poland still lacked a coordinated anti-corruption strategy.[40] The report also indicated that the European Union repeatedly criticised the Polish government in the *Regular Reports* for insufficient efforts to tackle corruption.[41] With accession negotiations finished, 2002 was the last year for the *Regular Reports* to be published. However, the European Commission was still monitoring candidates in 2003, regularly reported its findings to the Council of the European Union and wrote to the acceding countries signalling issues of concern. Afterwards, the Commission published the *Comprehensive Monitoring Reports* as the final, public and complete report on the state of preparations for membership.[42] The 2003 *Comprehensive Monitoring Report* reproached Poland for little progress in fighting corruption.[43] In support of their theses, the report referred to the results of GRECO's evaluation and the Supreme Chamber of Control's audits.

The European Union stresses explicitly that its instruments do not provide a genuine follow-up monitoring or evaluating mechanism comparable to those of GRECO or the OECD. It is explained by the fact that introduction of such mechanisms would run against

---

39. Open Society Institute, *Corruption and Anti-corruption Policy. Poland*, EU Accession Monitoring Program (EUMAP) (Budapest, 2002), 405 onwards, http://www.eumap.org/reports/2002/corruption/international/sections/poland/2002_c_poland.pdf (accessed February 8, 2010).

40. Several instruments were introduced by Leszek Balcerowicz's working group by the Council of Ministers to prepare a report on sources of corruption and to plan measures to eliminate them. The group referred to experts from the Supreme Chamber of Control, the World Bank, the Institute of Public Affairs, and the Stefan Batory Foundation's Anti-corruption Programme. In August 2000, the Economic Committee of the Council of Ministers approved the results presented by the working group. Unfortunately, they were never discussed by the government. Another initiative was the establishment, with the support of the World Bank, of the Anti-Corruption Working Group. In May 2001, the Group published *Premises for a Strategy of Combating Corruption in Poland*, suggesting a number of general anti-corruption measures. Nonetheless, the Group was not able to arouse authorities' interest in the initiative, especially after the September 2001 elections and the consequent change of government. Ibid., 405–6.

41. Ibid., 407–8; Commission of the European Communities, *Regular Report on Poland's Progress Towards Accession* (Brussels, 2001), 21, http://www.ukie.gov.pl/HLP/files.nsf/a50f2d318bc65d9dc1256e7a003922ed/dc76837a9620b5d5c1256e7b0048fd23?OpenDocument (accessed February 8, 2010); Commission of the European Communities, *Regular Report on Poland's Progress Towards Accession* (Brussels, 2002), 26, http://www.fifoost.org/polen/EU_Poland_2002/index.php (accessed February 8, 2010).

42. *Enlargement Archives*, http://ec.europa.eu/enlargement/archives/key_documents/reports_2003_en.htm (accessed February 8, 2010).

43. According to the report's authors, the governmental *Anti-corruption Strategy – First Stage 2002–2004* did not properly deal with high-level corruption, its actual impact was rather limited and the authorities failed to secure broad support for the strategy, which was one of the major assumptions for ensuring its effectiveness. Yet, some legislation, such as the amendment to the *Act on Political Parties* and *the Electoral Law* (2001), were regarded as being for the most part well implemented, thus leading to greater transparency in party funding. However, new legislation also contained some built-in loopholes, which could expose the system to abuse. The *Act on the Execution of Duties of Deputies and Senators* (2001) was also considered well-designed, as far as the submission of declarations of assets and their public disclosure was concerned. The report pointed out that the implementation of other provisions of the act needed to be improved. No anti-corruption office was established and a special anti-corruption unit within The Internal Security Agency, created in 2003, was regarded as unsatisfactory. European Comission, *Comprehensive Monitoring Report on Poland's Preparations for Membership* (2003), 16–17, http://ec.europa.eu/development/body/organisation/docs/CMR_PL.pdf (accessed February 8, 2010).

the Commission's general premise to avoid unnecessary duplication of efforts.[44] Therefore it was recommended for all EU members to ratify conventions on corruption established by the Council of Europe, the OECD and the United Nations.

The EC's 2003 *Communication on a Comprehensive Policy* serves specific guidelines for EU member states, e.g. it introduces, where appropriate, clear instructions for public administration staff, suggests the establishment of a single anti-corruption unit or a single coordinating body and encourages anti-corruption policies in the acceding, candidate and other countries on the basis of 10 general principles. Although anti-corruption policies were meant to be built during the accession negotiations (e.g. the pre-accession Phare programme), the Commission proposes that efforts should be intensified to ensure that its overall anti-corruption strategy is fully extended to acceding and candidate countries. [45]

After entering the European Union, Poland became a participant in the Twinning Project – *Transition Facility* 2004–2006. Within the project's framework, monitoring and evaluation of the implementation of anti-corruption activities in Poland is carried out and recommendations are developed to prevent and combat corruption.[46] The latest 2008 European Commission report *Enhancing Anti-Corruption Activities in Poland*, part of the *Transition Facility* programme, contains a summary of anti-corruption polices and reca- pitulates the status of Polish anti-corruption practices. This Polish–German project includes a comprehensive evaluation of anti-corruption strategy.[47]

As the European Union is not vested with a coherent system of combating corruption, the European Commission has not been able to compel member states to ratify anti- corruption conventions. One may, however, speak of the partial successes of the Conven- tions advanced by the Council of Europe, which were adopted by the candidate countries. The fact that most of the old member states did not ratify them shows a lack of instruments that could enable the Commission to influence member states. Pressure initiated by the Commission proved much more effective in the case of candidate countries on the verge of accession, in which the 1993 Copenhagen criteria obviously played an important role.[48]

---

44. Commission of the European Communities, *Communication from the Commission to the Council, the European Parliament and the European Economic and Social Committee on a Com- prehensive EU Policy Against Corruption* (Brussels, 2003), 5, http://eur-lex.europa.eu/LexUriServ/ LexUriServ.do?uri=COM:2003:0317:FIN:EN:PDF (accessed February 8, 2010).
45. Ibid., 12, 20.
46. *TF* 2004 *Strengthening of the Process of Implementation of the Anti-corruption Activities in Poland*; *TF* 2005 *Enhancing Anti-corruption Activities in Poland*; *TF* 2006 *Improvement of the Anti- corruption Activities in Poland*.
47. The report draws attention to a number of key issues, such as the necessity of depoliticising pub- lic administration. It contains a short list of specific recommendations: improvement of the anti- corruption strategy (lacking strategic elements), reinforcement of the central coordinating body (according to the requirements of the UN Convention), reinforcement of preventive anti-corruption (trainings, seminars, the need for a state educational strategy and a national anti-corruption cam- paign), more effective exchange of information between organisations responsible for combating corruption, decrease in the amount of acts concerning anti-corruption, an open attitude to mistakes, consistent conduct of financial investigations and uniform ethical standards. Claus-Peter Wulff and Marcus Ehbrecht, *Enhancing Anti-Corruption Activities in Poland, Twinning Project – Transition Facility 2005. Ekspertyza na temat skuteczności Strategii Antykorupcyjnej oraz podjętych w Polsce działań antykorupcyjnych* [Expert's report on the effectiveness of the anti-corruption strategy and undertaken anti-corruption activities in Poland] (Warsaw: European Commission, 2008), 17, 55–60, http://www.akop.pl/public/files/Ekspertyza_antykorupcyjna.pdf (accessed March 9, 2010).
48. Wojciech Kawa, 'Antykorupcyjne regulacje prawne Unii Europejskiej' [EU anti-corruption regula- tions], in *Korupcja. Oblicza, uwarunkowania, przeciwdziałanie* [Corruption. Aspects, conditionings, prevention], ed. Aniela Dylus, Andrzej Rudowski, and Marcin Zaborski (Wrocław: Zakład Narodowy

During the following rounds of Eastern enlargement, the European Union has remained one of the key players in anti-corruption. Reducing the level of corruption, development of research and anti-corruption strategies constituted some of the important conditions that had to be fulfilled by candidate countries. It certainly contributed to a faster and more effective implementation of anti-corruption measures in acceding states, even though a portion of the actions undertaken had a fictional nature directed towards fulfilling the requirements of the European Commission rather than an actual fight with this phenomenon. Also, paradoxically, the preparations for the entrance to the European Union were conduced by the SLD government that was itself involved in corruption scandals.

Currently, an aspect reinforcing the EU's influence upon member states' anti-corruption policies are structural funds. In November 2008, for the first time in the Community's history, the European Union decided to cancel its financial aid due to the non-fulfilment of certain conditionality criteria. Bulgaria irreversibly lost 220 million Euro of pre-accession Phare and Instrument for Structural Policies for Pre-Accession (ISPA) funding for shortcomings in judiciary reform and for failing to adequately tackle corruption and organised crime.[49] Although Poland was not regarded as totally successful in implementing anti-corruption requirements, it was not at any risk of sanctions similar to those imposed on Bulgaria. Withdrawing funding is the final measure that the European Union (and the European Commission) can undertake to fight corruption. As of now, it is unknown how effective it may prove.

In summary, even though the largest impact for implementing anti-corruption measures in Poland was motivated by the European Union, a particularly important instrument happened to be monitoring by the OECD and especially the GRECO programmes. Continuous evaluation of anti-corruption measures implemented by Poland, including the harmonisation of Polish law to ratified Conventions, and demarcation of areas requiring attention coupled with recommendations for future actions had a disciplinary and directional influence on the anti-corruption policies of the Polish governments. In the long perspective, the pressure of international organisations to implement the recommended anti-corruption measures undoubtedly contributed to the reduction of corruption in Poland; corruption started to be considered a serious social problem, which requires an equally serious government response to combat it.

Anti-corruption organisations in Poland

Pressure from international institutions for combating corruption had influence on the implementation of recommended anti-corruption solutions in the Polish legal system. However, success in fighting corruption is based largely on the effectiveness of the national institutions, which should realise the anti-corruption policies. Non-governmental organisations also play a vital role in this process. Their activities, on the one hand, contribute to supervising state institutions. On the other, they assist the development of social support for eliminating corruption, changes in social attitudes and reducing social tolerance for this phenomenon. Before proceeding with an analysis of advancements in the

---

Ossoliński, 2006). Although some of the old EU member states ratified the Conventions in the following years, others, e.g. Germany, Austria, Italy, and Spain, have never done so.
49. 'Bulgaria Loses 220 Million Euro of EU Funding', http://www.euractiv.com/en/enlargement/bulgaria-loses-220-euro-eu-funding/article-177496 (accessed February 8, 2010).

implementation of an anti-corruption policy in Poland, I will briefly discuss domestic anti-corruption institutions and organisations (Table 2).

Public institutions

The police are representatives of a state institution responsible for combating all types of crimes, including corruption that is dealt with by special anti-corruption police departments.[50] The amount of corruption incidents discovered by the police is increasing annually.[51]

The institution assigned to supervise the implementation of the governmental *Anti-corruption Strategy* is the Ministry of Interior and Administration. In accordance with the 2003 GRECO recommendations and the *Communication from the Commission to the Council, the European Parliament and the European Economic and Social Committee on a comprehensive EU policy against corruption*, a Team for Coordinating Anti-corruption Strategy was created. The Team's main tasks encompass the coordination and monitoring of government administration's actions in relation to the *Anti-corruption Strategy*, creating

Table 2.   Main institutions involved in combating corruption in Poland.

A	*Public institutions*
1	Police
2	Ministry of Interior and Administration
3	Ministry of Defense
4	Ministry of Finance
5	Tax Inspection
6	Supreme Chamber of Control
7	Internal Security Agency
8	Central Anticorruption Bureau
9	Government Plenipotentiary for Elaborating the Programme of Preventing Abuses in Public Institutions
B	*Non-governmental organizations*
1	Transparency International Poland
2	Stefan Batory Foundation (Anti-Corruption Programme)
3	Anti-corruption Coalition of Non-governmental Organisations
4	Helsinki Foundation for Human Rights
5	Foundation for Social Communication
6	Center for Citizenship Education, School for Leaders Association
7	Association of Leaders of Local Civic Groups
8	'Stop Corruption' Association
9	Local Social Group 'Citizens against Corruption'
10	'Normal State' Movement
11	'Transparent Poland' project carried out by the daily *Gazeta Wyborcza*, with participation of local governors

---

50. In 2004, 14 departments and 3 sections for combating corruption were formed as a part of the implementation of the first stage of *the Programme for Combating Corruption – Anti-Corruption Strategy 2002–2004*. An important role in combating corruption is also played by the Central Bureau of Investigation established within the framework of the General Police Headquarters, within which a specialised Team for Combating Corruption has been established.

51. In 1999, there were only 1359 identified cases of corruption; in 2005 there were 6126 and in 2008, 8337 cases, http://www.policja.pl/portal/pol/4/309/Korupcja.html (accessed February 8, 2010). This is partly due to an increase in the efficiency of the police but mainly due to broadening the scope of corrupt activities that have been determined as criminal in changes to the law in subsequent years. Notwithstanding, this continues to be the tip of the iceberg, as it is known that a majority of cases concerning corruption are never exposed.

analyses and evaluations of corruption in the public sphere and presenting opinions and conclusions thereof, as well as cooperation with non-governmental organisations and EU bodies in implementation of anti-corruption policy. An anti-corruption Internet portal was created as a joint initiative of the Ministry and the European Union.[52]

The Anti-corruption Procedures Bureau within the Ministry of Defense is another body implementing Polish *Anti-corruption Strategy*. The Anti-corruption Team, formed in 2003, operates within the Ministry of Finance. The Tax Inspection Unit also has substantial measures for reducing corruption through its extensive powers of auditing the financial status of institutions and private persons. Among its tasks, one finds, for example, the control of personal financial statements of public functionaries.

The chief auditing institution for the public sector is the Supreme Chamber of Control (NIK). According to the Polish Constitution, NIK is a state body subordinate to the Sejm (the lower house of the parliament). NIK has the authority to audit the budget, financial and asset management of the central state administrative bodies, the National Bank, other state bodies, for example, the parliament and senate office, regional and local self-government bodies, legal entities in which the state owns more than 50% stake and any other organisations in their use of public budget funds or fulfilment of public contracts. NIK also investigates the functioning of the internal audit systems in public administration, identifies areas threatened by corruption and mechanisms of corruption and highlights the necessity of undertaking preventive measures by public authorities. Its mission is promoting economic efficiency and effectiveness in the public service. Its reports are an expected and sought for source of information by state organs and the general public.[53]

An important role in fighting corruption is played by the Internal Security Agency (ABW), a governmental institution protecting the internal security of Poland and its powers. Its activity is regulated by the *Internal Security Agency and Foreign Intelligence Agency Act* of 24 May 2002. Its tasks include investigation, prevention and detection of corruption offences of public officials. In the 2004 report concerning corruption, the Agency warned that corruption would soon escalate to a critical point.[54]

The Central Anticorruption Bureau (CBA) was called into existence solely for the purpose of fighting corruption. The CBA is a government administration body created by the *Central Anticorruption Bureau Act* of 9 June 2006 as a special service, which is competent in criminal investigation of corruption, corruption prevention, anti-corruption information and operational activities. This specialised state service, with police powers, combats corruption in the public and private sectors, especially in the state and self-government institutions, as well as fights against any activity that may endanger the state's economic interests. Moreover, it verifies the correctness and authenticity of the financial declarations of public officials.[55]

---

52. http://www.antykorupcja.gov.pl (accessed February 8, 2010).

53. Supreme Chamber of Control, *Annual Report 2007* (Warszawa, 2008), 7, http://www.nik.gov.pl (accessed February 8, 2010); *The Act on the Supreme Chamber of Control* was passed on December 23, 1994. The Constitution of April 2, 1997 emphasises the NIK's independence of the government and stresses its subordination to the Sejm.

54. The report stressed a negative impact of corruption on social perception of the public administration, the level of foreign investments and Poland's international status. The report gave recommendations to the government to continue the process of implementation of anti-corruption law and to incorporate a motivational system for public administration. It also indicated the need to simplify the fiscal law, http://www.abw.gov.pl/Raporty/R_Korupcja.htm (accessed February 8, 2010).

55. The first legal definition of corruption in Polish legislation can be found in the 2006 *Central Anticorruption Bureau Act*, http://www.cba.gov.pl/portal/en/ (accessed February 8, 2010).

The CBA was created by the Law and Justice (PiS) government, which made anti-corruption its main electoral and political slogan; and it is known by the general public from media reports, which are usually concentrated on scandals. Since its inception, the Bureau's activity has sparked a great deal of controversy. The CBA was accused of being an instrument used for political means – to discredit an inconvenient coalition member [an unsuccessful attempt at entrapment, aimed at accusing deputy Prime Minister Andrzej Lepper of the Self-Defence (Samoobrona) political party of graft through involvement in the selling of land] and to fight the opposition [detecting and making public a corruption scandal in the Civic Platform party (PO) immediately before parliamentary elections, through a CBA-plotted operation of conveying a bribe to rig the sale of a plot of land at the Hel peninsula in northern Poland].[56] The Bureau was also used to conduct spectacular and public anti-corruption operations, serving to preserve the image of the ruling political party as fighting corruption networks and thus to boost its support in social surveys (e.g. in healthcare, as in the case of a dramatic arrest – with cameras and patients observing – of a well-known cardiac surgeon Mirosław Garlicki, arraigned on charges of corruption. This sole act resulted in the fall of Polish transplantology). Anti-corruption non-governmental organisations have from the very beginning of the CBA's existence advanced an opinion to subject the Bureau and the appointment of its head to parliamentary control.

In autumn 2009, the CBA revealed a 'gambling affair', which led to resignation of the Minister of Sport Mirosław Drzewiecki and head the of the Civic Platform parliamentary club and chairman of parliamentary committee for public finance Zbigniew Chlebowski accused of lobbying on behalf of gambling companies to block the change in the *Act on Games of Chance and Mutual Wagering* that would have imposed new fees on gambling operators. It was followed by the resignation of the deputy PM and the Minister of Interior and Administration Grzegorz Schetyna (a politician thought particularly close to the Prime Minister who, however, was moved to the position of the head of PO club left open by Chlebowski), Deputy Minister of Economy Adam Szejnfeld and Minister of Justice Andrzej Czuma whose support for his party colleagues casts doubts about impartiality of judicial system in solving the case. Donald Tusk decided to remove the Head of the CBA Mariusz Kamiński from his post, accusing him of pursuing political aims in the lobbing scandal as an ally of the opposition Law and Justice party and replaced him by the former Head of the CBS Paweł Wojtunik. The scandal resulted in appointing a special Parliamentary Investigative Committee for examining the legislative process of the amendments to the *Act on Games of Chance and Mutual Wagering* and its executive regulations when the SLD, the PiS and the PO governments were in power and researching legality of the activities of the government administration organs investigating this process.[57]

Documents summarising the work of the CBA are reports, prepared by the Bureau, on its activities in 2007 and 2008. They contain the number of operational-investigative,

---

56. The land-deal scandal resulted in the demission of vice-premiere Andrzej Lepper and, in consequence, early elections. After the fall of the Law and Justice government, a Parliamentary Investigative Committee was called for researching issues of illegal influence on special service and judicial functionaries to make them surpass their authorities or not fulfil their duties. The Committee is involved, among others, in analysing the actions by the CBA in both above mentioned cases. In 2009, the court issued a sentence in the case of Ministry of Agriculture, convicting two persons for trading influence. However, the alleged participation of Lepper in the affair was not considered.

57. The PiS members were at first excluded from the Committee by the PO parliamentarians due to their alleged involvement in legislative process (they gave opinions on 2007 amendment to the Act) and due necessity of examining them by the Committee. Finally, however, the Parliament voted for reinstating them.

control and analytical activities undertaken by the CBA, as well as more detailed information on selected cases conducted by the Bureau. In 2008, there was a dynamic increase in the number of cases undertaken in relation to the previous year. However, it is difficult, on this basis, to assess the effectiveness of the Bureau or to develop conclusions on the intensity of corruption.[58]

On 5 December 2007, Prime Minister Donald Tusk appointed Julia Pitera as the Government Plenipotentiary for Elaborating the Programme of Preventing Abuses in Public Institutions. The Plenipotentiary, being the Secretary of State in the Office of the Chairman of the Council of Ministers, is expected to prepare proposals for legislative changes (including those concerning the CAB), which will facilitate an effective struggle against abuses among top-level officials and within state administration structures.[59] Unfortunately, the results of the Plenipotentiary's work are scarce. A short report on the use of official credit cards by administration officials was published in June 2008, followed by a controversial report on the CBA, which was declassified by the Prime Minister in December 2008. Apart from these two documents, there is no further publicly accessible information on her activity in the field of combating corruption.

State institutions that are involved in combating corruption are generally assessed positively by the public.[60] It is generally believed that they perform their tasks fairly and in accordance with the law; however, accusation arise that they are being used for political goals. Aside from the examples discussed above, it is worth to make reference to the April 2007 attempt to arrest the former left-oriented Minister of Spatial Planning and Construction who served during the Democratic Left Alliance leadership, from 1993 through 1996. Barbara Blida, during steps to arrest her by ABW agents under suspicion of corruption and presumed ties to the 'coal mafia', fatally shot herself. Due to the accusations that the prosecutor's office did not have adequate evidence to undertake such an action (basing its decision on the testimony of unreliable witnesses) and pursued its investigation under political pressure[61] with the goal of 'breaking the leftist pact', in December 2007, after the

---

58. In 2007, 284 preparatory proceedings and operations were conducted, 169 persons were charged with 387 counts of allegations of crime, whereas in 2008, 670 preparatory proceedings and operations were conducted, and 346 persons were charged with 1075 counts of allegations of crime. *Informacja o wynikach działalności Centralnego Biura Antykorupcyjnego w 2007 roku* [Information on the results of activities of central anticorruption bureau in 2007], 2–4, http://www.cba.gov.pl/portal/pl/20/140/ Informacja_o_wynikach_dzialalnosci_Centralnego_Biura_Antykorupcyjnego_w_2007_rok.html (accessed February 8, 2010); *Informacja o wynikach działalności Centralnego Biura Antykorupcyjnego w 2008 roku* [Information on the results of activities of central anticorruption bureau in 2008], http://www.cba.gov.pl/portal.php?serwis=pl&dzial=20&id=242&search=412 (accessed February 8, 2010).
59. Kancelaria Prezesa Rady Ministrów, *Julia Pitera – Government Plenipotentiary for Struggle against Corruption*, http://www.kprm.gov.pl/english/s.php?id=1401 (accessed February 8, 2010).
60. In 2008, the Police have the best appraisal with over 70% of Poles giving it a positive evaluation and 20% assessing its work negatively. (Two years earlier, the institution was assessed positively by 55% of respondents and 30% evaluated it negatively.) Thirty-six percent of Poles assess the ABW positively; however, 20% evaluate its work negatively. The CBA is assessed positively by 35% of respondents, whereas 27% of those researched evaluate this institution negatively. NIK is accepted by 40% of Poles, however, almost one-fifth of respondents view its work negatively. CBOS, *Oceny instytucji publicznych* [Assessment of public institutions] (Warsaw, 2008), http://www.cbos.pl/ SPISKOM.POL/2008/K_149_08.PDF (accessed February 8, 2010).
61. As it was mentioned earlier, joining the functions of the Minister of Justice and the Prosecutor General creates significant doubts as to the possibilities for political control over investigations pursued by the prosecutor's office.

Civic Platform (PO) came to power as a result of parliamentary elections, a Parliamentary Investigative Committee was formed to research the tragic circumstances of the death of the official.

Domestic non-governmental anti-corruption organisations

The leading role in anti-corruption activity in Poland is played not, as one could expect, by the Polish office of the renowned international organisation TI but by the Batory Foundation (BF), an independent private Polish organisation established by the American financier and philanthropist George Soros. The organisation, registered in Poland in 1988, focuses on supporting the development of an open, democratic society in Poland and other Central and Eastern European countries.[62]

One of the main operational programmes run by the BF is the *Anti-corruption Programme*, which aims at reducing the scale of corruption in Poland by fostering attitude shifts among citizens with respect to everyday corruption, advocating new legislation to ensure transparency of decision-making and organising permanent community pressure on the government to enforce anti-corruption laws and regulations. The *Programme* consists of a number of initiatives and projects, such as activities aimed at amending electoral campaign financing law, monitoring of selected public funds spending, monitoring of the fulfilment of electoral promises to fight corruption made by political parties during the parliamentary election campaign (in cooperation with the Anti-corruption Coalition of Non-governmental Organisations AKOP[63]) and legal counselling for people who have encountered corruption. The Foundation has also assumed the monitoring of the governmental *Anti-corruption Strategy* by verifying every 6 months whether the government has fulfilled the adopted obligations and by directly informing the public opinion of its findings. In addition, the activities of the programme are concentrated on diagnosing corruption mechanisms in concrete areas of social life. One of the most important aspects of the Foundation's activity is *Corruption Barometer*, a project connected with annual conferences and presentations of public opinion poll surveys on the scale and perception of corruption in Poland. Another impressive project is monitoring legislative procedures, aimed to ensure the adoption of effective laws that will eliminate corruption, co-funded by the European Union within the confines of the *Transition Facility Programme 2005*. The BF is also known for organising numerous conferences, debates and for publishing expert reports that are available to the public.

Less active seems to be the national chapter of TI, created in 1998. Its statutory goals include undertaking actions against corruption and working to achieve clarity and honesty in public life. TI's main interest is reducing the level of corruption in Poland through lawmaking and influencing a new legal framework for transparency in public life.[64] TI's leading agenda is the Intervention Programme, aimed at determining the fields of corruption, characterising corruption mechanisms and putting forward solutions for exposed problems. This is from one perspective a programme designed to react to signals of corruption and from another a source of citizenship advice for individuals and institutions that have experienced corruption. The programme is concentrated largely at the local level and

---

62. http://www.batory.org.pl/english/index.htm (accessed February 8, 2010).
63. http://www.akop.pl (accessed February 8, 2010).
64. http://transparency.pl (accessed February 8, 2010).

on corruption in self-government administration.[65] TI's representatives take part in anti-corruption conferences. Likewise, TI undertakes on-going legislative monitoring, based on legal experts' reports, observations and press reports, as well as monitoring to formulate *de lege ferenda* guidelines for legislators. However, results of these projects are not known to the general public, unlike the annual CPI, which attracts much media coverage and public attention.

Other non-governmental organisations focused on fighting corruption in Poland include the already mentioned AKOP, which serves as an umbrella organisation associating the BF's Anti-Corruption Programme, the Helsinki Foundation for Human Rights, the Foundation for Social Communication, the Center for Citizenship Education, the School for Leaders Association and the Association of Leaders of Local Civic Groups. The main goals of AKOP is monitoring of electoral promises concerning corruption and raising the standards of public life. Its reports are available to the general public.[66]

Other societies dealing with corruption in Poland are the 'Stop Corruption' Association, the Local Social Group 'Citizens against Corruption', the 'Normal State' Movement and the 'Transparent Poland' project carried out by the daily *Gazeta Wyborcza*, with participation of local governors.[67] Another noteworthy initiative is the Kościuszko Institute's project 'Małopolska without Corruption', subsidised by the European Union within the confines of the *Transition Facility Programme 2005*. The programme focuses on the promotion and implementation of good anti-corruption practices.[68]

The activities of non-governmental organisations have without a doubt contributed to sensitising the society to the problem of corruption and resulted in a reduction of social tolerance for this phenomenon. At the same time, these organisations are an instrument of social control as they carry out the monitoring of anti-corruption activities undertaken by subsequent governments, the realisation of governmental anti-corruption strategies and the implementation of specified legal solutions. They have been observing the actions of the government leaders and hold them accountable to the obligations, which they have undertaken. In addition, the non-governmental organisations identify areas of social life with the largest risk of corruption and prepare their own legislative projects to counter corruption, which leads to the implementation of increasingly effective anti-corruption measures. All of this results in a decrease in the intensity of corruption in the most recent years observed in the research.

---

65. Julia Pitera, 'Wkład Transparency International Polska w przezwyciężanie korupcji' [Transparency international Poland's contribution to fighting corruption], in *Korupcja. Oblicza, uwarunkowania, przeciwdziałanie* [Corruption. Aspects, conditionings, prevention], ed. Aniela Dylus, Andrzej Rudowski, and Marcin Zaborski (Wrocław: Zakład Narodowy Ossolińskich, 2006), 150–3. Other undertakings realised by TI pertain to transparency in the sport of football, transparency and effective functioning of administrative units (Districts Building Construction Supervision Inspectorates), corruption risks in the governance of the water sector, and the proper conduct of Public Procurement tenders at the Ministry of Defense.
66. Until the present, three such reports pertaining to the elections campaigns of 2001, 2005, and 2007 were published. http://www.akop.pl/index.php?menu=4,1 (accessed February 8, 2010).
67. http://www.stopkorupcji.org (accessed March 9, 2010), http://www.lgo.pl/opk/news.php (accessed March 9, 2010), http://www.normalne.nazwa.pl/index.php?id=20 (accessed March 9, 2010), http://www.przejrzystapolska.pl/ (accessed March 9, 2010).
68. Instytut Kościuszki, *Małopolska bez korupcji. W poszukiwaniu dobrych praktyk antykorupcyjnych dla Polski* [Małopolska without corruption. In search of good anti-corruption practices for Poland] (Kraków, 2008), http://www.ik.org.pl/malopolska-bez-korupcji.html (accessed March 9, 2010).

Anti-corruption strategies: implementation of anti-corruption instruments within Polish legal systems

Adopting and implementing legal provisions

Before 2000, Poland's efforts to prevent corruption were dominated by a series of uncoordinated *ad hoc* actions. There was also no clear conception as to how to fight the problem. However, the first anti-corruption legal measures were adopted already in 1990 under Tadeusz Mazowiecki's government (Table 3). During this time, public administration officials were prohibited from managing commercial companies. In 1994, the then Minister of Justice Włodzimierz Cimoszewicz conducted a campaign 'clean hands', checking whether public officials did not breach the 1992 *Act on Restricting the Pursuit of Business Activity of Persons Performing Public Functions*, by being members of companies' supervisory boards. The new *Act on Restricting the Pursuit of Business Activity of Persons*

Table 3.   Selected anti-corruption legislation in Poland. List of Acts.

1	*Constitution of the Republic of Poland of 2 April 1997*, Articles 153 and 103 (Journal of Laws 1997, No. 78, item 483).
2	*Penal Code of 6 June 1997* (*Journal of Laws* 1997, No. 88, item 553, with later amendments).
3	*Act of 21 August 1997 on Restricting the Pursuit of Business Activity of Persons Performing Public Functions* (*Journal of Laws* 1997 No. 106, item 679).
4	*Act of 5 June 1998 on Voivodship Self-government* (*Journal of Laws* 1998, No. 91, item 576).
5	*Civil Service Act of 18 December 1998* (*Journal of Laws* 1999, No. 49, item 483, with later amendments); *Civil Service Act of 24 August 2006* (*Journal of Laws* 2006, No. 170, item 1218); *Civil Service Act of 21 November 2008* (*Journal of Laws* 2008, No. 227, item 1505).
6	*Civil Service Code of Ethics* (Regulation of the President of the Council of Ministers no. 114 of 11 October 2002 Establishing the Civil Service Code of Ethics).
7	*Act of 22 January 1999 on the Protection of Confidential Information* (*Journal of Laws* 2005, No. 196, Item 1631, with later amendments).
8	*Act of 7 May 1999 on Material Responsibility of Police, Border Guard, Government Protection Bureau, State Fire Service, Prison Service, Internal Security Agency, Foreign Intelligence Agency, Military Counter-intelligence Service, Military Intelligence Service, Central Anticorruption Bureau Functionaries* (*Journal of Laws* 1999, No. 53, item 548, with later amendments).
9	*Act of 16 November 2000 on Counteracting the Placement of Assets Originating from Illegal or Undisclosed Sources on the Financial Market and on Counteracting Terrorism Financing* (uniform text in *Journal of Laws* 2003, No. 153, item 1505).
10	*Act of 15 December 2000 on Competition and Consumer Protection* (*Journal of Laws* 2000, No. 122, item 1319); *Act of 16 February 2007 on Competition and Consumer Protection* (*Journal of Laws* 2007, No. 50, item 331).
11	*Act of 3 March 2000 on Remuneration of Persons Managing Certain Legal Entities* (*Journal of Laws* 2000, No. 26, item 306).
12	*Act of 6 September 2001 on Access to Public Information* (*Journal of Laws* 2001, No. 112, item 1198).
13	*Public Procurement Law of 29 January 2004* (*Journal of Laws* 2004, No. 19, item 177, with later amendments). In 2000 the *Public Procurement Act of 10 June 1994* (*Journal of Laws* 1994, No. 76, item 344) was amended to prohibit persons or companies whose members of statutory organs or managers were convicted for corruption from bidding for public contracts.
14	*Internal Security Agency and Foreign Intelligence Agency Act of 24 May 2002* (*Journal of Laws* 2002, No. 74, item 676).
15	*Act of 7 July 2005 on Lobbying in the Legislative Process* (*Journal of Laws* 2005, No. 169, item 1414).
16	*Central Anticorruption Bureau Act of 9 June 2006* (*Journal of Laws* 2006, No. 104, item 708, with later amendments).
17	*The Amendment of 9 October 2009 to the Act of 20 June 1998 on Public Prosecutor's Office and Some Other Acts* (*Journal of Laws* 2009, No. 179, item 1375).

Performing Public Functions was introduced on 21 August 1997 and has been in force despite numerous amendments, ever since. On 10 June 1994 the *Act on Public Procurement* was introduced for the first time in Poland. It was also one of the first laws regulating the problem of public procurement in Central-Eastern Europe. On 6 September 2001, as a result of an extra-parliamentary initiative, the *Act on Access to Public Information* was passed. Preliminary actions aimed at developing a formalised anti-corruption strategy were undertaken in 2000. A working group was assigned by the Economic Committee of the Council of Ministers, which prepared a report concerning compliance with anti-corruption principles and elaborated upon proposals for new solutions. Yet, because of the fall of the ruling coalition, the document was never used. The following year, a new group, working in cooperation with the World Bank, was created. Again, the intent of the report emitted by this group, *Premises for a Strategy of Combating Corruption in Poland*, was squandered in the midst of an electoral campaign. Even though subsequent governments declared a will to curb corruption, particularly during periods preceding parliamentary elections, there was a lack of genuine political will to systematically advance the pressure to combat this phenomenon.

Anti-corruption strategy: the 1st stage of implementation 2002–2004

The acceptance of the first governmental programme to combat corruption occurred during Poland's final negotiations for EU membership. In September 2002, the Polish government (coalition of the Democratic Left Alliance, SLD and Polish People's Party) adopted the first *Anti-corruption Strategy*.

Objectives of the *Programe for Combating Corruption – Anti-corruption Strategy* included detection of crimes of corruption, implementation of operative mechanisms of combating corruption in public administration, enhancing public awareness of corruption and promoting ethical behaviour.[69] In the framework of these generally formulated goals, specific projects were planned, which included legislative and organisational changes, as well as educational–informational initiatives, which were introduced into the activities of various areas in public life, e.g., the public administration, the civil service, the privatisation, the judiciary, the public services sector and the public finance sector. This concise 14-page document outlined the activities of the entire government, specific ministries and the central administrative units and also established a timetable specifying the date for the completion of each task.

In the government report summarising the realisation of the first stage of the *Programme for Combating Corruption*, from July 2004, which was next submitted to the European Commission, the introduction of new legal regulations and amendments of pre-existing legal statutes was emphasised with the achievement of heightened transparency in the interpretation of specific laws. The creation of new organisational cells and the realisation of new informational–educational initiatives were also stressed. A new *Public Procurement Law* of 29 January 2004 was adopted, along with the *Arbiters' Code of Ethics*, a project of the new *Civil Service Act*, in accordance with the recommendations of GRECO, was prepared, and a project to increase the ethical consciousness of members of the civil service corps was realised under the 2001 Phare framework. An amendment to the *Act* on *Commercialisation and Privatisation of State Owned Companies* of 30 August 1996 was adopted, and the amend-

---

69. *Program zwalaczania korupcji – Strategia Antykorupcyjna* [Programme for combating corruption – anti-corruption strategy], www.ceo.org.pl/binary/file.action?id=77326 (accessed February 8, 2010).

ment to the *Act on Self-Government Employees* was drafted. A very significant achievement was the adoption of the commonly called Anti-corruption Amendment, i.e. the *Act on Amendment of the Penal Code and other Acts* of 13 June 2003. The introduced changes were the result of harmonising the criminal code with international standards. The new regulations widened the scope of the criminalisation of corrupt actions in the public and private spheres. Likewise, a definition was introduced into the *Penal Code* pertaining to a person who performs public functions; this was a key idea for the crime of bribery in the public sector. In addition, the law introduced the criminalisation of electoral bribery, as well as the criminalisation of corruption in business transactions and in the area of professional sports.[70] New legal measures were introduced into the system of criminal law to come into compliance with a number of international regulations, in particular, the *Convention on the Protection of the Financial Interests of the European Communities* and the additional *Protocols*, such as the *Act on Liability of Collective Subjects for the Acts Forbidden under a Penalty* of 28 October 2002. Furthermore, Departments for Combating Corruption were formed at the offices of Regional (*Voivodship*) Police Headquarters, and a Department for the Prevention of Corruption, Terrorism and Organised Crime was formed within the ABW.[71]

Polish legislation's adaptation to international legal anti-corruption measures (conventions of the OECD, the Council of Europe and the European Union) was assessed as satisfactory in the BF report. Its author, however, pointed to several areas that were in need of alignment: private corruption, favouritism and trading in influence, which pose limits to the provisions included in the Conventions.[72] In the opinion of the Foundation, the implementation of the *Strategy* happened slowly and unevenly, which was the result of a lack of proper coordination of actions by the government. There were substantial delays in the execution of about 30% of the tasks listed in the government's document. Likewise, other tasks have not been initiated at all and some had already been finished before the adoption of the *Strategy*. Many tasks were only formally completed, which casts doubt on the sincerity of their execution. The lack of consistency was obvious, as legal amendments could in some cases be even conducive to corruption. Moreover, the European Commission, and not the general public, was the main recipient of the governmental reports on the *Strategy*'s implementation. The *Strategy* did not provide for an institution in charge of supervising the execution of tasks in ministries and coordinating anti-corruption efforts. Furthermore, no additional funding was planned for the implementation of the *Strategy*.[73] It appears, however, that the monitoring of the process of implementation of the *Strategy* by the BF resulted in a more effective realisation of its goals by the government.

---

70. However, immunity was granted to active corruption perpetrators informing the authorities of a corrupt act, with the intention of breaking solidarity between the one giving and the one taking material gratification. This solution has been widely criticised by both Polish and international experts. Celina Nowak, *Korupcja w polskim prawie karnym na tle uregulowań międzynarodowych* [Corruption in Polish Criminal Law in the light of international regulations] (Warsaw: Wydawnictwo C. H. Beck, 2008), 333–444.

71. Ministry of Interior and Administration, Sprawozdanie podsumowujące realizację I etapu programu zwalczania korupcji – strategia antykorupcyjna; stan prac – 31.07.2004 [Report summarising the implementation of the 1st stage of the programme for combating corruption – anti-corruption strategy], http://www.mz.gov.pl/wwwfiles/ma_struktura/docs/1_etap_korupcja.pdf (accessed February 8, 2010).

72. For a thorough analysis of legal changes with relation to their alignment with international anti-corruption measures, see Nowak, *Dostosowanie prawa polskiego do instrumentów międzynarodowych dotyczących korupcji*.

73. For a detailed analysis of implementation of the strategy, see http://www.batory.org.pl/korupcja/strategia.htm (accessed February 8, 2010). The AKOP report on the fulfilling of electoral promises made by political parties during 2001 campaign critically assessed certain solutions in the new Pubic

Adopting the governmental *Anti-corruption Strategy* was to a large degree an answer to the pressure of international organisations, especially the European Commission's. By that time Poland was preparing for accession, and annual EC reports stressed the threat of corruption and the lack of adequate concern for implementing anti-corruption measures. Even though changes were introduced in the Polish legal system to fulfil the requirements of the Commission, other aspects involving the realisation of the *Strategy* were not implemented to a satisfactory degree. For the most part, the governmental *Anti-corruption Strategy* remained a declaration rather than a serious initiative. It is worthwhile to remember that the implementation of the first stage of the *Strategy* happened during the Leszek Miller government, which fell as a result of corruption scandals at the highest levels of government.[74]

Anti-corruption strategy: The 2nd stage of implementation 2005–2009

In January 2005, the Council of Ministers adopted a document *Programme for Combating Corruption – Anti-corruption Strategy: The 2nd Stage of Implementation 2005–2009*. Its strategic objectives remain principally unchanged – preventing corruption and implementing mechanisms allowing for the employment of effective countermeasures, coordinating compliance with anti-corruption legal regulations, limiting social tolerance for occurrences of corruption by raising awareness and promoting suitable models of behaviour and creating transparent and citizen-friendly structures of public administration, adequate for the expectations of the open information society. The strategy envisages not only the engagement of the ministries and state offices but also the participation of local self-government authorities, non-governmental organisations, scientific research facilities and public broadcasters. The programme involves the completion of legislative, organisational, educational and informative actions supplemented with the monitoring of the efficacy of the undertaken activities. What is more, the tasks were prepared on the basis of information on the anti-corruption actions planned by particular ministries and institutions, analysis of the reports by the NIK and the ABW, as well as recommendations by GRECO drawn after the second Evaluation Round, documents and recommendations of the European Union and the Council of Europe concerning the prevention of corruption. An important point of reference was also provided by the UNCAC.[75]

The *Anti-corruption Strategy: the 2nd Stage of Implementation 2005–2009* is more complex and professional than its predecessor.[76] The document describes consecutive steps in the fight against corruption in a detailed way. Similarly as in the previous *Strategy*, the current one

---

Procurement Law, actions aimed at limiting corruption in the healthcare sector, the politicisation of senior posts in the civil service and also the fact that the reactions of the ruling SLD party, in case of revelation of conflict of interests among its members were dependant on the current level of popularity of the party in public opinion surveys and the strength of media pressure. http://www.akop.pl/public/files/Raport_Realizacja_Obietnic_Wyborczych_2001.doc (accessed March 9, 2010).

74. Aside from the 'Rywingate', several other affairs were then playing out at the central level, e.g. an affair regarding the *Act on Games of Chance and Mutual Wagering*, an affair associated with reimbursement for medications and an affair pertaining to the privatisation of the PKN ORLEN refinery group, which were accompanied by scandals at the local level. The negative social assessment of the seriousness of the government's efforts to implement an anti-corruption policy was shown through a systematic worsening in the TI's CPI during this period (see Table 1).

75. *Programme for Combating Corruption – Anti-corruption Strategy. 2nd stage of implementation 2005–2009*, pp. 5–6, http://www.mswia.gov.pl/portal/pl/83/2989/Program_for_Combating_corruption_Anticorruption_Strategy_2nd_stage_of_implement.html (accessed February 8, 2010).

76. Starting from the definition of corruption, its authors list international organisations, international and national legislation, Polish governmental and several non-governmental institutions dealing with

classifies its objectives and goals in accordance with the areas of public life that they refer to, such as the economy, the state's highest authorities, the public administration, the judiciary, the healthcare system, the public finance sector, the education system and the areas of culture and media. Specifically designated ministries and institutions are responsible for the implementation of the *Strategy* within a specified time-frame and the scope of their own budgetary resources. Some tasks, especially those related to the strengthening of public administration, are financially supported with EU funds as part of the Phare 2003 project the *Strengthening of the Implementation of the Anti-corruption Strategy* and the *Transition Facility* programme.

Although the *Strategy* was adopted almost 5 years ago, only three very general, half-page long, governmental implementation reports have been published ever since.[77] The conference summarising the project the *Strengthening of the Implementation of the Anti-corruption Strategy*, which took place in September 2006, was more of a propaganda event than a true informational meeting. In May 2008, a conference marking the conclusion of the European Commission Twinning Project – *Transition Facility* – 2005 was organised, and in November 2008, a subsequent conference took place to summarise the Twinning Project – *Transition Facility* 2006.

Conclusions concerning implementation of the second stage of the *Strategy* made by the head of BF's Anti-Corruption Programme, Grażyna Kopińska, are rather pessimistic.[78] Since no additional funding was planned for the implementation of the *Strategy*, from the very beginning, serious concerns arose over its proper implementation. Furthermore, similarly as in the case of the first stage of the *Strategy*, the second stage of the *Strategy* does not directly provide for an institution to supervise the execution of tasks in ministries and to coordinate anti-corruption efforts. According to Kopińska, the need for launching the second stage of the fight against corruption, when the first one has never been completed and constitutes a loose set of ideas, raises serious concerns. Another problem with the implementation potential of the document involves political factors. The right-wing Law and Justice (PiS) government of Jarosław Kaczyński was highly reluctant to implement the strategy designed by the left-wing administration of former Prime Minister Marek Belka, representing an ideologically conflicting political party. Instead, actions not envisioned by the *Strategy* were undertaken, such as creating the CBA, directly dependent on the Prime Minister and hence not free from political influence. However, despite Poland's ratification of the UNCAC in September 2006, an institution specialised in preventing corruption has not yet been created. Additionally, under the rule of the Law and Justice government, the new *Civil Service Act* and the *Act on the State Staffing Pool and High-rank State Posts* of 24 August 2006 were adopted, which practically constituted a renouncement

corruption, along with the latest data on the level of corruption in Poland. Referring to the Supreme Chamber of Control's reports, areas most prone to corruption and corruption mechanisms are named. Symptomatically, such an introduction accounts for half the volume of the document.

77. All three reports prepared by the Minister of Interior and Administration were published during Jarosław Kaczyński's government – in October 2006, April 2006, and June 2006. In reports, aside from the creation of the CBA, only educational–informational activities were mentioned, such as the organisation of training for civil servants, officers in the anti-corruption divisions of the police and the border guard, prosecutors in the appellate prosecutor's offices and ethical advisors for administrative units, as well as the creation of a contest 'A Friendly Self-Government Administration Office', initiated by the Ministry of the Interior and Administration. During the Donald Tusk's government no reports were issued concerning the realisation of the *Strategy*, http://www.kprm.gov.pl/s.php?id=467 (accessed February 8, 2010).

78. In her presentation 'Strategie przeciwdziałania korupcji' [Anti-corruption strategies], during the Kościuszko Institute conference, *Malopolska bez korupcji*, 30–1.

of the basic institutions and procedures within the civil service. Under the changes, the institutions of the Head of Civil Service and of the Office of Civil Service were abolished; their tasks were assumed by the Chief of the Chancellery of the Prime Minister. Senior civil service posts were to be staffed by way of appointment as the new regulation cancelled the provisions regarding competitions for high-ranking posts, thus leading to the politicisation of the public administration.

'Combating corruption' has become a political slogan, which brought the Law and Justice party to power in 2005. Similarly, the 2007 elections were dominated by political parties making anti-corruption promises. In a report published a year after the elections, the AKOP noted that among the promises made by the PO, who created a ruling coalition with the Polish People's Party after the elections, hardly any were kept.[79] The PO heralded improvement of the legislative quality and accuracy, i.e. simplification of the legal system, amelioration of its internal coherence and transparency, and advancement of law enforcement. Until now only a project involving a new type of legislative procedure, shifting preparation and drafting of legal acts from ministries to the Government Legislation Centre, has been adopted. The promised complex governmental anti-corruption system has still not been prepared. Shortly after the elections the position of the Government Plenipotentiary for Elaborating the Programme of Preventing Abuses in Public Institutions was created. Currently works on amendments to the *Act on Limitations on the Economic Activities Carried on by Persons Performing Public Functions* are underway. Anti-corruption provisions are to encompass a larger number of officials and sanctions for counterfeiting one's disclosure statements shall be more severe. The government is working on a bill aimed at the modernisation of the customs services and an improvement of the prosecution of offences committed against the state's finances. The declared closures of ineffective agencies and special purpose funds have not yet taken place. On the other hand, a new *Civil Service Act* of 21 November 2008 was passed, which helped depoliticise the civil service by re-establishing the posts of general directors, department directors and deputy directors as structural components of the civil service, and hence including their appointment into the open competition procedures, as well as by reinstating the position of the Head of the Civil Service. Some positive changes were also included in the *Act of Self-government Employees* of 21 November 2008, which introduced competitions for personnel recruitment. The government is also working on introducing clear and transparent rules of ownership supervision and open appointment to the supervisory boards of state-owned companies. On 6 December 2007, the ordinance was issued by the Minister of the Treasury on the *Principles and Methods for Electing Candidates to Supervisory Boards for Companies with State-Treasury Share Holdings*. However, at the same time, there have also been cases of tampering with the qualification procedures for membership in supervisory boards of state-owned companies, when the winning persons did not fulfil the necessary requirements for the position, yet they were found to be linked with one of the ruling parties. There were also few cases of manipulations involving contests for the positions of the presidents of the management boards of state-owned companies. A bill amending the *Central Anticorruption Bureau Act* and subordinating the CBA to the parliament is being prepared. The government has likewise

---

79. Antykorupcyjna Koalicja Organizacji Pozarządowych, *Realizacja obietnic wyborczych dotyczących przeciwdziałania korupcji złożonych przez partie polityczne podczas kampanii wyborczej 2007 roku* [The implementation of anti-corruption electoral promises concerning corruption prevention made by political parties during the electoral campaign of 2007] (2008), http://www.akop.pl/public/files/raport-realizacja-obietnic-wyborczych-2007.pdf (accessed March 9, 2010).

prepared a project of a new law on the *Customs Service* having the goal of modernising it. In December 2008, the government issued a statement that a new project named the 'Anti-corruption Shield' was prepared, the aim of which is to defend the process of privatisation of the state-owned companies and the procedures of public procurement from corruption; however, no public details were given regarding a plan of actions for this project. Finally, on 9 October 2009 the amendment to the *Act of 20 June 1998 on Public Prosecutor's Office and Some Other Acts* was passed that separates the functions of the Minister of Justice and the Prosecutor General, conducive to prosecution's better immunity against political influence.

From 2005, when Poland scored lowest in its history in TI's CPI report, its position in the ranking is systematically improving. On the one hand, this improvement is the result of the effectiveness of pressures by international organisations that made Poland introduce anti-corruption mechanisms into its legal system, but it is also the outcome of domestic efforts to combat corruption. After Poland joined the European Union, pressure by the European Commission no longer comprised such a strong motivation to fight corruption. One could therefore assume that the reversal of the increased trend in perceiving corruption is partially the result of a declaration by the then new Law and Justice government, after the parliamentary elections of 2005, to pursue a decided battle with corruption and the undertaking of tangible actions by this government to it.[80] In TI's assessment, the improvement of Poland's position on the CPI, in subsequent years, was impacted by the actions of the CBA and the 2007 campaign to the Sejm and Senate, during which the issues of combating corruption were addressed along with the criminal proceedings pursued by the prosecutor's office in cases against high-level public officials who faced corruption charges.[81]

From another perspective, the implementation of the *2nd Stage of the Anti-corruption Strategy* does not present a main concern in the scope of governmental priorities. The challenges before the cabinet of Donald Tusk have been obscured by the necessity to deal with the economic crisis. The government has not yet developed a clear and convincing vision for anti-corruption policy and has limited its actions to responding to chosen issues. Moreover, the variety of views for solutions to the problem of corruption by political parties and also the lack of desire of those governing to make use of methods developed by their predecessors do not bode well for the chance of creating an effective, long-term anti-corruption strategy, which goes beyond current party politics.[82]

---

80. TI experts indicated that Poland's improvement in the CPI ranking in 2006 was influenced by the creation of the CBA, as well as a series of arrests undertaken by the Central Bureau of Investigation, including civil servants in the Ministry of Finance, accused of issuing decisions for the benefit of criminals, prominent politicians from the SLD involved in insuring the power plant in the town of Opole, as well as members of the so-called Warsaw Pact who undertook decisions which were not beneficial to the city in the area of real estate management in exchange for bribes, http://www.egospodarka.pl/18321,Korupcja-w-Polsce-i-na-swiecie-2006,1,39,1.html (accessed February 8, 2010). On the other hand, accusations arose that these actions were directed towards political opponents and had the goal of marginalising them.
81. http://www.prawnik.pl/wiadomosci/wazne/86971 (accessed March 9, 2010).
82. Similar beliefs were expressed by the Government Plenipotentiary for Elaborating the Programme of Preventing Abuses in Public Institutions during the conference 'Anti-Corruption Strategies in Countries of Eastern and Central Europe: Is a Long-term Anti-corruption Strategy possible in Poland', organised in March 2008 by the Batory Foundation.

Conclusions

According to public opinion polls, 60% of Poles think that fighting corruption should constitute one of the priorities of the Polish government.[83] Even though TI indicates that from
2005, the level of perceived corruption in Poland is systematically decreasing, Poland continues to have the lowest CPI ranking position amongst the countries that entered the European Union in 2004.[84] At the same time, public opinion research reveals that in recent years
there was a decided decrease in the number of individuals admitting to giving bribes. In
2003, as many as 17% of respondents admitted to such actions, while in 2006 only 9% of
those researched admitted to giving bribes.[85] Additionally, in 2005, 67% of Poles believed
that corruption occurs very frequently, and 27% frequently, whereas research undertaken in
2007 indicates a change in the social perception of the expansion of this phenomenon: 42%
of respondents indicated that corruption in Poland takes place very frequently, and 45% frequently. However, these proportions are similar to the level in 1999.[86] Notwithstanding, it
can be argued that in recent years the society as a whole became less tolerant to corruption.

Developing an assessment of the impact of international organisations on the
effectiveness of fighting corruption in Poland is not an easy task. Initially, the institution
that drew attention to the problem of corruption in post-communist countries and called
for specified institutional solutions to limit this phenomenon was the World Bank. However, undoubtedly, it is the European Union which had the largest impact on implementing
an anti-corruption policy in Poland. Analysing the interplay between international and
national anti-corruption initiatives, it is necessary to notice that Poland ratified a number
of international anti-corruption Conventions, some before entering the European Union
and others after accession. By doing so Poland obligated itself to harmonise its legal system to these international instruments. A great number of the actions undertaken by
Poland to combat corruption were the result of pressures from the European Commission,
as limiting corruption by effective implementation of the anti-corruption measures was an
important condition that had to be fulfilled by candidate countries to be accepted into the
European Union; a successful fight with corruption was the next condition for allocating
EU funds for member states after accession. Nonetheless, several anti-corruption actions
undertaken by Polish governments aimed at formally conforming to the requirements of
the Commission rather than a real fight with corruption. An important instrument assisting
the battle against corruption was the continuous monitoring of Poland by the European
Commission, GRECO and to a lesser extent the OECD. Assessments of the anti-corruption
activities undertaken by Poland, including changes in the law connected to the ratification

---

83. CBOS, *Najważniejsze cele działań państwa – postulaty i oceny* [The most important goals of the
state – demands and opinions] (Warsaw, 2007), http://cbos.pl/SPISKOM.POL/2007/K_004_07.PDF
(accessed February 8, 2010).

84. While in the 2005 ranking of Central and Eastern European Countries only Romania was evaluated as a country more corrupt than Poland, in 2008 only the two new EU member states, Bulgaria
and Romania, scored lower than Poland in the CPI. Assuming that corruption perception is not only
a product of a given media reality (as is evident, the free media being an instrument for combating
corruption, at the same time increases corruption perception in the society), a positive change in the
actual level of corruption in Poland has taken place in recent years. For critical discussion of the TI's
CPI, see Makowski, *Korupcja jako problem społeczny*, 34–55.

85. CBOS, *Barometr Korupcji* [Corruption Barometer], for Batory Foundation, Anna Kubiak,
Codzienne doświadczenia korupcyjne Polaków [Everyday experience of poles with corruption]
(Warsaw, 2006), http://www.batory.org.pl/doc/doswiadczenia-korupcyjne-polakow.pdf (accessed
February 8, 2010).

86. TNS OBOP, *Korupcja: zmiana w latach 2005–2007.*

of the Conventions, indicating areas which require further attention, and recommendations regarding activities that should be undertaken in the future, that were contained in these reports, served as a mechanism that positively disciplined and directed the actions of the Polish governments. Although, in contrast to the European Commission, which repeatedly criticised Polish governments in its *Regular Reports* for insufficient anti-corruption efforts, neither GRECO nor the OECD had the privilege of initiating sanctions against countries that did not adjust to their recommendations.

Externally imposed initiatives meant to help combat corruption cannot be effective if they are not accompanied by domestic anti-corruption efforts, resulting in, on the one hand, top-down political and administrative projects, and on the other, bottom-up pressure. Even though since the beginning of the transition a number of legal acts have been adopted to fight corruption (Table 3), their simple enumeration does not show the correct image of the situation in Poland. Despite a lack of proper coordination of activities of international and state bodies, as well as of Polish organisations and institutions, which hinders the overall implementation of these regulations, some positive effects in the fight against corruption are apparent.

Poland, in contrast to countries like Bulgaria and Romania (see Ivanov in this volume),[87] after EU accession intensified its anti-corruption activities, the effectiveness of which is visible in the public opinion surveys. This directly coincided with a change in government. As discussed earlier, the slogan to fight against corruption, which in 2005 brought the Law and Justice party into power, was later used by this party as a weapon to fight-off its political opponents. Anti-corruption rhetoric also dominated the 2007 elections. However, it must be stressed that any form of politicising the problem brings about rather negative effects.[88] It is difficult not to agree with Ivan Krastev's thesis, that '[w]hat post-communist societies need are policies that reduce corruption, but not a rhetoric that leads to corruption-centered policies'.[89] Even though the Polish governments did not succeed in creating a long-term anti-corruption strategy that is beyond short-term party politics, with Law and Justice and next the Civic Platform parties unenthusiastically realising the second stage of the *Anti-corruption Strategy* developed by the Democratic Left Alliance government, they still undertook a fight against corruption and fulfilled a portion of their anti-corruption electoral promises. Domestic non-governmental organisations such as the BF, AKOP and TI, which have assumed the continued responsibility for monitoring of the implementation of the anti-corruption strategy by the subsequent governments, contributed to the progress against corruption.

It is often argued that the key to combating corruption is not only anti-corruption legislation, but above all the presence of well-designed state institutions governed by the rule of law.[90] As Antoni and Bartłomiej Kamiński aptly point out, a state anti-corruption battle confined to legal regulations and police actions may only lead to the alleviation of the symptoms but does not cure the disease. Good governance standards are necessary, while improvement of procedures should be complemented by the moral and intellectual

---

87. Kalin Ivanov, 'The 2007 Accession of Bulgaria and Romania: Ritual and Reality', *Global Crime* 11, no. 2 (2010): 210–219.
88. Wulff and Ehbrecht, *Enhancing Anti-Corruption Activities in Poland.*
89. Ivan Krastev, 'Corruption, Anti-corruption Sentiments, and the Rule of Law', in *Rethinking the Rule of Law after Communism*, ed. Adam Czarnota, Martin Krygier, and Wojciech Sadurski (Budapest and New York: CEU Press, 2005), 337.
90. Jan Stefanowicz, *Państwo minimum w stanowieniu prawa* [The minimum state in the law making process] (Warsaw: Centrum Adama Smitha, 1995). See also Rasma Karklins, *Wszystkiemu winien system. Korupcja w krajach postkomunistycznych* [The system made me do it: corruption in post-communist societies] (Warsaw: Wydawnictwo Sic!, 2009), chap. 7, 'Role of Institutions', 188–222.

development of the society.[91] The role of social and cultural norms in restraining corruption should not be underestimated. Institutional changes influence culture, thus the process of implementation of standard, internationally recognised measures into national laws, accompanied with the creation of institutions of the rule of law, in the long run, influences changes in norms and values of a society. But culture also has a reverse impact on the functioning of institutions. The success of actions designed to limit corruption is determined by social attitudes towards this phenomenon. Non-governmental organisations combating corruption, through the socially focused campaigns they have led, have contributed to an overall reduction of the social tolerance for corruption. They fostered attitude shifts among citizens with respect to everyday corruption and triggered social mobilisation against this phenomenon. Additionally, thanks to the actions of these organisations, social expectations regarding standards in political life increased along with expectations by citizens of government leaders in the area of combating corruption.

The most recent public opinion surveys reveal that one-third of Poles indicate that a struggle against corruption is the most important problem, which the elected politicians should currently pursue.[92] In the opinion of 52% of Poles, the current political climate surrounding corruption in Poland is conducive to a fight with this phenomenon. Only 25% of Poles are convinced that there is a lack of political will to initiate a great effort against corruption.[93] From another view, serious concerns arise regarding the success of the anti-corruption activities due to the fact that the politicians, who are responsible for implementing an anti-corruption strategy, are simultaneously pointed to as the most corrupt social group.[94] Moreover, the instability of the Polish political scene constitutes a major obstacle to the implementation of anti-corruption measures. Ruling coalitions change fairly frequently, leading to a lack of continuity in anti-corruption measures. Although political elites have become more aware of the need to combat the problem and to undertake genuine attempts at it, the fight against corruption is still used instrumentally as a part of one's political agenda. In summary, even though TI's CPI as well as the results of other Polish public opinion research on perception of corruption show the success of Poland's anti-corruption policies, it is hard to predict how durable this trend will be.

Acknowledgements

This article presents the personal views of the author. I thank Steven Sampson, Diana Schmidt-Pfister and an anonymous reviewer for their comments and useful suggestions. Any errors are my own.

Notes on contributor

Kaja Gadowska is an associate professor at the Institute of Sociology, Jagiellonian University in Krakow. She is the author and co-author of a number of articles on social, political and economic changes in post-communist countries published in academic journals and edited books, and the author of a book, *Political and Economic Clientelism: A Systemic Analysis of Clientelistic Networks*

---

91. Kamiński and Kamiński, *Korupcja rządów*, 272–3.
92. GfK Polonia for 'Rzeczpospolita' daily. Thirty-one percent of the respondents consider adopting a new anti-corruption law to be the most important task for the Parliament, whereas 28% indicate forbidding parliamentarians from pursuing business activity, http://www.rp.pl/artykul/10,354467.html (accessed February 8, 2010).
93. CBOS, *Opinia społeczna o korupcji w Polsce*.
94. In 2009, the social belief that corruption occurs most frequently in this group was expressed by as many as 55% of respondents. Ibid.

in the Restructuring of the Polish Coal Mining Industry After 1989 (2003), which received the First Klemens Szaniawski Prize and the First Stanisław Ossowski Prize for the best PhD dissertation in the Social Sciences and Humanities. Her research interests concentrate on the impact of clientelist networks on the processes of political and economic transformation in post-communist countries after 1989, as well as the problem of clientelism and corruption among Poland's political and economic elites. In the past several years she has led and participated in several research projects financed by the State Committee for Scientific Research Grants at the Ministry of Science in Poland.

The 2007 accession of Bulgaria and Romania: ritual and reality

Kalin Ivanov

Department of Politics and International Relations, University of Oxford, Oxford, UK

For both objective and subjective reasons, the European Union devoted unprecedented attention to the problem of corruption in Bulgaria and Romania. The European Union (EU) faced a complex challenge in wielding its arsenal of carrots and sticks to encourage reform in the two countries. Conditionality was further complicated by rivalries between Sofia and Bucharest. Despite its limits, EU pressure presented a rare opportunity to depoliticise anti-corruption policy. After accession, Romania regressed from its previous achievements against corruption, and Bulgaria remained reluctant to prosecute senior officials or confront organised crime. Nevertheless, the European Commission continued its monitoring activities, and its ability to freeze funds maintained a modicum of pressure for reform. More effective anti-corruption efforts are possible if a domestic constituency for reform gains sufficient momentum to replace the EU's waning influence.

Rite of passage?

Like pilgrims who must wash their feet before entering a temple, Bulgaria and Romania were commanded to clean up corruption before entering the European Union. With what level of seriousness was the ritual ablution performed? And what could the temple's high priests do if the entrants soiled the floor? This article analyses the impact of EU anti-corruption conditionality on Bulgaria and Romania before and after their accession on 1 January 2007. Varying Bulgarian and Romanian responses to EU demands reflect two forces: the conditionality of the European Union and the local 'politics of anticorruption' in each country, with roots in history, culture and the peculiarities of transition. This article analyses the motivations, opportunities and limits of EU policy. It then explores the two countries' uneven records against corruption before and after accession. Instead of motivating greater progress, rivalry between Bulgaria and Romania revealed scepticism about the objectivity of enlargement policy. More effective anti-corruption efforts would require domestic mobilisation to compensate for diminishing EU influence. A domestic constituency for reform has already sprouted but faces hurdles in both countries. Complementing a trend in the literature towards quantification, this article seeks to situate (anti)corruption in context.[1]

---

1. Regarding the dominance and limits of statistical research on corruption, see Ivan Krastev, 'The Strange (Re)Discovery of Corruption', in *The Paradoxes of Unintended Consequences*, eds. Ralf Dahrendorf, Yehuda Elkana, Aryeh Neier, William Newton-Smith, and István Rév (Budapest: CEU Press, 2000), 23–41.

Unprecedented focus on corruption

Bulgarian and Romanian corruption – and organised crime in the case of Bulgaria – evolved into an extraordinary problem in relation with the European Union, overshadowing other issues and threatening to impede accession. The EU's progressively stern warnings over corruption in Bulgaria and Romania represented the pinnacle in a complex landscape of domestic and international calculation and accusation, complicity and misunderstanding. In the European Union and in the two candidate countries, politicians promised, journalists exaggerated and citizens complained.

The European Union had virtually ignored corruption in previous enlargement rounds dating back to 1973. Ahead of the 2004 enlargement, the European Union did scrutinise and condemn corruption but without raising the stakes as high as it did in the lead-up to 2007. One reason for the special attention was that Bulgaria and Romania did suffer from serious corruption, combined with conspicuous organised crime in Bulgaria (exemplified by mafia-style contract killings that remained unresolved). A confluence of other factors included the growing confidence of the European Commission in addressing corruption, the onset of enlargement fatigue in the old member states and the ambiguous identity of the two Balkan countries as Europe's 'others within'.[2] Opprobrium and anxiety regarding Bulgarian and Romanian corruption – while often justified – were sometimes couched in terms reminiscent of historical stereotypes about the Balkans as inherently corrupt and unreliable.

In addition, growing attention towards corruption in the candidate countries was the result of a learning process within the European Commission, which was initially unsure how to tackle the issue. Upon stepping into office in September 1999, the Prodi team needed to restore the Commission's credibility, dented by a corruption scandal that had led to the resignation of the Santer Commission. Over time, the Commission's regular reports tended to become more detailed, differentiated and nuanced. This development was partly the result of candidates' efforts to 'pin down' the conditions and request more detailed targets.[3] Formulaic statements in early reports were followed by more specific recommendations, including an anti-corruption policy.[4] The Commission monitored the implementation (or otherwise) of action plans drafted by the candidates themselves, listing detailed anti-corruption measures.

The delay in the accession of Bulgaria and Romania meant that they faced EU conditionality at a stage when it included informal pressure for the prosecution of high-level corruption cases – a pressure experienced only weakly, if at all, by the cohort that joined in May 2004. By the same token, future entrants such as Croatia will deal with a Commission even better prepared to handle anti-corruption policy and even stricter in demanding evidence of results. The perception that the European Union made an error by admitting Bulgaria and Romania, because they were corrupt and unprepared, may raise the bar even higher for subsequent entrants.[5]

---

2. See Maria N. Todorova, *Imagining the Balkans* (New York: Oxford University Press, 1997).
3. Heather Grabbe, *The EU's Transformative Power: Europeanization through Conditionality in Central and Eastern Europe* (Basingstoke: Palgrave Macmillan, 2006), 195.
4. James Hughes, Gwendolyn Sasse, and Claire E. Gordon, *Europeanization and Regionalization in the EU's Enlargement to Central and Eastern Europe: The Myth of Conditionality* (Basingstoke: Palgrave Macmillan, 2004), 86–7.
5. George Parker, Sarah Laitner, and Kerin Hope, ' "Serious" Corruption Sparks EU Rift', *Financial Times*, April 26, 2007.

Corruption in Bulgaria and Romania topped political agendas and media headlines in the European Union as well as within the two countries. A safeguard clause in the accession treaty allowed the European Union to postpone the accession of Bulgaria and Romania by one year if they failed to tackle corruption to a satisfactory extent. Romania, initially considered to be behind Bulgaria in its preparations for membership, proved more responsive to the threat of postponement. In addition, after the 2004 elections, Romania's new government had an incentive to expose the corruption of its predecessors. Bulgaria's government found it difficult to follow suit, as virtually the same parties had been sharing power since 2001.[6] The weeks preceding the publication of Commission reports or important Council decisions were characterised by a rush of activity by both governments to demonstrate compliance. The local press exposed such efforts as belated ploys to impress the European Union when confronted with a looming deadline. Observers with a longer memory recalled the communist-era tradition of 'storming'.[7]

Lacklustre progress against corruption led some West Europeans to regard as premature the conclusion of negotiations with Bulgaria and Romania in June and December 2004, respectively. The 'rush' is often attributed to the desire of the then enlargement commissioner Günter Verheugen to complete the negotiations with at least one of the countries before his term expired. The Irish presidency in the first half of 2004 is also blamed for wishing to claim the achievement of closing accession talks with Sofia. Responding to such criticism, Verheugen later claimed that reforms often accelerate after accession and that Bulgaria and Romania were being unjustly held responsible for the French and Dutch 'No' votes to the draft Constitutional Treaty.[8] Such debates illustrate the complexity of EU decision-making on enlargement, which cannot be reduced to reward for compliance and punishment for non-compliance.

The policy and politics of anticorruption

Effective anti-corruption policy needs to be (seen as) impartial and even-handed. Without such credibility, it can easily be hijacked for partisan ends, breeding popular cynicism about the ulterior motives of corruption fighters. EU requirements provided an opportunity to rescue anti-corruption policy in Bulgaria and Romania from the depths of politicisation. The attendant risk was that candidate governments could become more accountable to the European Union than to their own electorate. However, candidate country citizens largely supported EU pressure for anti-corruption reform, even if not always for the same reasons.[9] Local citizens and EU officials did not always have the same goals in pursuing an anti-corruption agenda, but in the end both demanded high-level prosecutions, a rare concurrence of foreign pressure and domestic action.

One of the paradoxes of anticorruption conditionality is that to be effective, the European Union had to closely tailor its approach to domestic circumstances while remaining disinterested and neutral. Sometimes the European Union strengthened the hand of

---

6. After the 2005 elections, the Socialists joined the National Movement Simeon II and the Movement for Rights and Freedoms.

7. On 'storming', see William A. Clark, *Crime and Punishment in Soviet Officialdom: Combating Corruption in the Political Elite, 1965–1990* (Armonk, NY: M.E. Sharpe, 1993), 27.

8. George Parker, 'EU Expansion May Have Reached Its High-Water Mark', *Financial Times*, May 15, 2006.

9. On the discrepancy between popular sentiment and the international agenda against corruption, see Kalin Ivanov, 'Fighting Corruption Globally and Locally', in *Ethics and Integrity in Public Administration: Concepts and Cases*, ed. Raymond W. Cox III (Armonk, NY: M.E. Sharpe, 2009), 146–54.

domestic reformers such as Romanian justice minister Monica Macovei (2004–2007). At other times the European Commission's competing priorities, its formal approach and interest in bringing the enlargement process to a successful conclusion entangled the European Union into apparent alliances with officials whose anticorruption credentials were dubious.

The nature of the Commission's work requires it both to appear detached and to keep its finger on the pulse of domestic politics in member, candidate and even third countries.[10] It was difficult to remain above the fray when every action – or inaction – on the Commission's part was scrutinised through the lens of domestic politics. The process of negotiations created a mutual dependency between candidate country leaders and Commission officials whose own performance depended on the performance of the candidate country. According to Mungiu-Pippidi, the Commission's country teams came to hold a 'vested interest in the continuity of political and bureaucratic elites with whom they worked closely and to fear that elections might upset negotiations'.[11] In any event, the Commission had no option but to rely 'for both policy initiation and implementation on the very elites who can be expected to undermine' policies against high-level corruption.[12] This unavoidable reliance, even if tempered by Non-Governmental Organization (NGO) involvement, constrained the effectiveness of EU conditionality.

Romanian pro-reform groups frowned upon what appeared to them an unduly friendly relationship between enlargement commissioner Günter Verheugen and Prime Minister Adrian Năstase, hardly an anticorruption reformer.[13] A similar friendship between Bulgarian interior minister Rumen Petkov and justice commissioner Franco Frattini attracted domestic and even international censure after the two took a skiing holiday together in January 2007.[14] The European Union also risked being identified with another Bulgarian official who obstructed reform when a Bavarian EU twinning adviser publicly spoke out in favour of chief prosecutor Nikola Filchev in 2003.[15] Reformers greeted with open relief the end of Filchev's scandal-ridden reign in 2006.

At other times, EU officials and politicians defended reforms in domestic political struggles, going to unprecedented lengths to defend Romania's reformist justice minister Macovei from attempts to unseat her. In so doing they helped – even if provisionally – to prevent anticorruption policy from falling hostage to the feud between President Băsescu and Prime Minister Popescu-Tăriceanu. Measures against corruption had a greater chance of succeeding if they were couched in terms of a national effort to join the European Union rather than as an extension of domestic party politics by other means. The accession process could potentially anchor anticorruption policy from (perceived) partisan abuse. To understand the extent to which EU conditionality helped depoliticise anticorruption policy in Bulgaria and Romania, one must reach beyond the technicalities of 'anticorruption policy' and into the broader context.

---

10. An example is the 2002 steel tariff dispute with Washington, when Brussels threatened sanctions on goods from politically sensitive US regions, such as citrus products from Florida.

11. Alina Mungiu-Pippidi, 'EU Enlargement and Democracy Progress', in *Democratisation in the European Neighbourhood*, ed. Michael Emerson (Brussels: Centre for European Policy Studies, 2005), 15–37.

12. Open Society Institute, *Monitoring the EU Accession Process: Corruption and Anti-Corruption Policy* (Budapest: CEU Press, 2002), 71.

13. Such criticism echoed opposition disgruntlement at Western legitimation of Iliescu's regime in the early 1990s.

14. Parker et al., ' "Serious" Corruption Sparks EU Rift'.

15. Doroteya Dachkova, 'Filchev se hvali s podkrepa ot Briuksel', *Sega*, November 8, 2005.

Rivalry between Bulgaria and Romania

The European Union grouped Bulgaria and Romania together in 2001 when it excluded them from preparations for the 'Big Bang' wave of enlargement. Previously the two Balkan candidates had belonged to a larger cluster (along with Slovakia, Latvia and Lithuania) who began negotiating for EU accession in March 2000. The other members of this cluster managed to catch up with the frontrunners (who had started negotiating in 1998). Bulgaria and Romania now found themselves alone in the second-wave pool of candidates, and this isolation fostered the brewing rivalry between the two. Bulgaria's government publicly protested against being 'coupled' with Romania, then perceived as lagging behind.[16] Bulgarians took pride in closing negotiating chapters faster than Romania, in a vain attempt to join the frontrunners and leave Romania behind as the sole laggard. In a gesture loaded with symbolism for ordinary citizens, the European Union removed Bulgaria from the Schengen visa blacklist in December 2000. Romanians had to wait another year for visa-free travel to the European Union.

Ironically, as the accession process evolved Romania came to be seen as more effective at addressing corruption and better prepared to join the European Union. It was now Romania's turn to worry that its accession might be delayed because of being tied to Bulgaria. Minister Macovei even visited Bulgaria in May 2006 to urge faster reforms for fear that Bulgaria might hold back Romania's entry into the Union.

Potentially, jealousy between the two neighbours may have provided additional motivation for fulfilling EU requirements. However, longstanding mutual disdain meant that neither government was prepared to accept that the other could be truly more advanced. In the run-up to accession, Bulgarian officials privately attributed EU praise for Romania to a devious public relations campaign run by Bucharest. Such remarks reflected underlying scepticism about conditionality as an objective evaluation.

Romanians and Bulgarians have long used pejorative nicknames for each other.[17] When Bulgarians drive through Romania (or vice versa), they traditionally avoid stopping. (Romanians have increasingly bucked this trend by spending their summer holidays on Bulgaria's Black Sea coast.) Journalists from one country routinely adopted a superior attitude, referring to the other as the most corrupt, poor and backward country in Europe. By doing so, they were externalising the stereotypes that 'Europe' held about both countries. A peripheral location inspires, in the words of Romanian literary critic Matei Călinescu, feelings of envy, inferiority and 'frustration or distress at the marginality or belatedness' of one's culture. Conversely, Călinescu observed, peripheral inferiority could also trigger a compensatory 'superiority complex.'[18] Indeed, Balkan nations have long endeavoured to surpass their neighbours in being more European. Such competition forms a pattern of 'nesting orientalisms', reproducing the original dichotomy upon which Orientalism is premised.[19] The national historiographies of Balkan nations tend to ignore each other or even to belittle or negate each other's achievements.[20] This

16. As the *Financial Times* generalized, 'There is little doubt that as surely as Bulgaria moves towards integration and EU membership, Romania is virtually standing still and getting left further behind.' Phelim McAleer and Theodor Troev, 'When Just Desire Is Not Enough', *Financial Times*, October 24, 2000, 5.

17. Albena Shkodrova and Marian Chiriac, 'Special Report: Europe Heals Old Divide Between Bulgaria and Romania,' Balkan Crisis Report, 2005.

18. Matei Calinescu, 'How Can One Be a Romanian', *Southeastern Europe* 10, no. 1 (1983): 25–36.

19. Milica Bakic-Hayden, 'Nesting Orientalisms: The Case of Former Yugoslavia', *Slavic Review* 54, no. 4 (1995): 917–31.

20. Maria, *Todorova, Imagining the Balkans*, 183.

history of mutual disparagement provides a context for the rivalry – sometimes quiet, sometimes outspoken – between Bulgaria and Romania as they fought corruption to join the European Union.

At the same time, Sofia and Bucharest needed to maintain at least an appearance of partnership because the European Union required good neighbourliness. For similar reasons the two countries set aside their history of environmental and commercial disputes and made a joint effort for NATO membership. Occasionally, Romanians and Bulgarians even assumed that the grass was greener on the other side of the Danube. Such perceptions are linked to Jacoby's observation that 'familiarity often breeds contempt' when comparing Central and East European countries. Scholars (or citizens) closely familiar with one country tend to skewer its performance in comparison with 'some alternative CEE case where things supposedly have been done much better'.[21] In one such example, Romanian activist and academic Alina Mungiu-Pippidi lauded Bulgaria's 'massive grassroots anticorruption campaign', followed by the 'new and considerably cleaner government' of Saxe-Coburg-Gotha.[22]

After accession

The celebrations marking the entry of Bulgaria and Romania lacked the sparkle of May 2004, reflecting the onset of 'enlargement fatigue' in the old member states. Under the terms of the accession treaties, a 'cooperation and verification mechanism' was intended to ensure that both countries complied with their commitments. The Commission continued to publish reports on Bulgaria and Romania, now drawn up by the secretariat general under the authority of Commission President José Manuel Barroso and Vice-President Jacques Barrot. Bulgaria and Romania had their own commissioners who could potentially try to soften criticism in the reports drafted by the Commission's civil servants. As Bulgarian and Romanian authorities took control over remaining pre-accession funds, suspicions of wrongdoing deepened.

In Bulgaria, the Commission's pressure for results in the fight against corruption continued to impact domestic politics but not sufficiently to achieve a breakthrough. Two major corruption scandals shook the government, ending with the replacement of two powerful Socialist ministers. The first scandal erupted only 4 months after accession with a public exchange of recriminations between minister of economy and energy Roumen Ovcharov (deputy leader of the Socialists) and National Investigative Service (NIS) chief Angel Alexandrov. In an effort to avoid embarrassing the ruling parties ahead of European Parliament elections, both went on compulsory leave, never to return to their prior jobs. The government trumpeted its handling of the affair as evidence of its commitment not to tolerate corruption even at the highest levels. Sofia even invited Brussels to send experts to monitor the case – an invitation that was declined. However, instead of facing justice, Ovcharov went on to head the Bulgarian parliament's budget and finance committee.

The scandal tipped the balance of power within the Socialist party in favour of Interior Minister Roumen Petkov, accused by both European and domestic observers of thwarting reform. In a bid to limit Petkov's power and to step up efforts against corruption, Prime Minister Stanishev proposed an ambitious 'FBI-style' agency that would assemble elements of a fragmented security apparatus, including the interior ministry's counter-intelligence

---

21. Wade Jacoby, *The Enlargement of the European Union and NATO: Ordering from the Menu in Central Europe* (Cambridge: Cambridge University Press, 2004), 13.
22. Mungiu-Pippidi, 'EU Enlargement and Democracy Progress', 27.

unit. When the new agency was finally created, amid wrangling within the fractious coalition government, it failed to meet high expectations and became embroiled in scandals of its own.

The other powerful Socialist minister forced to resign, in April 2008, was Petkov, after it emerged that he had secretly met with organised crime bosses. According to Petkov's own interpretation, the meetings were intended to persuade organised criminal groups to desist from contract killings on the eve of accession in order not to jeopardise Bulgaria's chances. Petkov retained his post within the Socialist party and did not appear in danger of facing serious consequences.

In January 2008, the Commission cut off Bulgaria's funding for road construction after two road agency officials were arrested for bribery. The investigation was prompted by an article in the *Kapital* weekly.[23] In late February, the Commission froze further Phare funding over concerns about corruption at two agencies within Bulgaria's ministries of finance and regional development. Director-general for enlargement Michael Leigh demanded 25 'corrective actions' from the Bulgarian government to avoid irregularities. In March, the freeze extended to SAPARD agricultural funds, raising the total frozen resources above 30 million euro. Serious concerns over SAPARD dated from early 2007, when OLAF uncovered a scheme whereby old meat-processing equipment was exported from Bulgaria to Germany and then reassembled and re-imported as 'new'. The Bulgarian members of the scheme (including a donor to the Socialist party) faced protracted judicial proceedings, whereas Germany sentenced the German accomplices as early as October 2008.

In late November 2008, the Commission confirmed its decision to revoke the accreditation of two Bulgarian government agencies from disbursing Phare funds, resulting in the irreversible loss for Bulgaria of 220 million euro of pre-accession funding. A further 340 million euro remained frozen. The Commission charged that Bulgaria had failed to follow up on its commitments. Bulgarian government officials countered that the Commission had not taken into account recent progress and that the decision reflected double standards. These arguments were further developed by a Brussels-based lobbyist hired by the Bulgarian government. The lobbyist argued that the Commission was unfairly singling out Bulgaria for criticism whereas the corruption situation was no better in Romania or some of the 2004 entrants. As an example, the lobbyist pointed out that the Commission had interpreted the resignation of Romania's justice minister (Chiuariu) as a sign of progress against corruption whereas it had taken the resignation of Bulgaria's interior minister (Petkov) as a sign of rampant corruption.[24] The negative portrayal was allegedly due to miscommunication between Bulgarian and Commission officials. While this line of argument was not entirely devoid of substance, it reflected defensiveness and reluctance to implement anticorruption commitments. Bulgarian arguments regarding double standards also cited Transparency International's Corruption Perception Index – in which Bulgaria scored better than some 2004 entrants and Romania. Such arguments raised more general questions about the measurability and comparability of (perceived) corruption across countries and over time.[25]

---

23. Ivan Mihalev, '120 Milliona ot Batko', *Kapital*, January 11, 2008.

24. 'Lawyer: Bulgaria Wrongly Portrayed as EU's Bogeyman', *EurActiv.com*, November 18, 2008.

25. For a critical overview of CPI methodology, see Fredrik Galtung, 'Measuring the Immeasurable: Boundaries and Functions of (Macro) Corruption Indices', in *Measuring Corruption*, ed. Charles Sampford, Arthur Shacklock, Carmel Connors, and Fredrik Galtung (London: Ashgate, 2006), 101–30. See also Jens Christopher Andvig, 'The Challenge of Poor Governance and Corruption', Copenhagen Consensus Opponent Paper, (Copenhagen, April 2004).

The Commission's ability to freeze funds, and the attendant embarrassment for the government, maintained a degree of conditionality. On the other hand, the fact that Sofia replaced frozen EU funds with its own created the impression that corruption was somehow more tolerable at the expense of Bulgarian taxpayers. The episode highlighted the danger that the government might become accountable more to the European Commission than to its own citizens. The domestic constituency for reform remained patchy despite the efforts of investigative journalists at *Kapital* and elsewhere.

By contrast, Romania's Coalition for a Clean Parliament was a more decisive, if controversial, home-grown effort to curb corruption among the political class. The coalition of NGOs took matters into its own hands, publishing a list of politicians unfit for a clean parliament ahead of the 2004 elections. Such activism did not rely on EU funding or the formal framework of anticorruption strategies agreed between the government and the Commission. The coalition did make use of instruments available thanks to EU pressure – such as assets declarations – but also pushed for additional instruments such as freedom of information laws.

After the elections, coalition member Monica Macovei, head of the Helsinki Committee (APADOR-CH) became justice minister. In alliance with the Commission, she worked tirelessly to challenge the corrupt business as usual in Romania, even if she faced accusations of being partial to president Băsescu to whom she owed her appointment. Inevitably Macovei made enemies among Romanian politicians. The Commission and member states went to unprecedented lengths to keep Macovei at her post, which she ultimately lost in April 2007 when premier Popescu-Tăriceanu dismissed ministers backed by Băsescu. The dismissal heralded regression in Romania's anticorruption policy. Soon after accession, an emergency ordinance exempted 28 specific companies from anticorruption measures previously passed under EU pressure, which barred bankrupt companies from state aid. Băsescu himself was in danger of being impeached but remained in office, thanks to popular support at a referendum. In October 2007, the Commission threatened to freeze agricultural funds if Romania did not reform its payments system. Two months later, justice minister Tudor Chiuariu resigned over allegations of corruption in the sale of a plot of land in the centre of Bucharest.

In March 2008, the Romanian constitutional court ruled, to the dismay of Băsescu and the European Union, that parliament must give its approval before any investigation into high-ranking politicians.[26] To make things worse, parliament also amended the criminal code to require that senior politicians be warned in advance of judicial searches. Swift progress in the prosecutions of the former Prime Minister Adrian Năstase and the former Transport Minister Miron Mitrea seemed increasingly unlikely after the parliament refused to strip them of their immunity. However, in September 2008, the senate did give its assent to an investigation into Labour Minister Paul Păcuraru who was subsequently dismissed by Băsescu. Păcuraru stood accused of soliciting bribes and of arranging business contracts for his son's company.

The Romanian government undermined its credibility by attempting to sideline Daniel Morar, head of the national anticorruption directorate (DNA) appointed by Macovei. Morar was widely respected for his determination and integrity, even if he remained open to domestic accusations that the DNA was investigating mainly opponents to President Băsescu.[27]

---

26. 'Romania Angers EU over Corruption "Haven" ', *Euractiv.com*, July 4, 2008.
27. Judith Crosbie, 'Beacon of Hope', *European Voice*, December 11, 2008, 12.

These developments in Bulgaria and Romania were covered by a series of carefully crafted monitoring reports by the European Commission in June 2007, February 2008 and July 2008. Judging progress on a number of interlinked benchmarks, the Commission noted a lack of concrete results despite both governments' political commitment to reform the judicial system and to fight corruption. While Bulgaria and Romania readily adopted legislation and action plans, the Commission noted, implementation was lagging behind and progress against high-level corruption was insufficient. Likewise, the Council welcomed commitments undertaken by Bulgaria and Romania but repeatedly called on both countries to intensify their efforts without delay and to demonstrate tangible and lasting results.[28] Such statements appeared to fall largely on deaf ears. The Commission's ability to withhold funds was potentially more effective. In this respect the Commission made a clearer distinction between Romania and Bulgaria whereas reports assiduously avoided direct comparisons. The Commission did not propose triggering the safeguard clauses foreseen in the accession treaty in either country because such measures of last resort could be counterproductive.

Conclusion

The European Union addressed candidate country corruption with growing assertiveness and precision. Nonetheless, anticorruption advice remained patchy because of the lack of *acquis* in this area. The absence of clear benchmarks and consistent advice hampered the effectiveness of EU anticorruption conditionality. Principles sometimes gave way to practical considerations as in the case of EU preference for continuity of elites. The EU's greatest potential contribution was to help frame anticorruption measures in a non-partisan manner domestically. However, it was not always possible to do so because enlargement decisions depended on complex compromises.

The results on the ground in Bulgaria and Romania were mixed. Many anticorruption measures are to be credited to the European Union, even if their implementation requires further efforts. However, after accession Bulgaria continued to shy away from prosecuting high-level corruption, whereas Romania regressed from previous achievements. Any reversal of this trend would require the mobilisation of an effective domestic constituency for reform. The potential has already been demonstrated by investigative journalism, NGO activism and the May 2007 referendum against Băsescu's impeachment.

However, 'civil society' has its limits, especially in post-communist Europe.[29] In both Bulgaria and Romania, popular outrage at corruption is mixed with cynical resignation. Bulgarians and Romanians have elected too many leaders on an anticorruption ticket, only to see those leaders face corruption allegations themselves. Protests outside the parliament in Sofia in January 2009 failed to articulate an alternative to the corrupt *status quo*, indicating that domestic pressure for reform is difficult to focus and sustain.

With delays and variations, events in one country mirrored events in the other. As Bulgaria and Romania took turns playing laggard and frontrunner, their rivalry exposed doubts about the EU's professed policy of judging each candidate on its own merits. West European journalists and politicians did stereotype the two Balkan candidates. However,

---

28. See Council conclusions on the cooperation and verification mechanism with Bulgaria and Romania adopted on October 17, 2006, July 23, 2007, March 10, 2008, and September 15, 2008.
29. Marc Morjé Howard, *The Weakness of Civil Society in Post-Communist Europe* (Cambridge: Cambridge University Press, 2003).

Bulgarian attempts to justify lack of progress with complaints about double standards failed to cut ice.

In other policy areas, the European Union was more successful in encouraging reforms in candidate countries. For candidate governments, fighting corruption entailed a particularly high domestic cost of compliance, especially in cases like Bulgaria's, with no convenient predecessor to accuse of corruption. After 1 January 2007, the European Union no longer yielded its most crucial weapon – the carrot of accession. The Commission retained its ability to embarrass Sofia and Bucharest through critical monitoring reports or by freezing funds. Nonetheless, Romanian reformists lost ground while Bulgaria continued to frustrate EU officials by tolerating high-level corruption and organised crime. As a result, the European Union may well require future applicants to show tangible anticorruption results before accession, instead of giving them the benefit of the doubt.

Accession and the preparations for it were clearly not a panacea against corruption in Bulgaria and Romania. However, absent the prospect of EU membership, the situation is likely to have been worse. The ceremonial cleansing exercise may have left much of the dirt untouched on the two pilgrims' feet. Yet, the ritual fulfilled its symbolic functions. It channelled anxieties about 'Europe' being corrupted by the Balkans. It was also a rite of passage in the sense used by anthropologists to denote a ritual that begins by exclusion, proceeds with a liminal stage and ideally concludes with incorporation into the community on new terms.

Acknowledgements

This article reflects the author's personal views. Thanks to Steven Sampson, Martin Mendelski and an anonymous reviewer for comments on previous drafts. Any errors or omissions are my own.

Notes on contributor

Kalin Ivanov is completing a doctoral thesis in international relations at Oxford University, exploring the European Union's impact on the politics of anticorruption in Bulgaria and Romania. The thesis builds on over 60 interviews in Bucharest, Sofia and Brussels.

Anti-corruption interventions in Georgia

Lili Di Puppo

European Viadrina University, Frankfurt (Oder), Germany

The article aims at analysing the transfer of anti-corruption norms and standards as well as the instrumental use of anti-corruption efforts in Georgia. Drawing on the literature on anthropology and development, I use Georgia as a case study to analyse how an anti-corruption discourse is translated into local agendas. In the first part, I analyse three different perspectives on the fight against corruption in Georgia. In the second part, I examine three different types of anti-corruption interventions to illustrate the various agendas pursued by actors in the anti-corruption field. First, I study the implementation of the national anti-corruption strategy as an example of a conflict between two actors (government and international organisation) to assert the pre-eminence of a particular anti-corruption expertise. Second, I examine the reform of the Chamber of Control of Georgia (CCG), in particular the confrontation between the CCG and the Ministry of Education (MoE) in 2007, as an example of how an external anti-corruption agenda is adapted to local political struggles. Third, I analyse civil society anti-corruption projects as examples of the attempt to maintain a particular donor discourse.

Introduction

The article uses the literature on anthropology and development as a framework to study the transfer of anti-corruption norms and standards in developing and transition countries.[1] Anthropological studies of development challenge homogeneous views of development, notably two different approaches.[2] The first approach is instrumental and understands development policy as rational problem-solving. Anti-corruption research promoted by the World Bank reflects knowledge derived from the practice and the collection of empirical data that aims at being applied. The purpose of anti-corruption research is thus to gather sufficient documentation about situations and trends in order to draw practical recommendations for future anti-corruption work. This knowledge accumulation aimed at

---

1. See David Lewis and David Mosse, 'Encountering Order and Disjuncture: Contemporary Anthropological Perspectives on the Organisation of Development', *Oxford Development Studies* 34, no. 1 (2006): 1–13; Benedetta Rossi, 'Revisiting Foucauldian Approaches: Power Dynamics in Development Projects', *Journal of Development Studies* 40, no. 6 (2004): 1–29; and Norman Long, 'An Actor-Oriented Approach to Development Intervention' (background paper prepared for APO meeting, Tokyo, April 22–26, 2002); Barbara Orlandini, 'Consuming Good Governance in Thailand', *The European Journal of Development Research* 15, no. 2 (2003): 16–43(28).
2. See Lewis and Mosse, 'Encountering Order and Disjuncture'; Rossi, 'Revisiting Foucauldian Approaches'.

identifying 'best practices' is often separated from the social and political contexts of a given country, as the objective is to develop universal instruments. The second critical or deconstructionist approach inspired by Michel Foucault's work on discourse as power assumes that development 'problems' are constructed.[3] Development is seen as a rational-ising discourse concealing hidden agendas, for example a neo-liberal agenda, behind the veil of rational problem-solving. Critical approaches to anti-corruption are not interested in ways of improving these programmes, as they understand anti-corruption interventions as vehicles to promote certain interests.

Anthropologists may operate with both these approaches, but they also assume the heterogeneity of the local context and the multiplicity of interests. Local actors do not react in a uniform way to the export of external norms and standards, merely by resisting or accepting them. They follow various trajectories to translate and appropriate these development products. Orlandini refers to 'consumer practices' in her analysis of the appropriation of the concept of good governance in Thailand.[4] Different actors in Thai-land seize this concept, a process resulting in the existence of several 'good governances'. Similarly, in Georgia, an external anti-corruption discourse is appropriated in various ways. Local actors attribute different meanings to the fight against corruption, creatively assembling references to global standards with local meanings. My analysis of anti-corruption interventions in Georgia combines discourse analysis with a study of the actors' interests and behaviours in the anti-corruption field.[5] I am interested in how local actors in Georgia promote a particular interpretation of a broader anti-corruption discourse to advance their agendas. Georgia provides an excellent case study of the instrumental use of anti-corruption efforts.

In the following, I will first analyse three anti-corruption discourses in Georgia. In the second part, I will examine how local actors interact and compete in the 'anti-corruption field' by using these discourses to promote certain interests. Before turning to the analysis of three case studies, I will briefly explain how power relations between development actors have changed after the Rose Revolution.

Variety of anti-corruption discourses in Georgia

I have grouped anti-corruption discourses in Georgia into three ideal types corresponding to three groups of actors (government, international organisations and civil society organ-isations). More sub-discourses can be differentiated in Georgia within the government, the civil society sector as well as the world of international organisations.

---

3. See A. Escobar, *Encountering Development: The Making and Unmaking of the Third World* (Princeton: Princeton University Press, 1995); J. Ferguson, *The Anti-Politics Machine. 'Develop-ment', Depoliticization, and Bureaucratic Power in Lesotho* (Minneapolis: University of Minnesota Press, 1994 [1990]).

4. Orlandini, 'Consuming Good Governance in Thailand'; M. de Certeau, *The Practice of Everyday Life* (Berkeley and Los Angeles: University of California Press, 1984).

5. My analysis of the anti-corruption field in Georgia is based on about 100 interviews conducted in Georgia in 2007–2008. For reasons of confidentiality, the references to the interviews are anony-mous. I use Tisne and Smilov's classification of anti-corruption programmes in the Balkans to study anti-corruption interventions in Georgia: (1) omnibus programmes or national anti-corruption strategies, (2) civil society anti-corruption projects, (3) institutional reform programmes. Martin Tisne and Daniel Smilov, 'From the Ground Up – Assessing the Record of Anticorruption Assistance in Eastern Europe' (Policy Studies series, Central European University Center for Policy Studies, 2004).

The liberal technocratic discourse of international organisations

The liberal technocratic discourse is promoted largely by NGOs such as Transparency International (TI) and financial institutions such as the World Bank. Several assumptions on the nature of corruption underlie this discourse: (1) corruption is a universal problem; (2) corruption can be dealt with as a policy or managerial issue, without necessarily becoming 'political'; (3) corruption can be documented and measured so that the factors that stimulate or prevent corruption can be isolated. The challenge for the World Bank has been to design effective anti-corruption measures that can be applied in various countries. The World Bank presents corruption as a problem of dysfunctional institutions. Certain scholars attribute this new emphasis on fighting corruption to the legitimacy crisis faced by international financial organisations at the beginning of the 1990s. Corruption became depicted as a major obstacle to development, indeed the underlying explanation for why these programmes failed. Other scholars view the anti-corruption discourse as a means to promote neo-liberal policies.[6] Normally, the bank's approach would result in an appeal that recipient countries begin their own anti-corruption programmes. However, the bank promoted the need for external anti-corruption interventions on the premises that national governments lack the resources or will to fight corruption. In the view of international organisations, fighting corruption meant exerting pressure, via civil society monitoring or compulsory (conditionality-based) national anti-corruption strategies that would oblige these governments to be more accountable, with expertise provided from abroad as part of a loan package.

Georgia's national strategy

I conceptualise the anti-corruption discourse of the Georgian government after the Rose Revolution as a creative assemblage of diverse elements. Various elements are used depending on which constraints, national or international, the government is responding to. It is possible to distinguish between two official ways of fighting corruption in Georgia: one relying on law-enforcement agencies and domestically oriented, and one relying on economic liberalisation, inscribed in a modernisation programme, and more oriented towards the international community. These two approaches are unified rhetorically in a discourse emphasising the rupture with Soviet practices. The fight against corruption in Georgia is framed into a nation- and state-building project. While the economic liberalisation elements in the governmental discourse reflect the international anti-corruption discourse and its emphasis on the development of a market economy as a corrective to corruption, this discourse is also moralised through local references. External anti-corruption standards that are officially adopted to create Western-style institutions are juxtaposed with references to the national history. Georgian President Mikheil Saakashvili promoted this view in his inaugural speech, 'We must root out corruption. As far as I am concerned, every corrupt official is a traitor who betrays the national interest'.[7] In the discourse of the Saakashvili administration, 'good guys' are not corrupt; they are self-disciplined. After the Rose Revolution, the government has engaged in a process of regaining its lost legitimacy. During

---

6. See, for example, Ed Brown and Jonathan Cloke, 'Neoliberal Reform, Governance and Corruption in the South: Assessing the International Anti-Corruption Crusade', *Antipode* 36, no. 2 (2004): 272–94.

7. The inauguration speech of Mikheil Saakashvili on January 25, 2004, http://www.eurasianet.org/resource/georgia/hypermail/200401/0061.shtml (accessed May 2007) (Source: Georgian State Television Channel 1, Tbilisi, in Georgian 1115 gmt January 25, 2004 and BBC Mon FS1 FsuPol ws/ab).

Soviet times, the state had been perceived in Georgia as an alien object. As a result, corruption and the shadow economy were to some extent socially accepted as a form of national resistance. The post-revolutionary government wants to restore respect for the state and destroy parallel sources of legitimacy such as those generated through criminal authorities. The main outcome of the governmental anti-corruption measures has thus been the reinforcement of the executive. These measures had the effect of strengthening power within a narrow circle of insiders. This approach to fighting corruption was expressed by Saakashvili at the start of his presidency: 'We need to introduce in the parliament very drastic anti-corruption legislation that would give vast powers to a new elite, small, honest investigative unit that would really tackle high-level corruption'.[8] This top-down approach relies heavily on law-enforcement agencies and the prosecutor's office, while neglecting independent control bodies such as the judiciary and the Chamber of Control.

The bottom-up democratic discourse

In opposition to the governmental rhetoric, the discourse of civil society organisations in Georgia emphasises the need for democratic institutions to control the state. Public participation is seen as a major element in the fight against corruption, since pressure from the public is expected to render the government more accountable. Civil society and donor organisations emphasise transparency and accountability and a system of checks-and-balances as essential mechanisms to control corruption. The supposed moral integrity of public officials is not seen as a sufficient guarantee against corruption.[9] Civil society organisations challenge the government's libertarian vision that sees independent regulatory bodies as sources of corruption.[10]

Interactions in the 'anti-corruption field' in Georgia

These three discourses are used to justify different types of interventions in the anti-corruption field. The three groups of actors (government, international organisations, civil society) compete to ensure the pre-eminence of their anti-corruption approach.

After the Rose Revolution of November 2003, an active and committed government has had the effect of reducing the level of influence of non-state actors. Although Georgia was often described as a weak state and strong civil society before the Rose Revolution, now the reverse is true. Before the Rose Revolution, the state bureaucracy was seen as the embodiment of the corruption system, whereas donor-funded watchdog organisations were the drivers of the fight against corruption by pressuring the government to be more accountable. A major effect of the democratisation programmes of the 1990s in Georgia was the creation of an NGO elite, which was made immune to corruption through good

8. Citation in Don Hill, 'Georgia: Saakashvili Raising Hopes That Corruption May Be Tackled In Earnest', *RFE/RL*, January 9, 2004, http://www.rferl.org/featuresarticle/2004/1/0A0316B9-F4A4-495B-8C45-E27E30FB8282.html (accessed May 2007) and Molly Corso, 'Georgian President Saakashvili's Campaign Against Corruption', *Power and Interest News Report*, December 20, 2004.
9. An NGO representative describes the government's vision, 'The government says that there is no corruption at the top level, there is still corruption at the lower level because the lower level is more difficult to control . . . They think that top level people are people with integrity, they are motivated and there is much less corruption'. Interview with NGO head, Tbilisi, February 2008.
10. For example, the control of cars and the hygienic food agency were abolished after the Rose Revolution.

salaries.[11] After the revolution, power relations between development actors have changed. Government representatives often criticise the bureaucracy of international organisations as well as the lack of professionalism of NGOs. The Saakashvili administration has actively combated corruption through the arrests of low-level officials and different purges in the state administration. It tries to ensure a governmental monopoly in the field of anti-corruption by linking the fight against corruption to the project of regaining state-hood. The Saakashvili government has widely publicised its anti-corruption achievements on the international and domestic scene, making its efforts visible and immediate. Two different logics of fighting corruption are thus in opposition in today's Georgia: a strong executive versus strong control mechanisms on the state (parliament, civil society, auditing bodies). In this new environment, NGOs have seen their funding decreased, while they face a human resources crisis. A large number of qualified NGO staff has moved to government positions. Like in the rest of the former Soviet Union, Georgian NGOs have been artificially created by donor money. Few of them can claim to represent a large group of citizens and they are often more accountable to donors than to a particular constituency. International organisations face a similar legitimacy crisis, as the Georgian government is reluctant to accept their advice and openly question the efficiency of certain donor programmes.

The anti-corruption field in Georgia is characterised by competition: local actors try to legitimise their interventions by using a certain discourse while delegitimising other discourses and practices. The labelling of an activity as anti-corruption is a political act that opens an intervention field. For example, the Georgian government has described the arrests of high officials of the Shevardnadze administration in a speedy process after the Rose Revolution as an anti-corruption measure. This definition was contested by NGOs on the ground that these actions did not respect the rule of law and tended to target political opponents. The televised and staged arrests of public officials on television may well have had an impact on the levels of corruption by creating fear among public servants. However, the government's definition of these activities as anti-corruption was contested, since the rule of law is assumed to be inseparable from the fight against corruption in the discourse of international organisations and civil society. The vagueness of anti-corruption objectives, similar to the vagueness of concepts such as transparency, accountability and participation, allows these objectives to be interpreted in different ways, and therefore easily integrated into various agendas. As Sampson notes, 'Definitions of what constitutes corruption and assessments of the effectiveness of "fighting corruption" are sufficiently vague that they can be integrated into many political agendas or private projects'.[12] The following case studies illustrate the competition between local actors in the anti-corruption field as well as the instrumentalisation of the fight against corruption in Georgia.

The framework: the national anti-corruption strategy

The European Bank for Reconstruction and Development (EBRD) defines an omnibus programme as a coordinated assemblage of governmental structures and policies specifically

---

11. Interview with NGO leader, Tbilisi, June 2008.
12. Steven Sampson, 'Corruption and Anti-Corruption in Southeast Europe: Landscapes and Sites', in *Governments, NGOs and Anti Corruption: The New Integrity Warriors*, ed. L. de Sousa, P. Larmour, and B. Hindess (London: Routledge, 2008), 4.

geared towards fighting corruption.[13] Tisne and Smilov explain what assumptions exist behind omnibus programmes, 'corruption needs to be tackled through a comprehensive set of institutional and legislative measures encompassing most of the jurisdictional areas of government [. . .] the assumption posits that there exists a standardized list of measures to fight corruption and that there is a common understanding between the donors and the aid recipients on those measures'.[14] A further assumption is that these programmes will oblige a government in a transition or developing country to adopt anti-corruption measures, even if it is not willing to engage in anti-corruption activities. If a more committed government comes to power, the set of measures already in place will provide a direction to coordinate anti-corruption efforts. These programmes are seen as universal tools to combat corruption.

From the outset, the adoption of an anti-corruption strategy in Georgia appears to reflect more the demands of international organisations. Georgia's national anti-corruption strategy is not viewed as a serious basis for anti-corruption efforts by government officials.[15] The document was quickly drafted in 2005, as Georgia was risking violating its Council of Europe (COE) obligations. The implementation of the strategy was first placed under the responsibility of the National Security Council and then of the State Minister for Reforms Coordination headed by Kakha Bendukidze. When this ministry was abolished in 2007, it took almost a year to clarify which state organ would take over the responsibility to implement the strategy. The COE threatened to stop paying the salaries of Georgian experts working in a project to implement the strategy within the ministry if the problem was not solved.[16] Finally, it was decided in autumn 2008 that the Prime Minister would take over these tasks and they would be placed under the responsibility of the new head of the State Chancellery. The Georgian government was aware that it had to quickly find a way out of the situation to avoid risking its international reputation. The fact that the strategy was again placed under the responsibility of Kakha Bendukidze, who was named head of the State Chancellery in 2008, shows that the document is more a result of external constraints than it is an attempt to demonstrate the genuineness of governmental anti-corruption efforts to the Georgian public. The proponent of a libertarian vision, Bendukidze is a Georgian oligarch who has made his fortune in Russia. He is behind many of the radical policies of the post-revolutionary government. The lack of transparency in the privatisation process has made him an unpopular figure in Georgia, who is believed to have personally benefited from privatisation projects.

The lack of 'ownership' is seen by the COE as one of the major problems in the implementation of the strategy. The COE faced the typical dilemma of development agencies when trying to convince the Georgian government of adopting an anti-corruption strategy.

---

13. Tisne and Smilov, 'From the Ground Up', 39. Tisne and Smilov further define the attributes of an omnibus programme, 'Omnibus anti-corruption programmes generally contain all or a selection of the following attributes: an anticorruption law; a national anticorruption strategy or programme, a ministerial commission; specialized unit or dedicated agency; an action plan to implement the programme; and/or a monitoring mechanism', 40.
14. Tisne and Smilov, 'From the Ground Up', 40.
15. Interview with a senior official of the Saakashvili administration, Tbilisi, November 2008. A representative of a donor organisation explains, 'Although they [the Georgian government] have taken all the GRECO recommendations by heart, I have sometimes the feeling that they just do it because these are Council of Europe kind of conditions. They feel they have to do it to be on the good side with the international community'. Interview with representative of donor organisation, Tbilisi, July 2007.
16. Interview with representative of donor organisation, Tbilisi, November 2008.

While international organisations want to be seen as the actors giving the expertise that is assumed to fail in developing and transition countries or putting pressure on national governments lacking political will, the 'ownership' of projects has become the norm in development in recent years. The assumed demand for these tools from the part of recipient countries legitimate donor interventions. As a representative of a donor organisation explains, 'It is very important to have a counterpart in the country present, because otherwise you get very much this idea of another organisation flying into the country and telling people what to do. And this is not the way it should work'.[17]

The process of drafting and implementing a national anti-corruption strategy in Georgia reveals diverging views between the government and the COE. Georgian government officials wanted initially to draft a 'good governance strategy' instead of an 'anti-corruption strategy'.[18] The label 'good governance strategy' was seen as more appropriate to reflect the government's vision. The Saakashvili government tries to project the image of a champion of anti-corruption efforts. It has built its international reputation as well as its domestic legitimacy on its anti-corruption record and wants to defend Georgia's leadership position among transition countries.[19] A good governance strategy would better reflect Georgia's positive and innovative approach in fighting corruption, while indicating that it is already a step ahead of other neighbouring countries. A representative of a donor organisation explains that the document also implies an acknowledgement from the part of the government that corruption still exists in Georgia, 'It is also a political document and a political instrument. Again [it is about] showing that there is a commitment from the government side and we don't pretend that corruption has disappeared'.[20] Adopting a strategy sends the message to the international community and to citizens that the government in question is not able to deal with the problem of corruption and needs donor assistance. As Tisne and Smilov remark, it is a signal of incapacity: 'the appearance of anticorruption strategies, accompanied by commissions or agencies to monitor them, signal a dramatic inability on the part of the existing government institutions to deal with corruption'.[21] The Georgian government was reluctant to have Georgia stamped with the image of a transition country still struggling to fight corruption and unable to do so with its own resources. The COE, for its part, was not in favour of calling the document a good governance strategy, since the World Bank already plays a prominent role in the good governance field.[22] 'Anti-corruption' corresponded better to the profile of the COE.

These conflicting views on the labelling of the document show how different actors try to assert their position in the anti-corruption field. The COE wants to assert its profile as one of the leading organisations in the anti-corruption field, while leaving the field of good governance to the World Bank.[23] The position of worldwide anti-corruption expert gives the COE the legitimacy to comply national governments into adopting its instruments.

---

17. Ibid.
18. Interview with representative of donor organisation, Tbilisi, October 2008. A U4 report mentions, 'It is not easily understandable why development partners in the case of Georgia would urge the government to call its de facto good governance strategy an anti-corruption strategy when the goals clearly go beyond corruption'. Karen Hussmann, ed., 'Anti-corruption policy making in practice', U4 report 1:2007, Christian Michelsen Institute, p. 34.
19. Georgia was named the first 'world reformer' by the World Bank in 2007.
20. Interview with representative of donor organisation, Tbilisi, November 2008.
21. Tisne and Smilov, 'From the Ground Up', 52.
22. Interview with representative of donor organisation, Tbilisi, October 2008.
23. The global anti-corruption field can be understood as a market, where different organisations compete to position themselves.

The assumed possession of an expert knowledge by international organisations is the idea that sustains the 'hierarchies of knowledge' in the development field and provides the legitimacy behind external interventions. In the anti-corruption field, international organisations are interested in profiling themselves as 'givers' of anti-corruption knowledge, while the recipient countries are the 'takers'. They want to export 'their anti-corruption'. The field in itself is a product of and is dominated by international organisations, in particular the World Bank, but also the COE and the Organisation for Economic Cooperation and Development (OECD). These organisations tend to lay the blame on national governments when anti-corruption programmes fail, arguing that the political will is lacking. The assumed possession of an anti-corruption expertise also allows international organisations to direct funds for their own needs in the form of salaries for international consultants or the funding of trainings and workshops. Acknowledging that national governments also have a certain expertise in fighting corruption would imply that funds must be directed to the government itself without intermediaries.[24] Anti-corruption strategies can be seen as development products that donors want to market in different transition countries.[25]

The COE's promotion of an anti-corruption strategy in Georgia thus illustrates how international organisations secure their position in the anti-corruption field by asserting the pre-eminence of particular discourses. The fight against corruption in Georgia must be formulated and defined in the language of the international organisation. As one representative of a donor organisation explains, 'they [government representatives] have to define what they do'.[26] Every commitment of the government on paper opens a door for interventions in the form of the provision of expertise through international consultants or trainings. It also opens a door for giving recommendations and monitoring their implementation. The Georgian government is thus constrained into defining a certain number of anti-corruption activities and agreeing on a set of measures that are labelled 'anti-corruption'. The fight against corruption must depart from its spontaneous character and be framed into a specific document, which sets certain discursive boundaries. It defines appropriate ways of talking about anti-corruption as well as practicing it. Anti-corruption strategies appear to be promoted not because of their virtues in eradicating corruption, but as a tool to maintain a hierarchy of knowledge. The implementation of an anti-corruption strategy is used to demonstrate the existence of an exportable 'anti-corruption knowledge'. The assumption that international organisations must extract, formulate and provide an anti-corruption knowledge to the extent that national governments have failed to combat corruption legitimises global anti-corruption initiatives.

At the same time, the donor organisation cannot be considered as successful in imposing a particular way of talking about and practicing anti-corruption. While the COE has managed to set certain discursive boundaries by imposing the label 'anti-corruption strategy', it has a limited control over the practice. Local actors are constrained by the discourses of international organisations, but enjoy at the same time a room for manoeuvre and interpretation. The Georgian government has an ambivalent position regarding the strategy. While

---

24. In the case of the project funded by the Dutch embassy, the accent is put on the 'ownership' of the programme and national experts receive salaries, but international consultants are also hired and trainings organised.

25. Tisne and Smilov use this analogy, 'the risk is that donors should continue to market a seemingly successful product, while its added value and tangible effects have yet to be determined'. They add, 'it is a disturbing trend that national anticorruption strategies should be applied from country to country with little regard as to whether the solution matches the problem'. Tisne and Smilov, 'From the Ground Up', 51.

26. Interview with representative of a donor organisation, Tbilisi, November 2008.

certain statements tend to describe the strategy more as paper, others confirm the Georgian government's interest in having a coordinated approach.[27] Government representatives want to show at the same time their lack of conviction in the COE's approach to promote their own achievements, while not rejecting the strategy completely. They acknowledge that they have to honour their international commitments and that the strategy has some benefits.

The Georgian government seeks to contest the assumption that national governments are failing to combat corruption. It wants to demonstrate both its expertise and political will. Georgia is more interested in marketing its anti-corruption knowledge to other transition countries, than in importing external anti-corruption tools. The Georgian case is interesting insofar as governments not willing to fight corruption tend to adopt readily anti-corruption instruments, these documents remaining more like paperwork. On the contrary, the Georgian government appears more committed to the fight against corruption and less willing to adopt instruments that it does not see as efficient. The Georgian case is also in contradiction with the anti-corruption vision promoted by the World Bank. The fight against corruption initiated by the Saakashvili's government after the Rose Revolution is often described as spontaneous, lacking a strategy and coordination, while being based on ad-hoc policies and decisions. As one senior official of the Saakashvili administration explains, 'We were learning by doing'.[28] On the contrary, global anti-corruption efforts promoted by the World Bank and TI are based on an accumulation of knowledge. The assumption behind these efforts is that anti-corruption instruments must be based on a scientific analysis of the problem of corruption, its nature, causes and effects. The aim is to produce a universal knowledge. The spontaneous character of the fight against corruption in Georgia contradicts this assumption. The objective behind the adoption of a strategy is not primarily to reduce corruption, but rather to export an anti-corruption knowledge. The absence of a strategy would perhaps not be felt; its added value is not demonstrated. Anti-corruption instruments are void unless there is political will. But if there is political will, the same instruments may appear useless. The former head of an international organisation in Georgia explains, 'Donors are talking about anticorruption, but unless the government is serious, it is a waste of time. If the government is serious, they don't need the donors!'[29] He adds, 'They can't force the government to do it and if the government wants to do it, donors are irrelevant, they have nothing to contribute'.[30]

In conclusion, I do not conceptualise the tensions between the COE and the Georgian government as the result of a mismatch between the technical expertise of the international organisation and the conceptions of the Georgian government. The Georgian government's approach is not representative of an indigenous knowledge, as it also contains elements of a Western liberal approach to fighting corruption.[31] Neither is this confrontation the result of a lack of political will of the Georgian government to fight corruption. The government's reluctance to adopt the strategy is also not due to a lack of resonance of Western standards with domestic structures and identities or a fear that the strategy could

---

27. Interview with senior official in the Saakashvili administration and representative of donor organisation, Tbilisi, October–November 2008.
28. Interview with senior official of the Saakashvili administration, Tbilisi, November 2008.
29. Interview with former head of international organisation in Georgia, Tbilisi, November 2008.
30. Ibid. The former head of an international organisation further explains, 'What they [the donors] could do is write a case study of Georgia which is not perfect and sell it to all the countries that are worried about corruption. That's all, that would cost 1000 dollars'. Writing this case study would mean accepting that the anti-corruption knowledge stems from the recipient country itself.
31. For example, the deregulation of the economy.

threaten the entrenched interests of a political and business elite. The Saakashvili administration is rather not convinced of the efficiency of external anti-corruption instruments. On the contrary, international organisations argue that it is more efficient to have a coordinated approach and a clearly defined anti-corruption framework. The main argument of the Georgian government against international organisations is the lack of efficiency, the bureaucracy of development agencies. The government presents itself as being more efficient and results-oriented in working in an ad-hoc manner, while neglecting lengthy procedures. By assessing the efficiency of anti-corruption tools and other development instruments, the Georgian government wants to position itself on an equal footing with international organisations. The tensions between the Georgian government and the COE can thus be understood as a conflict to assert the pre-eminence of a particular anti-corruption knowledge and a struggle to maintain or reverse certain hierarchies in the anti-corruption field.

The reform of the Chamber of Control of Georgia

Different perspectives on the reform of the CCG serve as an example of the different approaches to the fight against corruption in Georgia. The reform of the CCG shows the difficulty of transforming institutions that were an integral part of the corruption system into bodies aimed at preventing corruption. Two main discourses on the reform of the CCG can be distinguished: a pro- and a contra-discourse. These two discourses reflect two distinct anti-corruption discourses in Georgia. The instrumental use of these discourses is visible in the confrontation between the CCG and the Ministry of Education (MoE) in 2007.

Rather than serving as an instrument to prevent corruption, the real purpose of the CCG before the Rose Revolution was to extort bribe payments from state agencies in a pyramid of corruption as well as tarnishing the reputation of political opponents. For example, the former chairman of the Chamber of Control, Sulkhan Molashvili, was reported to have collected compromising material ('kompromaty') on former Justice Minister Mikheil Saakashvili and former Prime Minister Zurab Zhvania in Shevardnadze's times.[32] After the Rose Revolution, the CCG is not used anymore to collect bribes, but remains the instrument of political interests. The reform of the CCG is aimed at transforming an institution, whose main function was to produce compromising material and collect bribes in Shevardnadze's years, into a tool to prevent corruption. A second challenge facing both the Georgian government and donors involved in the reform of the CCG is to transform a Soviet-style institution with the function of 'controlling' and punishing into a modern 'auditing' institution that will make recommendations to state agencies. The post-revolutionary government has used different tools to reform corrupt institutions. The solution has sometimes been to abolish these bodies or 'purge' them of their corrupt elements through the dismissal of staff.

A scandal involving the CCG and the MoE broke out in 2007. The CCG wrote a report about the MoE, indicating that money was missing in certain programmes. Opposition parties used these findings in a power struggle with the government, more precisely with the Minister of Education Kakha Lomaia and the loose grouping to which he belongs designed as the 'Liberty Institute group'.[33] Kakha Lomaia was reportedly in line to

---

32. He was one of the few public officials of the Shevardnadze administration to be imprisoned after the Rose Revolution and not allowed to avoid incarceration by paying back sums of money to the state.
33. The so-called 'Liberty institute group' includes former members of the NGO 'Liberty Institute' occupying influential positions in the current government.

become the next prime minister. One major finding in the CCG report was that documents failed to prove that funds allocated to buying material for different schools in Tbilisi were spent for this purpose. These funds were allocated within a project for secondary education co-financed by the World Bank. The MoE could not provide a record of signatures from every single school director stating that the material had been received. The CCG wrote in the report that the material did not reach the schools. The CCG refused to integrate the results of a World Bank evaluation on the same project on the ground that the report was written in English.[34] The World Bank evaluation did not report any instances of mismanagement.[35] The MoE reacted to the report by refusing to sign it and claiming that the findings were incorrect. Lomaia asked for a second mission to be sent. He expressed doubts about the professionalism of the CCG. Opposition parties used the CCG report to claim that 40 million dollars were missing from certain programmes. The MoE story quickly became one of the major scandals of the post revolutionary period. Two different narratives were used by the MoE and opposition parties to describe the scandal.

The MoE used two arguments to question the veracity of the CCG report: the lack of professionalism of the Chamber and its politicisation. The MoE camp argued that the CCG's investigation was not based on international accounting standards. The CCG staff was working with old Soviet standards, checking whether procedures were followed instead of whether the money was spent the way it was planned or in an effective manner.[36] The MoE described the CCG as a Soviet institution not able to conduct 'performance audits' or audits aimed at assessing the efficiency of money-spending.[37] Second, the MoE indirectly accused the CCG of partiality by arguing that its report and the way it was used by the opposition pointed to some political games.[38] Kakha Lomaia accused the CCG of being unprofessional and corrupt, while presenting proofs contradicting the CCG report before the Parliament in 2007.[39] An NGO leader close to the government describes the MoE scandal in the following terms.

> What I saw was a sort of monumental example of Soviet stupidity. The CCG was accusing the government that they did not have accounting at all because the MoE was carrying its accounting in accordance with World Bank standards. They were spending the World Bank money, so the World Bank was asking them to do their accounting in their standards, while the CCG was not recognizing these standards because they were in contravention with some Soviet standards [. . .] That was the main confusion. The CCG was not accepting the accounting documents which were not in conformity with their understanding of what accounting was about.[40]

On the other side, the opposition appeared to be using the CCG as a tool to unveil alleged corruption in the government. The CCG provided a guarantee of impartiality for the

34. Interview with former employee of the Ministry of Education, Tbilisi, November 2008.
35. A World Bank employee explains that it was more a case of poor filing than a case of mismanagement. Interview with World Bank employee, Tbilisi, November 2008.
36. Interviews with former employees of the Ministry of Education, Tbilisi, November/December 2008.
37. Ibid.
38. Ibid.
39. A Civil Georgia article writes, 'The Education Minister criticized the state audit agency for being staffed by many "non-professionals" who have been engaged in "corrupt deals" ', Civil Georgia, 'MPs Angered over Minister's Assertive Speech', Civil.ge, June 29, 2007, http://www.civil.ge/eng/article.php?id=15356 (accessed January 2009).
40. Interview with NGO leader, Tbilisi, November 2008.

opposition's allegations. One opposition leader explains what the scandal represented for the opposition.

> It became one of the greatest scandals. You know that the Georgian government made a lot of propaganda inside and outside the country [stating] that education reforms were one of the most successful reforms of the Georgian government and one of the most important achievements. And unexpectedly everyone found that it was not a great reform, but it was [a case of] great corruption and this was reported not only by opposition faction and parties, but it was reported by an official state body, a government-appointed body, the CCG.[41]

At the core of the MoE scandal, we can identify a political struggle involving two groups of actors referring to two different interpretations of the fight against corruption.[42] Each group of actors levels accusations of corruption and of using the CCG for political purposes against the other. The use of the label 'anti-corruption' is contested, for example in the reference to the dismissal of staff by the new management after the scandal. About 400 employees were forced to resign in the aftermath of the scandal. The CCG management under the chairmanship of Levan Choladze presented this vague of dismissal as an anti-corruption measure, a 'necessary ill' to fight corruption within the structure. The opposition portrayed the dismissal as an intervention of the executive aimed at limiting the independence of the CCG.[43] Opposition representatives claim that Choladze 'closed the system'.[44] Opposition parties also argue that they could not obtain material on the Tbilisi City municipality after the MoE scandal, claiming that the executive prevented the CCG from doing its work.[45]

The confrontation between the CCG and the MoE represents a local political struggle, where references to global integrity and transparency standards are integrated into local agendas.[46] Lomaia based its criticism of the CCG on a World Bank evaluation report conducted by a private auditing company that did not identify any wrongdoings or mismanagement from the part of the MoE. He refers to a private auditing company as being more impartial and professional than the CCG. The discourse used by Lomaia and the new team of reformers in the government emphasises the need of abolishing inefficient and corrupt state bodies, while outsourcing controlling functions to the private sector.[47] They

---

41. Interview with opposition leader, Tbilisi, November 2008.
42. The group of actors supporting the Chamber of Control is composed of opposition parties such as the Conservative Party and the Republican Party. Nino Burdjanadze, at the time Parliament Speaker, is alleged to have provided a certain support in the coulisses 'allowing' the CCG to do this report. Interview with leaders of opposition parties, Tbilisi, November/December 2008.
43. Ibid. CCG employees deny a link between the MoE scandal and this vague of resignation or see the link as very tenuous. Interview with CCG employees, Tbilisi, November/December 2008.
44. Interview with a representative of an opposition party, former MP, Tbilisi, November 2008. A former employee of the CCG, who had to resign during the restructuring, explains that people asked on the streets whether the CCG still existed. Interview with former employee of the CCG, Tbilisi, December 2008.
45. Interview with leaders of opposition parties, Tbilisi, November/December 2008.
46. As Sampson remarks, 'even the most localized rule-of-law conflicts are integrally tied to global forces. At the local level, these global discourses and resources are utilized in the local power struggles as they play themselves out in democracy promotion projects'. Steven Sampson, 'From Forms to Norms: Global Projects and Local Practices in the Balkan NGO Scene', *Journal of Human Rights* 2, no. 3 (2003): 329–37.
47. Interview with former employees of the Ministry of Education, NGO head close to the government, former head of international organisation close to the government, Tbilisi, November/December 2008.

argue that state agencies such as the CCG are not strong enough to resist political pressure. On the other side, opposition parties refer to the CCG as a tool to prevent government corruption. The CCG represents the idea of fighting corruption through independent control institutions and a checks-and-balances system holding the government accountable. They stress the need for strong and independent control institutions in view of high-scale corruption cases in the government. They underline the lack of democratic institutions in Georgia and invite international organisations to put pressure on the Saakashvili government to strengthen these institutions.[48]

In the first narrative of the MoE, the confrontation between the CCG and the MoE is presented as a 'lost in translation' story involving two different accounting styles. In this narrative, the country's institutions have not yet integrated international standards, while Soviet practices remain. The MoE paints the scandal as a confrontation between modernity and the Soviet past. The World Bank evaluation report is used as an 'approval stamp' for the MoE practices. In the other camp, opposition parties paint the same story as a struggle for democracy against a corrupt government. They refer to Western democratic standards of transparency and accountability. In this second narrative, Georgia has not yet left its authoritarian past behind and authoritarian features have re-emerged after the Rose Revolution. Control institutions are not independent and corruption is still rife. Opposition parties engage in a deconstruction of the Rose Revolution myth. In both narratives, Western actors are called as arbiters.

The confrontation between the CCG and the MoE shows that the reform of institutions is as much a political undertaking as an administrative improvement. The CCG is formally independent, but in reality dependent on the political context and alliances of the day. Donor projects aimed at increasing transparency and preventing corruption through the reinforcement of democratic control institutions tend to neglect the instrumentalisation of these institutions. They view them instead as apolitical tools that can be used to promote broader development objectives such as poverty reduction and good governance. However, the political context affects donor projects, for example changing power relations between the Parliament and the executive or cadre rotation.[49] Staff rotation is a tool employed by the government to prevent the formation of autonomous networks of loyalties in state organs.[50] Cadre rotation is presented as a way to combat corruption. Representatives of donor organisations working with the Georgian government regularly complain about this practice. They may lose a precious partner in a ministry with whom they have developed a working relationship. These changes clearly affect the implementation of donor projects, in particular trainings. Often, trained public servants lose their jobs and are moved to another ministry. In the case of the CCG, donor projects focused on the training of staff have seen the majority of the trained employees leave the CCG.[51] Especially in 2007, about 400 people were fired by the new management. The resignation of about 400 staff was justified by the new chairmanship as a method to fight corruption. Prior to this wave of forced resignations, two employees from a CCG department dealing with road construction were arrested by the Constitutional Security Department of the Ministry of Internal Affairs on charges of corruption and in the presence of television cameras. The

---

48. Interview with head of opposition party, Tbilisi, December 2008.
49. Tisne and Smilov remark, 'Institutional reform projects could hardly be seen as separate from the underlying political forces that shape a country's political climate and a public administration's working climate'. Tisne and Smilov, 'From the Ground Up', 60.
50. The same device was used during the Shevardnadze period.
51. Interviews with project managers, Tbilisi, December 2008.

objective was to make an example of these employees, create fear, and force the rest of the staff to resign. The new chairman Levan Choladze also restructured the CCG by assigning auditors to different sectors. They were not allowed anymore to control in one sector, but had to undertake controls in other sectors. While these changes were justified as anti-corruption measures, they affected the work of donor projects.[52] Donor projects were still ongoing during Choladze's time, but the new management did not show a great interest and certain activities were stopped.[53] Two different visions of the fight against corruption are thus in opposition in the reform of the CCG.

The current reforms undertaken by the new management at the CCG since the summer of 2008 appear to be motivated by the pressure of the international community for 'results' in Georgia. The European Commission has put pressure on the government to accelerate the process of transforming the CCG into an auditing institution working according to international standards. The pressure became higher after the Georgian–Russian war in the context of large amounts of donor aid coming to Georgia.[54] A new law on the CCG has been presented to the Parliament at the end of 2008. Certain observers view these reforms as cosmetic and doubt the willingness of the government to strengthen the CCG. After the MoE scandal, the government seems to have tightened its grip on the CCG. It seems as if the CCG itself is controlled by the government.

A civil society anti-corruption project

In this third part, I examine a project aimed at preventing and combating corruption through civil society pressure and public participation in Georgia. The project was implemented by two Georgian NGOs with the financial support of a donor organisation.[55] The general project objective was to prevent corruption through civil society pressure (NGOs' anti-corruption training) and active public participation (raising public awareness through discussions). An examination of the individual strategies of local project managers reveals that the main objective pursued during the implementation of the project is not the prevention of corruption. In the course of implementing the project, higher policy objectives (fighting corruption through civil society pressure and civic participation) are translated into practical interests (the training of NGOs and network-building with regional NGOs; the testing of a particular methodology imported from the United States; legitimisation of the work of NGOs in post-revolutionary Georgia as mediators between society and the state). An interview with a project participant reveals that the anti-corruption dimension is not a central aspect of the project. 'I'm not sure that it was a specific training for anti-corruption NGOs [. . .] I think the goal was to give them [local NGOs] some specific skills, not concretely how to deal with anti-corruption'.[56] Although the project was aimed at discussing different views on the fight against corruption, thus acknowledging that there are different ways to combat corruption and different opinions in society, the project is still inscribed into a particular anti-corruption discourse. This discourse states that the most appropriate means to combat corruption are more democracy, more public participation and increased civil society pressure on ostensibly weak or unwilling state institutions. By using a bottom-up anti-corruption discourse emphasising public participation, the NGOs

---

52. Interview with project staff, Tbilisi, December 2008.
53. Interview with project staff and CCG employees, Tbilisi, November/December 2008.
54. Interview with EU delegation representative, Tbilisi, December 2008.
55. For reasons of confidentiality, I will not name the two NGOs and the donor organisation.
56. Interview with project participant, Tbilisi, March 12, 2008.

implementing the project legitimise their own work by presenting themselves as mediators between society and the government. In interviews, project managers emphasise how the current government is disconnected from the general population, while NGOs mediate citizens' demands and opinions (one project objective was to 'convey the public voice'). One project manager explains, 'We wanted to tell our government that not all the ways they use in their fight against corruption are liked by the population or at least to see what really people want'.[57] The project indirectly undermines the government's anti-corruption practices by representing the government's actions as spontaneous and lacking a long-term strategy. For example, project managers question the professionalism of the government, for example, 'In my organisation we are doing our plan and we know that we have to do this, this, and this in order to get this. And I am not sure that the government has a similar plan'.[58]

The success of the project was not assessed through concrete outcomes such as the reduction of corruption.[59] Rather, the project was deemed successful because it was seen as strengthening civil society and public participation. Rather than a means to prevent corruption, civil society strengthening is viewed as an end in itself. Success is produced through an interpretive work that gives meaning to different events by binding them into a coherent sequence and connecting them to higher policy goals. The project is presented as successful, despite not having achieved some core objectives, such as influencing decision-making, preventing or reducing corruption, mobilising citizens for public actions and training NGOs to implement anti-corruption projects. The apparent conformity to an official discourse does not signify its acceptance. In particular, two project managers criticise the approaches of donor organisations after the Rose Revolution, which are seen as providing an uncritical support to the Georgian government, while having decreased their support to civil society.[60] Official representations are nonetheless reproduced and maintained by the NGO community in order to attract donor funding and secure positions. Contradictory statements during interviews reveal that depending on the context where they act and talk, local recipients of donor assistance can change their interpretations of the project results. One project manager implicitly admits that Georgian citizens might have different expectations towards NGOs, questioning the relevance of this project: 'Sometimes we thought that talking with these people about corruption is much too much, because they do not have even their basic needs satisfied and you are talking to them about corruption and policies'.[61] At the beginning of the project, the donor organisation imposes a certain view, constructing a representation of the project that corresponds to higher policy objectives. The final report on the project mentions the absence of applications from NGOs in a region of Georgia populated by an ethnic minority. Since this region is a priority target of the donor organisation, applications from local NGOs were directly solicited. The inclusion of the region does not correspond to specific local needs, but conforms to higher policy goals. One project manager mentions the irrelevance of this inclusion, referring to the public discussion in this region as the least successful.[62] The importance of the project as a 'representation' is also visible in the fact that half of the copies of the project results were published in English (the other half was published in

---

57. Interview with project manager, Tbilisi, February 1, 2008.
58. Ibid.
59. Project evaluation.
60. Interviews with project managers, Tbilisi, February 2008.
61. Interview with project manager, Tbilisi, February 1, 2008.
62. Ibid.

Georgian and given to public officials). Despite the fact that no public officials attended the final presentation of results, the presence of the media and international organisations is nonetheless seen as a success by project managers. Finally, the multiplicity of perspectives is mentioned in one interview with a project participant, showing that the project community is not a homogeneous group.[63] Project participants from local NGOs discussed the contents of a small brochure used during the public discussions. Some participants disagreed with defining the arrests of high officials from the Shevardnadze era after the Rose Revolution as an anti-corruption initiative and putting these initiatives in a positive light. One project participant explains, 'For example, there was one part which was saying that the new government began a very aggressive fight against corruption and some kind of anticorruptional activities. Not every participant in that project believed that these activities were assessed the right way and things like that . . . The anticorruptional movement, first anticorruptional steps of this government that we have in Georgia after the revolution were very problematic and discussed'.[64] He further adds, 'For example, the sentence [in the brochure] was that the Georgian government began to fight against corruption for example in November of 2005 or something like that . . . [. . .] and most of the participants thought that the thing that they had begun cannot be called a fight against corruption'.[65] This discussion between project participants shows that the definition of which measures belong to the anti-corruption domain is contested. The final report on the project says, however, that project participants' comments on the brochure were only aimed at making it more understandable. This shows how the inscription of the project into an official narrative conceals diverging interests while producing an appearance of consensus.

Conclusion

The article has analysed the translation and the instrumental use of an anti-corruption discourse in a local context. The three anti-corruption discourses and case studies of anti-corruption interventions in Georgia show the multiplicity of perspectives on the fight against corruption as well as the various trajectories that local actors employ to translate global anti-corruption standards. Three main conclusions can be drawn from this plurality of perspectives on the fight against corruption. First, the anti-corruption discourse is adapted and translated in a local context and integrated into various agendas, rather than merely resisted or accepted. Second, actors compete to assert their position in the anti-corruption field, using various rhetorics in order to legitimise their practices. This use of various interpretations of the fight against corruption is also visible in local political struggles. Third, success in anti-corruption projects is rather measured in terms of the maintenance of a particular discourse than in terms of reducing or preventing corruption. In the case of civil society anti-corruption projects, the reduction of corruption appears secondary, while these projects are more concerned with reproducing the NGO project culture and presenting NGOs as attractive recipients of donor funds. Fighting corruption appears to be a facade, or at best, a fundraising strategy. These findings contradict the assumption at the core of global anti-corruption initiatives that there is a single way to combat corruption and a universal knowledge that can be exported to developing and transition countries by international organisations. Furthermore, the analysis of anti-corruption interventions in

---

63. Interview with project participant, Tbilisi, March 12, 2008.
64. Ibid.
65. Ibid.

Georgia shows how institutions can be used as tools in political struggles and how anti-corruption efforts are instrumentalised.

Acknowledgements

The author would like to thank Diana Schmidt-Pfister and Holger Moroff for their helpful comments on an earlier draft of this article.

Notes on contributor

Lili Di Puppo is a PhD candidate at the European Viadrina University, Frankfurt (Oder) in Germany. Her research interests are transformation research, corruption and anti-corruption research, development studies and European studies. She has recently published an article 'The externalisation of JHA policies in Georgia: partner or hotbed of threats?' in the *Journal of European Integration*.

Elite perceptions of anti-corruption efforts in Ukraine

Åse Berit Grødeland

Rights, Democracy and Development Division, Christian Michelsen Institute, Bergen, Norway

Anti-corruption efforts introduced in Ukraine in recent years have predominantly been imposed from the outside. They have been vague, all-inclusive and lacking in political and public support. What is more, they have been fairly insensitive to the cultural context into which they have been introduced. While targeting corrupt behaviour, they have largely ignored its root causes. The impact of Ukrainian anti-corruption reform has therefore been limited. Drawing on extensive qualitative data from Ukraine, this article explores elite (i) perceptions of Ukrainian anti-corruption reform, (ii) familiarity with specific anti-corruption initiatives, and (iii) views on how best to combat corruption. Not surprisingly, Ukrainian elites are familiar with, and fairly negative in their assessment of, national anti-corruption reform. They advocate a number of measures targeting corrupt behaviour as well as its root causes with a view to reducing corruption in Ukraine".

unfortunately, we do not have such a person as Moses,
who could lead us (in the struggle against
corruption) . . . it is a pity . . .. (FB-K-4)

Introduction

The leaders of the Orange Revolution came to power largely as a result of public discontent with a corrupt regime that not only engaged in diverting public funds for private use but also in serious election fraud – including vote buying and the falsification of election outcomes.[1] Shortly after gaining power, the new regime launched a number of anti-corruption efforts. Five years on, their impact is limited.[2] Survey data tapping into public[3]

---

1. For an in-depth account of corruption and election fraud in Ukraine prior to the Orange Revolution, see Andrew Wilson, *Ukraine's Orange Revolution* (New Haven and London: Yale University Press, 2005). See also Jan Neutze and Adrian Karatnycky, *Corruption, Democracy and Investment in Ukraine* (Policy Paper; Washington, DC: The Atlantic Council of the United States, October 2007), 18–19.
2. Ukraine's score in Transparency International's Corruption Perception Index (CPI) improved by only 0.4 points from 2001 (score 2.1) to 2008 (score 2.5). While its score increased from 2001 (2.1) to 2002 (2.4), it decreased in 2003 (2.3) and 2004 (2.2). In 2005 – i.e. after the Orange Revolution – Ukraine's score went up to 2.6, continued to increase in 2005 (2.8), but has since decreased (2.7 in 2007 and 2.5 in 2008), www.transparency.org (accessed July 23, 2009).
3. MSI/KIIS, *Corruption in Ukraine. 2007 Baseline National Survey for the MCC Threshold Country Program* (Kyiv: MSI, May 10, 2007).

and elite[4] perceptions of corruption in Ukraine suggest that corruption is widespread, possibly even on the increase. The judiciary, which should in principle enforce anti-corruption legislation, is one of the sectors worst hit by corruption.[5] Political will to properly address the problem appears to be limited.

Explanations as to why corruption in Ukraine is so widespread, abound. Most of these focus on weaknesses inherent in Ukraine's anti-corruption programme as such,[6] or within the state institutions responsible for implementing them.[7] As noted by the General Prosecutor's Office of Ukraine: 'currently, the anti-corruption strategy in Ukraine is still in a reactive mode. That is to say to combat the consequences of corruption by investigating what had happened but not eradicating the problems at their roots. Meanwhile spontaneous reactions, lack of perseverance, unclear directions are the fundamental problems of the national anti-corruption strategy'.[8] Relatively few attempts have been made to identify and/or investigate these root causes of corruption.[9]

Ukraine has experienced considerable pressure on the part of the international community to reduce corruption. Efforts have largely been unsuccessful as they have mostly been derived from standard international anti-corruption strategies. These are not adequately sensitive to the Ukrainian cultural context. The political stalemate that has plagued Ukraine in recent years has further hampered anti-corruption efforts. Unless such obstacles are adequately addressed, the latter are not likely to be successful.

This article investigates Ukrainian anti-corruption policies as perceived by Ukrainian elites. The first part provides an account of internationally driven anti-corruption efforts both in the post-communist context more generally, as well as in Ukraine since the Orange Revolution. It is followed by a discussion of elite perceptions of Ukrainian anti-corruption efforts and their thoughts on how best to do away with corruption in the future. The concluding part of the article provides some thoughts on how to enhance the efficiency of anti-corruption efforts in Ukraine, including the need to address national 'mentality' and 'culture' facilitating corrupt behaviour.

Internationally driven anti-corruption efforts in the post-communist context

In recent years, the study of legal transplants[10] has gained prominence amongst legal sociologists and researchers of comparative law.[11] Gillespie defines a legal transplant as

4. Åse Berit Grødeland, 'Cultural Constants, Corruption and the Orange Revolution', in *Ukraine on Its Way to Europe. Interim Results of the Orange Revolution*, ed. Juliane Besters-Dilger (Frankfurt: Peter Lang Verlag, 2009), 79–101.

5. Ibid.; MSI, *Survey on Corruption within the Judicial System in Ukraine: Courts of the General Jurisdiction* (Kyiv: MSI, 2008).

6. Grødeland, 'Cultural Constants, Corruption and the Orange Revolution'.

7. Neutze and Karatnycky, *Corruption, Democracy and Investment in Ukraine*.

8. General Prosecutor's Office of Ukraine, 'Combating Corruption in Ukraine', http://www.icac.org.hk/newsl/issue32eng/button5.htm (accessed April 30, 2009).

9. For an analysis of some of these causes, see Grødeland, 'Cultural Constants, Corruption and the Orange Revolution'.

10. Alternative terms used to describe legal transplants include legal transfers, the circulation of legal models, legal influence, legal inspiration, legal cross-fertilisation, and reception. See Michele Graziadei, 'Comparative Law and the Study of Transplants and Receptions', in *The Oxford Handbook of Comparative Law*, ed. Mathias Reimann and Reinhard Zimmermann (Oxford: Oxford University Press, 2006), 441–76.

11. David Nelken and Johannes Feest, eds., *Adapting Legal Cultures* (Oxford/Portland, OR: Hart Publishing, 2001); Gunther Teubner, 'Legal Irritants: Good Faith in British Law or How Unifying

'the transfer of laws and institutional structures across geographical or cultural borders'.[12] Scholars disagree on whether such transplants are desirable, and also on whether they are feasible.[13] However, most of them agree that legal transplants do take place. Studies of legal transplants mostly focus on the outcome or impact of the legal transplant, which in turn depends on a number of factors – the crucial one being whether laws and institutions are 'imported' or 'exported' from one geographical and cultural context to another. Transplants that are initiated or actively encouraged by the society into which they are being introduced (i.e. 'imported'), rather than forced upon them from the outside (i.e. 'exported'), are more likely to be successful.[14] However, irrespective of whether a transplant is 'imported' or 'exported' it is likely to behave differently in the context into which it is being introduced, compared with the context within which it originates. Legal transplants, therefore, tend to act as 'legal irritants'.[15] Theories on legal transplants are not only applicable to the transfer of laws or institutional mechanisms. They may also explain how anti-corruption efforts – that is anti-corruption legislation, institutional models and best practices – generated within one cultural and/or geographical context behave when introduced into another. Following from the above, efforts that are sensitive to the cultural context within which they are introduced, are more likely to be successful than those that are not.

Anti-corruption efforts generated from the outside should be more successful if 'imported', that is initiated or welcomed locally, than if 'exported', that is forced upon a national or local community from the outside. Michael distinguishes between two waves of internationally driven anti-corruption efforts. The first wave, which took place in the 1990s, focused on creating awareness of the negative impact of corruption, largely by copying (read: 'exporting') anti-corruption programmes that had been developed for Africa some years earlier, to other geographical areas, such as post-communist Europe. The second wave, which started in the 2000s, focused on capacity building and involved a large number of national and international organisations.[16] In the post-communist world anti-corruption initiatives have mostly come about as a

---

Law Ends Up in New Divergences', in *The Europeanisation of the Law: The Legal Effects of European Integration. European Law*, ed. Francis Snyder (Oxford: Hart Publishing, 2000), 243–68.

12. John Stanley Gillespie, *Transplanting Commercial Law Reform. Developing the 'Rule of Law' in Vietnam* (Hampshire, UK: Ashgate, 2006), 1–6.

13. Alan Watson, *Legal Transplants: An Approach to Comparative Law* (Edinburgh: Scottish Academic Press, 1974); Pierre Legrand, *Fragments on Law as Culture* (Deventer: W.E.J. Tjeenk Willink, 1996); and Pierre Legrand, 'European Legal Systems are not Converging', *International & Comparative Law Quarterly* 45, no. 1 (1996): 52–81.

14. Gary Goodpaster, 'The Rule of Law. Economic Development in Indonesia', in *Indonesia: Law and Society*, ed. Tim Lindsey (Sydney: The Federation Press, 1998), 21–24.

15. Gunther Teubner, 'Legal Irritants: Good Faith in British Law or How Unifying Law ends up in New Divergences', *Modern Law Review* 61, no. 11 (1998): 24. Development experts acknowledge that the transfer of anti-corruption measures tend to produce different outcomes than those intended. See, for instance, Lili Di Puppo, 'Anti-Corruption Interventions in Georgia: From Rhetoric to Practice' (paper prepared for Changing Europe Summer School III, Central and Eastern Europe in a Globalized World, Bremen, July 28–August 2, 2008), http://www.changing-europe.org/download/Summer_School_2008/Di_Puppo.pdf (accessed July 22, 2009).

16. Michael, quoted in Diana Rucinschi, 'The Flourishing Anticorruption Industry', originally appearing in *Jurnalul National*, http://www.jurnalul.ro/articole/96022/industria-anticoruptie, users.ox.ac.uk/~scat1663/anticorruption_good.doc (accessed January 10, 2008).

result of external pressure – primarily from international organisations such as the World Bank, the IMF, the European Union, and the Council of Europe. Michael claims that 'the rhetoric of anti-corruption is used by organisations like the World Bank to re-establish dreaded conditionality and control over the governance of developing countries'.[17] INGOs, for their part, engage in a wide range of activities such as corruption monitoring, training programmes and workshops for government officials and civil society. They also work on strengthening the capacity of local NGOs to engage in anti-corruption monitoring and advocacy work.

Transferring legislation and best practices targeting corruption from one geographical and/or cultural setting to another appears to be fraught with the same type of problems as transplanting legislation and institutional arrangements intended to promote the rule of law and the market economy. One problem that arises in this regard is that key concepts and approaches may be alien to the 'receivers'. Another problem is that anti-corruption programmes developed by the international community and introduced in the post-communist context tend to be vague and all-inclusive,[18] leaving local decision-makers in disarray with regard to how best to adjust them to their own context. Further, the internationally developed or inspired anti-corruption strategies appear to be suffering from cultural bias. Social norms 'informing' people's behaviour in the cultural and/or geographical setting into which the programmes are introduced may therefore undermine them. Local political, administrative and legal culture,[19] for instance, may to quite some extent not be compatible with effective anti-corruption reform. Informal practice is an important part of such cultures in post-communist societies. It is partly rooted in the wider national culture, partly a left-over from communism, and it is used by people when dealing with the anomalies of, and difficulties caused by, transition.[20] Such behaviour is much more resistant to change than are formal rules.

Added to this, the international community has insisted on involving civil society in its anti-corruption efforts. Building civil society in post-communist states has been a priority throughout post-communist Europe. Bilateral organisations in particular work closely with INGOs and/or local NGOs on a number of issues. However, the excessive emphasis on civil society as an effective anti-corruption fighter has also been criticised. NGOs are generally not as active in the post-communist world as they are in Western Europe and to an even greater extent in the United States.[21] Besides, they are frequently viewed with suspicion not only by the authorities, but also by the general public.[22] As local NGOs engaged in anti-corruption efforts tend to be heavily funded by the international community, they have no need to engage in a dialogue with the

17. Michael, quoted in Rucinschi, 'The Flourishing Anticorruption Industry'.

18. Ibid.

19. Legal culture may be defined as a 'way of describing relatively stable patterns of legally oriented social behaviour and attitudes'. David Nelken, 'Using the Concept of Legal Culture', *Australian Journal of Legal Philosophy* 29 (2004): 1–28, at 1.

20. Åse Berit Grødeland and Aadne Aasland, *Informality and Informal Practices in East Central and South East Europe* [Working Papers Series, no. 3/2007, Contemporary Europe Research Centre, University of Melbourne (CERC)].

21. Marc Morjé Howard, *The Weakness of Civil Society in Post-Communist Europe* (Cambridge: Cambridge University Press, 2003).

22. Åse Berit Grødeland, 'Public Perceptions of Non-Governmental Organisations in Serbia, Bosnia and Macedonia', *Communist and Post-Communist Studies* 39 (2006): 221–46.

wider community within which they operate.[23] Besides, there are indications that local NGO representatives are as sceptical of the general public as the general public are of the NGOs.[24]

Despite the considerable funds and efforts that have been spent on anti-corruption efforts, the international anti-corruption industry has generated few, if any, visible results. In some instances rather than reducing, such efforts have facilitated, corruption.[25] Anti-corruption efforts in post-communist Europe – though very much 'inspired' by international pressure, are largely undermined by four key aspects of post-communist legal and political culture namely (i) the tendency to issue a large number of frequently contradicting laws and regulations; (ii) unclear and poorly coordinated institutional responsibility; (iii) too much support to civil society in fighting corruption even though its credentials in doing so are modest[26] and (iv) widespread elite and public disregard for the law. These factors are likely to negatively affect anti-corruption efforts in Ukraine.

Anti-corruption efforts in Ukraine since the Orange Revolution

While Leonid Kravchuk's presidency (1991–1994) focused on establishing Ukraine as an independent state, Kravchuk's successor, Leonid Kuchma (1994–2005) concentrated his efforts on building a viable economy and strengthening his personal control in the political sphere. As in most other post-communist states, corruption in Ukraine had become endemic by the late 1990s.[27] Not surprisingly, therefore, the country experienced considerable international pressure to introduce anti-corruption reform.

The first anti-corruption legislation dates back to 1991,[28] though most anti-corruption initiatives were introduced from 1995 onwards. The development of a coherent legal framework for combating corruption began that year and continued throughout the late 1990s, culminating with the 'Anti-Corruption Concept for 1998–2005'. Ukraine joined OECD's Anti-Corruption Network for Eastern Europe and Central Asia (ACN) in 2003. In December the same year it signed the United Nations Convention against Corruption (UNCAC). Despite these efforts, however, the OECD in its 2004 assessment of Ukrainian anti-corruption policies, noted that 'while Ukraine has a rich array of legal instruments and broad strategic documents (for fighting corruption), efficient coordination, implementation and enforcement remain insufficient . . . the effectiveness and interrelation of these

---

23. The unintended consequence of creating civil society NGOs which are reliant on external support has been that they are never forced to build their own base of popular support or take on the arguments or political programmes of the nationalists . . . ' Adam Fagan, 'Civil Society in Bosnia Ten Years after Dayton', *International Peacekeeping* 12, no. 3 (2005): 406–19, at 410.

24. Grødeland, 'Public Perceptions of Non-Governmental Organisations'.

25. Michael, quoted in Rucinschi, 'The Flourishing Anticorruption Industry'.

26. Ibid.

27. For an overview of low-level corruption in Ukraine in the late 1990s, see William L. Miller, Åse B. Grødeland, and Tatyana Y. Koshechkina, *A Culture of Corruption? Coping with Government in Post-communist Europe* (Budapest: Central European University Press, 2001).

28. GRECO, *Joint First and Second Evaluation Rounds. Evaluation Report on Ukraine. Adopted by GRECO at its 32nd Plenary meeting* (Strasbourg, March 19–23, 2007), 4.

legal acts is often difficult to assess, in part due to their overwhelming quantity'.[29] The ACN, for its part, has put forward a set of recommendations regarding the amendment of existing laws and regulations.[30]

Responding to both international and national criticism, President Yushchenko issued a presidential decree in November 2005 targeting corruption and the country's shadow economy. The largely inefficient Anti-Corruption Coordination Committee, established in 1995, was substituted by an Interagency Commission under the National Council for Security and Defence, tasked with developing a coordinated anti-corruption policy and strategy. Added to this, a Concept Paper 'On the Way to Integrity' was issued as a presidential decree in September 2006. It describes corruption as 'one of the most pressing problems to be resolved in Ukraine' and is critical of previous efforts undertaken in this area. Priority is given to reforming the executive branch, the legislature and the judiciary.[31] The Ukrainian government was tasked with elaborating an action plan based on the Concept Paper. Assistance with the work on such a plan has been provided by the European Union and Council of Europe through their 'Project against Corruption in Ukraine' (UPAC).[32]

Even though all parties contesting the 2007 parliamentary elections emphasised their commitment to anti-corruption reform,[33] their commitment has so far failed to translate into firm action and tangible results.[34] Yushchenko's efforts to fight corruption have been hampered by the recent years' drawn-out stalemate between the president, parliament and government.[35] Besides, just like their predecessors, the Orange forces also rely on wealthy business people for funds. Not all of these are uncorrupted.

As noted above, the international community has put considerable pressure on post-communist states to introduce measures intended to reduce corruption. It has also introduced a number of anti-corruption measures on its own with a view to (i) assisting Ukrainian authorities in creating legislation and introducing legal mechanisms aimed at reducing corruption and (ii) creating awareness amongst the Ukrainian public of the extent as well as the negative effects of corruption. Internationally driven anti-corruption efforts in Ukraine have not followed Michael's model in that they have been carried out in parallel rather than in sequence. While international organisations have primarily engaged in (i),

---

29. OECD, *Fighting Corruption in Transition Economies. Ukraine* (Paris: OECD Publishing, 2005), 15.

30. Amongst other, it recommended that Ukraine (i) update its national anti-corruption strategy with a focus on prevention; (ii) identify systemic gaps facilitating corruption; and (iii) utilise law enforcement capacity more effectively to combat corruption. ACN, *Istanbul Anti-Corruption Action Plan for Armenia, Azerbaijan, Georgia, Kazakhstan, the Kyrgyz Republic, the Russian Federation, Tajikistan and Ukraine. Ukraine. Update on Actions to Implement Recommendations. June 2006* (Paris: OECD, 2006).

31. The article also acknowledges the need for new legislation, revamped administrative structures, new accountability and control structures, codes of conduct and training.

32. GRECO, *Joint First and Second Evaluation Rounds*, 5.

33. Neutze and Karatnycky, *Corruption, Democracy and Investment in Ukraine*, 24–9.

34. The Cabinet of Ministers adopted a Decree on Measures Plan on the Implementation on the Concept on a Way to Integrity (Measures Plan) in August 2007. The Plan formulates several concrete benchmarks to be reached by 2010. In addition, it established the aims of the concept, defined the responsible state bodies, and created an implementation timetable for each of the measures. Freedom House in its assessment of corruption for 2008 notes that 'despite the adoption of the Measures Plan, corruption remains dominant in Ukrainian society', *Freedom House Report on Ukraine, 2008*, http://www.freedomhouse.org/template.cfm?page=47&nit=472&year=2008 (accessed May 2, 2009).

35. Author's interview with political officer Dimitri Gorchakov and JSF Project Manager Andriy Spivak, Delegation of the European Commission to Ukraine, Kyiv, June 14, 2007.

INGOs have predominantly concentrated their efforts on (ii). Some, such as the American Bar Association's Central European and Eurasian Law Initiative (CEELI), have done both.

The evaluation team that compiled GRECO's (The Council of Europe's Group of States against Corruption) assessment of Ukraine in its 2007 report states that 'the GET (GRECO Evaluation Team) was pleased to note that the international community is active in Ukraine as there is clearly a massive need for assistance and support'.[36] In the end, however, it is essentially not so much a question of what type of assistance or support the international community provides, but more a question of implementation. Michael criticises international anti-corruption initiatives for not making available financial support to those institutions tasked with investigating and prosecuting corruption so as to make them more efficient and independent.[37] As a rule, such initiatives typically fund fora within which to discuss corruption and 'problems learnt', surveys measuring public perceptions and personal exposure to corruption, various training activities, provision of expertise or other technical assistance, and access to expert literature.[38] The Council of Europe's UPAC programme represents a typical example in this regard.[39] Such activities do not necessarily contribute to the reduction of corruption on their own, or in the short term.

The American Bar Association, for its part, has linked up with the Parliamentary Committee on Combating Organized Crime and Corruption in the area of legislative work. It also collaborates with the Committee and the Ministry of Justice on preparing guidelines on the UNCAC and providing 'overviews of other international treaties and conventions to which Ukraine is a signatory'. In addition, it has established an Anti-Corruption Coordination Initiative, which effectively acts as a forum for Ukrainian governmental agencies, the donor community and civil society, allowing them to coordinate their efforts, share information and enter collaboration on specific projects.[40]

Since the second half of the 1980s, Ukrainian NGOs have successfully mobilised the Ukrainian public against nuclear power (Zeleniy Svit)[41] and dubious political regimes (Pora!).[42] For this reason, they enjoy a better reputation than NGOs in many other post-communist states. Assistance to civil society constitutes a key element in USAID's programme in Ukraine. USAID is currently running a 2-year $45 million anti-corruption programme funded by the US Millennium Challenge Corporation.[43] Management Systems International

---

36. GRECO, *Joint First and Second Evaluation Rounds*, 9.

37. For an assessment of the level of independence of the Ukrainian judiciary, see Walter H. Rechberger, 'Judicial Independence in Ukraine', in *Ukraine on its Way to Europe. Interim Results of the Orange Revolution*, ed. Juliane Besters-Dilger (Frankfurt am Main: Peter Lang, 2009), 61–78.

38. Michael, quoted in Rucinschi, 'The Flourishing Anticorruption Industry'.

39. UPAC provides funding for 'national conferences, expertise, work-shops, round tables and in-country training activities, study visits, surveys, awareness raising activities, translations and publications, risk analyses, development of the terms of reference for a grant program and IT equipment & advice'. European Commission. Council of Europe. 'Support to good governance: Project against corruption in Ukraine' – UPAC. 'Revised project summary' (Working Draft, March 18, 2008), http://www.coe.int/t/dg1/legalcooperation/economiccrime/corruption/Projects/UPAC/344-UPAC-Summary-Eng_March08-updated.pdf (accessed February 10, 2010).

40. For details, see www.abanet.org/rol/europe_and_eurasia/ukraine_programs.html# . . . (accessed May 10, 2009).

41. Åse Berit Grødeland, 'The "Greening" of Ukraine: An Assessment of the Political Significance of the Ukrainian Green Movement 1986–1994' (PhD-thesis, IREES, University of Glasgow, October 1996).

42. Wilson, *Ukraine's Orange Revolution*, 73–6.

43. For details, see USAID, *Ukraine Country Profile* (Washington, DC: USAID, November 2008), www.usaid.gov/locations/europe_asia/countries/ua/ukraine.pdf (accessed May 10, 2009).

(MSI), an American INGO, has been commissioned to implement a component aiming to reduce public sector corruption through the strengthening of civil society's ability to monitor and expose corruption. MSI has commissioned the Kyiv International Institute of Sociology (KIIS) to do several large-scale quantitative corruption surveys in Ukraine. It has also set up a network of NGOs throughout the country to enable Ukrainian civil society to monitor and expose corruption in the long term.[44] The 'Anticorruption Committee', a local NGO, has since 2007 been acting as Transparency International's national contact in Ukraine.[45] As a national advocacy group it has monitored election campaigns and political party funding and also monitored corruption in public procurement. More recently, it has been engaged in creating public awareness of corruption in higher education.[46] NGO impact in areas such as corruption advocacy and work with the public to date, however, is modest,[47] considering the financial and other assistance rendered by the international community.

Methodology

One of the first comprehensive surveys undertaken on corruption amongst the general public and various types of local government officials in Ukraine was carried out in 1997–1998.[48] Since then surveys have regularly been conducted amongst the general public. The largest one – a corruption baseline survey (below referred to as the MCC survey) – took place in 2007.[49] While there have been some surveys of Ukrainian elites, these as a rule focus on one particular group – typically businessmen (BEEPS), though also judges[50] have been surveyed – rather than on elites as such. What is more, they tend to be quantitative, thus missing out on the detail that qualitative surveys are able to provide.

We conducted a large-scale qualitative survey amongst elites of key importance in preparing as well as enforcing Ukrainian anti-corruption policies and anti-corruption legislation. The MCC survey suggests that public perceptions of corruption in Ukraine are strongly correlated to the urban–rural divide. As elites are few and far between in rural Ukraine, contrasting elites in urban and rural areas was not feasible. We therefore decided to conduct interviews at national and capital level (Kyiv), in one city in West (Lviv) and one city in the East (Donetsk).[51] We chose Lviv and Donetsk as

44. www.pace.org.ua (accessed May 10, 2009).

45. http://www.transparency.org/publications/newsletter/2007/march_2007/anti_corruption_work/ukraine (accessed May 10, 2009).

46. See Business Anti-corruption Portal, http://www.business-anti-corruption.com/en/country-profiles/europe-central-asia/ukraine/initiatives/private-anti-corruption-initiatives/ (accessed May 10, 2009).

47. Stewart suggests that 'the EU's expectation that Ukrainian NGOs would serve both as democratising agents and as supporting actors to achieve ENP goals has turned out to be overly ambitious in the current environment'. Susan Stewart, 'NGO Development in Ukraine since the Orange Revolution', in *Ukraine on Its Way to Europe. Interim Results of the Orange Revolution*, ed. Juliane Besters-Dilger (Frankfurt am Main: Peter Lang, 2009), 177–93, at 192.

48. Miller, Grødeland, and Koshechkina, *Culture of Corruption?*.

49. The survey was carried out by Management Systems International (MSI) and the Kyiv International Institute of Sociology (KIIS) for USAID and with funds from the Millennium Challenge Corporation's Threshold Country Program in Ukraine.

50. KIIS, *Final Report. Survey on Corruption and Service Delivery in the Justice System in Ukraine* (Kiev: KIIS, 2006), http://www.coe.int/t/DGHL/cooperation/economiccrime/corruption/Projects/upac/upac_en.asp (accessed May 10, 2009).

51. Ideally we would have liked to conduct interviews in Northern Ukraine, Southern Ukraine, and the Crimea as well. For financial reasons, however, we were not able to do so.

they are very different types of cities,[52] yet similar in terms of public perceptions of corruption.[53] Altogether, we conducted a total of 84 in-depth interviews[54] with the following types of elites: elected representatives, political party representatives, judges, prosecutors, representatives of local business and representatives of foreign business.[55] Interviews were conducted by SOCIS according to a pre-prepared interview guide, and tape-recorded. Complete transcripts in Russian and Ukrainian were coded and later analysed in QSR NUD*IST. Main findings appear in table-form in the text below and are 'illustrated' by representative quotes made by individual respondents.[56]

Elite perceptions of Ukrainian anti-corruption efforts

Corruption surveys as a rule either measure attitudes and experiences with 'bribery' or 'corruption'. However, notions of what exactly constitutes corruption are likely to differ across geographical and cultural borders. Therefore it is important to either clarify the concept – to ensure that it is understood in the same way by all the respondents – or to ask about specific types of corrupt acts.

---

52. Lviv is the largest city in West Ukraine, fairly ethnically homogeneous; ruled by the 'Orange' forces, historically and culturally rather distinct from other Ukrainian cities, and frequently referred to as the 'cultural capital' of Ukraine. Lviv has been a part of Kievan Rus, the Grand Duchy of Lithuania, the Polish half of the Commonwealth, the Austro-Hungarian Empire, the Second Polish Republic, and the USSR after the Yalta Conference. According to the 2001 census, Lviv had a population of 725,000 people. The large majority of these, 88%, were ethnic Ukrainians, 9% were ethnic Russians, and 1% was ethnic Poles. See Wikipedia, http://en.wikipedia.org/wiki/Lviv (accessed February 10, 2010). See also http://www.lvivbest.com/uk (accessed February 10, 2010). In contrast, Donetsk is a much younger city than Lviv, ethnically more diverse, primarily Russian speaking, heavily industrialised, and controlled by the 'Blue' forces. Donetsk is also the base of former Prime Minister Viktor Yanukovych and one of Ukraine's most powerful oligarchs, Rinat Akhmetov. In 2007 Donetsk had a population of 1,100,000 people, making it the fifth largest city in Ukraine. The majority of its population is Russian speaking and composed of 56.9% ethnic Ukrainians, 38.2% ethnic Russians, as well as a number of other ethnic groups. Donetsk was founded in 1869 by Welsh businessman John Hughes, who established a steel plant and several coalmines in the region. See Wikipedia, http://en.wikipedia.org/wiki/Donetsk (accessed February 10, 2010). See also http://encyclopedia.stateuniversity.com/pages/6076/Donetsk.html (accessed February 10, 2010).
53. Indices created based on findings from the MCC survey, suggest that in terms of perceptions of corruption, differences between Lviv and Donetsk are fairly small. Personal exposure to corruption, however, appears to be more common in Donetsk than in Lviv. See MSI/KIIS, *Corruption in Ukraine*.
54. Interviewing was conducted between February and April 2008 as part of project no. 182628 located at CMI and funded by the Research Council of Norway. A total of 16 interviews were carried out at national level (Kyiv), 28 at capital level (Kyiv), 20 in Lviv and 20 in Donetsk.
55. All representatives of foreign businesses interviewed, are Ukrainian nationals. The samples with elected representatives and non-elected political party representatives are composed of party representatives both from the position and opposition. Within each elite category we conducted a total of 14 interviews.
56. Tables were constructed from the total number of answers to questions – or text units – coded at each node (coding-category). Quotes from interviews with elected representatives are marked *ER*, interviews with non-elected political party representatives are marked *PP*, interviews with judges are marked *J*, interviews with public prosecutors are marked *PR*, interviews with local business representatives are marked *LB*, and interviews with foreign business are marked *FB*. *N* refers to national level, *K* refers to Kiev, *L* refers to Lviv, and *D* refers to Donetsk. The respondent number is also given. Thus *ER-N-3* refers to elected representative at national level number 3.

Corruption is commonly defined as 'the abuse of official position for personal gain'.[57] While a fairly large number of our respondents indicated that corruption is essentially the 'abuse of one's position', not all of them explicitly mentioned that the purpose of such abuse is personal gain. A fairly large number of respondents associated corruption with 'bribery', 'covert salary (making)', 'payment for kindness', 'payment for resolving problems' or 'paying' for (official service) – that is with some material benefit or compensation for services rendered. Business representatives – those representing local as well as foreign companies – understood corruption almost exclusively as 'bribery'. Others emphasised the illegal aspect of corruption, labelling such practice as 'illegal acts', 'illegal decisions', 'actions above or in conflict with the law', 'criminal acts' and 'the use of public resources to get around the law'. It is worth noting that nobody associated corruption with nepotism even though the latter is very widespread throughout Ukraine. Several judges, prosecutors and political party representatives referred to the definition of corruption given in the law – though without actually quoting it:

> Corruption is: 'the use of (one's) position with the aim of gaining some material profit, which may go against the interests of the state'. (Pr-K-2) 'to give and to receive a bribe . . . ' (PP-K-6); 'corruption is when (a) person does something prohibited by the law (in return) for money or some other remuneration'. (PP-N-5); '(when) he/she (i.e. the official) demands some additional money . . . ' (LB-K-6) 'the concept defined in the law'. (J-L-13)[58]

Elite familiarity with Ukrainian anti-corruption efforts

The leaders of the Orange Revolution pledged to combat corruption once in power. 'Orange' anti-corruption efforts have primarily been promoted by the presidential administration only to be stalled in parliament or government.[59] Still, several measures have been introduced and Table 1 suggests that Ukrainian elites are generally well aware of these.

Respondents' statements on anti-corruption efforts may be grouped into four broad categories, focusing on (i) *specific anti-corruption programmes*; (ii) *various formal measures taken to reduce corruption*, such as the introduction of new, and the amendment of existing, laws or decrees, as well as staff replacements in government administration and (iii) *the shortcomings of Ukrainian anti-corruption efforts*, including *corruption scandals* that have surfaced since the Orange Revolution. Statements indicating that respondents are *aware of Ukrainian anti-corruption efforts* may be put in a separate category (iv).

---

57. Transparency International defines corruption as 'misuse of entrusted power for private gain'. See http://www.transparency.org/news_room/faq/corruption_faq (accessed May 16, 2009).

58. The 1995 Law on Combating Corruption defines corruption as 'the unlawful active or passive use, reception or granting of advantages, privileges by a person of authority'. GRECO, *Joint First and Second Evaluation Rounds*, 8.

59. The presidential framework 'On the Way to Integrity', for instance, was stalled for almost a year in the Ukrainian parliament before being approved by the cabinet in August 2007. Business Anti-Corruption Portal. Ukraine. Country Profile, p. 1 of 22, www.business-anti-corruption.com/normal.asp?pageid=250 (accessed August 29, 2008). As a result of political stalemate, the 2nd session of the Ukrainian parliament (6th convocation), considered no more than 45 of 245 bills proposed by the coalition agreement between BYuT and OUPSD. Only 11 of these were approved. Ukrainian Center for Independent Political Research. Research Update: The 2008 Political Year: Review without Lessons. . . .

Table 1.   Awareness of Ukrainian anti-corruption
initiatives (in per cent).

	%
Aware of such initiatives	70
Not aware of such initiatives	22
Other statements	7
Don't know	1
N	(105)

Note: N = total number of text units. Decimals have been
rounded up or down to the nearest whole number and
numbers therefore do not always add up to 100.

The *anti-corruption programmes* best known to our respondents are those introduced in customs and the traffic police. The anti-smuggling programme, popularly referred to as 'Stop Contraband!' was endorsed by the Ukrainian Cabinet of Ministers in March 2005. The programme contained provisions for instantly dismissing customs officials reported to either demand or accept kickbacks.[60] In the view of some respondents, this campaign was launched more for show than to reduce corruption. Customs officials replaced as a result of this programme were simply substituted with 'equally corrupt people'. Respondents also criticised the campaign for being 'chaotic', 'unsystematic' and for being implemented by people not sufficiently motivated for the task. They also questioned its impact, claiming that bribery in customs has increased rather than decreased in recent years:[61]

'"Stop Contraband!" was implemented (in customs). As a result the unofficial price for slip-ping across the border increased threefold'. (ER-L-13); 'at customs stations the bribe rates increased considerably (as a result) . . . now bribes are taken for, as they call it, "honesty and risk". Secondly . . . those who were controlled (before the Orange Revolution) now have the possibility to abuse. The subjects have changed, the essence remains the same'. (ER-N-5); '"Stop Contraband!" . . . was done only for show'. (LB-L-13)

Respondents were also fairly aware of efforts introduced to reduce bribery in the traffic police and police.[62] The Ukrainian road 'business' has traditionally been one in which

---

60. The Cabinet of Ministers also passed a resolution to speed up customs clearance procedures from 12–15 to 1–3 days. A 24 hour telephone hotline to accept complaints against customs officials from Ukrainian importers was established somewhat earlier. Prime Minister Yulia Tymoshenko claimed that due to previous steps taken by the Cabinet to clean up customs, state earnings had increased 3.5 times. See 'Ukrainian Government endorses Comprehensive "Stop Contraband!" Pro-gramme', http://www.ukraine-eu.mfa.gov.au/eu/en/publication/print/2214.htm (accessed May 10, 2005).

61. For an assessment of anti-corruption efforts in Ukrainian customs, see Yuriy Skolotiany, 'Valeriy Khoroshkovskiy: Prychyna vsomu – useloglynaiucha, systema koruptsia', *Dzerkalo tyzhnia,* no. 41 (720), listopada 1–8, 2008, http://www.dt.ua/1000/1550/64564/ (accessed February 10, 2010).

62. At a session with Carnegie Endowment's Senior Associate, Andrew Kuchins, in February 2006, Ukrainian Minister of the Interior, Yuriy Lutsenko claimed that 3500 police officers had failed an examination and that 600 corruption cases had been launched against police. Carnegie Endowment for International Peace. 'Establishing the Rule of Law and Fighting Corruption. Yurii Lutsenko, Andrew Kuchins', Friday, February 10, 2006, http://www.carnegieendowment.org/events/index.cfm?fa=eventDetail&id=852&&pro . . . (accessed May 10, 2009). Yuriy Lutsenko was one of the key people orchestrating the Orange Revolution. He served as Minister of the Interior under

everything could be bought.[63] No wonder, therefore, that Ukraine has much higher accident rates than other European countries. The notoriously corrupt Ukrainian traffic police – DAI (derzhavna avtodorozhna inspektsia)[64] – was formally abolished by President Yushchenko in 2005, to be replaced by a '"European level" highway patrol service'.[65] New traffic rules and higher fines for traffic violations were introduced in 2008.[66] However, our respondents described these as 'chaotic', 'cosmetic', and as having 'no effect', just like they did when talking about anti-corruption reform in the Ukrainian customs service:

'there were some efforts inside the police. But here in Ukraine any efforts are reduced to changing a head – (be it) of policy (or) of region. It may simply be cosmetics – to catch a head of policy or a head of administration who took a bribe of $300 . . . ' (ER-L-13); 'the fight against corruption in the police . . . it is not an effort . . . '. (Pr-L-14)

Finally, there was considerable awareness of efforts to clean up the state vehicle inspection. But again, perceptions were fairly negative. At best, respondents simply stated that they were aware of such efforts. At worst, they described them as 'half measures', 'having no (real) effect'. Only one respondent, representing a foreign business, suggested that they had led to a 'slow improvement'.

Respondents referring to *formal measures*, that is, laws, decrees and replacements of administrative staff introduced to combat corruption, held the view that such efforts are made on paper only and that for this reason they are inefficient, producing no results:

'you see there are many programs. But they are only on paper'. (Pr-K-8); 'all efforts, presidential edicts (which were introduced), were declarative and produced no result'. (PP-N-2); 'they started replacing all the officials but nothing changed. New people came to work (in the same way) as before . . . '. (FB-K-3)

Although the victors of the Orange Revolution came to power partly as a result of their pledge to tackle extensive corruption, they have not been saved from corruption scandals themselves. One of the most recent allegations of corruption was put forward by Prime Minister Tymoshenko against the national Central Bank and the presidential administration,

Yanukovych (2005–2006), but was dismissed on allegations of corruption. Lutsenko was later cleared in court and appointed Minister of the Interior in December 2007, by Yulia Tymoshenko. For details on the corruption scandal, see Taras Kuzio, 'Ukraine's Elites remain above the Law', *The Jameston Foundation, Eurasia Daily Monitor* 4, no. 147 (July 30, 2007).

63. Until recently, a vehicle inspection without an inspector was typically charged $50, while obtaining a driver's license without a test would be somewhat more expensive at $200–500. Should one be so unfortunate as to run down and kill a pedestrian, charges could be avoided by paying a $5000 bribe – split between the prosecutor and the judge – provided that the deceased had no important friends or that his/her family had no money. See Kiev Ukraine News Blog, November 21, 2007. 'Yushchenko: Ukraine's Roads are Europe's most Corrupt and Dangerous', compiled by an American ex-pat based on Ukrainian newspaper reports, http://blog.kievukraine.info/2007/11/yushchenko-ukraines-roads-are-europes.html (accessed May 10, 2009).

64. DAI translates as 'give!' in Russian, and jokes were frequently made about traffic police flagging down cars and instructing the drivers to 'give' them something.

65. Valentinas Mite, 'Ukraine: Yushchenko Orders Law-Enforcement Overhaul', *Radio Free Europe/Radio Liberty*, July 19, 2004, http://www.rferl.org/articleprintview/1060025.html (accessed May 10, 2009); Andrew Osborn, 'Ukraine Scraps Traffic Police to End Corrupt Fines', *The Independent*, July 20, 2005, http://www.independent.co.uk/news/world/europe/ukraine-scraps-traffic-police-to-end-corrupt-fines-499464.html (accessed February 10, 2010).

66. Oksana Bondarchuk, 'Europe's Deadliest Roads', *Business Ukraine*, November 17, 2008, http://www.businessukraine.com.ua/europe-s-deadliest-roads (accessed May 10, 2009).

whom she accused of corrupt currency trading.[67] Several respondents referred to earlier corruption scandals, involving well-known politicians such as Oleksandr Zinchenko,[68] Petro Poroshenko,[69] Mykola Rudkovsky[70] and Oleksandr Tretiakov,[71] respectively:

'(there is) no real desire to combat corruption . . . those who struggled against corruption . . . are corrupted themselves: all these scandals (involving) Poroshenko, Zinchenko. . . ' (PP-N-4); 'there are many examples (of corrupt officials) from the highest echelons of power – Zinchenko, Martynyuk, Tretiakov . . . '. (PP-L-13)

Elite assessment of anti-corruption efforts

As already noted, respondents often provided spontaneous assessments of Ukrainian anti-corruption efforts when talking about their familiarity with them. When specifically asked *how they perceived Ukrainian anti-corruption initiatives*, most respondents were equally negative (Table 2).

Two main types of criticism were raised: (i) measures taken so far are inappropriate (majority of statements), and (ii) those in charge of implementing them are not 'qualified' for the task. Respondents suggested that there are too many anti-corruption measures, that they tend to be formal, lack a normative or legal foundation, frequently fail to translate into action, and consequently that their impact is either limited or non-existent:

'all (those) who should have been brought to responsibility for corruption . . . up to now successfully sit in parliament and were until recently in government . . . I can not give any example of any person who was punished for his corruption after the Orange Revolution . . . I can give a great number of examples when someone was not punished for this at all'. (PR-N-1); 'until at least one accusation is brought into court . . . we can't speak about any success in fighting corruption . . . '. (ER-N-2)

---

67. See 'Financial Fraud: Corruption Scandal over Ukraine's Emission Money', *Global Research*, December 20, 2008, http://www.globalresearch.ca/index.php?context=va&aid=11451 (accessed May 10, 2009).

68. Former State Secretary Oleksandr Zinchenko held a press conference in September 2005 at which he declared his resignation and alleged that several key officials close to President Yushchenko were corrupt. The press conference brought about a political crisis. The mentioned officials either resigned or were dismissed by Yushenko, while Prime Minister Yuliya Tymoshenko and her cabinet were fired. Zinchenko served as Secretary of State for President Yushchenko in 2005. He resigned in protest against alleged corruption amongst officials close to the President. His resignation triggered a set of dismissals, and Tymoshenko's government was fired.

69. Ukrainian businessman and politician Petro Poroshenko was appointed Secretary of the National Security and Defence Council in 2004. He was dismissed in September 2005, following allegations made by Former Secretary of State, Oleksandr Zinchenko. Poroshenko was re-elected to parliament in March 2006 and currently chairs the parliamentary committee on finance and banking.

70. Former Minister of Transport, Mykola Rudkovsky, was arrested in February 2009 on allegations that he had misappropriated some $200,000 to fund three chartered flights abroad. The Ministry of the Interior in addition filed criminal charges against him for allegedly having pilfered ministry property worth some $1.7 million. 'Former Minister jailed in Probe', *Ukrainians*, February 14, 2008, www.ukrainians.ca/political-news/403-former-minister-jailed-in-probe.html (accessed May 10, 2009).

71. Former first aide to the president, Oleksandr Tretiakov, was one of the high-ranking officials whom Former Secretary of State, Oleksandr Zinchenko accused of corruption. The Ukrainian parliamentary commission on organised crime and corruption declared the accusations against Tretiakov and former Minister of Transport, Yevhen Chervonenko, as 'groundless' in late 2005. 'Ukraine-Parliament-Commission-Corruption-Power', *Ukraine News*, November 30, 2005.

Table 2. Assessment of Ukrainian anti-corruption initiatives (in per cent).

	%
Positive	19
Mix	3
Negative	49
Other	25
DK	3
N	(59)

Note: N = total number of text units. Decimals have been rounded up or down to the nearest whole number and numbers therefore do not always add up to 100.

Those in charge of fighting corruption were generally perceived in a rather negative manner, and were frequently referred to as 'corrupt people'. Scandals involving higher-ups, frequently changing governments and lack of political co-operation between the position and opposition were also referred to in this regard. In contrast, none of the respondents referred to staff shortages and inexperienced staff:[72]

> 'there were many intensive efforts . . . to prevent corruption phenomena in (state) administration. I can't say they gave significant results . . . ' (ER-K-6); 'we see impunity in the highest echelons of power . . . '. (PR-D-11)

Respondents who thought anti-corruption efforts after the Orange Revolution have been positive, on the other hand, expressed their content without being overtly specific. They thought there 'had been changes', that there 'had been some results', 'more results' (as a result of more actions), that efforts to curb corruption had become 'more effective' or 'stronger' or that efforts 'had been successful but not sufficient'.

None of the respondents made any references to internationally driven anti-corruption efforts involving NGOs, nor did they refer to surveys on corruption. There were also surprisingly few mentions of anti-corruption measures undertaken in the respondents' own sectors. There may be a number of reasons for this. Respondents may simply not be aware of anti-corruption efforts undertaken by the international community as these are poorly advertised to the non-expert audience. Alternatively, the absence of such statements may simply reflect the fact that anti-corruption efforts initiated by the international community are carried out by 'local' government and other bodies and consequently primarily identified with these. Elites probably find it easier to talk about efforts to combat corruption in sectors other than their own. It is perhaps more worrying that Ukrainian elites do not seem to be aware of NGO-driven anti-corruption efforts, given that such NGOs are meant to create public awareness on the negative effects of corruption and also engage in advocacy work to bolster national and local anti-corruption efforts.

---

72. The Parliamentary Committee on the Struggle against Organized Crime and Corruption, for instance, recently assessed the performance of the SBU's Main Directorate on the Struggle against Corruption and Organised Crime as 'unsatisfactory' due to staff shortages, inexperienced staff, poor staff recruitment procedures, incorrectly set priorities, and insufficient interaction between national and foreign law enforcement bodies. *Eurasian Security Services Daily Review*, October 12, 2008, www.axisglobe.com/article.asp?article=1668 (accessed May 4, 2009).

Elite perceptions of how best to combat corruption

Although most respondents thought the judiciary was the most corrupt sector in Ukraine,[73] when asked how best to reduce corruption, the majority still favoured 'legal' measures. 'Cultural' measures were also favoured by a fairly large number of respondents. The latter were particularly popular amongst representatives of local business. 'Political', 'administrative' and 'socio-economic' measures aimed at improving living standards and combat corruption, trailed rather far behind. We will return to these measures in more detail, below (Table 3).

Respondents favouring *legal measures* primarily held the view that current legislation should be changed or replaced:

'I think that legislation concerning the struggle against corruption should first be improved'. (J-L-12); 'some (new) laws should be issued'. (LB-D-10); 'the laws should be maximally approximated to real life, to common sense. Second, they should provide the means of monitoring the observation of the law. And third, they should provide a possibility to defend someone's rights in court'. (FB-L-12)

Michael argues that amending old, and introducing new, legislation is not all that effective.[74] In Ukraine a more serious problem is access to existing legislation. Legal texts are generally difficult to get hold of. Even legal professionals do not always have access to relevant legislation. Although the State Judicial Administration is responsible for providing such access, in practice – due to a lack of funds – most judges have to purchase legal

Table 3. Preferred methods of fighting corruption in Ukraine (in per cent).

	%
Legal	25
Political	19
Socio-economic	16
Cultural	15
Administrative – incl. staff changes	6
Other	19
DK	0
N	(216)

Note: *N* = total number of text units. Decimals have been rounded up or down to the nearest whole number and numbers therefore do not always add up to 100.

---

73. Grødeland, 'Cultural Constants, Corruption and the Orange Revolution'. Freedom House in its 2008 Assessment of Ukraine note that the Ukrainian judiciary suffer from the following weaknesses: (i) lack of public respect for court decisions and the judicial system as a whole; (ii) insufficient funding of the court system; and (iii) an inefficient and non-transparent process of appointing judges. According to the report 'these problems remained untouched during 2007. The dismissal of the prosecutor general in May, along with the Constitutional Court decision revoking the president's right to appoint and dismiss heads and deputy heads of courts, led to imbalances in the overall judicial framework and raised broad public discussion over the need to reform the judicial system. Unfortunately, preoccupation with the election campaign and the subsequent process of creating a coalition drew main political players away from creating real initiatives'. *Freedom House report on Ukraine, 2008*, http://www.freedomhouse.org/template.cfm?page=47&nit=472&year=2008 (accessed May 2, 2009).
74. Michael, quoted in Rucinschi, 'The Flourishing Anticorruption Industry'.

texts at their own expense.[75] As familiarity with the law is limited,[76] observing the law is not the easiest of tasks. Possibly for this reason a fairly large share of our respondents favoured proper 'implementation' and 'observation' of the law as well as adequate 'control'. Violations of the law should in their view be properly punished:

'first of all laws must be observed and for that certain steps need to be made . . . ' (ER-N-3); 'there are many laws that are not applied because there are no government resolutions regulating the implementation of laws . . . ' (Pr-L-12); 'if a high-ranking official commits a crime . . . proceedings must be instituted against him . . . ' (Pr-K-8); 'tougher punishment for corrupt acts . . . '. (PP-N-4)

Ukrainians are generally unfamiliar with the law. Their trust in it is also limited.[77] Is it the unfamiliarity that breeds distrust or is it the lack of trust in the law that makes people less prone to familiarise themselves with it in the first place? Given the difficulty even legal professionals encounter in gaining access to relevant legislation,[78] the former explanation comes across as being the most plausible. Statements made by our respondents lend some support to this view. Respondents also thought citizens distrust laws as they contain loopholes, are constantly changing, are interpreted incorrectly, and/or may easily be evaded:

'I think people in Ukraine are generally unfamiliar with laws and do not trust them . . . ' (ER-N-1); '(people) are not aware of their rights and obligations and for this reason they cannot use the law'. (FB-D-10); 'I think people are totally unfamiliar with the law . . . the laws are constantly changing . . . ' (J-D-9); 'naturally they do not trust the law . . . because . . . different laws contradict each other . . . ' (LB-K-4); 'laws are interpreted incorrectly, we cannot rely on them'. (PP-D-10)

Acknowledging citizens' lack of familiarity with, and trust in, the law, some respondents called for the introduction of long-term measures, such as educating people about the law and forming a legal culture, as prerequisites for reducing corruption. By 'legal culture' they primarily understand a culture of 'law-abidingness'.[79] Some support was also voiced for reducing the powers of judges and prosecutors, promoting the rule of law and implementing the constitution:

'only legal culture, legal education obtained in school and precise laws (can combat corruption)'. (Pr-N-6); 'one should reform the judicial branch of power . . . ' (PP-N-2); '(people) lost trust in justice . . . you will not go to the police if you have no money. You will not go to the prosecutor's office without money because your question will not be resolved. No money (means) no answer to the question'. (Pr-D-10); '. . . limiting the authority of the judges . . . such people consider themselves sovereign rulers and they do what they want'. (PP-N-4); 'honesty and legality, correctness of court and judicial activity in Ukraine are the first and most important . . . having changed the court we can improve the legal situation in Ukraine'. (PR-N-1)

---

75. Rechberger, 'Judicial Independence in Ukraine', 76.
76. Grødeland, 'Cultural Constants, Corruption and the Orange Revolution', 85–6.
77. Grødeland, 'Cultural Constants, Corruption and the Orange Revolution'.
78. Rechberger, 'Judicial Independence in Ukraine', 76.
79. Legal culture may be defined as a 'way of describing relatively stable patterns of legally oriented social behaviour and attitudes'. Nelken, 'Using the Concept of Legal Culture'.

Respondents favouring *political measures* called for a thorough overhaul of the Ukrainian political system. They thought there is a need for strengthening the power of Ukraine's political leadership and streamlining the power vertical to improve its performance.[80] In the opinion of one respondent, what Ukraine needs is a strong hand ('a dictator') and more and better control of Ukrainian politicians:

> '(there should be) clear and strict demands on behalf of the President to the power ministers'. (ER-K-8); 'the state vertical . . . should be strengthened. Strong dictatorship should be applied . . . there should be a stronger executive power with wider authorities . . . ' (LB-L-12); 'the political system needs to be changed because the present political system makes both state officials and ordinary people use corruption in their (mutual) relations'. (ER-N-4); 'well, there is a perfect way: totalitarianism, but it will pull off our common way of life . . . '. (PP-L-12)

Respondents also called for better quality and more responsible politicians. Top politicians should set a good example and also be more accessible to the Ukrainian people. Better control of elected representatives could be achieved by lifting deputy immunity and change the election system. This, in turn, would transform Ukraine into a more transparent and democratic society. Finally, calls were made for improving the level of political culture:

> 'first of all it is necessary to raise the level of political culture . . . the executive power has to be in the hands of people who care about their reputation . . . who understand that their honest name is the largest (political) capital . . . ' (ER-N-2); 'if people see that corruption is being fought at the top level, (they) will start contributing to this (fight) more energetically . . . ' (Pr-K-8); 'there should be more institutions that control power. Abolishing deputy immunity is one of the possibilities'. (ER-D-10)

There was limited support for special anti-corruption bodies tasked with reducing corruption in Ukraine. However, Ukraine could do with 'an anti-corruption campaign', 'an all-Ukrainian anti-corruption campaign' or even 'a global anti-corruption campaign', which in turn requires a proper and comprehensive plan.

The third type of measures required to curb corruption that our respondents identified may be referred to as *socio-economic measures*. Mauro notes that 'corruption discourages investment, limits economic growth, and alters the composition of government spending, often to the detriment of future economic growth'. He also points out that low wages in the civil service relative to wages in the private sector constitute a source of low-level corruption.[81] There also appears to be a link between GDP per capita, communist-style, and to some extent also illegitimate, lobbying.[82] Not surprisingly, therefore, respondents argued in favour of improving people's – including those of state officials and judges – socioeconomic conditions in order to reduce corruption. However, none of them had any specific ideas as to how this could be achieved.

In a study of Ukrainian judges, Rechberger notes that judges receive inadequate remuneration for their work. As both remuneration and access to state-supplied housing – a

---

80. Measures listed to facilitate stronger government include the 'improvement of the power vertical', 'a strong power vertical', 'a united power vertical', 'unified political power', 'reconsidered government functions', and 'less high level power groups'.
81. Paulo Mauro, *Why Worry About Corruption?* (Washington, DC: IMF, Economic Issues 6, 1997), 3–5.
82. Åse Berit Grødeland, 'Political Lobbying in Post-Communist States' (Article currently being reviewed by *Slavic Review* – and available from the author upon request.)

benefit bestowed upon judges – depend on the executive, local government has put itself in a position where it can exert 'undue influence on judges, because in practice they have the power to decide when and how this benefit (i.e. state-supplied housing) is provided'.[83] Our data lend some support to Rechberger's observations. One respondent who is himself a judge held the view that the social and economic conditions of judges will have to be raised if the courts are to effectively combat corruption. Only a limited number of respondents thought staff replacements would improve matters. Those who did, called for 'professionals' to be placed in positions tasked with combating corruption – implicitly suggesting that those holding such positions at present are not up for the task:

> '(one should) fight against poverty, because poverty generates corruption'. (ER-N-3); 'state officials who are responsible for something in the country should get a salary (that is so) . . . high (that they) will not be willing to receive a bribe . . . ' (FB-D-7); 'it is still necessary to provide professionals to those organs and structures that would be busy fighting corruption . . . it is necessary to prepare personnel . . . '. (Pr-K-4)

In the end, however, the success or failure of such efforts is linked to 'culture', be it individual, institutional or political. Enhancing public awareness – including by raising new generations in a different mould and providing children with proper education in school – was perceived as a highly popular measure. In addition, respondents specifically argued in favour of strengthening 'national consciousness', 'national mentality' and 'cultural standards'. Some even called for a 'national catharsis'. Yet others were somewhat more resigned, hoping that time would do its job. A small minority held the view that nothing could be done – that is that corruption in Ukraine is endemic. These views should be taken as an acknowledgement on the part of Ukraine's elites that corrupt behaviour has deeper root-causes and that these must be addressed to successfully combat corruption. Long-term measures specifically targeting these root-causes must therefore accompany more short-term measures targeting corruption as such. Respondents emphasised that there can be no short-term fix:

> 'there is already a certain generation that has grown on this corruption. They just don't imagine that it's possible to live differently and I think it is not that easy to change this consciousness . . . ' (J-K-6); '(anti-corruption work) starting with the upbringing of children in the family, at school and in the institute'. (LB-L-14); 'first we must outlive a certain national catharsis (acknowledging) that it's impossible to live like this any more. It should come from the people . . . ' (ER-N-5); 'more than one generation should pass . . . it is still passed on with the mother's milk . . . ' (J-D-9); 'it is (the) mentality . . . maybe it will change in 100 years . . . ' (J-K-1); 'really nothing (can be done). For this purpose, DNA must be changed'. (LB-K-4)

Elite preferences regarding who should be responsible for anti-corruption efforts

Ukrainian experts occasionally voice their assessment of anti-corruption efforts and their suggestions regarding how best to combat corruption, in the local media or in various expert reports.[84] We know less about their preferences regarding who should actually be

---

83. Rechberger, 'Judicial Independence in Ukraine', 72–3.
84. See, for instance, Serhii Rakhmanin, 'Dobri namiry?', *Dzerkalo tyzhnia,* no. 20 (649), travnia 26–chervnia 1, 2007, http://www.dt.ua/1000/1550/59415/ (accessed February 10, 2010); Liudmyla Shangina, '. . . I rik pry tsiy vlady, abo den' lososia', *Dzerkalo nedeli,* no. 28 (657), serpnia 4–10, 2007, http://www.dt.ua/1000/1550/60021/ (accessed February 10, 2010); Ukrainian academic Yevhen Nevmerzytskiy and political scientist, Andriy Saphonenko have also written on corruption,

Table 4.   Who should be in charge of fighting corruption in Ukraine (in per cent).

	%
Government	20
President	17
Special and independent anti-corruption body	11
Society at large (i.e. the general public)	10
Parliament	9
Judiciary	9
Police	3
Foreign donors, foreign experts	1
Other	19
DK	2
N	(174)

Note: N = total number of text units. Decimals have been rounded up or down to the nearest whole number and numbers therefore do not always add up to 100.

in charge of these efforts. As shown above, Ukrainian elites are not particularly satisfied with anti-corruption efforts carried out by these institutions and organisations to date. It is therefore useful to investigate preferences on the part of the elites regarding (i) who should be in charge of anti-corruption efforts, (ii) their level of trust in these institutions and (iii) their reasons for trusting or distrusting them. Then if institutions supervising anti-corruption efforts are not trusted, the specific policies undertaken by them are less likely to be complied with – even if the quality of the measures targeting corruption are improved.

Anti-corruption activities in Ukraine after the Orange Revolution have been the shared responsibility of the president, government, parliament and the judiciary. The international community has also been fairly active. The latter's efforts have primarily been carried out through INGOs and local NGOs. As seen in Tables 4 and 5, the executive – that is the president and the government – were perceived as the most appropriate hosts of Ukrainian anti-corruption efforts. While the president enjoys a high level of trust amongst elites, government trails somewhat behind. In the view of our respondents a special anti-corruption body, independent of existing political structures and entrusted with widespread powers, would also be useful. Ukrainian elites acknowledge the role of society at large in the struggle against corruption.

Respondents preferring the president to be in charge of domestic anti-corruption efforts pointed out that the presidency is the highest office in the country – an office vested with considerable power. Those preferring the government to take on this task had in mind either the Cabinet of Ministers (majority of statements) or specific branches of government such as the Ministry of the Interior or the Security Service of Ukraine (SBU). A fair share of the respondents preferred both. Since the Orange Revolution, relations between president, government and parliament have been strained. More often than not, these institutions have pulled in different directions. As a result, a number of anti-corruption

---

but their works are not publicly accessible on the internet. See Halyna Kokhan, 'The Challenges of Political Corruption in Ukraine' (paper prepared for the Changing Europe Summer School III. Central and Eastern Europe in a Globalized World, Bremen, July 28–August 2, 2008), http://www.changing-europe.org/download/Summer_School_2008/Kokhan.pdf (accessed July 22, 2009).

Table 5. Trust in institutions (in per cent).

	Most (%)	Least (%)	Net dif (%)
President of Ukraine	18	9	9
Local business	12	2	10
Media	10	12	−2
NGOs	9	1	8
Parliament	8	7	1
Government	7	11	−4
Judiciary	7	17	−10
Foreign business	7	n.a.	7
Government officials	4	6	−2
Public prosecutors	2	10	−8
Foreign donors	2	5	−3
Public procurement officials	n.a.	6	−6
Other	11	10	−10
DK	2	4	−2
N	(123)	(112)	

Note: N = total number of text units. Decimals have been rounded up or down to the nearest whole number and numbers therefore do not always add up to 100.

initiatives have been stalled. In terms of trust, the Ukrainian president enjoys considerably more trust amongst elites than does the government. The net difference between high and low trust in these institutions is 9% for the president and −4% for the government. Trust in both the president and government is primarily linked to the personalities of President Yushchenko and Prime Minister Tymoshenko. Anti-corruption efforts are initiated by the most trusted institution (i.e. the president), whereas one of the least trusted institutions (i.e. the government) is responsible for implementing them:

> '(the initiative must come from) the President . . . because he is the head of state . . . the leader of the nation . . . ' (ER-N-2); 'let it be the President and the Prime Minister, in an informal way . . . these people, their subordinated systems should show that they do not use corruption and live with the help of those means that they have, and that they do not buy suits for 15,000 (hryvnia) on 3,000 hryvnia salaries'. (Pr-K-7); 'I trust the president most of all . . . the president is a person who keeps his word . . . ' (Pr-D-10); 'because the President tries to do something . . . and the parliament and government don't'. (J-D-10); 'the head of the government commands the bigger respect . . . the name of the prime minister – Julia Tymoshenko – speaks for itself . . . ' (ER-L-12); 'at present (the government's) policy is open. They strive to make it transparent . . . '. (LB-K-3)

As already noted, legal measures are the most preferred measure in combating corruption. More specifically, such measures include better or new legislation, better law enforcement and proper punishment for corrupt behaviour. Some respondents therefore thought the judiciary should be in charge of anti-corruption efforts. However, Ukrainian elites are highly critical of judges and to some extent also of public prosecutors.[85] Both groups received the lowest net scores for trust (i.e. the difference in per cent between trust and distrust), at −10% and −8%, respectively. While a fair share of the respondents voiced their distrust in courts without explicitly stating why, the majority indicated that their lack of trust

---

85. Although judges also received a reasonably good score for high trust, most of the statements suggesting that judges may be trusted, were generated by the judges themselves. Four judges, two prosecutors and one elected official expressed high trust in judges.

in judges is due to corruption. In their view, 'everything is for sale' in Ukrainian courts. Courts are plagued by 'bribery', and (legal) 'problems cannot be solved without money':

'the judiciary would be the best, but it is the most corrupt . . . ' (ER-N-5); 'I have the least belief in judges and public prosecutors, because corruption is very developed (in the judiciary)'. (LB-D-8); 'I don't trust judges very much since in our country everything can be bought and sold'. (FB-K-3); 'I trust judges less because there is corruption (in courts). If you have no money you cannot approach (the court) . . . '. (Pr-D-10)

Despite having launched a large number of anti-corruption efforts, neither foreign donors and anti-corruption experts nor local NGOs were perceived as appropriate anti-corruption fighters – even though the latter enjoy considerable trust in Ukrainian society. As concerns the former, Ukrainian elites may resent interference from abroad. Or they may simply not be aware of anti-corruption efforts made on the part of the international community, as such efforts target expert audiences rather than society as such. Our data show that Ukrainian elites are wary of the motives attached to foreign development assistance:

'(I trust) international donors (the least), because they defend their own interests'. (FB-D-8); 'one cannot deal with charity in the political sphere. Such people . . . lobby their program, (their) points of view, therefore I trust them the least'. (Pr-K-5)

Foreign donors in general and American ones in particular, have a preference for involving civil society organisations in anti-corruption efforts. Evidence from post-communist states in South East Europe suggest that anti-corruption NGOs fail to properly coordinate their activities, largely fail to engage the public and also fail to influence state institutions responsible for national anti-corruption efforts.[86] What is more, in many post-communist states NGOs are generally perceived with suspicion given their close links with the international donor community[87] and their generally closed nature.[88] Although donors claim that the NGOs they support do achieve results, few independent reports corroborate such claims.[89] Still, local NGOs enjoy considerable trust amongst Ukrainian elites. However, the latter do not suggest that NGOs should engage in anti-corruption efforts. Besides, none of them referred to anti-corruption activities when explaining why they trust or distrust Ukrainian NGOs. Ukrainian elites predominantly trust NGOs because they are independent of the authorities and for having no vested interests of their own:

'I think that non-governmental organizations are the most trustworthy. If they are real non-governmental organizations then they really do not depend on anybody'. (Pr-D-9); 'I trust NGOs the most, because they . . . have no power, no seats . . . ' (J-D-9); 'I am more inclined

---

86. Martin Tisne and Daniel Smilov, *From the Ground Up. Assessing the Record of Anticorruption Assistance in Southeastern Europe* (Budapest: CPS Policy Studies Series, 2004).
87. Grødeland, 'Public Perceptions of Non-Governmental Organisations'; 'Russia extends Deadline for Obligatory NGOs Registration', *Moscow News,* October 26, 2006, http://www.mosnews.com/news/2006/10/26/deadline.shtml (accessed December 5, 2006).
88. Grødeland, 'Public Perceptions of Non-Governmental Organisations'.
89. Home-grown Ukrainian NGOs receiving limited funding from abroad and having properly committed activists in their midsts appear to have been more successful than 'donor-created' NGOs – with the exception of NGOs such as 'Pora!' that were actively engaged in the Orange Revolution and also fairly heavily supported from abroad. Grødeland, '"Greening" of Ukraine'; Wilson, *Ukraine's Orange Revolution*, 183–9; Katalin E. Koncz, ed., *NGO Sustainability in Central Europe: Helping Civil Society Survive* (Budapest: Opoen Society Institute, 2005).

to trust non-governmental organizations, though I wouldn't say that . . . (my trust in them) is absolute . . . '. (PP-N-1)

We have earlier argued that in order to enhance the impact of anti-corruption efforts these must address not only the manifestations of corruption but also their root causes. Informal practice facilitating corruption is deeply embedded in Ukrainian national culture and the communist past.[90] Anti-corruption measures must therefore also target the mindset of Ukrainian citizens – be they elites or ordinary people. A fairly large share of the statements made by our respondents suggests that a prerequisite for reducing corruption is that society at large be transformed. This finding resonates well with their notion that 'mentality' causes people to behave in a corrupt manner and that for this reason legal and institutional measures are in themselves not sufficient to fight corruption. From our respondents' statements it is clear that awareness of the negative effects of corruption will have to emerge from within society itself. Such awareness cannot be imposed upon society from the outside and there can be no short cuts or easy solutions:

'our society has to mature from within . . . ' (LB-K-6); '(ordinary) people must understand that they should be in charge of this fight, because . . . the authorities cannot initiate this as they are . . . corrupt'. (ER-N-3); 'everybody (should be in charge of the struggle against corruption), starting with the cleaner and ending with the President'. (FB-K-2); 'everybody should do this (i.e. fight corruption) together. A single person (on his own) won't do this'. (PP-K-7)

Conclusions

Anti-corruption programmes in post-communist states have primarily been introduced as a result of pressure on the part of the international community – i.e. 'exported'. In some instances such pressure has been resisted by local political elites who have vested interests in maintaining the status quo. In other instances it has proven difficult to 'translate' vague and all-inclusive anti-corruption programmes into viable anti-corruption policies. Lack of sensitivity to local cultures has further complicated this task. Four factors seem to be particularly relevant as regards the success or failure of Ukrainian anti-corruption efforts: (i) the design and content of the anti-corruption measures; (ii) absence or presence of political will to implement such measures; (iii) public awareness of, and support for, anti-corruption measures and (iv) adequate responses to corrupt individuals, in accordance with current legislation.

As regards the *design and content of the anti-corruption measures*, Ukraine has been under considerable external pressure to reduce corruption. As a non EU applicant state it has not been formally required to adopt the EU's anti-corruption acquis. However, the EU has, through its European Neighbourhood Policy exerted considerable pressure on Ukraine to reduce corruption. The EU and the Council of Europe have actively supported Ukrainian national anti-corruption efforts through its UPAC programme and exposing Ukraine to peer pressure through GRECO. Anti-corruption efforts implemented by Ukrainian authorities thus appear to be the result of 'best practices' having been 'exported' rather than 'imported' to Ukraine. These efforts appear not to have been adequately tailored to suit local conditions. A local business representative indignantly stated that 'it seems to me that all of them (i.e. the anti-corruption decrees) were made on the order from abroad' (LB-L-14).

---

90. Grødeland and Aasland, *Informality and Informal Practices.*

As already noted, international anti-corruption requirements cover a large number of areas and are fairly vague. In addition, they are not sufficiently sensitive to the cultural context – individual as well as institutional – into which they are being introduced. Consequently, 'translating' them into effective policies 'on the ground' is not easy. The discontent expressed by our respondents when referring to Ukrainian anti-corruption policies may in part reflect such problems of 'translation'. Added to this, despite the expressed will of the Ukrainian president and later also government to combat corruption and despite the expressed commitment on the part of all major political parties during the 2007 election campaign to engage in anti-corruption efforts,[91] results have been few and far between. What is more, Ukraine has since the Orange Revolution been plagued by several corruption scandals. Some of the statements made by our respondents seem to suggest that corruption levels dropped sharply immediately after the Orange Revolution as people feared the consequences of being corrupt given the new regime's pledge to combat corruption. Once convinced that corruption would not automatically result in punishment, however, the situation soon returned to 'normal'. Ukraine's score on Transparency International's Corruption Perceptions Index, however, has slightly improved since the Orange Revolution,[92] suggesting that the latter has had some impact on corruption levels. *Absence of political will* when it comes to implementing anti-corruption policies is a problem throughout the post-communist world. This was also the case in Ukraine before the Orange Revolution.[93] Ukrainian elites consider it to be largely absent also at present.[94]

As regards *elite awareness of, and support for, anti-corruption measures* awareness is fairly extensive. However, it has not translated into any significant support neither for the institutions in charge of implementing the measures, nor for the measures themselves. Such measures are perceived as inadequate and the people responsible for implementing them are perceived as incompetent or corrupt. What is more, most of the institutions responsible for Ukrainian anti-corruption efforts enjoy limited trust amongst Ukrainian elites. Lack of trust seems primarily to be a result not only of the perceived quality of the anti-corruption measures as such, or the qualifications of those in charge of implementing them. However, the fact that corrupt behaviour rarely results in criminal proceedings does not help matters. To the extent corrupt officials are dismissed, they seem to simply be replaced by equally corrupt officials. Consequently there are no incentives for not being corrupt. The preference on the part of the majority of our respondents to fight corruption by enforcing existing laws should be understood against this backdrop. As such they also lend some support to Michael's argument that the most effective manner in which to curb corruption is to ensure that judicial institutions work – that is that they are sufficiently independent and provided with adequate resources to properly investigate, prosecute and sanction corrupt behaviour.

In our view, an important flaw of Ukrainian anti-corruption policies is that they fail to address the root causes of corruption – such as informal behaviour shaped by social norms

---

91. For an overview of the anti-corruption platforms of Ukrainian political parties ahead of the 2007 parliamentary elections, see Neutze and Karatnycky, *Corruption, Democracy and Investment in Ukraine*, 24–9.
92. See note 2.
93. Wilson refers to estimates suggesting that 300 out of the 450 Ukrainian MPs who entered parliament in 2002 were dollar millionaires. Wilson, *Ukraine's Orange Revolution*, 149.
94. Grødeland, 'Cultural Constants, Corruption and the Orange Revolution', 97: some 49% of all statements given in response to the question 'do you think there is sufficient political will in this country to reduce the level of corruption?' suggested that such will is absent, though 32% suggested the opposite.

rooted in the country's historical, cultural and political past. As we have shown previously, such behaviour to quite some extent motivates corrupt practice. Survey data indicate that Ukrainians are generally negative to corruption. However although they are against being forced to give bribes they are not necessarily against voluntarily giving them to somebody if this might help them solve their problems (faster) or to gain unlawful advantages.[95] It would therefore be wrong to refer to Ukrainian citizens simply as victims of corruption. They are also accomplices.[96] Added to this, to the extent Ukrainian citizens perceive corruption as a problem, they have no real incentive to discontinue giving bribes themselves as long as they perceive other people as being corrupt. The prisoner's dilemma is thus a very real dilemma for many Ukrainians and not one which is likely to find a solution in the near future.

In their effort to introduce swift political, economic and judicial reform in the former communist states and consequently turn them into Western-style democracies, international organisations and foreign donors have at best overlooked, at worst ignored, the need to accompany such efforts with measures aimed to change the mindset both of those in charge of implementing these measures as well as those affected by them. Our respondents' preference for fighting corruption also by changing people's 'mentality' and 'society at large', as well as their call for involving the general public in anti-corruption efforts to bring about such change, should be acknowledged and endorsed. Efforts in this direction will, as respondents rightly point out, have to be long-term and they are not likely to produce immediate results. Building awareness around corruption as an issue is a prioritised issue on the part of the international community. Seeking to build awareness through internationally funded 'designer' NGOs may not be the most suitable, indeed not even the only, suitable forum. Some of our respondents suggested that involving the Orthodox Church may be an appropriate alternative.

Acknowledgements

I would like to thank the editors of the special issue on 'Anti-Corruption for Eastern Europe' for inviting me to contribute an article on Ukraine and also the anonymous reviewers for their useful comments and suggestions.

Notes on contributor

Åse Berit Grødeland works as senior researcher at the Chr. Michelsen Institute in Bergen, Norway. She has previously held positions at University of Glasgow, International Crisis Group and the Norwegian Institute for Urban and Regional Research. Currently she is directing projects on informal practice and corruption and on European legal cultures in transition. Recent publications include 'Culture, Corruption and the Orange Revolution', in *Ukraine on its Way to Europe? Interim Results of the Orange Revolution*, ed. Juliane Besters-Dilger (Frankfurt am Main: Peter Lang, 2009), 79–102; and 'Informal Practice, Cultural Capital and Politics in the Czech Republic, Slovenia, Bulgaria and Romania', in *State and Society in Post-Socialist Economies*, ed. John Pickles (Basingstoke, Hampshire/New York, NY: Palgrave/Macmillan, 2008), 229–52.

---

95. Miller, Grødeland, and Koshechkina, *Culture of Corruption?*
96. Ibid.

Experience versus perception of corruption: Russia as a test case

Richard Rose[a] and William Mishler[b]

[a]Centre for the Study of Public Policy, University of Aberdeen, Aberdeen, Scotland, UK;
[b]Department of Political Science, University of Arizona, Tucson, AZ, USA

Corruption is important because it undermines bureaucratic predictability and is a potential threat to support for a political regime. The perception of corruption is the most commonly used measure of the actual incidence of corruption. This article marshals the New Russia Barometer survey data to challenge this assumption. Even though most Russians perceive a variety of everyday public services as corrupt, this assessment is not based on first-hand experience. Only a minority pays bribes. We test four hypotheses about differences in individual perception and experience of paying bribes: the ability to pay, contact with public services, normative acceptability and political awareness. Contact is most important for paying bribes whereas political awareness is most important for the perception of corruption. We also test how much the perception and experience of corruption, as against other forms of political and economic perform-ance, affect support for the regime. Support is driven by the substantive performance of government, especially its management of the economy, rather than by the perception or experience of corruption.

Political corruption, the misuse of public power for private material gain, is important as an indicator that institutions of governance fall short of the Weberian paradigm of political sys-tems that operate predictably by bureaucrats impersonally applying rules and laws and pol-icy-makers accepting their constraints when making decisions.[1] The cash cost is higher when corruption involves large government purchases, but the number of people affected is much greater when corruption involves health care and education services affecting many millions of citizens. In the former case, the cost of wholesale corruption is indirectly distributed and in small sums to individuals in the population, whereas in the case of 'retail' corruption the payer of the bribe bears the whole burden. In so far as decisions affected by corruption result in the misallocation or waste of public funds or in illegal and criminal activities that are inef-ficient and costly, then corruption reduces the benefits of economic growth to society as a whole. This is a problem of particular importance in developing countries.[2]

---

1. This article was prepared with the assistance of a grant from the British ESRC(RES-062-23-03441) Testing the Durability of Regime Support.
2. See, for example, Michael Johnston, *Syndromes of Corruption: Wealth, Power and Democracy* (New York: Cambridge University Press, 2005); Susan Rose-Ackerman, *Corruption and Government: Causes Consequences and Reform* (New York: Cambridge University Press, 1999); and Vito Tanzi, 'Corruption Around the World', in *Governance, Corruption and Economic Performance*, ed. G. Abed and S. Gupta (Washington, DC: International Monetary Fund, 2002), 19–58.

In democratic political systems, making decisions on the basis of illegal payments is a departure from accountability to the electorate. Corruption can breed popular distrust in government with consequences for lower participation in politics and support for protest parties or, in authoritarian regimes, demonstrations that may even lead to regime change.[3] In societies in which there is widespread awareness of corruption and a belief that everybody is doing it, an equilibrium can be arrived at in which public officials and citizens engage in 'I-let-you-corrupt-me-and-you-let-me-corrupt-you' transactions[4] until an 'optimal' level of corruption is achieved.[5] Thus, corruption can maintain a 'low level equilibrium trap' that becomes 'the natural result of efficient predatory behaviour in a lawless world'.[6]

In principle the substance of corruption – the exchange of money or tangible benefits for identifiable public services – is observable. Therefore, it should be less difficult to collect empirical evidence of corruption than to measure an abstract concept such as democracy. However, because corruption is illegal, participants in corrupt political practices normally conceal such activities. Individual cases of corruption offer a starting point for analysis. Journalists, lawyers and historians provide thick descriptions of particular cases involving the payment of a large sum of money to an individual politician or party to obtain the passage of legislation, an administrative ruling, a license to exploit natural resources or a multi-million dollar contract from the government. If the media obtains evidence of such an activity, the prominence of those involved is headline news. Opposition politicians and anti-corruption campaigners have an incentive to encourage the belief that the government as a whole is corrupt.[7] Ethnographers can draw on experience of living in a village or being embedded in street corner activities to produce a thick description of corruption in a given community. However, the generalisability of a single example is problematic.

The most commonly used measure is the perception of corruption.[8] It is assumed that perceptions of corruption provide a reliable if not perfectly accurate indicator of the extent to which corruption actually exists in a society. Perceptions of corruption can also be treated as important correlates of political attitudes and behaviour. The Corruption Perception

---

3. See, for example, Christopher J. Anderson and Y.V. Tverdova, 'Corruption, Political Allegiances and Attitudes Toward Government in Contemporary Democracies', *American Journal of Political Science* 47, no. 1 (2003): 91–109 and Mitchell A. Seligson, 'The Impact of Corruption on Regime Legitimacy: A Comparative Study of Four Latin American Countries', *Journal of Politics* 64, 2 (2002): 408–33.

4. Elemer Hankiss, 'Games of Corruption: East Central Europe, 1945–1999', in *Political Corruption in Transition: A Sceptic's Handbook*, ed. S. Kotkin and A. Sajo (Budapest: Central European University Press, 2002), 248.

5. Eram Dabla-Norris, 'A Game Theoretic Analysis of Corruption in Bureaucracies', in *Governance, Corruption, and Economic Performance*, ed. G. Abed and S. Gupta (Washington, DC: International Monetary Fund, 2002), 111–34.

6. Joel S. Hellman, 'Winners Take All: The Politics of Partial Reform in Postcommunist Transitions', *World Politics* 50 (1998): 203–34 and Joshua Charap and Christian Harm, 'Institutionalized Corruption and the Kleptocratic State', in *Governance, Corruption, and Economic Performance*, ed. G. Abed and S. Gupta (Washington, DC: International Monetary Fund, 2002), 137.

7. C. McManus-Czubinska, W.L. Miller, R. Markowski, and J. Wasilewski, 'Why Is Corruption in Poland "A Serious Cause for Concern"?' *Crime, Law and Social Change* 41 (2004): 107–32.

8. For reviews, see Johann Graf Lambsdorff, *The Institutional Economics of Corruption and Reform* (Cambridge: Cambridge University Press, 2007); Daniel Treisman, 'What Have We Learned about the Causes of Corruption from Ten Years of Cross-National Empirical Research?', *Annual Review of Political Science* 10 (2007): 211–44; Global Integrity, *A User's Guide to Measuring Corruption* (New York: United Nations Development Programme, 2008); and Diana Schmidt, 'Anti-corruption: What Do We Know? Research on Preventing Corruption in the Post-Communist World', *Political Studies Review* 5, no. 2 (2007): 202–33.

Index (CPI) of Transparency International (TI) is the best-known example. Its purpose is to characterise the political system as a whole and it does so in more than 150 countries worldwide. Its raw data come from a multiplicity of desk-based studies and interviews with elites likely to be in the know about how decisions are made in one or more countries. They are asked to assess the level of corruption in national governments familiar to them, drawing on their own undisclosed experience, what they are told by others whom they know in policy-making circles, and on the government's reputation. The Index converts these assessments into a standard set of metrics to assign a government a single Index rating from 10, least perception to 1, most perception.[9] Similarly, the World Bank includes an evaluation of transparency, accountability and corruption as part of its international system of governance indicators.[10]

Methodologies for scoring countries have attracted a variety of critiques.[11] Aggregate indexes do not specify the context in which bribes are paid, whether to secure a big public works contract or a simple local service. It is thus not possible to differentiate perceptual judgements based on a single outstanding case of elite corruption from low-level corruption in the delivery of everyday services to ordinary citizens. There is also a danger of 'echo chamber' effects, as evaluators repeat the conventional wisdom about particular countries, in part reflecting awareness of TI's rating of a country. Such an interpretation is consistent with the strong correlation between different aggregate corruption indexes; these are indicators of reliability but not necessarily of substantive validity.

Public opinion surveys can ask about mass perceptions of corruption in government as a whole. In addition, questions can be asked of individuals about their experience of corruption. For example, TI has begun to include a short module of questions about the experience of corruption in a 60-country global survey organised by Gallup International (http://www.transparency.org/). The surveys, however, do not collect data of social science interest about the consequences of individuals perceiving or experiencing corruption. Although aggregate indexes of perception give the impression that 'everybody is doing it', surveys of individuals find that the percentage of people having experience of bribery is limited to a minority.

The use of perceptual measures to analyse corruption can be justified by W.I. Thomas's theorem: 'If men define situations as real, they are real in their consequences'.[12] National indexes of the perception of corruption can be related to other holistic characteristics, such as a country's level of democracy, or to growth in its Gross Domestic Product. Such assessments normally find that corruption depresses economic growth and is also negatively correlated with the levels of democracy.[13] Survey-derived measures of individual perception can be related to individual attitudes towards the political system. If a regime is

---

9. See http://www.transparency.org/policy_research/surveys_indices/cpi/2009.
10. See www.governance.org; Daniel Kaufmann, Aart Kraay, and Massimo Mastruzzi, *Governance Matters VI: Aggregate and Individual Governance Indicators, 1996–2006* (Washington, DC: World Bank Policy Research Working Paper 4280, 2007).
11. See Christine Arndt and Charles Oman, *Uses and Abuses of Governance Indicators* (Paris: OECD Development Centre Studies, 2006) and Stephen Knack, 'Measuring Corruption: A Critique of Indicators in Eastern Europe and Central Asia', *Journal of Public Policy* 27, no. 3 (2007): 255–92.
12. W.I. Thomas, *The Unadjusted Girl* (Boston: Little Brown, 1923).
13. George T. Abed and Sanjeev Gupta, eds., *Governance, Corruption and Economic Performance* (Washington, DC: International Monetary Fund, 2002) and Johann Graf Lambsdorff, *The Institutional Economics of Corruption and Reform* (Cambridge: Cambridge University Press, 2007): Chapter 5.

widely perceived as corrupt, this may substantially depress trust in political institutions and support for the regime[14] and foster an 'uncivic' or exploitative culture among subjects.[15]

The object of this article is to test empirically whether mass perceptions of corruption are an accurate proxy for the experience of corruption; whether the causes of perceptions and experience are the same or different and what consequences such attitudes and experience have for support for the political system. It draws on the New Russia Barometer (NRB) survey, which has a full module of questions about the experience as well as the perception of corruption. Russia is a suitable test case for analysis because corruption was integral to the working of Communist political systems and its persistence since then has been persistently denounced by Vladimir Putin with little observable effect. As it is a major emerging market, corruption in Russia is also of major concern to foreign investors and to the World Bank.[16] The TI Index consistently evaluates corruption there as high by both comparative and absolute standards.

Theories of corruption

Although aggregate measures of corruption are limited to testing theories about the systemic causes and consequences of corruption, survey data from individuals make it possible to test attitudinal and behavioural theories about why people living in the same political system differ in their experience and perception of corruption and its consequences.

Why people pay bribes

Hypothesis 1 (Ability to pay). Bribe-paying varies with the ability of individuals to meet the cost of a bribe. Economic theories of crime and corruption adopt a clinical cost–benefit approach.[17] Bribery is deemed acceptable if you get what you pay for. Public services that would be expensive to buy privately, such as a place in a good school or privileged medical treatment, offer profit to providers and cash savings to those who can pay a bribe. An ability to pay predicts that higher income citizens will be more likely to engage in bribery because they can. Alternatively, theories of inequality propose a victimisation hypothesis: those who are poor and uneducated are more likely to be forced to pay bribes because they lack the non-pecuniary resources for obtaining services without bribery.

Hypothesis 2 (Contact). Bribe-paying varies with the extent to which individuals contact public services. An alternative theory is that the likelihood of paying a bribe depends on the need to make use of public services. The more contacts that people have with public services, then *ceteris paribus* the more likely they are to pay a bribe. Contact with services varies with the life cycle; older people do not have children of school age and have little

14. cf. Donatella Della Porta and Yves Meny, eds., *Democracy and Corruption in Europe* (London: Pinter, 1996); Susan J. Pharr and Robert D. Putnam, ed., *Disaffected Democracies: What's Troubling the Trilateral Countries?* (Princeton: Princeton University Press, 2000), 173; and Mitchell A. Seligson, The Impact of Corruption on Regime Legitimacy: A Comparative Study of Four Latin American Countries, *Journal of Politics* 64, no. 2 (2002): 408–33.

15. cf. Edward Banfield, *The Moral Basis of a Backward Society* (Glencoe, IL: The Free Press, 1958).

16. For example, Joel S. Hellman, 'Winners Take All: The Politics of Partial Reform in Postcommunist Transitions', *World Politics* 50 (1998): 203–34; Rasma Karklins, *The System Made Me Do It* (Armonk, NY: M.E. Sharpe, 2005); and S. Kotkin and A. Sajo, eds., *Political Corruption in Transition: A Sceptic's Handbook* (Budapest: Central European University Press, 2002).

17. Gary Becker, 'Crime and Punishment: An Economic Approach', *Journal of Political Economy* 76 (1968): 169–217.

contact with educational institutions and officials whereas younger people do not seek medical services as much as their elders. Insofar as contact is also affected by social status, low-income people may experience less corruption by virtue of being excluded from ready access to public services.

Hypothesis 3 (Awareness). The more individuals hear about corruption in public services, the more likely they are to pay bribes. Awareness of bribery need not come from experience. It can be created through conversations and observations within one's community or media reports of cases of corruption nationally. Anti-corruption campaigns heighten awareness of corruption as part of a pressure group strategy to force political leaders to take steps to reduce the level of corruption. However, the first step, raising awareness, may succeed much more than the second, stopping corruption.

Hypothesis 4 (Everybody's doing it). The more individuals perceive paying bribes as normal and legitimate, the more likely they are to pay bribes. Anti-corruption campaigners denounce bribery as normatively wrong. For example, Gambetta[18] describes corruption as the degradation of agents' ethical sense, their lack of moral integrity or even their depravity. However, norms can also refer to operational rules for behaviour. If corruption is considered normal, that is, 'everybody's doing it', then people may decide to go along with prevailing practices and pay a bribe.[19]

Why people perceive government as corrupt

Hypothesis 5. The degree to which government is perceived as corrupt reflects experience of the payment of bribes. This hypothesis builds on the foregoing discussion. It postulates that people who make use of public services often pay bribes and therefore will be more likely to perceive government as corrupt. Insofar as paying a bribe is both a necessary and a sufficient condition for perceiving government as corrupt, then measures of perception can be treated as equivalent to evidence of the payment of bribes.

However, experience of government is not necessary to form judgements about political institutions.[20] Survey research finds that many people are willing to offer personal assessments about the trust and integrity of many national institutions with which they have little or no contact. Their assessments are second hand based on national television and press or informal discussions with others who act as opinion leaders and establish a consensus within a face-to-face group. Depending on the extent to which media reports and opinion-leader attitudes about corruption are themselves second hand, then public assessments may be third or even fourth hand. This is the basis of Hypothesis 3.

Consequences for regime support

Corruption is not only important in itself, but also because of its potential political consequences. When a citizen must pay a bribe to receive a public service, the public official

---

18. Diego Gambetta, 'Corruption: an Analytical Map', in *Political Corruption in Transition: A Sceptic's Handbook*, ed. S. Kotkin and A. Sajo (Budapest: Central European University Press, 2002), 33–56.
19. Bo Rothstein, 'Social Trust and Honesty in Government: A Causal Mechanisms Approach, in *Creating Social Trust in Post-Socialist Transition*, ed. Janos Kornai, Bo Rothstein, and Susan Rose-Ackerman (Basingstoke: Palgrave Macmillan, 2004), 20–21.
20. William Mishler and Richard Rose, Seeing Is Not Believing: Measuring Corruption Perceptions and Experiences (paper presented at Midwest Political Science Association, Annual Meeting, Chicago, April 2–5, 2009).

benefits whereas the citizen not only loses money but also may feel aggrieved at being exploited. When a million-dollar bribe is paid by a private-sector company to public or party officials to secure a multi-million dollar contract from the government, from the participants' perspective this may appear to be a 'win–win' outcome, because the bribe payer gains a contract and the public official gains a material benefit. The taxpayer loses, however, and insofar as such cases occur frequently, this may have negative consequences for the public perception of government as a whole.

Hypothesis 6. The more individuals perceive government as corrupt or themselves pay bribes, the less likely they are to support the political regime. Political performance is regarded as of central importance for support for a political regime[21] and the extent to which political institutions deal honestly or corruptly with the public is integral to political performance. In David Easton's[22] model of a political system, political support is generated through a continuing interaction between the demands of the public, the response of government and the feedback of this information to citizens. Insofar as people expect government to treat each person fairly, then a higher degree of corruption, however, measured, should reduce support for the political regime.

Hypothesis 7. The better a regime's overall economic and political performance, the less effect corruption will have on support for the political system. Theories of political support are multivariate: even if corruption is recognised as contributing to support, it may be only one influence among many. A host of theories predict that support depends on economic performance.[23] Citizens may be more influenced in their political judgements by the payoff from a buoyant economy than by any side payments that government officials receive or that they are required to pay to use public services. For example, this is important in the claim of the People's Republic of China for mass support of a regime that delivers high economic growth and a high level of political corruption.

There is widespread agreement among theorists that corruption detracts from the quality of democracy.[24] Although statistical evidence can often be found that measures of corruption have a negative effect on political support, it may often be offset by other measures of political performance, such as the maintenance of democratic electoral competition, personal freedom and, in some cases, the appeal of political personalities. If a regime is perceived as corrupt but as relatively free and fair, then it may be supported on the grounds that it is a lesser evil than alternative regimes that are undemocratic as well as unfree.[25]

21. Russell Dalton, *Democratic Challenges, Democratic Choices: The Erosion of Political Support in Advanced Industrial Democracies* (Oxford: Oxford University Press, 2004).

22. David Easton, *A Systems Analysis of Political Life* (New York: John Wiley, 1965).

23. W. van der Brug, C. van der Eljk, and M. Franklin, *The Economy and the Vote* (New York: Cambridge University Press, 2007); Raymond Duch and Randolph T. Stevenson, *The Economic Vote: How Political and Economic Institutions Condition Election Results* (New York: Cambridge University Press, 2008).

24. See, for example, Leonardo Morlino, 'Good' and 'Bad' Democracies: How to Conduct Research into the Quality of Democracy, *Journal of Communist Studies and Transition Politics* 20, no. 1 (2004): 5–27.

25. See Richard Rose, William Mishler, and Christian Haerpfer, *Democracy and Its Alternatives: Understanding Post-Communist Societies* (Oxford: Polity Press and Baltimore: Johns Hopkins University Press, 1998) and William Mishler and Richard Rose, 'Political Support for Incomplete Democracies: Realist vs. Idealist Theories and Measures', *International Political Science Review* 22, no. 4 (2001): 303–20.

Measuring the incidence of corruption

Because corruption usually involves exchanges between public officials and citizens or organisations outside government, people can learn from their own experience and direct observation whether public officials are corrupt. Just as crime victimisation surveys can collect data about experiences not recorded by the police, so a nationwide corruption survey is even more likely to uncover evidence than that found in official documents and court records.

A survey turns attention from elite corruption involving large sums of money on a grand scale to petty corruption involving the payment of small sums for the delivery of public services to large numbers of citizens. It also raises questions of the meaning of terms in colloquial language. The academic literature is replete with the classification of concepts by which rules can be 'bent' or 'broken' to get things done. In Russian, the term 'blat' is used to describe the use of connections to get prompt action on a legal request or a favourable ruling on a request that violates the law; the Chinese use a similar term to describe connections, 'guanxi'.[26] Favouritism can be shown when public officials give preference to friends or friends of friends in expediting actions without breaking rules. When this is systematically organised, it can become clientelism. Bribery goes further, it involves a public official breaking a rule in exchange for a bribe, that is, cash or some other significant material benefit. It thus differs from 'gratitude' offerings of money or incidentals, such as fresh eggs, flowers or some other gift after a public official has provided a benefit.

The analysis that follows draws on a module of questions about corruption and bribery included in the fifteenth NRB survey fielded on behalf of the Centre for the Study of Public Policy by Russia's oldest not-for-profit survey institute, the Levada Centre (http://www.levada.ru/). A nationwide stratified random sample of 1606 adults was interviewed at home between 12 and 23 April 2007.[27] Although a single-country survey cannot claim to be globally representative, for four decades Russia was the central reference point for governments of hundreds of millions of people.[28] Moreover, the transformation of Communist into post-Communist regimes in the 1990s created many opportunities for corrupt behaviour through the privatisation of state-owned assets.[29] Presidents Vladimir Putin and Dmitry Medvedev have frequently spoken of the need to 'do something' about corruption in Russian government. A Google search of the terms Putin and corruption turns up 2,480,000 entries, and a comparable search for Medvedev returns 463,000 entries. The substantial level of corruption perceived in Russia places it closer to the median country on the TI Index. However, this leaves open whether the experience of ordinary Russians matches what is reflected in TI's perception-based aggregate Index.

Public officials widely perceived as corrupt

When the NRB asks the broad question – How widespread do you think bribe-taking and corruption are among public officials? – the result is unambiguous: five-sixths of Russians

---

26. Mayfair Mei-hui Yang, *Gifts, Favors and Banquets: The Art of Social Relationships in China* (Ithaca: Cornell University Press, 1994) and Alena V. Ledeneva, *Russia's Economy of Favours* (Cambridge: Cambridge University Press, 1998).

27. For the full text of the questionnaire and the sample report, see Rose, 2007.

28. Rasma Karklins, *The System Made Me Do It* (Armonk, NY: M.E. Sharpe, 2005).

29. See Chrystia Freeland, *Sale of the Century: The Inside Story of the Second Russian Revolution* (London: Little Brown, 2000) and Paul Klebnikov, *Godfather of the Kremlin: Boris Berezovsky and the Looting of Russia* (New York: Harcourt Brace, 2000). While carrying out further investigations into corruption in Russian government, Paul Klebnikov was murdered in Moscow in 2004.

perceive most officials as corrupt. The only difference is between the 35% who believe that 'almost all' public officials are corrupt and the 51% thinking 'most' officials are corrupt. Only 9% say that 'less than half' of officials are corrupt and 5% think 'very few' lack integrity. These views are consistent with perceptions of specific public officials and institutions. For example, only 20% of NRB respondents trust the police and less than one in eight trust members of parliament or political parties.

Generalised perceptions, like the aggregate TI Index, are consistent with ideal-type 'vending machine' theories of bureaucratic administration[30] that treat all kinds of public services as procedurally uniform. However, such theories fail to take into account the differences between public services that can affect the capacity of public officials to extract bribes. Klitgaard[31] postulates that corruption is most likely to occur under two conditions: public officials are unaccountable monopoly suppliers and they also have substantial discretion. At high levels of government, contracts for the purchase of military hardware involve few potential suppliers, technical specifications that inhibit transparency and large sums of money. At the street level, police can take decisions without supervision by superiors and a teacher can award a student a good grade without further verification.[32] By contrast, there is far less discretion in the computerised calculation of pension payments based on information obtained from a computerised database of social security payments. An important implication is that it is misleading to characterise the whole of government as corrupt, as the extent of corruption is not constant within government.

To test the pervasiveness of the perception of corruption, Russians were also asked the extent to which they perceive a variety of public institutions as corrupt. Instead of focusing on national institutions such as the Duma, which are remote from everyday experience or only known through the national media, the NRB survey asked about seven public services found in every community, that respondents are likely to know about from their own experience or that of other members of their family or friends. Most of these services give officials a degree of discretion, including that of professionals whose skills are difficult to challenge, such as doctors or teachers.

The extent to which Russians see specific public services as corrupt varies substantially. A total of 89% regard most police as corrupt, and more than three in four see hospitals and doctors as corrupt. Two-thirds or more regard most schools, the military, offices issuing permits and tax inspectors as corrupt. The most bureaucratised service, social security, where the qualification for a pension is based on a birth certificate, employment records and payments routinely entered in the public record, is least likely to be seen as filled with corrupt officials (Figure 1).

Actual experience of corruption is limited

Following questions about perceptions, NRB respondents were asked whether in dealing with any of seven public services did they or anyone in their family pay a bribe.[33] In economic terms each is a private good because access could be restricted to those who pay

---

30. Max Weber, *The Theory of Social and Economic Organization* (Glencoe, IL: The Free Press, 1947).
31. Robert E. Klitgaard, *Controlling Corruption* (Berkeley: University of California Press, 1988), 75.
32. Michael Lipsky, *Street-Level Bureaucracy: Dilemmas of the Individual in Public Services* (New York: Russell Sage, 1980).
33. The Russian word used, *vzyatka*, has similar connotations to the English word for bribe.

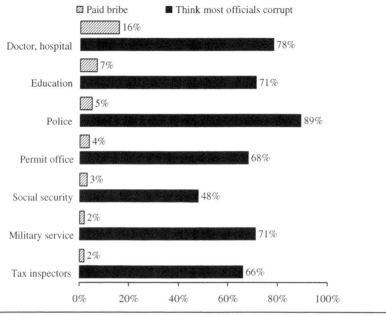

Q. To what extent do you see the following institutions as affected by corruption?
Q. In dealing with any of these institutions in the past two years, was it necessary for you or anyone in your household to give a bribe?

[Number of respondents: 1,606.]
Source: Centre for the Study of Public Policy, New Russia Barometer XV, 13–24 April, 2007.

Figure 1.   Gap between perception and experience of corruption.

for it and those who do not pay could be excluded, even if they have a legal entitlement.[34] The time frame was the past 2 years to avoid memories of Communist times, while capturing interactions that might not occur annually, such as contacting the police or a tax office.

Although big majorities see public services as corrupt, the proportion reporting that their household has recently paid a bribe for a public service ranges from 2% to 16% (Figure 1). It was lowest for tax inspectors and military service, and almost as low for social security and for permit offices. Bribery was most often mentioned in two pillars of the welfare state, education and medical treatment. Even though these services may be nominally free, nonetheless officials can collect bribes for making them available or for giving better treatment to patients or better marks to pupils.

In the absolute sense, the percentage of Russians reporting the payment of a bribe is very low. In a cross-national context, however, it is not so low. The proportion of people paying bribes is lower in old member states of the European Union, whereas it is similarly

34. Taxation, encounters with the police and military service may colloquially be described as private 'bads'. As such, people have an even greater incentive to pay a bribe in order not to be subject to such exactions.

high in most post-Communist states of Eastern Europe and even higher in many develop-ing countries in other continents.[35]

The gap between perception and experience is greatest for the police: whereas 89% regard most police as corrupt only 5% report anyone in their household paying a bribe in the past 2 years. The gap between perception and experience is not quite as high for education and for health care, but that is because the incidence of paying bribes is higher.

The perception of corruption cannot be treated as a proxy for experience; a big majority of those perceiving corruption do not base their judgement on personal experience of pay-ing bribes. The correlation between a generalised perception of corruption and paying a bribe is surprisingly weak ($r = 0.09$). As far more people perceive government as corrupt than pay a bribe, the consequence is that 75% of Russians who see most officials as corrupt have not had anyone in their family pay a bribe in the past 2 years.

The gap between perceptions and experience of corruption is a caution against assum-ing that what people say about government is what they experience in their everyday lives. Moreover, it is consistent with surveys in other continents that have found the experience of corruption far below what perception data imply.[36] On a priori grounds, it could be argued that Russian respondents are unwilling to speak openly to an unknown interviewer, but surveys have documented that this is not the case,[37] and people who are made to pay bribes have an incentive to complain about this experience. Another explanation is that paying a bribe leaves an impression of generalised corruption that endures for many years after the event. Insofar as this may be true, it would undermine the validity of the perception of corruption as an indicator of current corruption.

Testing causes of experience and perception

The hypotheses outlined above can, up to a point, be applied to both the experience and perception of corruption. However, the big difference in their incidence implies a need to test the hypotheses separately and this is also consistent with the two measures being set in different theoretical contexts. The NRB collects a multiplicity of indicators suitable for testing each hypothesis (see Appendix for details). However, statistical analysis shows that their salience is not the same for the two dependent variables.

Paying bribes

Because most households make use of multiple public services, the cumulative reach of corruption is noteworthy. A total of 23% report that someone in their household had paid a

---

35. European Commission, *The Attitudes of Europeans towards Corruption* (Brussels: Special Euro-barometer 291, 2008) and Transparency International, *Report on the Transparency International Global Corruption Barometer 2006* (Berlin: Transparency International, 2006).
36. Mitchell A. Seligson, 'The Impact of Corruption on Regime Legitimacy: A Comparative Study of Four Latin American Countries', *Journal of Politics* 64, no. 2 (2002): 418ff.; Mireille Razafindrakoto and François Roubaud, 'How Far Can We Trust Expert Opinions on Corruption? An Experiment Based on Surveys in Francophone Africa', in *Global Corruption Report 2005* (London: Pluto Press, 2005), 292–5; William L. Miller, Ase B. Grodeland and T.Y. Koshechkina, *A Culture of Corruption?* (Budapest: Central European University Press, 2001), Tables 4.5, 4.6; Transparency International, *Report on the Transparency International Global Corruption Barometer 2006* (Berlin: Transparency International, 2006); and European Commission, *The Attitudes of Europeans towards Corruption* (Brussels: Special Eurobarometer 291, 2008).
37. Richard Rose, 'Going Public with Private Opinions: Are Post-Communist Citizens Afraid to Say What They Think?', in *Journal of Elections and Public Opinion* 17, no. 2 (2007): 123–42.

Table 1. Influences on paying bribes.

Dependent variable: number of bribes paid 0–7				
Variance accounted for:	1.6%	14.3%	18.7%	21.3%
	Beta	Beta	Beta	Beta
H1: Capacity to pay				
Age	−0.11***	−0.07**	−0.04	−0.04
Education	0.03	0.01	0.00	−0.01
Social status	−0.02	−0.02	0.01	−0.01
Income quartile	0.04	0.05	0.03	0.02
Female	−0.00	0.00	0.00	−0.01
H2: Contact with officials				
Number of contacts	–	0.36***	0.35***	0.35***
H3: Political awareness				
Learn from friends	–	–	–	0.11***
Learn from what I see	–	–	–	0.10***
Learn from media	–	–	–	0.06*
Political interest	–	–	–	0.01
H4: Everybody is (not) doing it				
Bribery acceptable	–	–	0.18***	0.16***
Perception of corruption	–	–	0.10***	0.05*

Number of respondents: 1606.
***Significant at 0.00, **Significant at 0.01, *Significant at 0.05.
Source: Centre for the Study of Public Policy, New Russia Barometer XV, 13–24 April, 2007.

bribe in the past 2 years, including 10% who paid bribes for more than one public service. Thus, our dependent variable is the number of bribes that the respondent's household has paid.[38] From the full-length NRB survey, initially we chose more than two dozen indicators of potential influences on paying a bribe. Those that added nothing significant were dropped. The results reported in Table 1 concentrate on those indicators that significantly influence the likelihood of paying a bribe or else are important because they provide evidence of a lack of support for the above hypotheses. Given the importance of different hypotheses, a series of ordinary least squares regressions were run in which indicators relevant to different hypotheses were added sequentially.

Contrary to Hypothesis 1, bribe-paying is not influenced by individual ability to pay or vulnerability to being exploited (Table 1). Income has no significant influence on bribe-paying. Likewise, individuals with less education and lower social status are not especially likely to be victimised by having to pay a bribe for nominally free entitlements. Age is the only social-economic influence that initially appears significant, but this is not sustained when additional hypotheses are tested. Altogether, five socio-economic indicators at most account for only 1.6% of the variance in the payment of bribes.

To test Hypothesis 2, bribe-paying varies with the use of public services, questions were asked about whether anyone in the respondent's household has had contact with each of seven public services in the past 2 years. Even though the services are locally available, from two-thirds to seven-eighths of Russian households have not had contact with six of

---

38. Since there is a skew distribution in the number of bribes paid, we also ran regression equations which collapsed respondents into three categories, paying a bribe more than once, paying a bribe once, and not paying a bribe. The results are the same as those reported here.

Table 2.   Contacts with services and payment of bribes.

Q. In the past two years have you or anyone in your household contacted any of the following public institutions?

Q. (IF answer is yes, there was contact) In dealing with this institution, was it necessary to pay a bribe?

	No contact	*Contact*	
		No bribe (% all respondents)	Bribe
Doctor, hospital	24	60	16
Police	75	20	5
Education	74	19	7
Permit office	78	19	4
Social security	67	30	3
Army recruiting	84	14	2
Tax inspectors	87	11	2

Note: Number of respondents: 1606.
Source: Centre for the Study of Public Policy, New Russia Barometer XV, 13–24 April 2007.

them (Table 2). The health service is the only public institution with which a majority of Russian households have a regular contact. However, because contacts are cumulative, 84% have been in contact with at least one public service in a 2-year period. Moreover, the median household has used two public services and 10% have contacted as many as five. When all of a household's contacts with public services are taken into account, Russians divide into three groups: 23% have had contacts that included payment of a bribe; 61% have had contact with public officials without paying a bribe and the remaining 16% have not been vulnerable to corruption because they have not had any contact with a public service.

Contact with public services does have a major influence on the payment of bribes. After controlling for capacity to pay, the more contacts a household has with public services, the more likely people are to pay a bribe. The effect is strong as well as significant; it boosts the amount of variance accounted for from almost nothing to 14.3% (Table 1).

Hypotheses 3 and 4 emphasise awareness of corruption as an important influence on paying bribes, insofar as it encourages people to regard bribery as both normal behaviour and normatively acceptable. To identify how people become aware of the possibility of corruption without experiencing it, the NRB survey asks: There are different ways in which people learn about corruption. To what extent are your views informed by what you learn from the media and television, friends and neighbours, what you see on the street around you and at work? National television and newspapers are by far the most important sources of information: 86% say they learn a lot or something about corruption from these media. Talking with friends and neighbours is considered important by 73%. What people see in the streets around them comes third, 59%, whereas 49% find that work provides information about corruption.

When Russians are asked whether corruption is acceptable if it is the only way to get what you want from a public official, more than two-thirds say it is not, whereas 29% adopt the pragmatic view that it is. After controlling for contact with public services, those who view bribery as an acceptable means of working the system are significantly more likely to pay a bribe. The perception that public services are corrupt has some influence too, but its effect is weaker (Table 1).

Learning about corruption from friends and what you see yourself has the most influence. Because the media is only marginally significant, this suggests that 'normalisation', that is, learning about bribery, is more likely to occur in a local context. Awareness of corruption is not driven by political interest. People with the most interest in politics are no more likely to see their government as corrupt than are those who have no interest in politics. Together, being exposed to information about corruption and regarding it as acceptable as a means to get what one wants raises the variance the regression accounts for to 21.3%.

Perceiving corruption

Paralleling the experience of bribery, the perception of corruption is measured as the mean of individual perceptions of corruption across the seven specific public services (cf. Figure 1). As expected, the mean is high, 3.2, on a four-point scale. However, the standard deviation of 0.58 shows that Russians differ in the extent to which they perceive services as corrupt. An ordinary least squares regression accounts for 16.4% of the variance in perceptions of corruption (Table 3). However, the hypotheses that are most important in explaining this are not the same as those accounting for the experience of corruption.

There is no support for Hypothesis 5; the payment of a bribe has no significant influence on the perception of corruption. Similarly, people who have more frequent contacts with government are not significantly different in their perceptions of corruption. Thus, it is empirically misleading to treat perceived corruption in Russian society as if it were a proxy for the extent of corruption there.

Table 3.   Influences on the perception of corruption.

	b	SE	Beta
H1: Capacity to pay			
Age	−0.00	0.00	−0.01
Education	0.00	0.02	0.00
Social status	−0.02	0.01	−0.04
Income quartile	0.02	0.02	0.03
Female	−0.01	0.03	−0.01
H2: Contact with officials			
Number of contacts	0.00	0.01	0.00
Number of bribes paid	0.02	0.02	0.03
H3: Political awareness			
Learn from friends	0.10	0.02	0.16***
Learn from what I see	0.09	0.02	0.15***
Learn from media	0.08	0.02	0.11***
Political interest	−0.02	0.02	−0.03
H4: Everybody's (not) doing it			
Officials act fairly	−0.17	0.02	−0.21***
Bribery acceptable	0.02	0.02	0.03

Note: Dependent variable: perception that seven public services are corrupt; variance accounted for 16.4%; range 4, almost all corrupt to 1, very few. Mean: 3.2.
**Significant at 0.00 *Significant at 0.01
Source: Centre for the Study of Public Policy, New Russia Barometer XV, 13–24 April, 2007.

Nor is there support for hypothesis 2: contact with public officials does not encourage an increased perception of corruption. Hypothesis 1 is also rejected: none of the five socio-economic indicators has a significant influence on the perception of corruption. People whose income may lead to public officials soliciting bribes on the assumption they can afford to pay them are no more likely to perceive the system as corrupt. Even though educated people ought to be more aware of how the political system works, the most educated Russians do not differ significantly from the least educated in their evaluation of the integrity of government.

A bad press and cynical friends and neighbours are more important than bad experiences in shaping popular perceptions of corruption, as Hypothesis 3 predicts. Many Russians are exposed to news of corruption on television and in the press; in conversations with friends and see conspicuous consumption by new-rich Russians as proof-positive of corruption. The more people are made aware of corruption by friends, what is seen in the community, and by the national media, the more they perceive public services to be corrupt. This is true whether or not they have paid a bribe or contacted public services. However, if what people hear about corruption is contradicted by an expectation that, whatever their degree of venality, public officials will treat people like themselves fairly, then Russians are less likely to perceive their political system as corrupt (see Table 3).

The dissociation of the experience and perception of corruption is confirmed by the regression analyses showing that the biggest influence on paying bribes – contact with public officials – has no statistical influence on the perception of corruption. The chief hypothesis positively supported in both analyses concerns political awareness. More frequent exposure to news about political corruption through multiple sources boosts the belief that most public officials are corrupt; it also has a significant but less dominant influence on the readiness to pay bribes. Beliefs about what everybody is doing are doubly significant: a belief that bribery is normal to get things done influences the readiness to pay bribes, whereas the expectation that public officials will treat one fairly reduces the perception of corruption.

Consequences for regime support

The fact that perceptions of corruption are not driven by personal experience merits treating this phenomenon as distinct from the actual payment of bribes. Hypothesis 6 summarises the expected consequences for regime support: the perception of corruption is likely to have a negative effect independent of individual experience. However, Hypothesis 7 cautions against a reductionist approach that makes corruption appear all important by calling attention to other features of political and economic performance that can influence the evaluation of government.

Support for the Russian regime

Although Russians tend to see their regime as corrupt, in itself this is not evidence that they reject its legitimacy. Samuel Huntington[39] argues that in badly governed countries corruption can be positively valued as 'providing immediate, specific and concrete benefits'. In such circumstances, 'the only thing worse than a society with a rigid, over-centralised dishonest bureaucracy is one with a rigid, over-centralised honest bureaucracy' that cannot

---

39. Samuel P. Huntington, *Political Order in Changing Societies* (New Haven: Yale University Press, 1968), 64, 69.

be circumvented by paying a bribe. A similar view is summed up in the Russian saying: 'The law is like a door in the middle of a field. You can go through it if you want, but you don't have to.' When an earlier NRB survey asked for an evaluation of the effect of laws, 61% of Russians felt they were hard on ordinary people and 73% endorsed the view that the harshness of Russian laws is softened by their non-enforcement.[40] Such views imply that a generalised perception of corruption will have no effect on support for the regime or even the perverse hypothesis that such a view will increase toleration for a repressive regime.[41]

In the NRB, support for the regime is measured by asking respondents to rate 'the current political system', a phrase which avoids the misleading assumption that the regime is democratic simply because it holds multi-candidate elections. Replies are invited on a scale that runs from +100 to −100, thus giving equal weight to positive and negative views. In the April 2007 survey, those positive about the regime greatly outnumbered those negative: 70% were positive, 8% neutral and 22% negative. The standard deviation of 46 shows substantial variation around the mean of +19.

Consistent with Hypothesis 7, our regression model of regime support includes not only measures of perception and experience of corruption but also political and economic performance indicators that were found to be significant in earlier research.[42] These include trust in political institutions, a sense of greater personal freedom than under the Soviet regime, a belief the regime is now democratic and an evaluation of the performance of the economic system (see Appendix for details).

Our multivariate model of regime support shows a very good fit: 39.6% of the variance is accounted for (Table 4). The chief influences on whether Russians support the current regime are five indicators of political and economic performance. Consistent with political economy models of voting, by far the biggest impact on support is how people evaluate the current economy. Oil prices were booming at the time of this NRB survey and 66% of Russians had a positive evaluation of the economy. Net of all other influences, for each additional point on the economy scale, support for the regime went up half a point. Four measures of political performance also have a significant effect on support for the regime. Russians who trust their political institutions and expect officials to treat them fairly are more positive in their view of the regime. The same is true of the big majority who feel much freer now than under the Soviet regime and the minority who consider that the regime is democratic rather than dictatorial.

Contrary to theories of the corroding consequences of corruption, after controlling for political and economic performance, none of the five corruption variables has any significant influence on support for the regime. Behavioural measures, such as the number of bribes paid or the number of contacts with public officials, have no influence. The perception of corruption likewise has no effect nor does the acceptability of bribery. The Huntington argument that corruption is acceptable because it makes government tolerable is not endorsed. Likewise, all the measures of awareness of corruption lack statistical significance.

---

40. Richard Rose, *Getting Things Done with Social Capital: New Russia Barometer VII*. Studies in Public Policy Number 303 (Glasgow: Centre for the Study of Public Policy, 1998), 48.

41. On this, see Janine R. Wedel, ed., *The Unplanned Society: Poland During and After Communism* (New York: Columbia University Press, 1992).

42. See Richard Rose, William Mishler, and Neil Munro, *Russia Transformed: Developing Popular Support for a New Regime* (Cambridge: Cambridge University Press, 2006), Chapters 5–8.

Table 4. Corruption has little effect on regime support.

	b	SE	Beta
H6: General perception of corruption			
Number of contacts	−06	07	−02
Number of bribes paid	−17	13	−03
General perception corruption	−10	14	−02
Mean perception, corrupt services	24	20	03
Bribery acceptable	00	12	00
H7: Economic and political performance			
Evaluation current economy	51	02	54**
Trust political institutions	35	10	09**
Officials act fairly	59	16	09**
Feel freer now	38	14	06*
Regime is democratic	16	06	06*
H3: Political awareness			
Learn from friends	27	13	05
Learn from what I see	13	12	03
Learn from media	−15	14	−02
Political interest	24	12	05
H1: Ability to pay			
Age	−00	01	−00
Education	−20	12	−04
Social status	14	09	04
Income quartile	−02	11	−00
Female	31	21	03

Note: Dependent variable: support for political regime; variance accounted for 39.6%; range +10 to −10. Mean: +1.9.
**Significant at 0.00 *Significant at 0.01
Source: Centre for the Study of Public Policy, New Russia Barometer XV, 13–24 April, 2007.

Implications

The low incidence of reported bribery in Russia challenges the view generalised from aggregate ratings and headline cases of elite corruption that 'everybody's doing it'. Nonetheless, it leaves open the question: How do people get things done in countries where activities of government do not conform to strict Weberian rules of procedure? The answer is that the payment of bribes is but one alternative in a relationship between a person who wants a public service and the provider of that service. Instead of paying a bribe, a person can pay to secure a service in the market place, for example, private school. For those who do not have the money, use can be made of connections – friends, friends of friends or a patron in a clientelistic relationship. Begging or pleading to be granted a service as an act of sympathy or charity is another alternative. Relying on the system to work as it ought to do may be sufficient in countries where bureaucratic responsiveness is predictable but in Russia it can be a counsel of despair.

An earlier NRB social capital survey[43] explored alternatives to bribery, offering people options of getting services by the book (filling out forms and waiting), by hook

---

43. Richard Rose, *Getting Things Done with Social Capital: New Russia Barometer VII*. Studies in Public Policy Number 303 (Glasgow: Centre for the Study of Public Policy, 1998).

Table 5.   Getting things done by the book, by hook or by crook.

Q. What should you do to get prompt admission to a hospital; a government-subsidized flat you were not entitled to; a permit or official document?

	Hospital	Housing	Permit
	(endorsing: more than one answer allowed)		
Use connections	44	24	38
Offer a "tip"	24	25	32
Beg, tell a story, write letter	22	5	27
Buy in the market	20	30	7*
Wait, nothing can be done	17	25	20

*Percent saying do what you want without a permit
Source: Centre for the Study of Public Policy, New Russia Barometer VII, 6 March – 13 April 1998. Number of respondents: 2002.

(e.g. connections) or by crook (paying a 'tip' or bribe). Three services were asked about; getting admission to hospital for immediate treatment of a painful disease; securing a subsidised flat without being entitled to do so or getting a permit required by a cumbersome bureaucracy. More than one reply was accepted on the grounds that people who want something that they value will try more than one alternative to get what they want (Table 5). For example, if a lengthy wait makes people impatient, then they can turn to a connection or beg for action from an official.

The most frequently invoked strategy is to bend rather than break rules, that is, invoke connections to get speedy and preferential treatment from an official without offering a material benefit. Such behaviour is entirely consistent with the norms of societies in which people depend on a network of contacts in which the reputation for being helpful, rather than having a hand out for money, is important in maintaining ongoing exchanges of assistance and benefits. If a person can afford it and a service is available in the market, then buying it there is an alternative; about one-quarter indicate that they can afford to do so. If money is lacking, then a 'tip' or bribe can get what is wanted at a sub-market price. People who lack both money and connections are likely to beg or plead. The inhibition against openly breaking the law is shown by only 7% saying they would do what they wanted without a necessary permit, by comparison with 32% saying they would 'expedite' a permit by offering a bribe. The proportion of Russians who feel they could only depend on their administrative system was between one in four and one in six. The fact that most Russians chose only one alternative when a second alternative was allowed implies that many have a reliable strategy to get what they want straightaway.[44]

The disjunction between the experience and perception of corruption is not limited to Russia. A Eurobarometer survey of European Union citizens found that 75% perceived corruption as a major problem in their country, but only 7% reported being involved in bribery in the past year.[45] In the 60 countries covered in the 2006 TI Global Corruption Barometer, an average of 77% perceived most public officials as corrupt, whereas only 9% reported that anyone in their household had paid a bribe in the past year. On every

---

44. For comparative Asian answers, see Takashi Inoguchi, ed., *Human Beliefs and Values in East and Southeast Asia in Transition* (Tokyo: Akashi Shoten, 2009), 305.
45. European Commission, *The Attitudes of Europeans towards Corruption* (Brussels: Special Eurobarometer 291, 2008), 3, 12.

continent, big majorities see government as corrupt although everywhere the gap between perception and experience is large. In the mean Global Barometer country, for every nine persons who perceived government as corrupt, only one reported that their household had recent experience of corruption. The gap is least large in Africa, where the experience as well as the perception of corruption is high.

Global evidence of a big gap between the perception and experience of corruption implies the need for an explanatory theory that is general rather than country- or culture-specific.[46] However, because perceptions of corruption appear high in countries where its incidence tends to be low as well as in countries where it is high, this implies the need to take some contextual characteristics into account. One possible explanation is that perceptions are driven primarily by elite conceptions of how their political system ought to work. In countries where the integrity of public administration is relatively high, any departure from high absolute standards may produce an over-reaction, generalising such behaviour to the whole of the political system. On the contrary, in countries where corruption is relatively frequent, foreign observers from countries with high integrity may interpret this as a characteristic of the national culture. When corruption involves major infrastructure investment and military procurement, areas which do not directly involve ordinary people, elites may project their own corrupt practices onto the mass population to exculpate themselves on the grounds that 'everybody is doing it'. However, this argument is based on elite misperceptions about what their citizens think and do. A survey of elites and the general public in eight African countries found that elites over-estimated by 4 times the mass experience of paying bribes.[47] Elites also greatly over-estimated the general public's readiness to tolerate bribery. In other words, elites may justify their own corrupt behaviour with arguments inconsistent with the experience and values of the mass of their citizens.

Notes on contributors

Richard Rose is Director of the Centre for the Study of Public Policy and Professor of Politics at the University of Aberdeen. His most recent publications are *Understanding Post-Communist Transformation* (Routledge, 2009) and *Parties and Elections in New European Democracies* (ECPR Press, 2009). For further details, see www.abdn.ac.uk/cspp

William Mishler is Professor of Political Science at the University of Arizona and Co-Editor of *The Journal of Politics*. A specialist in democratic theory and political behaviour, he has published widely on popular support for democratic leaders, institutions and regimes.

---

46. See William Mishler and Richard Rose, 'Seeing Is Not Believing: Measuring Corruption Perceptions and Experiences' (paper presented at Midwest Political Science Association, Annual Meeting, Chicago, April 2–5, 2009).
47. Mireille Razafindrakoto and François Roubaud, 'How Far Can We Trust Expert Opinions on Corruption? An Experiment Based on Surveys in Francophone Africa', in *Global Corruption Report 2005* (London: Pluto Press, 2005), Table 26.1.

Appendix Table   Variables included in regression analysis

	Range		Mean	SD
	Minimum	Maximum		
Mean, services perceived as corrupt	1	4	3.2	0.58
Contacts with public services	0	7	2.2	1.62
Number of bribes	0	6	0.4	0.88
Bribery acceptable	1	4	1.9	0.94
Officials act fairly	1	4	2.5	0.73
Support for political regime	−10	+10	1.6	4.6
Learns about corruption from:				
Media	1	4	3.4	0.75
Friends	1	4	3.0	0.91
What I see	1	4	2.7	0.97
Interest in politics	1	4	2.2	0.91
Age in years	18	89	44	17
Education	1	4	2.7	1.00
Social status	1	7	3.3	1.34
Income quartile	1	4	2.6	1.10
Gender female	0	1	0.57	0.50

Note: General perception of corruption Min = 1; Max = 4. Mean 3.1; SD 0.79.
Source: Centre for the Study of Public Policy, New Russia Barometer XV, 13–24 April, 2007.

Civil society between the stools[1]

Diana Schmidt-Pfister

Corruption is a phenomenon primarily associated with the public and commercial sectors. Civil society, as the so-called third sector, is therefore naturally seen as one of the key agents in the anti-corruption arena.[2] Indeed, at the level of international governance, contemporary forms of global civil society have substantially contributed to the birth and growth of the global anti-corruption venture. Within countries, however, effective civil society involvement has remained challenging and controversial (DCD/DAC 2003; EUMAP 2003; OECD 2003; WMD 2010).[3] With the articles compiled here, the question about the limited impact of the numerous anti-corruption activities of domestic civil societies is back on the table. As shown by the in-depth case studies in this volume, and as recently underlined by a database compiling almost 500 civic anti-corruption projects that were realised in 16 eastern European countries, post-communist civil societies have been very actively involved in anti-corruption efforts during the 2000s.[4] That their practical impact has remained unsatisfactory seems particularly puzzling since post-communist civil society organisations (CSOs) have been maintaining strong links with both the international and governmental spheres where larger scale anti-corruption action is taking place. Their simultaneous embeddedness within the global and domestic cultural contexts, however, does also present the very crux of the matter.

In an effort better to understand the apparent weakness of domestic civil societies in the anti-corruption field, this chapter outlines key challenges that spring from the entanglement of three cultural contexts where crucial developments have occurred over the past two decades. These have not always been positively synergetic. Two of these contexts are pertinent to civil society involvement in anti-corruption efforts in any country: civil society in general has changed its character, especially at the global level, and, closely related, the anti-corruption venture has evolved as a global movement of its own kind. With regard to the eastern European and possibly other transition countries, these developments are complemented by the contextual dynamics of an ongoing search for viable state–civil society relations at the domestic level. In such countries in particular, civil society in the anti-corruption arena has been sitting oddly between a growing number of stools reserved for an increasingly diverse set of international and governmental actors as well as for global civil society, while often referred to the ranks of 'traditional civil society' as associated with protest, awareness raising and large-scale public mobilisation.

General context: global and domestic civil societies

Civil society in general has changed its character in the context of global governance. Yet it still tends to be widely associated with political protest and street action as the main channels for raising public awareness of political problems. Moreover, its inherent mandate, mediation between the programmatic action of governments, the entrepreneurial action of business, and the everyday needs of the populace, may still be valid within domestic contexts. However, that domestic civil societies are today supplemented by global civil society requires for new distinctions, not only of scope but also of kind.

At the global level, the practices of civic advocacy have not completely renounced public protest and mobilisation. Transnational CSOs such as Greenpeace or Human Rights Watch continue to be actively engaged in highly visible awareness-raising actions. However, since their foundation and spread during the 1970s and 1980s, organisations like these have fundamentally changed their styles of internal organisation and interaction with international and national policymaking and business. A large proportion of global civil society has become more institutionalised, professionalised and better equipped with financial, technical and legal resources. Increasingly specialised organisations and ever larger coalitions have become involved on a routine basis in the transnational negotiation of policies and related distribution of funds and information.

This has not been a smooth transition. At the level of the United Nations (UN), civil society participation has presented one of the key controversies ever since the creation of the UN and the entitlement of its Economic and Social Council (ECOSOC) in 1945 to consult international and national nongovernmental organisations (NGOs).[5] As much as this framework has effectively structured the everyday relations between the UN, national governments and civil society, it has restricted the scope and nature of civic participation. Despite the recognition of access barriers, especially for southern NGOs, such as the complicated and expensive accreditation process and the veto power of the member states, and despite an ongoing search for solutions (e.g. United Nations 2004a), these and other limitations persist (Zettler 2009). So do the controversies (Clark 2008). Similarly, the distinct civil society sector that has emerged in Europe with institutionalised links into Brussels-based policymaking has faced challenging access conditions and other limitations (Ruzza 2004). Coalition building within and beyond the civic sector has become a key strategy for civic organisations to better their access and bundle their influence at policymaking pivots such as the EU and the UN (Florini 2002b; Ruzza 2004). Importantly, all these developments have triggered questions about the legitimacy and accountability of civil society organisations acting at a supranational level (Ruzza 2004; Saurugger 2006; Steffek and Hahn 2010).

Domestic civic spheres are supplemented by this parallel global civil society, but they cannot be equated with the latter. Indeed, many domestic organisations have embodied crucial changes in style as they have become highly professionalised, specialised and formalised, better budgeted and networked, and have turned from mobilising citizens to targeting specialised audiences of administrators, policymakers, scholars and other experts. However, as much as in the global civic sphere (Forgarty 2011), this applies only to a certain proportion of each domestic civil society sector. Depending on their individual goals and contextual opportunities, some organisations are managing these shifts better than others, and many domestic organisations prefer to abide by traditional styles of action that are more in tune with their societies' cultural contexts. Yet the latter may be hardly visible to international actors and foreign donors.

There is one feature that all kinds of civil society organisation seem to share: while civic action has become highly diversified, the normative views towards civil society have generally remained rather narrow and stable over the past two decades. The image of civil society as a mere mediator, as a protestor, and as the most intangible part of political processes has persisted, especially among international actors. At the same time, and somewhat paradoxically, civil society is largely viewed as synonymous with one of its many units, namely NGOs as the most concrete and formally attestable parts of the whole.

General context: the global anti-corruption venture and civil society

In the context of global governance and global civil society participation, the anti-corruption venture has evolved as a transnational advocacy arrangement of its own kind. If global civil society in general has become more professionalised, more heavily based on formalised links with policymaking, and better budgeted, these characteristics have from the very beginning applied to the civil society that has spearheaded global anti-corruption advocacy, most notably on the part of Transparency International (TI) (De Sousa 2009; Sampson in this volume: 185-202; Wang and Rosenau 2001). Also coalition building has become a particularly strong normative suggestion in the anti-corruption venture in general. This is now best illustrated by the 2006-founded UNCAC Coalition, a prototype contemporary global civil society arrangement with more than 300 member organisations that seeks to represent civil society at the UN level in the process of implementing the United Nations Convention against Corruption (UNCAC).[6]

The early beginnings of transnational political advocacy in fields such as environmental protection or human rights could well be conceptualised from a social movement perspective as combined pressure from above and below, exerted onto certain target states by domestic civil society and international actors. This pressure proved most effective where international actors entered the scene in response to distressed calls from domestic NGOs (Keck and Sikkink 1998; Risse and Sikkink 1999). Global anti-corruption advocacy, however, started out from the opposite direction, with pressure from above, on the part of an increasingly influential global civil society organisation and powerful international (financial) organisations, and sought to reach out into domestic contexts. Along this route, it was faced with the double challenge to get on board both governments and civil societies in the target states. These two main addressees have been approached via rather parallel structures, with intergovernmental and international financial institutions focusing on governments and international and western donor organisations on civil societies (see Schmidt-Pfister 2010: 55–56). Coalition building has been promoted by donors as a preferred form of action in the civic domain.

Another characteristic of the global anti-corruption venture is its foundation on a pre-existing comprehensive system of international actors and structures for channelling financial, human, technical and ideational resources. This has substantially contributed to the fact that global anti-corruption efforts could proceed towards establishing intergovernmental legal instruments at the level of the Organisation for

Economic Co-operation and Development (OECD) and at European levels within less than a decade (McCoy and Heckel 2001), and could mount in the entering into force of the UNCAC as a truly global convention within another five years. In contrast, the negotiation and adoption of the first international treaties in the realm of human rights took several decades (see Risse and Sikkink 1999). However, it also meant that, first, the anti-corruption theme was adopted by 'diverse actors normally at odds with each other' (Sampson 2005: 110) and, second, that anti-corruption was adopted as an add-on task by most international actors, except for TI and very few other newly founded organisations with a special focus on corruption.

The currently strong focus on the implementation of the international anti-corruption conventions also means a turning away from the terrain of civic engagement. These conventions are inherently focused on triggering legal and administrative reforms in the signatory countries and have become accompanied by rigorous and formal intergovernmental monitoring regimes that aim at mutual evaluation and peer pressure among the signatory parties. Accordingly, the general commitment to civil society involvement on the part of those international organisations that have adopted international anti-corruption conventions, namely the OECD, the Council of Europe (CoE), and the UN, has become increasingly contradicted by their actual practices along longstanding diplomatic routines. The following discussion shall focus on the agendas and actions of the CoE and the UN as the most relevant organisations with regard to eastern Europe.[7]

The CoE did in the anti-corruption field always specify its general commitment to civil society involvement by employing a narrow definition of civil society as comprising the media, lobby organisations, and institutions capable to realise research projects (Council of Europe 1996, 1997). With the development of the monitoring regime accompanying the CoE Criminal Law and Civil Law Conventions on Corruption, which has been realised under the umbrella of the Group of States Against Corruption (GRECO) since 1999, civil society has become gently pushed towards more distanced margins. Civil society participation in the review process came to be conceptualised as an option in case of demand, namely in the form of consultation during onsite visits.[8] The frequently amended monitoring guidelines (GRECO 2010), presenting the most important guiding document for the country evaluations, have remained silent about civil society participation while detailing the procedures for consulting national authorities during onsite visits and for forming the evaluation teams. The latter are recruited from a pool of experts to be appointed by the member states. Only 'exceptionally' and 'where appropriate' additional and scientific experts may be involved as part of the evaluation teams. Moreover, the evaluation procedures provide little access for awareness raising and information politics as all persons involved are obliged to keep confidential any information gathered.

Even more public actions by the CoE provide little space for meaningful civic participation, as illustrated two recent conferences, GRECO's 10th anniversary conference in 2009 and an international conference on 'Fighting corruption at local and regional level' in 2010. Both conferences were announced as events involving civil society. In practice, however, they reveal a quantitative and qualitative restriction stemming from an equalisation of TI and civil society in this field. While the 2010 conference was open to the media and interested public, among the speakers civil society was represented by only one leading TI delegate. In case of the 2009 anniversary conference, civil society was officially represented among the 200 official participants by not more than three representatives of CSOs, including TI and the Global Organisation of Parliamentarians against Corruption (GOPAC) as the most leading and most specialised transnational civic organisations in the field. With the sole exception of Germany, where TI has its headquarters, none of the 50 national delegations was equipped with civic experts. Moreover, the delegations were markedly dominated by the representatives of the ministries of justice and governmental investigation services.[9] The refreshed design of the CoE webpage, where corruption-related activities are placed within the 'Law' category of action, is perhaps the best symbolic expression of the CoE's strengthened emphasis on spurring legal reform in this field.

Also regarding the UNCAC, rhetoric commitment to civil society involvement has been relativised in the light of actual practices at the UN level. Despite the long-standing formal ground for such involvement, as outlined above, it is far from commonly accepted among the participating state parties. On the part of the UN Office on Drugs and Crime (UNODC), the body under which the UNCAC is to be implemented, the explicit emphasis on 'specialised NGOs' is awkwardly contradicted by a persistent reluctance to associate NGOs with more than awareness-raising functions.[10] Given the increasing professionalisation of civil society, this comes at the expense of additional expertise embodied in many civic organisations today. Moreover, UNODC has arrived at a particularly hierarchised interaction with mainly three large umbrella organisations, including the above-mentioned UNCAC Coalition that has its secretariat at TI and includes many other global networks among its members.[11] Despite such powerful appearance, civil society participation in the UNCAC implementation and monitoring has remained limited and contested.

As for the types of UNCAC-related events, the celebration of the International Day against Corruption on 9 December has remained the only one explicitly open to active civil society collaboration with UNODC. The most fertile bodies and procedures concerning the implementation of the UNCAC, the intergovernmental working groups, the Conference of the State Parties (CoSP, since 2006) and the Implementation Review Group (IRG, since 2010) have remained reserved to governmental experts. It may be true in principle that NGOs have 'actively participated' in the CoSP.[12] Recent controversies, however, have shown that participating governments are deeply divided about the issue of NGO admission (see Dell 2011a, 2011b). This divide has essentially become one between western and less democratic countries since the Russian Federation started an initiative to block civil society organisations from attending the IRG meetings, or at least to confine them to a separate briefing session at the margins of IRG meetings. Despite an opinion of the UN Office of Legal Affairs (United Nations 2010) confirming the observer status of NGOs at CoSP and IRG sessions, these organisations have remained barred from subsequent IRG meetings in 2010 and 2011. At the CoSP, their attendance has remained confined to general plenary sessions, while they have remained excluded from the actually decisive informal discussions. Oddly enough, the latter have been the space for addressing the issue of NGO participation. At the same time, the professional expertise of NGOs has been acknowledged, although in a non-deliberative fashion, by including civil society review reports submitted by the UNCAC Coalition in the official conference documentation. More light on this matter may be shed with the 6th CoSP, which Russia has offered to host in 2015.

With a growing emphasis on the implementation of the international anti-corruption conventions in general, and the UNCAC in particular, this tendency that international actors and governments proceed along proven diplomatic routines, seems to be destined to further intensification.[13] In any domestic context, this implies the challenge that these routines and concerns leave little space for civil society participation. For eastern European civil societies, this has only added to other challenges in the context of an ongoing search for viable state – civil society relationships.

Post-communist contexts: anti-corruption, states and civil societies

As illustrated by most case studies in this volume, some of the unfavourable circumstances hampering civil society involvement in transnational anti-corruption efforts have become particularly pronounced in the post-communist countries. The diversity of post-communist transitions notwithstanding, there are some shared challenges resulting from the simultaneous embeddedness of post-communist civil societies in the overlapping cultural contexts of their home countries as well as of global civic activism and global anti-corruption advocacy.

Eastern Europe may well be labelled as the 'birthplace of the anti-corruption industry' (Sampson in this volume: 185), not only because the high levels of corruption invited much counter-action across the region, but also because transnational anti-corruption efforts have been implemented on the basis of pre-established democracy promotion structures and discourses, which had reached into eastern Europe since the early 1990s and which were reinforced with the EU eastern enlargement during the 2000s. Moreover, since post-communist civil societies were commonly viewed as part and parcel of both democratisation and opposition against political corruption, they have been assigned a key role by anti-corruption promoters in this region. On the positive side, the adoption of the anti-corruption idea under the wing of democracy promotion has provided many vantage points. As shown in preceding chapters, chances have been particularly high that relevant measures on the part of international, governmental and civil society actors coincide with heightened synergy potential, quite in the sense of the mainstreaming idea. Accordingly, eastern European countries have shown exceptional records of anti-corruption measures, especially in the course of the 2004 and 2007 EU eastern enlargements (see Wolf in this volume: 11-33). Clearly, in this region strong emphasis has been placed on the ratification of the international legal instruments, most notably the CoE and UN anti-corruption conventions.[14]

However, some of the complex questions raised with regard to external democracy promotion in eastern Europe, including mismatches between rhetoric and action, interventionism and sovereignty, Euroscepticism, anti-westernism, or lacking successes (Carothers 1999; Lord and Harris 2006) and not least lacking understanding of the precise interaction between international factors and domestic change (Magen and Morlino 2009), have been sharply mirrored in the anti-corruption field. Despite widespread discontent with the extent of corruption, externally promoted anti-corruption measures have become criticised in many eastern European countries for their lack of local relevance and lack of effectiveness. In this context, the participation of domestic civil societies in anti-corruption efforts is particularly challenging. Most civic organisations in this field are intensely interconnected with both the international and the governmental levels and are thus easily exposed to tensions between these levels.

Post-communist NGOs have in their current form only emerged since the early 1990s and with substantial support from western and international sources. They thus grew up in the global civil society spirit outlined in the beginning of this chapter. In the absence of domestic sources, including state subsidies or membership contributions, these NGOs have remained overly dependent on foreign donor funding. Also in the anti-corruption field, this implies several challenges. On the part of international anti-corruption promoters, as mentioned, donor support to domestic civil societies and technical assistance to governments have been provided in a parallel rather than in a concerted fashion. Both governmental and civic anti-corruption efforts have been affected by the overall 'projectisation of anti-corruption' (Sampson 2005: 109), that is, the conversion of a moral campaign issue into grant categories and technical assistance contracts with emphasis on visible, measurable outputs over a short-term horizon. However, due to the overdependence of eastern European CSOs on the acquisition of donor-funded projects, they are more heavily bound to realising their objectives within preconceptualised programmes and fixed timeframes. Most donor-funded civic anti-corruption projects across the region have usually lasted one year or less (Mungiu-Pippidi 2010: 20). In procedural respects, one cannot deny the difficulty, or even impossibility, to provide donor support exactly at those times when viable opportunities for civic action are coming up within a particular domestic context. The timescales of international institutions and foreign donors regarding their funding, training, or monitoring programmes but also regarding their internal staff rotation or their presence within the countries concerned are rather stiff. Public outrage about corruption within any country, however, requires longer term popular dissatisfaction with corruption problems in combination with spectacular events involving (usually political) corruption. That all donor-funded civic projects in the above-mentioned database have been reported as successful (Mungiu-Pippidi 2010: 21) indicates a reinterpretation of success with regard to sheer project activity rather than to outcomes of a specifically measurable decline in corruption (see also di Puppo in this volume: 113). This interpretation is not always shared by the grant recipients who are indeed often dissatisfied with the prescribed agendas and styles of action that hardly fit their cultural context. For example, the idea of coalition building, which has become a predominant feature in anti-corruption grants, has been particularly difficult to realise in the post-communist contexts where a fierce competition exists among CSOs and where relations with actors outside the CSO sector are often far from smooth.[15]

Another important aspect is that domestic NGOs primarily rely on foreign donor support for realising their aims rather than seeking active involvement at the international or governmental level, where most anti-corruption policymaking is negotiated. At the UN level, eastern European NGOs have remained even more underrepresented with consultative status than southern ones (see UN/ECOSOC 2011) and are also meagrely represented at the UNCAC Coalition with only 26 among over 300 member organisations, including 9 TI chapters.[16] At this level, domestic organisations are faced with two kinds of misplaced expectation: many cannot meet even the basic eligibility requirements, including a democratically adopted constitution, a representative structure, appropriate mechanisms of accountability, democratic and transparent decision-making processes and official registration for at least two years, and many object the watchdog function primarily assigned to civil society.

Moreover, the dominance of TI in representing civil society at this international level is reproduced within the countries, where the globally well-connected TI chapters have become the most visible civic address to be approached by international actors.[17] This does not only seem to weaken the nodes required for anchoring transnational civic activism in domestic realities (Florini 2002a: 217), it also overrides much valuable anti-corruption expertise residing with native CSOs that have implemented a large number of locally oriented projects.[18]

Post-communist CSOs have remained deeply embedded within their countries' particular post-communist cultures also with regard to their persisting reliance on informal practices (EUMAP 2003; Grødeland and Aasland 2011: 134–136), which, of course, presents a particularly controversial theme in the anti-corruption field. Moreover, in countries where the distance between the state and the populace has remained particularly large, CSOs tend to engage either in social service provision or in political advocacy rather than positioning themselves somewhere in the middle of that spectrum. Political advocacy, including anti-corruption advocacy, is often characterised by blurred boundaries between the state and civil society sectors on a personal level, because many CSO activists have come from positions in public administration or international organisations (Grødeland and Aasland 2011: 144; Schmidt-Pfister 2010: 119–120, 123) or have left the civic sector for government positions (e.g. Ivanov and di Puppo in this volume, chapters 6 and 7). In some countries, where CSOs have experienced a return to Soviet-style control, such as Belarus, Russia or Ukraine, civic engagement seems to be more functional from within the state than in opposition to it, just as in Soviet times (Lewin 1991). Also the Hungarian case illustrates that oppositional leverage enjoyed by CSOs in a more democratic climate may be suddenly lost when the political environment becomes less democratic (see Batory in this volume: 57-70; Batory 2011).

Civil society between the stools – or back at the jump seat?

Civil society remains a contested concept. However, its meaning is rarely negotiated overtly among practitioners. Rather, implicit tensions crop out where actual practices and normative views are getting out of tune. This becomes more complex with the ongoing internal differentiation of civil society and with the simultaneous embeddedness of its various parts in both international and domestic contexts. International actors, in particular, maintain rather stable normative expectations towards civil society, as presenting a key awareness-raising and mass-mobilising force, while allowing for civil society participation in their activities on an increasingly formalised basis.

As shown in the case of transnational anti-corruption advocacy in eastern Europe, post-communist civil society organisations thus find themselves entrapped in a struggle for legitimacy on all fronts, vis-à-vis authorities and the general public in their home countries (Grødeland and Aasland 2011: 130) as much as vis-à-vis western donors and international organisations. They tend to be viewed as agents of western agendas by the state, as unduly privileged by peers and citizens, or as merely oppositional or somehow unprofessional by western and international organisations. That the financing and networking of post-communist CSOs are the key bones of contention in all these respects turns out to be particularly challenging for organisations in the anti-corruption field. Mutual distrust here is particularly intense because the value commitments inherent in both the anti-corruption agenda and civil society mandates are particularly vulnerable to being contradicted by more pragmatic practices needed for facilitating global advocacy. Distrust on the part of governments and citizens is further intensified by the fact that, in comparison to income dimensions in this region, relatively large sums are at stake by participating in the anti-corruption industry.

These challenges are stepped up by the above-outlined turn towards intergovernmental action in the anti-corruption field, most notably the implementation of the CoE and UN conventions. Despite the clause that UNCAC state parties should ensure civil society participation (United Nations 2004b, Article 13), experience to date has indicated that the general focus on the international conventions implies a relocation of anti-corruption efforts towards the international-governmental nexus. In the post-communist and possibly other transition countries, where the anti-corruption agenda has tended to be instrumentalised by governments against their political opponents, this increases the potential that strategic top-down anti-corruption efforts will gain even more weight. Not least, surveys and studies in many eastern European countries continue to show that this is bolstered by the tendency that anti-corruption, as much as any other socio-political issue, is perceived as the prime task of governments and presidents by authorities and citizens alike.

Research about transnational advocacy has devoted a great deal of attention to the operational conditions of successful transcultural norm promotion, such as the importance of strategically framing the problem or issue at stake, in order to make it resonate within particular domestic contexts, or the involvement of three main actor categories, namely international organisations, states, and civil societies. What has remained largely neglected, however, is a thorough assessment of the tensions that emerge when such concerted action is not necessarily based on shared normative views and practices concerning the very roles of each actor category.

Notes

1 This chapter builds on the articles that are re-issued in this volume, on updated comments provided by our authors, and on my own extensive research on anti-corruption efforts and the involvement of post-communist civil societies therein (see Schmidt-Pfister 2010, especially Chapters 1, 3, and 7 for more general findings). I am also grateful to Holger Moroff and Steve Sampson for their insightful comments on an earlier version of this chapter.

2 In this chapter, civil society is understood as comprising any collective civic engagement outside the spheres of the state, the economy, or private households.

3 See also World Bank, Anticorruption, Civil Society Participation, http://go.worldbank.org/NULF579BT0 (accessed 18/12/2011).

4 See Civil Society Against Corruption, Projects Database (http://www.againstcorruption.eu/resources/projects-database/, accessed 08/01/2012) and Mungiu-Pippidi (2010) for an analysis of the projects compiled therein.

5 See UN Charter, Chapter 10, Article 71, http://www.un.org/en/documents/charter/index.shtml (accessed 02/12/2011).

6 UNCAC Coalition, http://www.uncaccoalition.org/ (accessed 11/01/2012).

7 For similar criticisms of the OECD, see Transparency International (2008: 8) and consider the fact that the OECD consultations inviting documents like this have only reached out to international auditing organisations and the TI secretariat as representations of civil society.

8 Council of Europe, How does GRECO work?, http://www.coe.int/t/dghl/monitoring/greco/general/ 4.%20How%20does%20GRECO%20work_en.asp (accessed 02/12/2011).

9 See Council of Europe, GRECO's 10th Anniversary Conference (Strasbourg, 5 October 2009), http://www.coe.int/t/dghl/monitoring/greco/10th%20Anniversary%20Conf/10thAnniversaryGRECO_en.asp, International Conference: "Fighting Corruption at local and regional level" (Messina, 7 May 2010), http://cor.europa.eu/pages/EventTemplate.aspx?view=detail&id=0eeb3c70-c734-423a-9ef8-c551a639773b (accessed 05/12/2012).

10 See, for example, UNODC, About Civil Society and UNODC, http://www.unodc.org/unodc/en/ngos/ index.html?ref=menuside (accessed 09/01/2012).

11 See, UNODC, Main Civil Society Partners with the UNODC, http://www.unodc.org/unodc/en/ngos/main-partners.html (accessed 09/01/2012).

12 See UNODC, About Civil Society and UNODC, http://www.unodc.org/unodc/en/ngos/index.html?ref=menuside (accessed 09/01/2012).

13 That attention has been substantially distracted towards the UNCAC is mirrored in the ratification patterns. Since the UNCAC entered into force in December 2005, the CoE and OECD conventions have not seen any new ratification, whereas 155 countries have ratified the UNCAC during that time, including 24 eastern European and Balkan countries (i.e. all but the Czech Republic and Macedonia).

14 The impressive ratification record of eastern European countries is summarised in Schmidt-Pfister (2010: 46–52; for an overall picture; see Table 4). Today, the ratification of the UNCAC by Ukraine (in December 2009) and Estonia (in April 2010) would need to be added.

15 For a detailed analysis of the tensions entailed in a western-promoted anti-corruption coalition project in Russia, see Schmidt-Pfister (2010: 149–156).

16 See UNCAC Coalition Members, http://www.uncaccoalition.org/en/about-us/members-list.html (accessed 18/01/2012).

17 Own interviews with representatives of the CoE, the EU, and the UNODC regional office in Moscow (2005–2007).

18 Almost half of a sample of 417 anti-corruption projects realised by eastern European civil society actors between 1999 and 2009 have been focused towards the local level or specific sectors (Mungiu-Pippidi 2010: 20).

Literature

Batory, Agnes (2011), *Venue Shopping in the EU: Multi Level Politics and the Hungarian Media Law Debate* (unpublished manuscript).

Carothers, Thomas (1999), *Aiding Democracy Abroad. The Learning Curve* (Washington, DC: Carnegie Endowment for International Peace).

Clark, John (2008), 'The UN and Civil Society: Three years after the Cardoso Report', *Journal of Civil Society*, 4(2), 153–160.

Council of Europe (1996), Programme of Action Against Corruption (GMC (96) 95).

Council of Europe (1997), *Resolution (97) 24 on the Twenty Guiding Principles for the Fight against Corruption* (Adopted by the Committee of Ministers on 6 November 1997 at the 101st session of the Committee of Ministers).

DCD/DAC (2003), *Synthesis of Lessons Learned of Donor Practices in Fighting Corruption* (DCD/DAC/GOVNET(2003)1, Report prepared for the DAC Network on Governance by a team of consultants led by Mr. Bruce B. Bailey, commissioned by the OECD: DAC Network on Governance).

De Sousa, Luis (2009), 'TI in Search of a Constituency: The Institutionalization and Franchising of the Global Anti-corruption Doctrine', in Luis de Sousa, Barry Hindess, and Peter Larmour (eds), *Governments, NGOs and Anti-Corruption: The New Integrity Warriors* (London / New York: Routledge), 186–208.

Dell, Gillian (2011a), 'The IRG Suspends NGO Participation Again'. http://www.uncaccoalition.org/en/home/183-irg-suspends-ngo-participation-again.html, accessed 08/01/2012.

Dell, Gillian (2011b), 'What Happened at CoSP4? Overview'. http://www.uncaccoalition.org/en/home/189.html, accessed 08/01/2012.

EUMAP (2003), *Is Civil Society a Cause or Cure for Corruption in Central and Eastern Europe?* (EUMAP: EU Monitoring and Advocacy Program, Online Journal, Feature (29/07/2003)).

Florini, Ann M. (2002a), 'Lessons Learned', in Ann M. Florini (ed.), *The Third Force: The Rise of Transnational Civil Society* (Washington, DC: Carnegie Endowment for International Peace), 111–239.

Florini, Ann M. (ed.) (2002b), *The Third Force: The Rise of Transnational Civil Society* (Washington, DC: Carnegie Endowment for International Peace).

Forgarty, Edward (2011), 'Nothing Succeeds Like Access? NGO Strategies Towards Multilateral Institutions', *Journal of Civil Society*, 7(2), 207–227.

GRECO (2010), *Rules of Procedure* (GRECO (2010) 9E; Strasbourg: GRECO Secretariat/ Council of Europe).

Grødeland, Åse B. and Aasland, Aadne (2011), 'Civil Society in Post-Communist Europe: Perceptions and Use of Contacts', *Journal of Civil Society*, 7(2), 129–156.

Keck, Margaret E. and Sikkink, Kathryn (1998), *Activists Beyond Borders. Advocacy Networks in International Politics* (Ithaca/London: Cornell University Press).

Lewin, Moshe (1991), *The Gorbachev Phenomenon. A Historical Interpretation* (Expanded edition edn; Berkeley/Los Angeles: University of California Press).

Lord, Christopher and Harris, Erika (eds) (2006), *Democracy in the New Europe* (Houndmills and New York: Palgrave Macmillan).

Magen, Amichai and Morlino, Leonardo (2009), *International Actors, Democratization and the Rule of Law. Anchoring Democracy?*, eds Amichai Magen and Leonardo Morlino (New York and London: Routledge).

McCoy, Jennifer and Heckel, Heather (2001), 'The Emergence of a Global Anti-Corruption Norm', *International Politics*, 38(1), 65–90.

Mungiu-Pippidi, Alina (2010), *Civil Society as an Anticorruption Actor. Some Lessons Learned from the East Central European Experience* (additional paper for the workshop 'Neopatrimonialism in Various World Regions' 23 August 2010, GIGA German Institute of Global and Area Studies, Hamburg).

OECD (2003), *Fighting Corruption. What Role for Civil Society? The Experience of the OECD* (Paris: Organisation for Economic Co-operation and Development).

Risse, Thomas and Sikkink, Kathryn (1999), 'The Socialization of International Human Rights Norms into Domestic Practices: Introduction', in Thomas Risse, Stephen C. Ropp, and Kathryn Sikkink (eds), *The Power of Human Rights. International Norms and Domestic Change* (Cambridge: Cambridge University Press), 1–38.

Ruzza, Carlo (2004), *Europe and Civil Society. Movement Coalitions and European Governance* (Manchester/New York: Manchester University Press).

Sampson, Steven (2005), 'Integrity Warriors: Global Morality and the Anti-Corruption Movement in the Balkans', in Dieter Haller and Cris Shore (eds), *Corruption. Anthropological Perspectives* (London/Ann Arbor, MI: Pluto Press Ltd), 103–30.

Saurugger, Sabine (2006), 'The Professionalisation of Interest Representation: A Legitimacy Problem for Civil Society in the EU?', in Stijn Smismans (ed.), *Civil Society and Legitimate European Governance* (Cheltenham: Elgar), 260–276.

Schmidt-Pfister, Diana (2010), *Transnational Advocacy on the Ground. Against Corruption in Russia?* (Manchester: Manchester University Press).

Steffek, Jens and Hahn, Kristina (2010), 'Introduction: Transnational NGOs and Legitimacy, Accountability, Representation', in Jens Steffek and Kristina Hahn (eds), *Evaluating Transnational NGOs – Legitimacy, Accountability, Representation* (Basingstoke: Palgrave Macmillan), 1–25.

Transparency International (2008) *Responses to the Consultation Paper on the Review of the OECD Anti-Bribery Instruments*, http://www.oecd.org/dataoecd/7/46/40498398.pdf, accessed 08/12/2011.

UN/ECOSOC (2011), *List of Non-governmental Organizations in Consultative Status with the Economic and Social Council as of 1 September 2011* (E/2011/INF/4).

United Nations (2004a), *We the Peoples: Civil Society, the United Nations and Global Govern-ance* (A/58/817).

United Nations (2004b), *United Nations Convention against Corruption* (New York: UN/UNODC).

United Nations (2010), *Conference of the States Parties to the United Nations Convention against Corruption, Legal Opinion from the Office of Legal Affairs* (CAC/COSP/IRG/2010/9).

Wang, Hongying and Rosenau, James (2001), 'Transparency International and Corruption as an Issue of Global Governance', *Global Governance*, 7(1), 25–50.

WMD (2010), 'How Can Civil Society Help Ensure the Effectiveness of Anti-Corruption Efforts?', *World Movement for Democracy. The Sixth Assembly*, 83–85. http://www.wmd.org/sites/default/files/FINALREPORT_smaller_2.pdf, accessed 02/12/2011.

Zettler, Angela (2009) *NGO Participation at the United Nations: Barriers and Solutions*, http://csonet.org/content/documents/BarriersSolutions.pdf, accessed 08/01/2012.

The anti-corruption industry: from movement to institution

Steven Sampson

Department of Social Anthropology, Lund University, Lund, Sweden

This article describes the concept of 'industry', often used pejoratively in critiques of international development, and applies it to the field of anti-corruption. The characteristics of the anti-corruption industry, including anti-corruptionist discourse, resemble that which has taken place in development aid, human rights, civil society and gender equality. The anti-corruption industry thus includes key global actors, secondary actors who look for 'signals' and an apparatus of understandings, knowledge, statistics and measures, all of which tend to prioritise anti-corruption institutions over anti-corruption activism. It is argued that the questionable impact of anti-corruption programmes enables the anti-corruption industry to coexist along with the corruption it ostensibly is combating. Instead of viewing anti-corruption as hegemonic, we need to critically examine the consequences of the global institutionalisation of anti-corruptionist discourse and anti-corruption practice.

Introduction

All the articles in this issue of *Global Crime* focus on one major issue: how was an anti-corruption regime established in the emerging democracies of post-socialist Europe? As outlined in the introduction, they describe interactions between local civil society, national policy elites and international pressures. The questions, then, are several: to what degree was there a national political will to fight corruption in these countries? And, to what degree was anti-corruption imposed upon them? What incentives were offered, pressures employed or norms adopted for anti-corruption to enter the policy agenda in post-socialist Europe? What was *happening* in these countries that enabled some civil society actors to be heard, a voice which presumably led governments to prioritise corruption? Or in some cases, why did governments who were normally *not* pressured by civil society nevertheless enact anti-corruption policies?

Theories of cultural globalisation, as developed by anthropologists and others, are of relevance to these fundamental issues. Such theories try to explain why certain practices, tastes or value systems can move from one society to another; in some cases, these practices are enthusiastically accepted by local cultures (American hip-hop among European youth, Protestant evangelism in Africa), whereas in other cases they can be bitterly resisted (electoral democracy). Researchers in cultural diffusion describe various intermediate states of 'hybridity' or 'creolisation'.[1] In Indonesia, for example, a study of a forest protection movement shows how external or universal discourses about 'rights' and 'protecting nature'

---

1. Ulf Hannerz, 'Notes on the Global Ecumene', *Public Culture* 1 (1989): 66–75.

are appropriated by local actors for their own local projects.[2] In a manner similar to that of environmental protection, anti-corruption discourse presents itself as a global movement, circulating in a rarefied space of international conventions and platforms. As a global discourse, anti-corruption can embrace local communities, national governments in North and South, international organisations, civil society and an enlightened private sector into a common project. Anti-corruption now appears as an idea whose time has come. But why this idea? And, why at this particular time? What is it that makes an otherwise diverse set of international and local actors coalesce into what seems to be a single project? *Why is anti-corruption 'hot'?*

I argue in this article that we need to view anti-corruption not simply as an idea but as a complex of resources. These resources are knowledge, people, money and symbols. Together they operate as a complex of practices that I call 'anti-corruptionism'. Today, we can identify a conglomeration of activities carried out by governments, intergovernmental organisations, private sector actors, NGOs, media and citizens, which take the form of 'campaigns' or programmes. Anti-corruption activities have now institutionalised themselves into what some scholars would call an 'anti-corruption regime'. The resources, rhetoric and organisational interests of the anti-corruption regime now lead an existence independent of the actual phenomenon of corruption itself. Anti-corruptionism now projects itself onto the global landscape as a series of policies, regulations, initiatives, conventions, training courses, monitoring activities and programmes to enhance integrity and improve public administration. In short, anti-corruption has become an 'industry'.

The purpose of this article is to describe the implications of anti-corruption as an industry. Every industry brings with it a new language, a new way of thinking about the world, a new discourse. I call this discourse 'anti-corruptionism'. Anti-corruptionism lies behind the hundreds of millions of dollars, hundreds of projects, and dozens of anti-corruption agencies pursuing anti-corruption agendas. Anti-corruptionism is articulated in the key international conventions, national laws, regulations, NGOs platforms, training sessions, congresses, meetings, measurement tools and statistical indicators, which comprise the anti-corruption industry.

Anti-corruptionism is a complex ideology. It is a set of postulates about what corruption is, how it emerges, why it needs to be controlled, and how to control it. Like other discourses, anti-corruptionism is not about absolute truths but about the unstated limits on questioning these truths. There are controversies, of course: anti-corruptionism is full of debates about the precise definition of corruption, and whether corruption is a cause or effect of poverty, and whether corruption is a cause or effect of state inefficiency. That corruption is a 'global issue', however, is not a subject of debate. The controversies within anti-corruptionist discourse help to consolidate the anti-corruption industry. The purpose of this paper is to outline the elements of the anti-corruption industry, and to show its implications for actually reducing corruption. The goal of 'reducing corruption', 'fighting' or 'preventing' corruption is not as clear-cut as may seem. Since corruption itself is a slippery concept, summarising a whole gamut of attitudes and practices, the concept of an 'anti-corruption intervention', may be similarly difficult. These difficulties are indicative of the main feature of the anti-corruption industry: its ongoing expansion at the same time as so few anti-corruption programmes actually reduce corruption. The anti-corruption juggernaut marches on.

---

2. Anna Tsing, *Friction: An Ethnography of Global Connections* (Princeton and Oxford: Princeton University Press, 2005).

Why 'industry'?

The term 'industry' is normally used with respect to manufacturing or to refer to a specific branch of business (e.g. 'the advertising industry'). Used in other contexts, the term 'industry' is a pejorative. To talk about the 'anti-corruption industry', then, is to describe the institutional investment made in solving a problem. In a policy context, a successful industry expands: it maintains a problem on the policy agenda, attracting ever more attention and resources. The anti-corruption industry resembles its forerunners in the development industry, the human rights industry, the civil society/NGO industry or the 'rescue industry' that tries to save prostitutes from trafficking. As this article is being written, we are witnessing the consolidation of a 'climate change industry' (understood as those who want to 'do something' to inhibit man-made global warming).

Here I would like to take the word 'industry' seriously, discussing what features characterise such an 'industry' and how it might evolve, flourish or collapse. In economic history, our industrial society evolved out of a simpler 'craft-based' economy. Industrial society replaced agrarian society, and industrial organisation is usually considered having replaced something we call 'craft'. Many of us, when perturbed by the dysfunctions of industry, even suffer from 'craft nostalgia'.

Economic historians have endeavoured to identify the forces that gave us industrial development. In the world of anti-corruption, a world which I study as an anthropologist,[3] I have tried to isolate those forces which spawned the anti-corruption industry. What made anti-corruption 'hot' over the past decade? It is this perspective that I will offer in this article, on the background of the myriad of studies of anti-corruption initiatives that have taken place in the former Soviet block countries over the last 20 years, and especially in the last decade with EU enlargement.

It would be convenient to swiftly dismiss anti-corruptionism as a smokescreen for some kind of insidious neoliberal agenda.[4] The sudden embrace of anti-corruptionism, by major transnational corporations, with its accompanying rhetoric of corporate social responsibility, transparency, integrity and accountability is indeed remarkable. Yet the participation of transnational corporations in anti-corruption work does not necessarily make it some kind of capitalist plot. Anti-corruption practices often make life harder for transnational corporations, and in addition, there is a genuine alarm in the private sector to do something about exorbitant amounts of bribe-taking and waste in the developing world. We are still left with the question of why the private sector has taken on corruption-fighting as a priority.

We might also explain the rise of corruption in terms of bureaucratic self-interest. In this perspective, corruption becomes yet another issue that these interest groups can use to sustain themselves. Various organisations, associations or NGOs seem to benefit in exaggerating the extent of corruption and their need for more anti-corruption programmes, in order to obtain access to funds or staff. This explanation of self-interest suffers from two weaknesses. First, it does not explain why the particular discourse of anti-corruptionism

---

3. Steven Sampson, 'Corruption and Anti-Corruption in Southeast Europe: Landscapes and Sites', in *Governments, NGOs and Anti-Corruption: The New Integrity Warriors*, ed. Luís de Sousa, Peter Larmour, and Barry Hindess (Abingdon: Routledge, 2009), 168–86. Steven Sampson, 'Integrity Warriors: Global Morality and the Anticorruption Movement in the Balkans', in *Understanding Corruption: Anthropological Perspectives*, ed. Dieter Haller and Chris Shore (London: Pluto Press, 2005), 103–30.
4. Barry Hindess, 'Anti-Corruption as a Risk to Democracy: On the Unintended Consequences of International Anti-Corruption Campaigns', in *Governments, NGOs and Anti-Corruption: The New Integrity Warriors*, ed. Luís de Sousa, Peter Larmour, and Barry Hindess (Abingdon: Routledge, 2009), 19–32.

has come to the forefront in the first decade of the twenty-first century. Nor does it explain the unified character of the anti-corruption industry. The anti-corruption industry does not contain a single dominant actor, but a whole gamut of them, each with their own interests, strategies and world views. Here we concentrate on what it is that unites them. How was this unified character achieved? How were these diverse interests (states, global regimes, market actors, civil society) forged into a single anti-corruption industry?

This article will therefore constitute a preliminary attempt to sketch out the anti-corruption industry and to describe what might be called the tenets of anti-corruptionism. It applies firstly to Eastern Europe, the region that Leslie Holmes called 'rotten states'.[5] By any measure, the post-Soviet transition countries were not the most corrupt states in the world. However, their transition from isolated, state-managed economies into democracies with uncontrolled privatisation, a history of suspicion between citizens and the state and the context of EU accession pressures gave them special characteristics that made them the birthplace of the anti-corruption industry. Hence, Eastern Europe and the Balkans constitute a fruitful point of orientation for understanding how the global anti-corruption industry has evolved.[6] In the third world, those countries with natural resources (Africa) or major markets (China, India) or both (Russia) were less affected by pressures to conform to European anti-corruption regimes. Nevertheless, they, too, have adopted much of the rhetoric of anti-corruptionism.

In highlighting the key features of the 'anti-corruption industry', my goal here is to identify those points where anti-corruptionist discourse was created and sustained, as well as those moments when we should be critically interrogating the concept of anti-corruption.

A critical interrogation of anti-corruptionism is necessary because, like other policy issues such as global crime, anti-corruption has a fundamental problem. It is the problem of impact: deciphering whether the resources used for anti-corruption actually affect the phenomenon it is intended to reduce. Any kind of policy intervention is supposed to produce some kind of change. Anti-corruption practices are supposed to reduce corruption. The issue of impact, or of measuring impact, is common in all areas of policy formation and implementation. Insofar as policies have goals – increasing employment, reducing HIV/AIDS, achieving a cleaner environment, reducing crime, preventing corruption – this requires a whole set of practices to achieve these goals. Measuring impact requires agreement on what phenomenon is to be observed, a system of gathering data and coding observations, and an interpretation of what these observations 'mean'. Measuring the impact of a policy requires baseline data, or to use the more popular word, 'evidence'. Clearly, some impacts are easier to observe, classify and measure than others. On the other hand, some policy interventions may have unintended impacts. Anti-bribery campaigns, for example, may cause bribe transactions to become more sophisticated or hidden, without actually reducing the amount of cash that changes hands. Corruption awareness campaigns often lead to an increase in

---

5. Leslie Holmes, *Rotten States? Corruption, Post-Communism, and Neoliberalism* (Durham: Duke University Press, 2006).
6. See note 3 on anti-corruption in the Balkans, as well as M. Tisne and S. Smilov, 'From the Ground Up: Assessing the Record of Anticorruption Assistance in Southeastern Europe. Budapest Center for European Police Studies', http://www.soros.org.ba/docs_pravo/wp-anticorruption.a1.pdf (accessed November 10, 2009). This paper is based on a long-term perusal of certain key sources, as well as on my own involvement with civil society development, democracy export and anti-corruption research and training. In particular I have been studying the anti-corruption movement associated with Transparency International (TI) and anti-corruptionism in Eastern Europe, where I have expertise. In Scandinavia, where I live (Denmark) and work (Sweden), I have also participated in a variety of anti-corruption and TI-related activities.

perceived corruption (according to surveys) even though actual corruption levels may not have changed. One of the features of the anti-corruption industry, therefore, is the parallel 'careers' of corrupt practices and anti-corruption measures.

Corruption and global crime

Global crime and corruption are connected. The smuggling, arms trafficking, money launder-ing, drug trade and other illegal entrepreneurial activities of global crime would be inconceiva-ble without the involvement of corrupt officials at the customs checkpoints, financial agencies, contracting boards or police, any of whom may receive payments for looking the other way.

What makes anti-corruption relevant for those interested in global crime is that both crime and corruption are more than just issues of gathering data, deciphering trends and setting up units to 'coordinate' measures. Behind the issues of policy, strategy and resources lie moral projects and cultural worldviews. Anti-corruptionism connotes the idea of a global moral project to compel states to be more transparent, to keep officials honest, and to reward integrity; hence the stated need to build a 'culture of anti-corrup-tion', a term that now yields 1.5 million hits on Google.[7] The issue of global organised crime carries similar moral and cultural implications that go beyond the problem of pre-venting illegal imports or making states more secure. Policy discussions on crime and cor-ruption take on moral overtones. Everyone – state leaders, private sector and oppositional NGOs – are against global organised crime and corruption. Even the most authoritarian states have their anti-corruption campaigns and commissions.

In their transnational scale and spider-web penetration into the most benign areas of society, both corruption and organised crime have become global security issues. As a result of their security threats and border-crossing character, both crime and corruption are now objects of international measures that attempt to assess, control and reduce them. Incentives are offered to states or governments to take action: cheaper loans, better credit ratings and promises of entry into international organs or the EU club. There are conditionalities or even penalties for not doing something about crime or corruption. There are appeals to governments for political will, and for more trust between citizens and their governments. Citizens and governments must be made to understand that crime and corruption 'hurts everyone'. Hence, the need for 'awareness-raising' campaigns. At the national level, there is the usual complement of strategies, policies, laws, measures and establishment of inde-pendent agencies to fight crime and corruption. Bureaucratic agencies require ever more documentation: surveying, defining and assessing incidents of crime or corruption in, say, the customs service or procurement. Since measuring corruption and organised crime is notoriously difficult, both because they are illegal and because the concepts themselves are slippery, it generates political discussion about the effectiveness of anti-corruption or anti-crime campaigns. Government, political opposition, civil society groups and interna-tional donors make claims and counterclaims, so that both issues become politicised.

This scenario above provides the background for the emergence of the anti-corruption industry, and it has parallels in the 'struggle against global organised crime'. It is a trajectory of events that has occurred before, in the field of international development, human rights, environmental protection, sex trafficking, children's rights, or conflict resolution. A previ-ously limited or esoteric problem becomes an area of public concern, moral campaigning

---

7. The phrase 'culture of corruption' generated 4.5 million 'hits' on google.com (accessed December 31, 2009), plus an additional 545,000 hits for a 2009 book by Michelle Malkin about the Obama administration also entitled *Culture of Corruption* (Washington: Regnery Publishers).

and policy initiatives. Coalitions are formed between previously hostile actors (grassroots NGOs, government agencies, international organs, private companies).

Both anti-corruption and global crime-fighting are 'industries'. They bring together international initiatives, governmental programmes and civil society advocacy. The goal is to get as many actors 'on board' as possible. Such industries become institutionalised policy areas, with associated organisations, conferences, conventions, secretariats, and the usual academic discussions over concepts, measurement, progress, and above all, impact.

Industrial systems produce products in what appears to be an orderly, efficient way. But behind the assembly line (or today, behind the Policy Paper or web portal) are grey zones where issues are debated and strategies ironed out. These academic discussions often revolve around basic definitions. In almost all such industries, including those of 'transnational organised crime' and 'corruption', the phenomena itself are subject to definitional debates. While discussions often bring to mind the most typical practices (bribes, money-laundering, etc.), there is invariably a dilemma of whether activity X is or is not corruption, whether this measurement tool is actually measuring 'corruption' or something else.[8] This slippery definition can be 'hidden' as the industry emerges In studying the anti-corruption industry, we can begin to understand how institutional actors and organisations 'combat' a phenomenon that remains difficult to define and to measure. The parallel with pornography ('you know it when you see it') comes to mind here. The slippery character and the moral aspects are what make corruption and global crime difficult policy issues. In measuring the impact of all the myriad programmes, conventions, laws, commission and projects, the irony of the anti-corruption industry is that despite the universal appeals to transparency made on government and private business, and despite the technologies of transparency, such as the Internet or the Wikileaks, 'corruption' (however defined) seems to be more prevalent than ever. If this is true, then we need to understand not only the problem of corruption, but also why the now vibrant anti-corruption industry seems to lead a life of its own. We need to understand how anti-corruptionism can persist *alongside* corruption. Perhaps the 'industry' concept can help us in this understanding.

The anti-corruption industry

The practices of corruption – bribery, nepotism, clientelism, etc. – are by nature hidden from view. They are not formally observed or officially recorded. They are, rather, disguised as 'gifts', 'facilitation fees' or 'networking'. Solutions to the problem of corruption involve not simply new laws and regulations, but a new awareness and engagement on the part of officials and citizens. Changes in attitude take longer and are difficult to identify, so it is difficult to determine whether programmes to combat corruption actually have much of an impact. Judgements about impact lead to the politics of anti-corruption. The political struggle involves inflating the severity of the problem in order to obtain more resources to combat it and publicising exaggerated success statistics to demonstrate political will. With our 'trust in numbers'[9] as value-free, abstract measures, there is a constant problem of accurately measuring statistically slippery phenomena such as 'crime' or 'corruption', not to mention interpreting these data. In the area of corruption, the most widely used measure is the Transparency International (TI) Corruption Perceptions Index (CPI), which measures

---

8. See Holmes, *Rotten States?* or especially Charles Sampford, Arthur Shackock, Carmel Connors, and Frederik Galtung, eds., *Measuring Corruption* (Aldershot: Ashgate, 2006).
9. Theodore M. Porter, *Trust in Numbers: The Pursuit of Objectivity in Science and Public Life* (Princeton, NJ: Princeton University Press, 1999).

experts' opinions of how much corruption they believe exists in a given country. Such opinions say little about actual corrupt practices. Other indices, for example, those which measure whether or not a country's parliament has ratified a convention, may be accurate, but irrelevant to the practice of corruption. It is instructive, therefore, to take a step back and assess what it is we are doing when we participate in industries set up to combat undesirable social phenomena such as crime or corruption.

I will begin by outlining some of the characteristics of an 'industry'. We are speaking here of the work of hundreds of specialists, embedded in a myriad of programmes, initiatives and institutions, using hundreds of millions of dollars to combat corruption. The impact of these activities is, at best, unclear. We can only observe that those European countries considered most corrupt – the South-eastern European countries – have the largest number of good governance/public administration reform/anti-corruption programmes.

Let me start with a description of the phenomenon of corruption and the efforts to define it.

What is corruption?

Robert Harris[10] has emphasised the academic dilemma of researching corruption: 'We [reject] the possibility of a unitary definition of corruption: it is such a variegated activity that a single sentence could not encapsulate it, while a comprehensive definition would . . . have too many qualifications to be useful' (p. 199). Nonetheless, Harris defines corruption as the use of public position for private advantage and the subversion of the political process for personal ends. Most descriptions of corruption would typically include solicited or extorted bribery of public officials, nepotism in awarding public goods, contracts or jobs and 'borderline' practices such as inflated facilitation payments made by foreign companies to officials or misuse/embezzlement of public funds by officials. Conventional understandings of corruption tend to focus on collusion between a public official and a citizen who desires or needs a service. Virtually all definitions of corruption highlight the contrast between a public official's formal duties and their private interests or allegiances. In its most generalised form, corruption is simply a breach of any sort of public trust or mandate. Corruption can thus take place within a private company (the trust of shareholders breached by the CEO), in an NGO (members' trust breached by the NGO project manager), or an aid donor in some kind of partnership (the aid donor's trust breached by a dishonest government 'partner'). With corruption now possible in domains beyond the sphere of public administration, it means that the total amount of corruption has increased because the concept is now inflated. Corruption is now potentially possible in any organisation of entrusted power (private firms, government, NGOs, international organisations). Corruption need not be collusion, insofar as it may be the work of a single individual, as in cases of fraud or embezzlement. Purely due to this semantic inflation, then, there is simply more corruption 'out there' than previously thought. Finally, the inflation of corruption also reflects a problem of scale. Corruption is now transnational, insofar as foreign donors, Western firms, local NGOs, local governments and local firms can interact in complex transnational relations of cooperation, partnership, sub-contracting and corruption. Accountability can thus be breached at various links in this chain. Corruption is now more than just the speed payment to a corrupt traffic cop, customs official or government bureaucrat. Insofar as it also includes corrupt heads of state and secret bank accounts, its impact can

---

10. Robert Harris, *Political Corruption: In and Beyond the Nation State* (London: Routledge, 2003).

be measured in the billions of dollars. The problem, however, is that much corruption cannot be measured, since it consists of networking/nepotistic practices that give intangible benefits. Of importance here, however, is that these complexities of conceptualising corruption may be both a cause and an effect of the now vibrant anti-corruption industry.

Characteristics of the anti-corruption industry

The following list summarises the distinguishing characteristics of a generic 'industry' as defined here. By 'generic' is meant that it could apply to many kinds of moral projects or policies – development, trafficking, climate, etc. The listing of features is roughly chronological (the industry 'evolved'), but it would be more accurate to say that these characteristics tend to evolve in synergistic fashion. For each item, I then provide an example specifically from the anti-corruption industry.

(1) There exists, initially, an articulated grassroots concern, in which a politician or media story highlights a specific case or issue. In the case of corruption it is generally something of a 'scandal', a major open breach of trust. 'Fighting corruption' emerges as a priority among several major policy actors, seemingly at the same time.

(2) A variety of initiatives are taken and 'measures' enacted to set up a framework for dealing with the issue. These measures include (a) declarations of intent or statements of 'commitments', (b) signing of agreements and conventions, (c) efforts to enforce or monitor these commitments/agreements by governmental and nongovernmental actors, and (d) setting up of civil society monitoring coalitions. In the anti-corruption field, key governmental and intergovernmental organs are the Global Compact and the Group of States against Corruption (GRECO), and in civil society organisations such as TI, the Extractive Industries Transparency Initiative (EITI) and the UNCAC coalition (an advocacy group pressing for stricter adherence to the UN Convention against Corruption).

(3) The policy area takes on institutional autonomy, with specific organs, office and bureaus established to deal with the problem. The problem becomes its own budget line. Those organs with the largest budget lines (World Bank, UNDP, USAID, OECD, EU, the UK foreign assistance unit DFID) become the major actors. Bureaucratic interests develop to sustain or expand budgets by expanding, mainstreaming or exaggerating the definition of the problem and including ever more areas of concern. In the 'anti-corruption' field, for example, we obtain new policy areas: 'corruption and crime', 'corruption and security', 'corruption and climate', etc.

(4) A diverse group of secondary actors emerge who seek to influence the major actors by 'pushing' certain issues or priorities. These secondary actors include Western European bilateral aid agencies, donor foundations searching for new areas of concern, major NGOs and large consulting firms seeking to expand their activities. These secondary actors are at once donors, recipients of aid funds, stewards of funds, implementers of programmes and advocates for certain priorities. Hence, they may be combining fundraising activities with project management, being ever more integrated with the major policy decision-makers.

(5) A corpus of key texts emerges to which everyone pays reference, most especially the international or regional conventions. These declarations are invoked at international gatherings, meetings, ritual celebrations (10 years since passing of Convention X) and in formulating new initiatives. Typically, the documents are broad on principle, whereas measures for monitoring and implementation are less

clear and subject to further negotiation. What took place in the areas of human rights, development aid, women's equality and environmental protection has now been replicated in the field of anti-corruption. Key UN, OECD or European conventions are followed up by various monitoring and compliance mechanisms. Getting countries to ratify or fulfil their commitments to these conventions is now seen as a key tool for fighting corruption.

(6) An array of tools and indicators is developed to measure, assess and evaluate the extent of the phenomenon and the effectiveness of policy measures (in this case, measuring corruption and effectiveness of anti-corruption measures). These tools and methods, called 'diagnostics', become abstract, complex, standardised and comparable across countries and sectors. Qualitative, intensive studies keyed to specific situations or countries are downgraded in favour of standardised, context-free methods. The issue of quality of baseline data (measuring corruption levels in, say, Burma or North Korea) is downgraded in favour of comparable statistical measures and rankings that can be easily 'crunched'. 'Diagnostics' becomes a branch in itself, accessible only to specialists. Various actors attempt to make their indicators the standards of the industry. In the anti-corruption industry, for example, the comprehensive World Bank Governance Indicators competes with the Bertelsmann Transformation Index, the TI Bribe Payers Index, the Global Corruption Barometer, the Freedom House index, the TI CPI and the more qualitative country studies of Global Integrity.[11]

(7) The major players who dominate the discourse – be they governmental, multilateral, private-sector or NGO – can effectively marginalise those who question the conventional approaches, or even limiting grassroots input. These players coordinate with each other, harmonising their terminologies, statistical categories, understandings and view of appropriate solutions. Meanwhile, the initial grassroots 'movement' behind the problem evolves into more professional activities. Staff and personnel also become more professional and stable. Civil society leaders, government aid specialists and business leaders become more comfortable with each other, sharing similar perspectives, strategies and tactics. Deciphering 'donor priorities' and strategic fundraising becomes a key field of action for civil society organisations. In the anti-corruption industry, the governments within the UNCAC monitoring mechanism have succeeded in eliminating NGO input and country inspections. In the NGO sector, TI is administering its own Integrity Analysis of 27 European countries, with funds from the EU. The study is to contain the same kinds of data, gathered in the same way, from Sweden to Macedonia, from Hungary to the United Kingdom. Anti-corruption grassroots organisations, often loose affiliations of activists, now evolve into coalitions and organisations.

(8) Knowledge about the phenomenon, its causes, consequences and remedies is systematised into knowledge regimes in which academics, specialist training, and project implementation overlap. Academic specialists move in and out of policy implementation areas, while policy specialists receive certified training in areas such as Governance, Project Management, risk assessment or CSR. A cadre of specialists emerges, whose major talent is to determine donors' priorities. In the case of anti-corruption, there is now a whole retinue of specialists, trainers, project managers,

---

11. See Sampford, Shackock, Connors, and Galtung, *Measuring Corruption,* for a fuller discussion of these measures.

diagnosticians, centring around foreign aid, public administration reform and private sector CSR. Anti-corruption knowledge banks have emerged, such as the U4 group of European foreign ministries, the World Bank's http://www.fighting-corruption.org, TI's Research and Policy unit, and the Business Anti-corruption Portal. These data banks contain risk assessments, project evaluations, and the inevitable catalogues of 'lessons learned' and 'best practices'. TI, for example, assists anti-corruption activists with its Corruption Fighters Toolkit, Global Integrity assists aid professionals with its Country Assessments, the Danish Global Advice Network, financed by several European foreign aid ministries, assists businesses with information about corruption, the OECD offers information for government actors, the U4 assists European development aid organs, and the Internet Center for Corruption Research offers anti-corruption training.

(9) A standardised, 'industrial' terminology develops in which key terms, problems and solutions are framed and understood. In the field of anti-corruption, for example, this terminology refers to types of corruption, understandings about the causes of corruption, extent, impact, the need for broad solutions and coalitions, the use of sanctions, and about the urgency of the corruption problem. One of these under-standings, for example, is that it is possible to change people's corrupt practices if the right 'tools' are found. And the tools include a package of structural reforms, openness, enforcement, and raising awareness that corruption is bad, including bad for business. Among anti-corruption activists, TI has now developed a Plain Lan-guage Guide so that its members understand the phenomenon they are dealing with.

(10) The industry produces a standardised product (of knowledge, measures, activities), which is then marketed by major actors as absolutely essential. Clients for the package – countries, municipalities, private sector associations or firms – are those seeking entry into key associations (EU, chambers of commerce), those who need credit worthiness, those who want additional foreign assistance, or those who do not want to lose these resources for lack of compliance. The anti-corruption indus-try, for example, produces an 'anti-corruption package', which some governments 'purchase' only reluctantly. The 'customer' (Romania prior to EU accession, for example) may lack 'political will' or may never really 'come on board', but they are compelled to accept the package anyway. The marketing of the package may be stimulated by a combination of external pressures, a trusted local 'champion', a public relations campaign ('raising awareness') and 'capacity building' among those clients who now see the value of the package (or the consequences of not accepting it). In the anti-corruption field, for example, the establishment of anti-corruption agencies and commissions, with the accompanying foreign consultants and advisors and the continuing training, is one such trajectory.[12]

(11) Various actors attempt to expand the industry so as to overlap or include neigh-bouring industries. The expansion can take place by linking previously separate policy areas ('corruption and climate', 'corruption and gender', 'corruption and

12. Nicholas Charron, *Mapping and Measuring the Impact of Anti-Corruption Agencies: A New Dataset*, http://ancorage-net.org/index.jsp?page=documents&id=82 (accessed December 14, 2009); John R. Heilbrunn, Anti-Corruption Commissions: Panacea or Real Medicine to Fight Corruption? (World Bank Institute, 2004). Stock No. 37234, http://siteresources.worldbank.org/WBI/Resources/wbi37234Heilbrunn.pdf (accessed December 15, 2009); 'Local Anti-Corruption Agencies: Pros and Cons', U4, http://www.u4.no/pdf/?file=/helpdesk/helpdesk/queries/query141.pdf (accessed December 1, 2009).

post-conflict aid', 'corruption and human rights') or by connecting sectors of social activity (corruption and private business, corruption and NGOs). As a result, anti-corruption initiatives that were once limited to international business and corruption in foreign aid have now expanded into issues of environment/climate, water, organised crime, security, sport, and issues of whistle blowing and access to information.

(12) As the industry comes of age, local initiatives are increasingly tailored to the needs and donor priorities of the major industrial players. Public outreach, fundraising, branding and deciphering the donor landscape all become standard activities in the 'home office' or 'secretariat'. The problem of 'certification' becomes an issue, insofar as local governments or NGOs need to ensure the public and their donors that they are indeed doing what they say they are doing. In the anti-corruption field, based as it is on integrity in public affairs, there have been several scandals or near-scandals in connection with foreign aid to anti-corruption agencies and bogus anti-corruption NGOs. Even TI now has an entire monitoring and certification process to ensure that none of its national chapters abuse the TI brand.

(13) The final sign that an industry has come of age is that it spawns an *academic critique*. The critique of the industry poses questions as to its political correctness, adequacy of its programmes, its motives, effectiveness and interests. These critiques of development, humanitarian aid, of NGOs and of democracy promotion, often with a post-structuralist, discourse-analysis perspective, are well known. Yet the critiques tend to dwell on the margins of the industry and do little to substantively alter the established knowledge regimes, techniques or policies. The critique of the anti-corruption industry, for example, has centred on the misuse of the CPI, the lack of impact of anti-corruption programmes and the notion that anti-corruption policies are but a handmaiden of neoliberal capitalism.[13] These critiques have had little impact on the evolution of the anti-corruption industry.

Today, anti-corruption has arrived. To use a term from feminist theory, anti-corruption is now 'intersectional', touching on a wide variety of issues in different manifestations. Just as feminist scholars (or environmentalists) conceive of no issue that can be free from gender (or environmental) impact or policy relevance, we are now at a stage where all policy issues must now be considered in light of their implications for transparency or potential corruption. Anti-corruption has become a burgeoning industry with hundreds of millions of dollars in project funds, hundreds of anti-corruption professionals and a continuing stream of reports, indicators, conferences, action plans, conventions and evaluations. In the space of a decade, the world has now obtained dozens of national anti-corruption agencies in even the poorest third world countries. There is now a UN Convention against Corruption, a monitoring apparatus, a World Bank anti-corruption unit, a private sector anti-corruption initiative (http://www.fightingcorruption.org), a USAID anti-corruption programme and generalised anti-corruption budget lines or programmes in every major West European aid agency. TI leaders are now permanent invitees to Davos and TI's chairperson, Hugette Labelle, can command op-ed pages in major newspapers. The anti-corruption industry is starting to peak.

---

13. See for example Hindess, 'Anti-Corruption as a Risk to Democracy' or Frederik Galtung, 'Measuring the Immeasurable: Boundaries and Functions of (Macro) Corruption Indices' in *Measuring Corruption*, ed. Charles Sampford, Arthur Shackock, Carmel Connors, and Frederik Galtung (Aldershot: Ashgate, 2006), 101–30, and in http://www.u4.no/pdf/?file=/document/literature/Galtung%282005%29-boundaries.pdf (accessed February 10, 2010).

Anti-corruptionist rhetoric, the rhetoric of integrity, accountability and transparency, is present not just in government. The discourse of tranparency and openness pervades the private sector, in NGOs, and our universities. A variety of actors are all trying to make the invisible visible (transparency), trying to clarify responsibility (accountability), trying to ensure legitimacy (certification) and providing evidence of good performance (evidence-based evaluation). Anti-corruption programme managers are all trying to get higher rankings, better ratings, and more effective outputs. Like other mature industries, the anti-corruption industry has a small number of major players producing roughly the same product in different mixes: new laws, more monitoring, wider sanctions, more awareness raising, whistleblower protection, ethics management, getting everyone 'on board'. But the complexity of 'corruption' and the inadequacy of measuring short-term impact create frustration, which means that fashions and novelty approaches may suddenly enter the picture. Evaluations and documentation of past corruption initiatives tend to be filed away and overlooked, as the 'wheel' of project design, SWOT analysis[14] and stakeholder analysis is reinvented by each new actor. European aid agencies, for example, are now enacting various 'zero tolerance' policies for their work in countries or aid situations where such codes of conduct may simply not be feasible. The expansion or inflation of the industry leads more actors to be invested in it, and the impetus is for the very meaning of the term 'corruption' to be inflated. Corruption becomes amalgamated with white collar crime, bad judgement, or inefficient management. In the meantime, fighting corruption itself becomes a political issue. One can now accuse opponents not just of being corrupt, but of being slack in the fight against corruption. Accusations of anti-corruption organs as themselves corrupt can now take their place on the political stage.

As the industry matures, we observe the institutionalisation of a policy area, and its derivative regimes of knowledge, funds, organisations, specialists and problems. This creates the foundation for a discourse of anti-corruptionism. Here it is essential to emphasise that the 'industry' itself is not an actor. It does not have its own project or programme, a consolidated ideology nor even its own 'missionaries'. Rather, there are a whole set of actors who both cooperate and compete with each other at the same time. Like traditional industries (think of Big Tobacco or the Big Three Automakers in Detroit), there is cooperation and competition, subcontractors and peripheral players, creative types and cautious managers; there are the disillusioned, the critics and the wannabees. We have an institutional complex containing national and international organs, national aid programmes, ministries and EU directorates, NGOs in the North, consulting firms, donors, private industry and the CSR field, private foundations; and in the South, a set of aid-receiving ministries, erstwhile 'champions of reform' and local NGO coalitions. Dwelling along all this are the media, who can uncover periodic scandals as Northern aid is lost in the South, or can ask, 'Where was the anti-corruption agency?', a question that could not have been asked some years ago.

The development of a comprehensive anti-corruption 'industry' based on both policy and morality, is not unique. The rise of the anti-corruption industry resembles similar developments in development aid, human rights, civil society, women's (now gender) issues, and in environmental (now climate) protection. The trajectory is one where an issue which was formally marginal or unmanageable is 'boxed and packaged' so that it can 'put on the agenda'. If industries are anything, they are 'agenda setters'. Individual or sporadic activism by outsiders is gradually replaced, or enveloped by a process of institutionalisation, standardisation and by a globalised elite discourse that ensures that the issue remains on

---

14. Strengths, Weaknesses, Opportunities, Threats, a well-known technique for strategic planning in firms and organizations.

the agenda and obtains its own budget line, even if in revised or 'new improved' form (evidence-based anti-corruption, for instance). Coalitions must be formed so that everyone comes 'on board'. What began as a movement or campaign now becomes organised and institutionalised. Movements become projects. Projects become policies. Governmental and non-governmental actors now emphasise common interests. Additional conventions or amendments are formulated, ratified and monitoring mechanism set up at international or regional levels. Non-governmental actors – private business or NGOs – are brought in and made into 'stakeholders'. The media 'discovers' the issue, as do Hollywood celebrities or the Nobel Peace Prize committee. With new budget priorities from major actors, the secondary players – the think tanks, consulting companies, development aid strategy offices – also begin to rethink their priorities. Anti-corruption is now 'mainstreamed' into previously established programmes or made into a 'crosscutting issue' in foreign policy, competing with already established priorities. The more glamorous, new industry begins to push the other out of the way.

Is the anti-corruption industry different from other industries? Here we might cite one major difference, in that the issue of 'corruption' seems to be less clear, and therefore less amenable to measurement than issues of poverty, literacy, AIDS, environmental degradation, etc. In these other issues there are the well-known polices, commitments, budget lines, parameters, impact measures and critiques. We seem to have more reliable measures of impact: rates of measles, cases of AIDS, or BNP per capita can be measured and assessed more easily, and alternative solutions can be tried out. Assessing and measuring corruption seems to be more problematic, more akin to measuring and assessing 'the informal sector' or 'illegal migration'.

How did this happen?

The anti-corruption industry did not emerge overnight. Indeed, corruption and corruption fighting have been practices and government policies since there have been governments. In 1977, the US Government enacted the Foreign Corrupt Practices Act, which penalised US corporations for corrupt behaviour in foreign transactions. Governments as diverse as Mexico and China have had anti-corruption programmes and platforms for decades, and foreign leaders in the most authoritarian states have frequently spoken out against abuse of public office or corruption. The struggle over corruption seems to transcend regime type. However, the development of a corruption industry is new. It required a general conclusion that good governance is a precondition for development and a move towards greater openness, accountability and transparency in the affairs of governments and private firms. The demands for transparency are now louder and the penalties for opacity seemingly greater. While some kinds of corruption with impunity are now eliminated, it is unclear whether this means that we have less corruption, or whether corruption has become more sophisticated (bribes could be replaced by nepotism, facilitation payments and consulting fees). What is new over the last decade is some kind of *international consensus about corruption being a major problem* for development. The full story of how this consensus was achieved has yet to be written. We can only observe that driven activists, pressured institutions, and hard-nosed businessmen seem to have come together to put anti-corruption onto the policy agenda.

Every industry has its founders and milestone events. Anti-corruption is no exception. Anti-corruption as an industry begins with two such events, and both are centred around the major institution of third world development, The World Bank. The first is the founding, in 1993 of the NGO TI by a former World Bank official, Peter Eigen, and several colleagues from international development, business and diplomacy. The second is the famous 'cancer of corruption' speech by World Bank President James Wolfensohn in 1996, in which the agenda of economic development was tied together with the effectiveness of government, leading to new conditions of loans. Tied into these events is a third, general trend in public administration and market-based management, what academics tend to call 'neoliberalism'. The neoliberal model combines the privatisation of services and new techniques for measuring and assessing performance. In short, programmes must work effectively, and leaders, organisations and governments are responsible for establishing the mechanisms to show that that these programmes do indeed work properly. This trend takes on many labels, in which terms such as 'accountability', 'transparency', and 'openness' are the most frequent.

Let me discuss these two events and the neoliberal trend in more detail, as they inform our understanding of how the anti-corruption industry evolved. We begin with TI.

The birth of TI

Frustrated by the waste of aid in East Africa, where he had worked for the World Bank, and by the Bank's failure to put more conditions on its loans to corrupt leaders, the German economist Peter Eigen brought together a network of ex-diplomats, international lawyers, businessmen and government civil servants, including some from the Third World, to form TI in 1993. With a secretariat in Berlin, Eigen's home town, TI has since expanded to form independent national chapters, which today exist in about 85 countries. Crucial in this expansion was the development of the CPI, a ranking of the most and least corrupt countries, and the closest thing TI has to an acknowledged 'brand'. Today, TI produces a Global Corruption Report, corruption assessments such as National Integrity Studies, the Bribe Payers' Index, and it organises a biannual International Anti-corruption Conference for all anti-corruption actors from government, private sector and NGOs. With a budget of 8–10 million Euros, largely from West European governments/aid agencies, TI is the major non-governmental player in the anti-corruption industry. It provides knowledge, conducts advocacy and lobbying campaigns and attends or organises meetings as a responsible member of civil society. Its activities have now evolved from simple awareness-raising – the naming and shaming' of the CPI – to include the various tools for measuring corruption and determining where anti-corruption inputs should be made. TI's members include activists, business people, former aid workers, ex-diplomats, civil servants, lawyers and journalists. TI chapters carry out country studies of potential for corruption in various sectors (customs, health, procurement) and help establish 'integrity pacts' between governments and contractors. TI is active in programmes to monitor government or private sector actions in corruption-prone sectors (extractive industries, development aid, health). Their strategy, as developed by Eigen, is called 'coalition building', which means the forging of alliances with any group who will listen. As articulated by Eigen, coalition building should be seen in contrast to confrontation or demonstration in which groups are kept outside the decision-making bodies. As such, TI has celebrated its inclusion in various UN and World Bank forums on anti-corruption, which has given it some influence on formulating policy. Concretely, TI was part of the lobbying process for a UN Convention against Corruption, now ratified by 80 countries and is presently active in advocating monitoring provisions for the Convention. TI's CPI is used in journalistic, academic and policy communities as an instrument for measuring governance performance and may even play a role in determining a country's eligibility for foreign development assistance. At local levels, TI chapters have begun to establish anti-corruption legal aid centres (ALACs) which support whistle-blowing activities. TI cooperates with governments in drafting laws or setting up programmes. Local TI chapters do not necessarily pursue individual cases, but they do try to comment on government or non-governmental initiatives. As it receives its support largely from Western government donors, TI is constantly in dialogue with these donors in various forms of fundraising, advising and cooperation. TI has modelled itself in some ways on Amnesty International in terms of gaining influence, but without the activist or provocative image of Amnesty or Human Rights Watch.

Cancer of corruption

The second milestone event is the famous 'cancer of corruption' speech by James Wolfensohn when he headed the World Bank. The speech, held in 1996, also marked the acknowledge-ment of TI's mission by the Bank, and set the stage for the Bank beginning to include stip-ulations about government effectiveness and legitimacy in its loan policies. In more general terms, the 'cancer of corruption' speech also marked the entry of governance criteria into World Bank lending, and spawned the engagement of the Bank in establishing various indicators of good governance by the researchers in the World Bank Institute. The key operational concept in the governance diagnostics became that of 'state capture', here understood as the illicit control of public policy by private actors in the form, say of undue influence or purchasing of judges or politicians. The Bank was able to develop indicators to show 'high capture' and 'low capture' societies and to tie it to corrupt behaviour under privatisation, especially in the former Soviet countries. The Bank thus began the compara-tive ranking of countries on various good governance scales (called 'Governance Matters', and published by the World Bank Institute). These indicators could now be used as a baseline on which to develop policy. The key problem however, remained that of tying anti-corruption programmes to demonstrably improved governance. To date, it has been next to impossible to demonstrate that a specific anti-corruption measure (change in public procurement, for example) has reduced the general level of corruption. On the contrary, it remains the case that those countries with the most extensive anti-corruption programmes also tend to be the most corrupt according to the existing indices (in the same manner, the country with the largest TI organisation, is Bangladesh, which constantly ranks near the bottom of the CPI).

New public management

Aside from these two milestones, the third factor in the development of the anti-corruption industry is the general change in public administration towards market orientation. Indicators of public administration performance were now developed along with an 'audit culture' stressing accountability, openness, transparency and unambiguous indicators.[15] The slogan, or rather epithet, for this change is known as 'neoliberalism', in which a market mentality and market tools are applied to the gamut of public services, social welfare measures and individual careers under the influence of flexible capitalism. As such, local and national governments, and even donors, transformed themselves from providing services to pur-chasing them from outside contractors. This led to a new type of corruption, by which bureaucrats who previously sold direct access to government resources or embezzled aid could now profit by collecting a facilitation fee from private contractors or otherwise influence the procurement process. The movement of money in the global economy also led to a new set of anti-corruption activities, known as 'asset recovery', in which the hidden

---

15. On the concept of audit culture see especially Michael Power, *The Audit Society: Rituals of Verification* (Oxford: Oxford University Press, 1997) and Marilyn Strathern, ed., *Audit Cultures: Anthropological Studies in Accountability, Ethics, and the Academy* (London: Routledge, 2000).

foreign bank accounts of corrupt leaders were located and returned to the state treasury. In this function, anti-corruption became a new instrument for making governments more effective and introducing criteria of ethics into public life. This strategy of greater transparency could be applied both in the South and in the developed Western democracies. As a result, new target areas are developed for 'selling' the anti-corruption package. Now it is not only governments who need an anti-corruption policy, but NGOs and private companies as well. Anti-corruption became an element of risk assessment, due diligence and monitoring foreign aid abroad. It became part of controlling abuses in procurement at home, integrity in contracting, getting firms to sign on to the Global Compact's anti-corruption principle, new initiatives to support whistleblowers and combating abuse of authority within private companies or organisations. In its mature stage, the anti-corruption industry is thus coupled with other such 'industries'. Hence, conferences are now held and reports written on issues such as corruption and health, corruption and media, corruption and post-war reconstruction, corruption and human rights, corruption and extractive industries, corruption in security, corruption in the arms trade. And now, of course, corruption and climate change. This coupling would not have occurred had it not been for the general neoliberal changes in public management.

Conclusions: industry or craft? Movement or institution?

As described here, the anti-corruption industry contains key global actors with considerable resources and policy reach. It contains local NGOs who look to these global actors for signals about 'The Next Big Thing', and it includes an attractive rhetoric highlighting integrity, trust, accountability and openness. Those who are part of the industry, those who articulate the discourse of anti-corruptionism, call it a 'movement'. In reality, it is more a flexible organisation. The discourse of anti-corruptionism is sufficiently generalised so that new actors can enter the field, each with their own agenda, but appropriating the anti-corruptionist discourse. We have a marketplace of anti-corruption initiatives, organised and prioritised by actors in the anti-corruption industry, now using hundreds of millions of dollars in projects. More important, these projects now have their own, solid budget lines, sometimes coded directly as 'anti-corruption', other times subsumed under 'good governance' or 'public administration reform'. Certainly these millions of dollars are far below the kind of 'industry' we could observe in the field of security and defence, or even of global crime-fighting. The total anti-corruption budget for all Western aid agencies is far below the cost of a few fighter planes or a single Halliburton contract. And in the field of global crime, there is no anti-corruption equivalent of Interpol or the various cooperative institutions for fighting global organised crime. Nevertheless, for local and global NGOs operating within the larger framework of governance and democracy assistance, as well as the private consulting firms whose staff contain former aid workers, civil society activists and government experts, anti-corruption is now an attractive market for moral entrepreneurs. One of the reasons it is attractive is that success/impact is so difficult to measure. A drug enforcement programme, for example, might measure its success by the amount of drugs captured or arrests made. Anti-corruption has no such scale, and tends to rely on more spectacular news that this ex-leader's assets have now been recovered or this new law enacted. As a result, a well-organised programme, with many events, reports, coalitions formed and training modules conducted, with the setting up of action plans, formulation of anti-corruption strategies and self-evaluations, such a programme will be considered 'successful' even though 'reduction of corruption' itself will be next to impossible to measure over the short term. It is here that we see the emergence of group interest within the anti-corruption industry, even though the actors are also in competition with each other for donor funds. International gatherings such as the (governmental) Global Forum or the (non-governmental) International Anti-corruption Conference attempt to iron out these differences. It is in such fora that diverse actors are forged into 'industries'.

It is instructive to compare this 'industry' with what came before it. In this sense, we might see industry as the opposite of 'craft'. Craftsmen work with a limited set of tools, are sensitive to local variation and adapt their work to local conditions. A crafted product lasts longer and feels more authentic than an imposed, standardised industrial product. Craftsmen pass on their knowledge in a traditional, practice-oriented form, improvising as they go along, and they are often so passionate about their work that it is almost a passion rather than occupation. They figure things out locally, in their context. Craftsmen are therefore the opposite of the 'industry' approach. The handicrafts scene is varied; innovative local, adaptable, passionate enthusiasts pass on oral, flexible traditions. It resembles a 'movement' in the sense of being less hierarchical, less codified into texts, with fewer formalised instructions and guidelines. Industry, on the other hand, is standardised, global, elitist and codified. Industry now contains 'training' or 'project' or 'strategic planning' specialists who in fact have no specific 'craft', but who can move from one policy domain to another. These people are experts in 'project management', in 'programme development' or fundraising, no matter whether the goal in question is humanitarian aid, anti-corruption, or children's rights. They move from one industry to another, committed not to the cause as such (the craft), but to their own career within whatever industry offers opportunities. In this sense, they are the opposite of a movement. The anti-corruption *industry* is full of anti-corruption assessments, programmes and projects. The industry is overshadowing the anti-corruption *movement,* with its limited number of activists and mobilisation. Entry into this movement, in fact, is now increasingly limited to those who can articulate anti-corruptionist discourse. Aside from the conventions, training programmes and diagnostics, however, there are also courageous local activists exposing brutal corruption in their home countries; individuals and groups who are harassed, jailed, and even murdered for exposing corruption in their local environments. Such people speak and act in a manner that is wholly foreign to the everyday activities of actors in the anti-corruption industry. They act as symbolic beacons for the 'movement', but symbolic only because they are celebrated in ritual gatherings. When the rituals are concluded, the budget negotiations and fundraising overtures start up again.

The 'industry' concept has often used in cynical or pejorative terms. Yet the rise of the anti-corruption industry is not to be condemned as such. The generalised skills found in industries are not to be devalued. We all want to see efficient organisations achieving their goals. My point here is to examine the price we pay when such activities become codified as the *only* way to reach such goals, when a global discourse and standardisation, under the rubric of 'coalition building' and the number crunching of 'diagnostics', an approach that stigmatises other approaches as 'confrontational' or 'unprofessional', begins to dominate. What is the price we pay when international anti-corruption forums, conventions and EU programmes swallow up those very grassroots initiatives that can shed light on ineffective government and bring down dishonest officials?

Industries do not last forever. Insofar as they refuse to innovate, lose touch with their customer base or fail to adapt to new conditions, any industry can become a dinosaur. The American rust belt and the European shipyards are evidence of industries that declined. In the world of development and international assistance, the emergence of new policy priorities can also lead to 'policy evaporation', as the exigencies of poverty alleviation and development are now absorbed into the climate change industry. The Paris Declaration on Aid Effectiveness (2005), intended to 'harmonise' foreign aid, would seem to present a pressure towards more such standardisation. In the meantime, major players and donors can suddenly gravitate to new, fashionable priorities. One can only speculate what will happen to 'integrity' and 'anti-corruption' as the climate change juggernaut takes over.

There is a long tradition in social science to study movements and protests. But it is equally important to study what happens when the movement and protest that moves individual 'believers' become institutionalised. The struggle against corruption, which has always involved courageous activists, whistle-blowing civil servants and enterprising journalists, has now become mainstreamed, projectified and 'organised'. This is what happened to human rights some two decades ago. It happened to civil society and the NGO sector over the past decade. And it is happening now with anti-corruption, which is itself part of a general trend towards 'good governance', and 'global integrity'. In this process, the object of the movement, corruption itself, recedes into the background as anti-corruptionism obtains its own rhetorical influence and budget lines.

One of the most famous studies in industrial sociology is called the Hawthorne experiment. In this series of experiments, conducted in the 1930s at an American plant making telephone parts, a group of researchers instituted various improvements in the working environment on the factory floor. The researchers noticed that regardless of what change they instituted – increasing the light, decreasing the light, changing work breaks, revamping pay schedules – that workers' productivity increased. What began as a test of improving productivity ended up showing that people react positively to researchers who pay attention to them. For the workers, it was not about improving output but feeling good. Anti-corruption, I submit, has this feel-good character. Like other moral projects, anti-corruptionism has its own set of career-oriented actors with personal or institutional vested interests. The message conveyed is that 'we are doing something', rather than the more critical, 'Is what we are doing any good?' Examining the EU measures for anti-corruption, and others elsewhere, we find two parallel universes: one where anti-corruption measures are increasingly systematised and institutionalised into the anti-corruption industry; the other where corruption, increasingly more sophisticated, thrives unabated, even within some anti-corruption units. We need, therefore, to study not just the concrete ways in which we can reduce corruption. *We need to study how anti-corruption has been making us feel so good over the past decade.* Anti-corruption, like so many other industries in the sphere of development, might just be another therapeutic, feel-good industry. Hence, we need to ask whether the anti-corruption industry is really a kind of Hawthorne experiment, a feel-good pill, a kind of policy-Prozac that we take while we examine the latest corruption rankings and recite the tenets of anti-corruptionism. There are indeed 'rotten states' out there, and there is a thriving anti-corruption industry. But it is not clear that anti-corruption is having any effect on them.

Acknowledgements

I thank Diana Schmidt-Pfister and Holger Moroff for their helpful critiques and extraordinary patience in allowing me to complete this article.

Notes on contributor

Steven Sampson is an Associate Professor of Social Anthropology at Lund University, researching anti-corruption in the Balkans. Recent publications include 'Corruption and Anti-Corruption in Southeast Europe: Landscapes and Sites', in *Governments, NGOs and Anti-Corruption: The New Integrity Warriors*, ed. Luís de Sousa, Peter Larmour, and Barry Hindess (UK: Routledge, 2009). And 'Integrity Warriors: Global Morality and the Anticorruption Movement in the Balkans', in *Understanding Corruption: Anthropological Perspectives*, ed. Dieter Haller and Chris Shore (London: Pluto Press, 2005).

The intricate interplay of multi-level anti-corruption: a conclusion

Holger Moroff

This chapter argues that a three-level analysis of anti-corruption efforts provides an essential matrix for identifying relevant actors as well as understanding the motivations, mechanisms and effects of their actions. The detailed case studies in this book testify to its explanatory strength and serve as a basis for a general evaluation. By way of connecting and extending these cases light is shed on more recent developments in eastern European anti-corruption policies and possible future trajectories are delineated.

Analytical frame

Domestic civil society, national governments and international society constitute the three levels of analysis in the studies at hand. Several actors can be identified on each of these levels who can, in turn, be connected to actors on the other two levels. Domestic civil society is often thought of as consisting purely of NGOs. However, in a western context, civil society is usually much more broadly defined than that.[1] It can comprise all kinds of pressure group whether based on values, beliefs or material interests such as businesses, trade unions or the media. In many post-communist countries values and ideals based NGOs are the ones targeted most by international donors for helping to promote and monitor anti-corruption policy goals. Herein also lays the connection between the international and the domestic civil society levels. The national governmental level can be thought of as comprising the political decision makers and administrative implementers as well as opposition parties with a history or at least the potential ability to truly challenge and take over the government.[2] International society then consists of international organisations, transnational actors such as private foundations, think tanks, multinational businesses, international NGOs and internationally active, norm entrepreneurial governments who in their aggregate set the international anti-corruption discourse and practices through awareness campaigns, aid programmes, international law, advocacy scholarship as well as by economic and political conditionality.

The mix of spontaneous outbreaks of anti-corruption protests on the domestic level, power political instrumentalisation on the governmental level, as well as legal and aid efforts originating at the international level have resulted in rather coincidental breakthroughs and setbacks without any overarching coordination or common frame of reference. Nevertheless, there seem to be cyclical developments in anti-corruption on all three levels that can at times result in interlocking mutual reinforcement or in interblocking stalemates. Such temporal dynamics can encompass: the attention dedicated to corruption cases and their scandalisation by the domestic and international media, election cycles that might or might not lead to a periodic change in government, intermittent crackdowns on corruption by governments as either a genuine policy or as means to rid themselves of rivals and critics, growing popular dissatisfaction with corruption leading to intervals of mass protests or alienation from and cynicism about the political system, general trends of dis/satisfaction related to the momentary position of a country's economy in the business cycle, the changing degree of trust international money lenders have in the clean and efficient administration of a government and thus the ability of countries to pay back their public debt. All these dimensions show dynamic patterns that affect anti-corruption efforts in a wider sense. Any analysis of a particular national or international legal, aid or political measure has thus to be placed in the context of a three level game played out on the changing tides and cycles of scandalisations, elections, governmental crackdowns, economic performances, trust in the sustainability of public debts, and popular protests, all leaving their mark on anti-corruption policies.

Three illustrative new cases

In recent times and after the studies in this volume had been concluded, three major exemplary events were playing themselves out in eastern Europe on the three levels of our analysis, involving all types of actor as identified already. Two are more directly anti-corruption related, namely the Yulia Timoshenko case in Ukraine and the mass demonstrations against Vladimir Putin in Russia while the third one is more connected to perceived financial mismanagement by governments with direct consequences for government oversight and thus also for anti-corruption policies. These are the implications of the financial crisis for Hungary, Romania and Bulgaria among others.

The first case again illustrates how a national government instrumentalises anti-corruption as a means to punish and potentially eliminate political rivals. On 11 October 2011 Yulia Timochenko, the former prime minister of Ukraine, received a 7-year prison sentence for allegedly abusing her power by signing an arguably unfavorable gas treaty with Russia.[3] Besides underlining the fact that the judiciary is not an independent branch of government, ensuring the equal application of the law, but used rather as a political tool by the current president Viktor Yanukovych, it showed once again how anti-corruption rhetoric and instruments can be applied in power political gambits.[4] In this case it served several purposes. Besides the obvious flogging of a former opposition leader who helped stage the Orange Revolution seven years earlier against the then and now again current president of the country, it is also used to break the conventional discourse portraying Yanukovych as being pro-Russia and anti-western while Timoshenko is standing for the reverse orientation. Domestic civil society is supposed to see that its former revolutionary leader was not acting in its interest but in her own and even worse in the interest of a foreign government. Major external powers felt uncomfortable about this as well: Russia because it implied it bought off or at least duped then Prime Minister Timoshenko and the EU because it epitomised a blatant politicisation and miscarriage of justice that put the rule of law further into jeopardy.[5] The EU reacted strongly by putting on hold already signed association agreements. However, no strong outcry or even mass demonstrations against such cynical power politics under the label of anti-corruption could be witnessed in Ukrainian society. This seems to confirm Grødeland's assessment in this volume that both the elites and masses are disillusioned with anti-corruption measures and have resigned to a fatalistic and cynical perspective as well as her finding that the judiciary is perceived as the most corrupt branch of government.

Similar judicial retribution against former government members – also framed in a broad anti-corruption mould – could be observed in an EU member country, namely Hungary.[6] Even though it lacks the trimmings of a show case trial, the Hungarian method was equally questionable as the new government passed laws and used them retroactively against the former government and its appointees. In both cases, former government leaders are retroactively prosecuted for corruption in a broad sense, delegitimising the former government and by implication undermining the present opposition's claim to be ready and competent for switching roles in future.

The second case, public mass protest against Vladimir Putin, demonstrates how domestic civil society and a long time silent and cynical public start taking to the streets rather spontaneously. The protests were triggered by an event that symbolised business as usual rather than a scandal out of the ordinary, namely the rigged parliamentary elections in Russia 2011. Nevertheless, it provided only the occasion in the wake of which broad dissatisfaction with a semi-authoritarian regime was voiced and whose governing methods were widely perceived as corrupt and summed up in slogans such as 'Putin is a thief' and 'United Russia – party of crooks and thieves'.[7] The speaker of the Russian parliament, the Duma, was forced to resign in the aftermath and the events will certainly have implications for the presidential elections in 2012 after which it might become clearer on which side the regime will come down, more democratic or authoritarian. In either case, the anti-corruption discourse is destined to play an important role for both the government and civil society alike. In a climate of widespread mistrust in a leadership that tried to paper over the gap between its own self-aggrandisement and its dismal performance on the ground it took only a minor event to reach a tipping point seemingly spontaneously. The government took the acquiescence of a seemingly apathetic if not subservient and deferential people for granted when announcing in November 2011 that it was a long-planned gambit to keep switching roles between president Medvedev and prime minister Putin, with the latter potentially staying in power till 2024 or beyond. While the government invoked the mantra of stability and painted threats of chaos if its grip on power was ever challenged and loosened – emulating the leaders of the old regimes during the Arab Spring – its reactions followed a predictable pattern. Initially, Putin accused the US and other western governments of sponsoring protest groups as well as meddling in internal affairs and thus using the international anti-corruption discourse from above and the domestic one from below to corner and weaken a national government. These attempts appeared so rehearsed and threadbare that they were quickly taken up and ridiculed by protesters themselves.[8] The rigged election was then only the condensation kernel around which public protests crystallised. As shown time and again in this volume's studies, it seems unpredictable when the tipping point for mass protests is reached. The previous colour revolutions in eastern Europe and the more recent Arab Spring uprisings all used new media and methods of communication such as cell phones, the internet, blogs or twitter and also exposed corruption through video posts on the web. Of course, these new technologies cut both ways and can be used as investigative and surveillance instruments by civil society and governments alike. All these protest movements have vented their anger over mismanagement and corruption at the governmental level and it constitutes a permanent theme in their criticism. What connects these movements as well is that they took place in countries without a functioning opposition, an opposition that could truly monitor and challenge the government, including its extended patron–client web, and can reasonably be expected and thus prepare for potentially taking over as a new government. This structural feature of most modern democracies, the checks and balances provided not only by a separation of the three branches of governments but also by the bipolar interplay of government and opposition as an anti-corruption tool in and of itself, has rarely been studied and seems to be of great importance for the country cases in this volume.[9] This situation calls for further research that links anti-corruption to political and democratic theory for which eastern European transition countries would constitute good test cases.

The third case, the implications of the financial crises in Hungary, Bulgaria and Romania, reveals the impact financially powerful non-state actors can have on governments once those actors lose trust in those governments and perceive them as a source of mismanagement and corruption. Starting in 2010 international private actors such as banks, pension funds and private investors who grew suspicious of certain governments' ability or willingness to pay back their debts and thus refused to lend them money (or only against prohibitively high interest rates) for refinancing. It does not seem a coincidence that the two lowest ranked EU countries on the corruption perception index, namely Greece and Italy, had to change their governments under market pressure virtually overnight in 2011 whereas Ireland, Portugal and Spain did so in the regular electoral way. Latvia, Hungary, Romania and Bulgaria were those eastern European countries hardest hit by this loss of trust and all will have to undertake efforts not only to put their fiscal house in order but also to improve accountability, oversight and good governance of their administration. Whatever the origins of the unsustainable balance sheets of public finances, its consequences are closer scrutiny of their financial management at the international level not least through the European Commission[10] whose assessments and sanctions can only be altered by a two-thirds' majority of the member states. This will very likely have consequences for all large-scale, state-centred, patron–client-based corruption networks as they directly impact the public coffers and transparency. Greece already announced that it will comply with the EU Commission's request to put all public contracts up as open tenders via the internet and make all bidding processes public.[11] Public administration itself has been thrown into the limelight. Where it is seen as a bloated, self-serving machine for generating secure jobs, contracts and sinecures for friends, family and mutual support networks of any kind it is a target for criticism by international financial institutions who make further lending conditional on cleaning up – and for the most part that also means shrinking – the state apparatus. This dovetails with the neoliberal anti-corruption discourse as expounded by Steven Sampson and Lili Di Puppo in this volume. It also reinforces the view that a smaller government displays less surface area for public–private corrupt exchanges and thus supposedly leads to a cleaner and more transparent government. Such a view is buttressed by the fact that the governments in the two countries with the highest levels of perceived corruption, Greece and Italy, were forced to transfer their leadership not to another major political group – which might just have served another patron–client network – but to 'technocrats' who were not closely affiliated with those larger political forces and their machines.

Other forms of corruption such as paying bribes for public services in hospitals, schools, universities, police etc. are likely less affected by cleaning up the high-level corruption at the governmental top. Petty corruption on the ground mainly to supplement meager salaries as studied by Richard Rose and William Mishler for Russia in this volume is usually not anchored in larger political patron–client networks. The public and private debt crises in Hungary and to a lesser extent in Romania, Bulgaria, Latvia and Poland has already resulted in more stringent budget oversight that will also encompass issues of good governance, clean administration and thus by implication anti-corruption measures. More supranational oversight not only over EU money[12] but also over national budgets is the first tangible outcome of a crisis brought about by international, private money lenders suddenly losing faith in national governments. The unpredictable nature of this loss of faith becomes apparent when it is pointed out that the public debt to GDP ratio did not change overnight and had been at such high levels for a long time before markets perceived them as unsustainable and stopped lending money.

These three recent cases illustrate how anti-corruption still plays a central role on the domestic civil society, national governmental and international levels. The major actors on the domestic level are civil society defined as anything but directly government and state related or employed; on the national level we find governments, their appointees and employees; whereas the international level is comprised of international organisations, international financial institutions, private investors and international donors whether governments, NGOs, or individual philanthropists that support reforms abroad by helping foreign civil society to organise and monitor their national governments and their implementation of international anti-corruption treaties and measures. All these levels and their actors are potentially interlinked and their analyses reveal an intricate interplay of multi-level anti-corruption policies.

Comparative conclusion

The studies brought together in this volume reflect developments on these three levels in eastern Europe up until 2009 and could thus not consider the aforementioned cases. However, the authors provided updates to their analyses in December 2011 that are weaved into the concluding summary that follows.[13] It provides thus a first assessment of the studies with some benefit of hindsight and a new installment in the continuously unfolding stories of corruption and anti-corruption in eastern Europe and beyond. Starting at the international level the implementation of legal anti-corruption instruments in eastern Europe is analysed followed by a closer look at the EU's efforts in its eastern neighbourhood. The individual country case studies reflect different degrees of association with the EU and support the assumption that anti-corruption efforts are less successful the weaker that association is. A critical assessment about the origins and questionable results of the global anti-corruption industry concludes the set of studies in this volume.

From the perspective of international legal anti-corruption efforts as represented by the OECD and the Group of States against Corruption (GRECO), Sebastian Wolf asserts that their monitoring mechanisms have remained crucial for follow up and implementation efforts in eastern Europe. While the UN anti-corruption monitoring is a purely intergovernmental affair both OECD and GRECO are obligated to also include civil society actors in their assessments. After the second round of GRECO evaluations were almost completed by the end of 2011 the trend that eastern European countries are ahead of their western neighbours in transposing the GRECO norms into national law has been reconfirmed. A notable exception is a lag in implementing the OECD rules on criminalising bribery of foreign public officials, whereas all countries seem to be reluctant in following the GRECO recommendations on the financing of political parties thus indicating a red line for law based international anti-corruption efforts. As soon as they affect core elements of the political game and party competition it is shunned.

Tania Börzel, Andreas Stahn, and Yasemin Pamuk offer an overview of corruption in the EU's eastern neighbourhood, noting that these countries exhibit all three of the main factors contributing to corruption: their (semi-)authoritarian political structure, distorted markets marked by state intervention, and complex regulatory frameworks, in addition to cultural explanations. Compounding these problems, the transition from communism to democracy and market economies has increased opportunities for corruption. In the neighborhood countries, in contrast to the new EU members, these transitions have been only partial and incomplete. The lack of democratic reform in particular seems to have hampered anti-corruption policy development and implementation. The prevalence of high level corruption on the input side – meaning legislation – has rendered anti-corruption efforts fairly ineffective because of their focus on the output side – that is law implementation and general administration.

The authors offer three basic approaches for combating corruption. The reform of the state approach attacks corruption by reforms of the existing political structure regarding administration, monitoring, and the judiciary. The reform of the economy approach focuses on eliminating opportunities for corruption through a deregulated market economy. The democratic reform approach focuses on increasing the involvement of non-state actors in the narrow sense of value- and belief-based NGOs. A focus on the third approach allows international actors to affect both input and output legitimacy.[14] Which approach is most appropriate to a given country depends on the particular strengths and weaknesses of that state. In general, the authors recommend that the EU should focus much more on the democratic reform approach in the European Neigbourhood Policy (ENP) states.

The ENP, which built on previous bilateral agreements between the EU and the post-Soviet states after the fall of communism, was developed in response to new concerns raised by the eastern enlargement and the need to develop a coherent policy towards the EUs new neighbours, especially because of their relative development lag. The action plans are rather comprehensive and touch on all three approaches, some even explicitly demanding involvement of non-state actors. However, the implementation of these plans has been hampered by vague language and broad recommendations within the context of a broad political dialogue, which has largely left out non-state actors. The EU lacks the membership carrot and other incentives seem too weak or untenable. Some effect has been had through negative conditionality but here too the neighbourhood lacks a strong disincentive, leaving the EU to rely largely on reforming financial assistance packages and to a lesser extent market access. Though the new financial assistance programmes focus on transparency and accountability, but also on the involvement of non-state actors and the protection of civil liberties, the ENP is unlikely to achieve substantial anti-corruption reform in the targeted states. Reliance on cooperation with elites in states that suffer high levels of state capture is unlikely to yield positive results. The lack of the 'membership carrot' and the lack of differentiation, fine tuning and adjustment among plans for different countries are also likely to hamper the EU's efforts to effect the desired changes in the region.

The ENP and its implementation underscore the difficulty faced by international anti-corruption efforts. The lack of a willing and competent domestic political regime renders many efforts ineffective, and efforts to bring about change in such regimes may prove these international programmes wasted or even counterproductive in some cases. According to Börzel et al. attention to domestic conditions and differences is crucial to the effective implementation of any international anti-corruption effort, but seems to be precisely what the ENP Action Plans lack. The real effects of the ENP remain to be seen even after a decade of its inception, but the prognosis is far from inspiring.

The active leverage of the EU is rather limited, however its passive leverage – that is its power of attraction to the elites and the citizenry – seems to be of greater though much less noticed relevance.[15] This becomes clear when one looks at the slogans and publicly stated rationales of the colour revolutions in eastern Europe from Georgia (2003), Ukraine (2004) and Kyrgyzstan (2005) to Russia (2011). Demonstrators demanded western European standards of democracy, political competition, and freedom of expression and of the media as well as accountability of politicians and the bureaucratic apparatus.[16] Without the EU's explicit or implicit sponsoring of these movements it exerts a strong power of attraction by serving as a model to point at. This so-called soft power might very well be the strongest force even though or maybe because of its non-direct, non-intentional character. A cautious approach in the direct sponsoring of the value- and belief-based civil societies – which for the most part, it can be assumed, would aid the political opposition – was most likely a wise strategy, whether by design or default. Thus the governments of the day could not credibly claim that public dissent was orchestrated by the west and their efforts to do so did not carry far and appeared as a rearguard effort that would quickly be ridiculed. The growth of dissent with an entrenched regime that appears more and more petrified speaks to the dynamic aspects of modern democracies that can gain stability and legitimisation only by alternating at least once in a while the roles of government and opposition.

For Russia, our case study by Richard Rose and William Mishler shows that citizens' perception of corruption depends heavily on the state of the economy. Whatever works in making citizens feel better off is pragmatically deemed permissible. The equal and transparent participation in the governance process – i.e. input legitimacy – seems less important than the problem-solving capacity of the system that provides output legitimacy by delivering better standards of living through whatever means. International actors and their monitoring mechanisms tend to use corruption perception indicators in their evaluations as good proxies for actual levels of corruption. This common practice should be viewed more critical in the light of these findings, suggesting that the perception of corruption is linked to a country's business cycle which points to another cyclical dynamic in the patterns of anti-corruption processes. Given another finding in this study based on the New Russia Barometer, caution is also called for even when using more sophisticated surveys. Thus the authors show that the perception of corruption is not based on the personal experiences of paying bribes.

Agnes Batory argues that Hungarian accession to the EU in 2004 may have been less of a watershed moment in the anti-corruption campaign than incentive-based conditionality explanations suggest. In terms of legislation and institutional mechanisms, the EU's policy of membership conditionality has been widely viewed as a major success. Indeed, the pre-accession period was marked by a significant jump in national anti-corruption activities, followed by an 'anti-corruption fatigue' on achieving official EU membership status. Considered together, these two developments are widely interpreted as evidence for the success of EU conditionality. However, beyond criticisms relating to the double standards of EU conditionality, Batory raises two more pragmatic criticisms that cannot be overlooked when assessing the effectiveness of EU conditionality-induced reforms. The first is that conditionality over-emphasised the adoption of laws and institutions in line with EU Commission requirements with little attention paid to whether and how legislation was actually implemented on the ground. Thus governments were able to tick off Commission requirements without making any serious efforts to affect substantive changes. The second, related criticism is that the conditionality did not provide a clear and systematic approach to anti-corruption policies. Thus, while Hungary's institutional anti-corruption framework (inspired by the EU) looks impressive, implementation of related laws and regulations is rather patchy. This type of symbolic compliance suggests that the EU's impact may be less far reaching than the conditionality literature suggests. Beyond the EU, other international organisations have had, perhaps, a more lasting impact on national governments insofar as anti-corruption would never completely disappear from the political agenda even when EU pressure is absent. Here, the influence of the OECD convention, UN agencies and the Council of Europe's GRECO are most important. However, lacking a credible sanction, international organisations are effective only in combination with domestically rooted forces. Although, the most recent post-accession revivals of anti-corruption efforts occurred in the absence of conditionality pressures, and it seems a product of the interplay among international, non-governmental and governmental actors. In the last case, the impetus came from low-key actors within the administration itself rather than from the political leadership. Batory stresses that it was low-level civil servants from within the administration rather than civil society who seem to take over from the EU as the main driving force behind anti-corruption. It is also apparent that the absence of civil society's involvement in the accession process (concerning negotiations, policymaking, and reforms) weakened this strand of the anti-corruption matrix.

Finally, the underlying motivation of relevant actors may be more significant in terms of hindering or helping anti-corruption than was previously realised. In particular, politicisation of corruption issues, frequently used as part of smear campaigns against opponents, both discredits anti-corruption as a worthy political goal and makes it difficult for actors outside government to frame it as a policy issue that should be tackled through targeted, sustainable interventions not unlike other social problems. Thus, political motivations of such interventions have come under fire and undermine the credibility of interventions of any kind in the anti-corruption field. As in Ukraine and many other countries the electoral cycle has a decisive impact on the anti-corruption momentum and direction. Since 2010 the constitution changing super majority of one party, Fidesz, led to a weakening of constitutional checks on executive power and anti-corruption rhetoric being used to legitimise new laws that punish the previous government without involving civil society at large.[17] Legally questionable methods of retroactive laws and curtailing the supreme court's competencies in financial matters of state are similar to those seen in Ukraine after Viktor Yanukovych regained power. Fidesz also changed the rules for nominating the central bank leaders and appointed an active party member to head the national audit agency, which is also in charge of overseeing party finances, as well as lowering the retirement age for judges so as to appoint new ones earlier and in greater numbers. A large part of Fidesz election campaign that resulted in its landslide victory focused on fighting corruption and the promise that corrupt government politicians (meaning the socialists) would be held accountable. Soon after the election Fidesz created the post of a government commissioner for uncovering the previous government's corrupt practices, even charging the former prime minister Gyurcsany with abuse of power. The parallels with the Timoshenko case in Ukraine are striking though as of yet without any major show case trials.[18]

The Polish case reveals what was argued earlier by Wolf, namely that even though symbolic legal mechanisms induced by the international level are in place, they remain largely ineffective due to a lack of implementation because of machine politics on the national level. Kaja Gadowska also delineates how foreign actors influenced the Polish anti-corruption discourse. It was first and foremost George Soros, an American financier and philanthropist, who helped set up the Batroy Foundation as a major NGO. Together with the EU, Soros also established the 'Corruption Barometer', which conducts public opinion polls on the scale and perception of corruption. Administrative patterns can also be changed by weaving them into parts of the EU. Thus the use and joint management of EU structural funds seems to also have altered the domestic bureaucracy in charge of administering these funds. The cyclical nature of anti-corruption in political campaigns is shown once again. However, unlike the 2005 and 2007 elections, combating corruption was not among the leading issues in the 2011 parliamentary campaign. The outfit responsible for implementing the various anti-corruption laws and strategies, the chamber of control, was somewhat depoliticised by appointing a new head on a purely meritocratic basis. However, the audits the chamber has conducted in several ministries remained rather low key as they have only affected officials in deputy and lower rank positions, indicating that the chamber has more power than before but still not enough for significant overhauls.

As shown by Kalin Ivanov for Bulgaria and Romania, popular outrage and scandalisation of corruption cases by domestic civil society may be mixed with cynical resignation of the masses. By discussing the peculiar competitive scramble for EU accession between these two countries, Ivanov shows the impact of the international system on domestic politics and their interdependence. Domestic NGOs and media in Bulgaria and Romania were both motivated by conviction and material benefits. Initially, the change of government in Romania presented an opportunity for a strong anti-corruption campaign by the new government while Bulgaria's corruption scandals were viewed differently, due to a lack of media attention and the reentry of implicated elites back into the political system. In Romania, we find a similar outcome by different means. Amendments to the legal code that provide for giving advance notice of major search and seizure operations allows for high-level corruption to remain unchecked. The abilities of the EU and other international actors to tailor efforts to the domestic context were indeed limited by the complexity of the material and power struggles. Governments also fear that they become more accountable to the European Commission than to their own citizens. The EU had an excellent opportunity with the accession process for Bulgaria and Romania effectively to disconnect anti-corruption policies from the common pitfall of politicisation and instrumentalisation. Yet, many contentious issues concerning the definition, monitoring and gauging of corruption as well as finding ways to impose reforms before accession forestalled such efforts. Most importantly, the EU's ability to freeze assets (mainly its structural funds) for member states that seem to drag their feet about effective anti-corruption measures was pioneered in the case of Bulgaria and serves as a stern and credible warning to other member states. Moreover, concerns about sluggish judicial reforms and corruption led several EU member states to block the entry of Bulgaria and Romania into the pass-port-free Schengen zone.[19]

For Georgia, Lili Di Puppo shows that international organisations such as the World Bank but also Transparency International promote a liberal technocratic discourse premised on the notion that national governments lack the resources or the will to fight corruption. She makes out two official ways in which the Georgian government fights corruption. First, there is a domestically oriented approach working through law enforcement. Second, with an eye toward the international community, economic lib-eralisation is framed as an anti-corruption tool. Both methods of battling corruption emphasise a rupture with Soviet practices. Prior to the Rose Revolution, Georgian citizens saw corruption and the shadow economy as a legitimate form of national resistance to state control. The post-revolution Georgian government has been eager to assert its legitimacy by referring to both western norms and national history in its dis-course on corruption. This top-down approach relies heavily on law enforcement, as opposed to the bottom-up discourse from civil society, which emphasises the need for democratic institutions to control the state. Di Puppo points out that in Georgia international organisations, the national government, and civil society compete rather than cooperate to ensure the pre-eminence of their anti-corruption approach. Georgian NGOs have been artificially created by donor funds and anti-corruption measures in Georgia reflect the demands of international organisations. Again, this claim is con-sistent with observations in the other country studies. By asserting the dominance of particular discourses, international organisations are able to market their anti-corrup-tion strategies in different transition countries. However, the anti-corruption discourse is adapted and translated in a local context and integrated into various agendas, rather than merely resisted or accepted, while actors compete to assert their position. Whether or not an anti-corruption project is considered a success has come to be measured more in terms of the maintenance of a particular discourse than in terms of its impact on corruption itself.

In the case of Ukraine, measures taken by the post-revolutionary Yushchenko and Timoshenko government clearly represent a response to the international anti-corrup-tion discourse and demands, even though they are not properly adjusted to domestic circumstances according to Åse Grødeland. She argues the majority of anti-corruption efforts have been 'transplanted' into Ukrainian society as a result of external pressure from the international community while NGOs have received a considerable amount of funding and technical assistance from outside sources. However, both the international organisations supplying the funding and the local NGOs utilising those funds are viewed with great suspicion by domestic elites. Moreover, elites view the institution charged with implementation of reforms, namely the judiciary as the most corrupt. Ultimately, these imported anti-corruption measures have been ineffective in Ukraine. The primary reason Grødeland cites for this is that the international community and the Ukrainian government have not properly addressed the root causes of corruption, which she identifies as laying in a post-communist political culture. The three levels – domestic, national, and international – that should be working together on anti-cor-ruption efforts are all out of sync in Ukraine. Civil society organisations are not well respected or trusted by political elites and the public mentality in general is tainted by remnants of the communist political culture. At the national level, the aftermath of the

Orange Revolution – which also relied on very wealthy businessmen and oligarchs – has fostered strained relations among the president, government and parliament; thus anti-corruption efforts have been at a political stalemate in recent years. After the old establishment regained power through democratic elections in 2011 their efforts to use anti-corruption tools against the previous 'orange' power holders by using the judiciary – which is perceived as the most corrupt governmental institution – has further added to wide spread apathy and mistrust.

All these developments in the region must be seen before a wider international setting. Steven Sampson discusses the transformation of anti-corruption efforts from localised, grassroots, and crafts-based movements to a global, institutionalised bureaucratic industry. This industry is a complex of knowledge, people, money, symbols, and discourse termed 'anti-corruptionism'. It operates as a conglomeration of activities carried out by actors on all levels and operates or exists more or less independent of actual incidences of corruption. Important characteristics include the development of an array of texts, conventions, and tools to assess and measure corruption, and the development of a standardised discourse and terminology unique to anti-corruption efforts. The actual ability of this industry to reduce corruption is viewed sceptically. Instead, Sampson argues this industry actually creates new opportunities for careers. Anti-corruption efforts began in many places as grassroots movements by individual actors focused on actual incidences of corruption. Since the emergence of the anti-corruption industry in the late 1990s the focus has shifted towards the broader terms of good governance, global integrity, and transparency. Concepts which have traditionally been associated with business and economics and can be viewed as results of the neoliberal market mentality of the international anti-corruption industry. Three trends converged and elements of development economics, administrative science of effective government, and the tendency of using a neoliberal model of privatising assets coupled with performance assessments all fitted the cases of the eastern European transition countries in the 1990s. Actors on all three levels – civil society, national, and international – interact and actively participate in the anti-corruption industry in a variety of ways as the promulgation of anti-corruption measures has created a multitude of opportunities for careers. This provides incentives to individuals from businessmen, NGO officials, and opposition leaders to heads of state for exaggerating the corruption problem to keep their businesses, parties and funding going. Thus there is a danger that the goal of anti-corruption might shift from eradicating corruption to sustaining the anti-corruption industry.

Most countries studied in this volume have subscribed to international anti-corruption conventions such as those of the UN, the OECD or the Council of Europe. Monitoring the domestic implementation will thus constitute a continuous element in any future developments. A further insight from our studies is that newly elected governments are more likely to initiate new anti-corruption policies and in many cases to target their predecessors as in Ukraine and Hungary. External actors are often more concerned about stability and administrative continuity in these countries than civil societies' capacity for scrutiny, criticism and protest. This, however, seems to be the basis for successful anti-corruption measures as the studies collected in this volume strongly suggest. The vital role of a broad societal constituency is essential in any anti-corruption efforts on all three levels of our analysis. The cyclical nature of corruption scandalisation in the media, in governmental anti-corruption crackdowns, in electoral anti-corruption campaigns and potential retroactive punitive measures taken by newly elected governments as well as the impact of the business cycle on the perception of corruption and the dynamics of mass protests as well as changing levels of trust in governments by money lenders all point to temporal dimensions in the processes of anti-corruption movements, mechanisms and machines that call for further research on both the empirical as well as analytical level.

Notes

1 Grødeland, Åse Berit and Aasland, Aadne, 'Civil Society in Post-Communist Europe: Perceptions and Use of Contacts', *Journal of Civil Society*, 7(2) (2011): 129–156, here p. 130.
2 This is predicated on the assumption that the interplay between government and opposition is constitutive of modern democracies as its inbuilt tension generates both: constant criticism and conflict as well as their non-violent resolutions. See Robert Dahl (ed.), *Political Oppositions in Western Democracies*, Yale, 1966; Richard Hofstadter, *The Idea of a Party System*, Berkeley, 1970; Annna Grzymala-Busse (2006) 'The Discreet Charms of Formal Institutions: Postcommunist Party Competition and State Oversight', *Comparative Political Studies* 39(4): 271–300.
3 New York Times 'A Sentence against Ukraine', 11 October 2011, http://www.nytimes.com/2011/10/12/opinion/ 12iht-edgetmanchuk12.html, accessed 12/1/2011.
4 Financial Times, 20 December 2011, 'Yanukovych Citing Fight against Corruption'.
5 EU press release PRES/11/514, Kyiv, 19 December 2011 'Statement by Herman Van Rompuy, President of the European Council, after his meeting with Ukrainian Civil Society representatives', http://europa.eu/rapid/ pressReleasesAction.do?reference=PRES/11/514, accessed 12/1/2011.
6 More on the Hungarian case further later.
7 The Economist, 17 December 2011; BBC 'Russian Election: Biggest Protests since Fall of USSR', http://www.bbc.co.uk/news/world-europe-16122524, accessed 12/1/2011.
8 New York Times, 23 December 2011, page A1.
9 Conor O'Dwyer (2004) 'Runaway State Building: How Political Parties Shape States in Postcommunist Europe', *World Politics*, 56(4): 520–553.
10 In conjunction with the International Monetary Fund and the European Central Bank. See European Voice, 'Hungary Slammed for Failure to Cut Deficit', 11 January 2012, http://www.europeanvoice.com/article/2012/ january/hungary-slammed-for-failure-to-cut-deficit/73154.aspx, accessed 12/1/2012.
11 EU Commission press release, IP/11/1441, 24 November 2011, 'Public Procurement: Commission Acts to Ensure that Greece and Malta Comply with EU Rules', http://europa.eu/rapid/pressReleasesAction.do?reference= IP/11/1441&type=HTML, accessed 12/1/2012.
12 This has been the case with EU structural funds for Bulgaria and Romania as analysed by Kalin Ivanov in this volume.
13 I would like to thank all authors for taking the time and scrupulous efforts to respond to Diana Schmidt-Pfister's and my request for sending us relevant updates on each of the case studies in this volume.
14 Input the legitimacy is derived from democratic elections, political participation of and governmental responsiveness to the electorate, whereas output legitimacy is derived from the degree of effectiveness and efficiency with which a government can implement its policies and deliver on its promises regardless of their democratic merits.
15 For an in-depth analysis of active and passive leverage in EU's external and enlargement policies, see Milada Vachudova, *Europe Undivided: Democracy, Leverage, and Integration After Communism*, Oxford 2005.
16 Whether the realities in western democracies live up to all these demands is less important than the fact that they seem to strife for these ideals and politicians who deny them quickly lose legitimacy and are more easily challenged.
17 Agnes Batory, *Venue Shopping in the EU: Multi-level Politics and the Hungarian Media Law Debate* (unpublished manuscript, 2011).
18 New York Times, 'European Union Gives Hungary an Ultimatum', http://www.nytimes.com/2012/01/13/world/ europe/ european-union-gives-hungary-an-ultimatum.html, accessed 16/1/

2012. See also EUBusiness.com, 'Under-fire Hungary Faces Threat of EU Financial Sanctions', http://www.eubusiness.com/news-eu/finance-public-debt.erc, accessed 25/1/2012.

19 Spendzharova, Aneta and Vachudova, Milada, 'Catching Up? Consolidating Liberal Democracy in Bulgaria and Romania after EU Accession', *Western European Politics*, 35(1) (2012): 39–58.

Index

Page numbers in *Italics* represent tables.
Page numbers in **Bold** represent figures.

www.routledge.com/9780415676076

Eastern Partnership: A New Opportunity for the Neighbours?

Edited by Elena Korosteleva

This volume offers a collective assessment of the development and impact of the European Neighbourhood Policy and the Eastern Partnership Initiative on its eastern neighbours - Belarus, Ukraine and Moldova in particular, with Russia's added perspective. Founded on extensive empirical and conceptual research, the volume uniquely bridges the perspectives of all parties across the EU's eastern border, in an attempt to understand advantages and problems related to the effective implementation of the EU policies in the eastern region.

This book was published as a special issue of the *Journal of Communist Studies and Transition Politics*.

Elena Korosteleva is Senior Lecturer in European Politics and Director of the Centre for European Studies at Aberystwyth University.

September 2011: 216 x 138: 200pp
Hb: 978-0-415-67607-6
£85 / $133